Mosaic 2

Grammar

4th Edition

Patricia K. Werner

John P. Nelson

McGraw-Hill/Contemporary 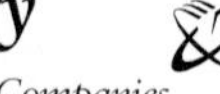

*A Division of The **McGraw-Hill** Companies*

Mosaic 2 Grammar, 4th Edition

Published by McGraw-Hill/Contemporary, a business unit of The McGraw-Hill Companies, Inc., 1221 Avenue of the Americas, New York, NY 10020.

 This book is printed on recycled, acid-free paper containing 10% postconsumer waste.

3 4 5 6 7 8 9 0 QPD/QPD 0 9 8 7 6 5 4

ISBN 0-07-232963-7
ISBN 0-07-118020-6 (ISE)

Editorial director: *Tina B. Carver*
Series editor: *Annie Sullivan*
Developmental editor: *Jennifer Monaghan*
Director of marketing and sales: *Thomas P. Dare*
Project manager: *Joyce M. Berendes*
Production supervisor: *Kara Kudronowicz*
Coordinators of freelance design: *Michelle M. Meerdink/David W. Hash*
Cover image: © *Corbis*
Senior photo research coordinator: *Lori Hancock*
Photo research: *Pam Carley/Sound Reach*
Supplement coordinator: *Genevieve Kelley*
Compositor: *Interactive Composition Corporation*
Typeface: *10.5/12 Times Roman*
Printer: *Quebecor World Dubuque, IA*

The credits section for this book begins on page 413 and is considered an extension of the copyright page.

INTERNATIONAL EDITION ISBN 0-07-118020-6

www.mhcontemporary.com/interactionsmosaic

Mosaic 2 **Grammar**

Boost your students' academic success!

Interactions Mosaic, 4th edition is the newly revised five-level, four-skill comprehensive ESL/EFL series designed to prepare students for academic content. The themes are integrated across proficiency levels and the levels are articulated across skill strands. The series combines communicative activities with skill-building exercises to boost students' academic success.

Interactions Mosaic, 4th edition features

- updated content
- five videos of authentic news broadcasts
- expansion opportunities through the Website
- new audio programs for the listening/speaking and reading books
- an appealing fresh design
- user-friendly instructor's manuals with placement tests and chapter quizzes

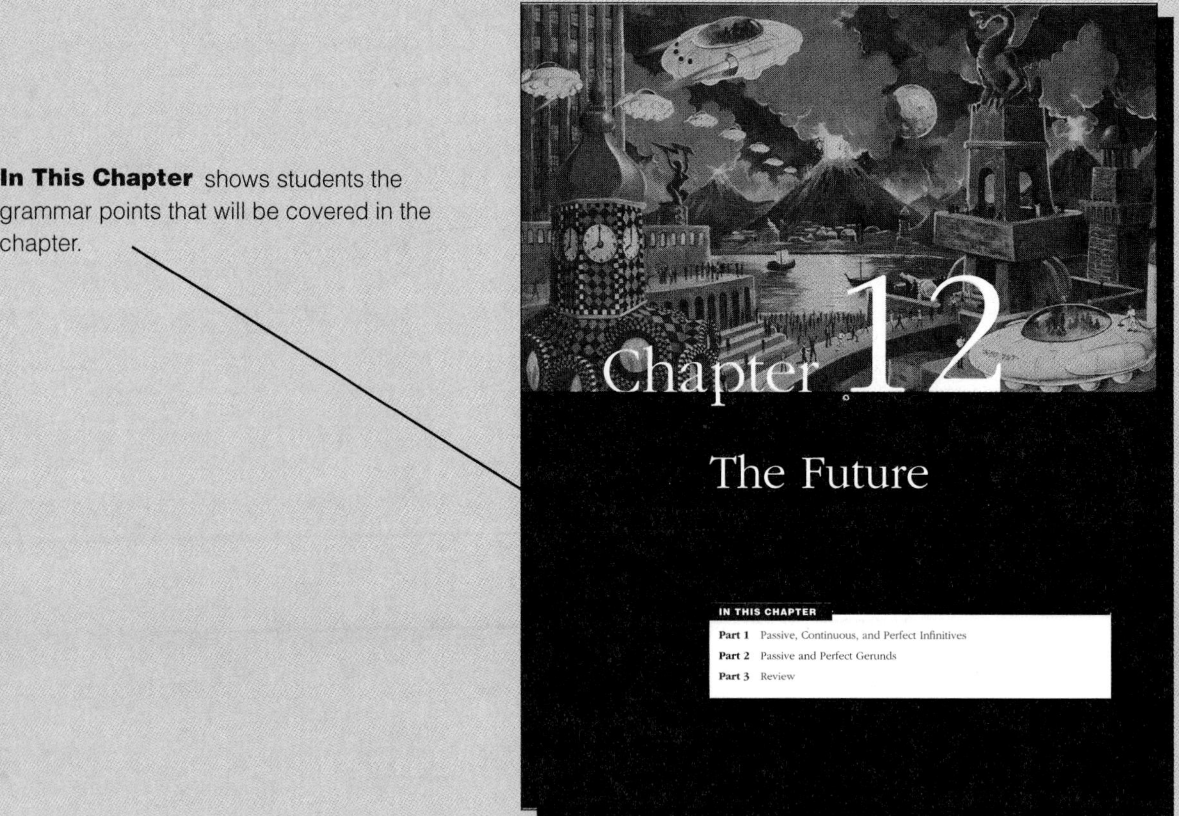
In This Chapter shows students the grammar points that will be covered in the chapter.

Chapter 12

The Future

IN THIS CHAPTER

Part 1 Passive, Continuous, and Perfect Infinitives
Part 2 Passive and Perfect Gerunds
Part 3 Review

2 Mosaic 2 Grammar

Introduction

In this chapter, you will review key terminology and the uses of all the verb tenses and the modal auxiliaries. As this chapter is review, you should study it quickly; the terminology and structures reappear throughout the text. While you are reviewing the tenses, pay close attention to time expressions used with each. Also notice the shifts from one tense to another.

The following passage introduces the chapter theme "Language and Learning" and raises some of the topics that you will cover in the chapter.

Language

Language is the most important development in human history. The arts, sciences, laws, economic systems, and religions of the world could not exist without language. Humans have not changed biologically for some 40,000 years. However, our ability to communicate has led us from the cave all the way to the moon.

Little is known about the birth of language. Written records that are more than 4,000 years old have been found, but anthropologists agree that humans were speaking thousands of years before that.

Today, most of us learn to talk by the age of three, and for the rest of our lives we rarely stop. Even while we are reading or just thinking, we are in a sense "talking," if only to ourselves. Language is so much a part of human existence that we will be talking as long as we inhabit the earth. As linguist David Thompson notes, "When language dies, so will man."

Discussing Ideas. How important is language to humans? Could we "think" the same way without language? Do you have thoughts that do not take the form of words?

PART 1

The Sentence and Its Parts

Setting the Context

Prereading Questions. How many languages do you think there are in the world? What similarities does your first language share with English? Do you know of any similarities that all languages share?

Language Similarities

In all, there are at least 1,500 different human languages. Although each [...] a distinct set of words and grammar, they all have similar "parts of speech." [...] example, all languages have certain elements that function as nouns *(Jack, ten[...] house)* and others that act as verbs *(play, love, sing)*. In addition, every langu[...] uses one class of words to modify nouns *(slow, red, beautiful)* and anothe[...] modify verbs *(slowly, beautifully)*. All languages have rules that can convert ve[...] either into nouns *(sing, singer)* or into adjectives *(interest, interesting)*. Finally[...] use both proper nouns *(Janet Blassey, Seattle)* and pronouns *(she, it)*.

Introduction sections introduce both the theme and the grammar points that will be covered in the chapter.

Discussing Ideas questions reinforce students' understanding of the topics through comprehension questions and encourage students to express themselves.

Setting the Context activities introduce key vocabulary and further familiarize students with the chapter theme. Introductory activities include model conversations, readings, class discussions, prediction activities, previewing, and pair interviews.

Prereading Questions encourage students to share what they know about the topic before they read.

314 Mosaic 2 Grammar

Culture Note

People in the United States often use petitions as a way of focusing on a problem or of getting support for or against possible solutions. A petition is a request, usually to a governmental body or authority. A petition can be signed by only one person, but it will generally carry more weight with more signatures. Specific interest groups may gather thousands of signatures in support of or against an issue.

5. We wish that people everywhere had more concern for the world around them. ____________
6. We wish that governments had faced the problems of drugs and arms trafficking long ago. ____________
7. We wish that people had cared more about the environment many decades ago. ____________
8. We wish there were a way to end all civil wars. ____________
9. We wish that all countries were working together to create a better world. ____________
10. We wish that all nations could live in peace. ____________
11. We hope that future generations will have a peaceful, healthy environment. ____________
12. We hope that the leaders of the world will face these problems so that today's young people will have a world in the future. ____________

B. Subjunctive Forms with Wish

In general, the verb *wish* is followed by a verb in the subjunctive mood. Modal auxiliaries are sometimes used with present and future forms. *That* is optional in sentences with *wish* and *hope*.

	Examples	Notes
Wishes About the Future	I **wish** that the situation **were going** to change. I **wish** the situation **would (could)** change.	Present and future wishes are expressed by using *would, could,* or a subjunctive verb form. In most cases, this form is the same as the simple past tense. In formal English, *were* is used for all forms of the verb *be*. In informal English, *was* is often used with *I, he, she,* and *it*.
Wishes About the Present	Tony **wishes** he **were** still young. I **wish** I **could leave** right now. I **wish** that we **saw** them more often.	
Wishes About the Past	I **wish** they **had arrived** earlier. I **wish** that they **hadn't stayed** so late. She **wishes** she **could have gone.**	Past wishes use the past subjunctive. The past form is the same as the past perfect (*had* + past participle). In conversation, perfect modals are sometimes used.

2 Quickly reread the passage "Taking Responsibility." Then do the following:

1. Find the two clauses that follow *wish* in the second paragraph. Underline the verb(s) in each of these clauses. What is the time frame in the first clause? What about the second?

Culture Notes offer interesting cultural insights related to the chapter theme.

Grammar explanations and charts provide clear, easy to understand, and visually appealing grammar presentations.

390 Mosaic 2 Grammar

2. Japan is a world leader in the use of robots, and Japanese industry is committed to ____________ (protect) that lead.

3. As a result of ____________ (use) robots in the semiconductor industry, Japanese companies have been able to acquire a significant share of the world semiconductor market.

4. Although Japanese industry is committed to ____________ (use) robots, Japanese workers are not overly concerned about ____________ (replace) by machines. This is because human and robot workers typically perform different tasks. For example, a French reporter recently told of ____________ (visit) a Japanese engine factory that operated with a small crew of human workers during the day and continued ____________ (produce) engines at night by ____________ (use) robots. In an automated equipment factory, parts are assembled into finished products during the day after ____________ (make) by robots during the night.

5. Currently, the Japanese are working on ____________ (develop) a new generation of robots that will be able to handle objects with great precision. ____________ (accomplish) this goal will lead to the robots' ____________ (use) in many new industries.

Web Note

Learn more about Japanese robotics. Try these Websites:
Honda: *http://world.honda.com/robot/;*
Koganei System: *www.koganei.co.jp/;*
The University of Tsukuba: *www.roboken.esys.tsukuba.ac.jp/;*
Toray Engineering: *www.toray-eng.com/.;*
And don't forget to check Tomoe Co., *creators of sushi-making robots!: www.sushi-master.com/.*

5 Working in pairs, interview one another about the following topics. Write your partner's answers in complete sentences.

Example: something you enjoy doing early in the morning
A. Tell me something you enjoy doing early in the morning.
B. Early in the morning, I enjoy sleeping!

Ask about something your partner . . .

1. hates doing alone
2. likes having done for him or her
3. regrets not doing (not having done) when he or she had the chance
4. enjoys doing on a rainy day
5. resents being asked to do
6. feels guilty about not doing more often

Web Notes offer suggestions for students interested in using the Web to find more information about a particular topic.

Pairwork activities encourage students to personalize and practice the target language.

206 Mosaic 2 Grammar

Using What You've Learned

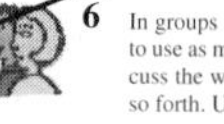

6 In groups of two or more, discuss the meanings of the following adjectives. Then try to use as many of them as possible in a two-minute conversation. You may want to discuss the weather, your apartment, a place near your home, various types of food, and so forth. Use the example as a model.

Example: cold

It's so cold today that there is ice on the road.
or
We're having such cold weather that I hate to go outside.
or
We've had so much cold weather lately that my tan has totally faded.
or
We've had so many cold days that the river may freeze.

soft	humid	foggy	hot	exhilarating
slippery	rough	tart	dreary	pungent
harsh	bitter	fragrant	acrid	nauseating
tense	painful	shrill	bumpy	frightening
sweet	repulsive	bright	ice	salty

Video Activities: Social Phobia

Before You Watch. Answer these questions in small groups.

1. A phobia is ____________.
   a. a need b. a fear c. an idea
2. What kinds of phobias do you know of?

Watch. Answer these questions in small groups.

1. What kind of phobia does Katherine Whizmore suffer from? ____________
2. Circle the things that people with this disorder believe.
   a. People are judging them all of the time.
   b. People want to physically hurt them.
   c. People are unfair to them.
3. Which kinds of treatments help these people?
   a. education about their illness
   b. antidepressant drugs and behavioral therapy
   c. surgery

Watch Again. Choose the correct answers.

1. By the age of 20, Katherine Whizmore was afraid to ____________.
   a. go to work b. cross the street c. go shopping alone

Using What You've Learned provides students with opportunities to do less structured, more communicative activities.

Groupwork activities maximize opportunities for discussion.

Video news broadcasts immerse students in authentic language, complete with scaffolding and follow-up activities.

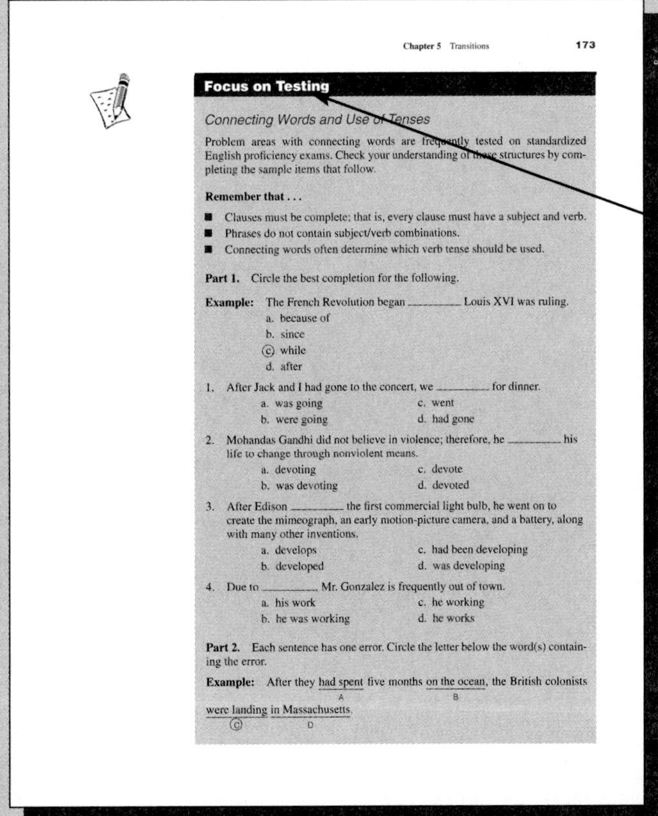
Chapter 5 Transitions 173

Focus on Testing

Connecting Words and Use of Tenses

Problem areas with connecting words are frequently tested on standardized English proficiency exams. Check your understanding of these structures by completing the sample items that follow.

Remember that . . .

- Clauses must be complete; that is, every clause must have a subject and verb.
- Phrases do not contain subject/verb combinations.
- Connecting words often determine which verb tense should be used.

Part 1. Circle the best completion for the following.

Example: The French Revolution began ________ Louis XVI was ruling.
a. because of
b. since
ⓒ while
d. after

1. After Jack and I had gone to the concert, we ________ for dinner.
a. was going c. went
b. were going d. had gone
2. Mohandas Gandhi did not believe in violence; therefore, he ________ his life to change through nonviolent means.
a. devoting c. devote
b. was devoting d. devoted
3. After Edison ________ the first commercial light bulb, he went on to create the mimeograph, an early motion-picture camera, and a battery, along with many other inventions.
a. develops c. had been developing
b. developed d. was developing
4. Due to ________ Mr. Gonzalez is frequently out of town.
a. his work c. he working
b. he was working d. he works

Part 2. Each sentence has one error. Circle the letter below the word(s) containing the error.

Example: After they had spent (A) five months on the ocean (B), the British colonists were landing (ⓒ) in Massachusetts (D).

Focus on Testing helps students prepare for academic exams and standardized tests, such as the TOEFL.

Don't forget to check out the new ***Interactions Mosaic*** Website at www.mhcontemporary.com/interactionsmosaic.

- Traditional practice and interactive activities
- Links to student and teacher resources
- Cultural activities
- Focus on Testing
- Activities from the Website are also provided on CD-ROM

Chapter	Grammar Structures	Contexts	Video Topics
1 **Language and Learning** **Page 1**	■ The sentence and its parts ■ The simple tenses ■ The continuous tenses ■ The perfect and perfect continuous tenses and verb tense review ■ Modal auxiliaries	■ Similarities among languages ■ Animal versus human communication ■ Why is grammar important? ■ History of languages ■ Language and politeness	The School of Success
2 **Danger and Daring** **Page 45**	■ Review of nouns, pronouns, and possessive adjectives ■ Indefinite articles and quantifiers ■ The definite article with count and noncount nouns ■ The definite article with proper nouns ■ More on nouns and noun modifiers	■ Marco Polo ■ Polynesian voyages ■ The age of discovery ■ Exploring the polar regions ■ Climbing Mt. Everest	Extreme Sports
3 **Sex and Gender** **Page 85**	■ Commands and exclamations ■ Compound sentences ■ Transitions ■ Complex sentences ■ Sentence problems	■ Male versus female behavior: innate or learned? ■ Are there intelligence differences between genders? ■ Biological differences between males and females ■ Language differences between males and females ■ Wife/husband roles	Seeking Love
4 **Mysteries Past and Present** **Page 113**	■ Adjective clauses: restrictive versus nonrestrictive ■ Adjective clauses: replacement of subjects ■ Adjective clauses: replacement of objects ■ Other adjective clause constructions ■ Review: Chapters 1 to 4	■ The Great Pyramid of Cheops ■ Early Mayan civilization ■ The Nazca Lines ■ Easter Island ■ Stonehenge	Abduction by Aliens
5 **Transitions** **Page 145**	■ Clauses and related structures of time: future time ■ Clauses and related structures of time: present and unspecified time ■ Clauses and related structures of cause and result ■ Clauses and related structures of time: past time	■ Personal transitions: the stages of life ■ Social transitions: the evolution of societies ■ Transitions: the role of leaders ■ Countries in transition: revolution	College Graduation
6 **The Mind** **Page 175**	■ Clauses and related structures of contrast: concession ■ Clauses and related structures of contrast: opposition ■ Clauses and phrases of purpose ■ Clauses and related structures of comparison ■ Clauses of result	■ The central nervous system ■ The two hemispheres of the brain ■ Alzheimer's disease ■ Comparing humans and animals	Social Phobia

Chapter	Grammar Structures	Contexts	Video Topics
7 **Working** **Page 209**	■ Clauses with *that;* reported speech ■ Clauses with embedded questions ■ Statements and requests of urgency ■ Clauses as subjects of sentences ■ Reduction of noun clauses to infinitive phrases	■ The changing U.S. job market ■ Talking about a job interview ■ Economic inequality in a capitalistic system ■ Job satisfaction ■ Job stress	Telecommuting
8 **Breakthroughs** **Page 241**	■ The simple tenses ■ The perfect tenses ■ The continuous tenses ■ The modal auxiliaries ■ Review: Chapters 5 to 8	■ The importance of technology in today's world ■ Miracles in medicine ■ Developments in agriculture ■ The search for alternatives to fossil fuels ■ Breakthroughs in cinematography	Advances in Medicine
9 **Art and Entertainment** **Page 279**	■ Gerunds ■ Infinitives ■ Verbs followed by either infinitives or gerunds ■ Infinitives and gerunds as subjects and complements; parallelism	■ Jazz ■ Pre-Colombian gold work ■ Impressionism ■ African art	Women in Jazz
10 **Conflict and Reconciliation** **Page 311**	■ *Hope* versus *wish* ■ Imaginary conditions: present and unspecified time ■ Perfect modal auxiliaries ■ Imaginary conditions: past and present time ■ Factual conditions: present, future, and unspecified time	■ Taking responsibility and addressing problems ■ Creating model societies ■ Solving the world's problems: is it too late? ■ The high price of progress ■ The conflict of humans versus the earth	A Strike
11 **Medicine and Science** **Page 349**	■ Adjective clause to phrase reduction ■ Verbs followed by participial constructions; the verbs *lay/lie, raise/rise* ■ Adverb clause to phrase reduction ■ Causative and structurally related verbs	■ Medical and nutritional advances increase the average life span ■ The oldest woman alive ■ The search for the secret to longevity ■ The quest for eternal youth	Stealth Surgery
12 **The Future** **Page 377**	■ Passive, continuous, and perfect infinitives ■ Passive and perfect gerunds ■ Review	■ Space colonies ■ Robots and robotics ■ The family of the future	Concept Cars

Appendices
1 Irregular Verbs
Page 406

2 Spelling Rules and Irregular Noun Plurals
Page 409

3 Pronunciation Guidelines for *-s* and *-ed* Endings
Page 411

4 Verbs Not Normally Used in the Continuous Tenses
Page 412

Skills Index
Page 415

Chapter 1

Language and Learning

IN THIS CHAPTER

Part 1 The Sentence and Its Parts

Part 2 The Simple Tenses

Part 3 The Continuous Tenses

Part 4 The Perfect and Perfect Continuous Tenses and Verb Tense Review

Part 5 Modal Auxiliaries

Introduction

In this chapter, you will review key terminology and the uses of all the verb tenses and the modal auxiliaries. As this chapter is review, you should study it quickly; the terminology and structures reappear throughout the text. While you are reviewing the tenses, pay close attention to time expressions used with each. Also notice the shifts from one tense to another.

The following passage introduces the chapter theme "Language and Learning" and raises some of the topics that you will cover in the chapter.

Language

Language is the most important development in human history. The arts, sciences, laws, economic systems, and religions of the world could not exist without language. Humans have not changed biologically for some 40,000 years. However, our ability to communicate has led us from the cave all the way to the moon.

Little is known about the birth of language. Written records that are more than 4,000 years old have been found, but anthropologists agree that humans were speaking thousands of years before that.

Today, most of us learn to talk by the age of three, and for the rest of our lives we rarely stop. Even while we are reading or just thinking, we are in a sense "talking," if only to ourselves. Language is so much a part of human existence that we will be talking as long as we inhabit the earth. As linguist David Thompson notes, "When language dies, so will man."

Discussing Ideas. How important is language to humans? Could we "think" the same way without language? Do you have thoughts that do not take the form of words?

PART 1 The Sentence and Its Parts

Setting the Context

Prereading Questions. How many languages do you think there are in the world? What similarities does your first language share with English? Do you know of any similarities that all languages share?

Language Similarities

In all, there are at least 1,500 different human languages. Although each has a distinct set of words and grammar, they all have similar "parts of speech." For example, all languages have certain elements that function as nouns *(Jack, tennis, house)* and others that act as verbs *(play, love, sing)*. In addition, every language uses one class of words to modify nouns *(slow, red, beautiful)* and another to modify verbs *(slowly, beautifully)*. All languages have rules that can convert verbs either into nouns *(sing, singer)* or into adjectives *(interest, interesting)*. Finally, all use both proper nouns *(Janet Blassey, Seattle)* and pronouns *(she, it)*.

Discussing Ideas. The passage indicates that there are 1,500 languages. What do you think the difference is between a language and a dialect? Are there several dialects of your first language? How do they differ from each other?

A. Parts of Speech

Parts of speech are the smallest grammatical units: *adjective, adverb, article, conjunction, noun, preposition, pronoun,* and *verb*. They are shown as follows.

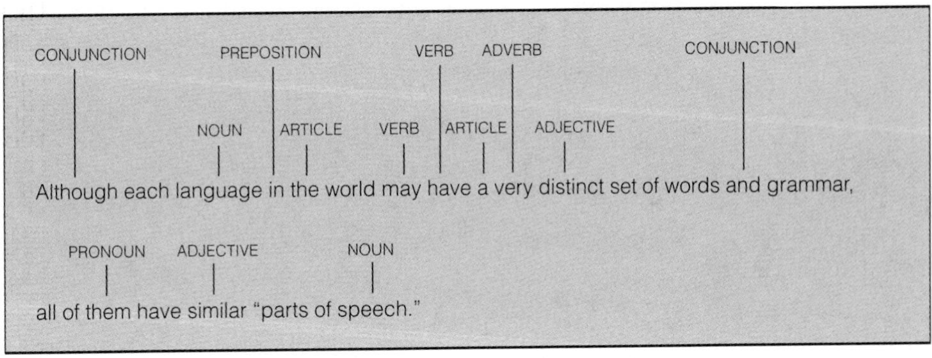

1 Identify the part of speech (noun, pronoun, verb, adjective, adverb, article, preposition, conjunction) of each italicized word. The first one is done as an example.

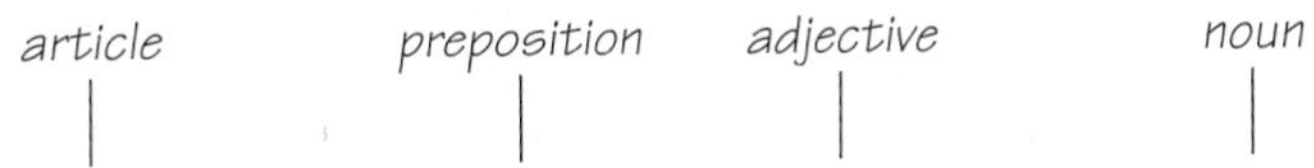

Example: *A* growing number *of* people are *fluent* in several *languages*.

1. *The* most common first language in the *world* is *Mandarin* Chinese, *but it* is widely spoken only *inside* China.
2. There *are* almost a billion Mandarin Chinese *speakers*.
3. *Almost* half of the world's *population* speaks one of the *Indo-European* languages.

4. *English* is the most *popular in* this group, *and its popularity* is growing.
5. *If* second-language speakers *are included,* English is the most common language in the world.

B.C.

B. Sentences

A sentence is a group of words that expresses a complete idea. Every sentence includes at least one subject and verb. (The verb may be followed by an object or a complement.) There are four basic types of sentences:

	Examples	Notes
Statement	English is a wonderful language. I just bought my books.	A statement gives information or opinions.
Question	What is your native language? Have you found a roommate yet?	A question asks for information.
Exclamation	What a pretty red dress you have!	An exclamation expresses surprise, pleasure, or other emotions.
Command	(you) Stop that train! (you) Be quiet, please.	A command tells what to do. The subject *you* is understood.

C. Subjects

The subject is normally the most important person, place, thing, or idea in the sentence. Subjects commonly take four forms:

	Examples	Notes
Noun	**Tony** just arrived from Italy.	A noun is a person, place, thing, or idea.
Pronoun	**He** has studied English for three years.	A pronoun is used in place of a noun.
Phrase	**Several Italian students** study here. **To study in this country** is popular.	A phrase is a group of related words with a noun or a verb form.
Clause	**Why he left Italy** is a mystery.	A clause is a group of related words with a subject and a verb.

D. Verbs, Objects, and Complements

Some verbs tell what the subject does. In general, these verbs can be grouped as transitive or intransitive. Intransitive verbs do not have objects, but a transitive verb *must* have an object. Other verbs tell what the subject is, feels, etc. This type of verb is called a linking verb because it connects the subject to the complement. A complement is a noun, pronoun, adjective, verb form, phrase, or clause that describes the subject. Common linking verbs include *be, appear, become, feel, get* (when it means *become*), *look, seem, smell, sound,* and *taste.*

	Examples	**Notes**
Intransitive Verbs	Martin **arrived** on Thursday.	An intransitive verb is complete without an object.
Transitive Verbs and Objects	He **found** a nice place to live.	A transitive verb *must* have an object. It is incomplete without one.
Direct Object	He brought **some gifts.**	Direct objects answer the questions *who(m)?* or *what?*
Indirect Object	He gave **us** the gifts.	Indirect objects answer the questions *to/ for who(m)?* or *what?*
Linking Verbs and Complements	Sam **is** a dentist. He **appears** quite intelligent. He **looks** rather tired. He **sounds** upset.	Linking verbs are followed by information that describes the subject. Adverbs cannot be used as complements after these verbs.

2 Underline the subjects once and the verbs twice in the following sentences. Circle the object(s) or complement(s).

Example: Humans have been using (language) for at least 40 thousand years.

1. Linguists have identified over four thousand languages.
2. Some languages are relatively new in human history.
3. Others were used for thousands of years and then mysteriously disappeared.
4. Over four thousand languages and dialects are currently being used.
5. Many have no written form.
6. Linguists have given writing systems to some of these languages.

3 Find and underline the clauses in the following sentences. If the sentence has more than one clause, underline one of the clauses twice and circle the word that connects the clauses.

Example: (Although) some societies are technologically underdeveloped, their languages are quite complex.

1. The Aranda people, who live in the Australian desert, lead simple lives.
2. Still, their language is incredibly complex.
3. While the English verb system is considered complex, it is much simpler than the Arandan system.
4. Every Arandan verb can take about a thousand different endings, and each ending changes the meaning of the verb.

5. It is as if English verbs like *run* had one thousand different forms.
6. Nobody knows why the Arandan verb system is so complex.

E. Preview of the Tense System

English has twelve verb tenses, eleven modal auxiliaries, and a variety of verb expressions. The forms of these structures follow specific rules. However, the functions can change: Each has a time frame that depends on the context of the sentence. For example, compare the following sentences: *We **had** lunch at 12:30. We **had** better leave soon.* The time frame of the first sentence is past, while the time frame of the second is present-to-future.

Through the rest of this chapter, you will review all verb tenses, modal auxiliaries, and related structures. Before you start, however, check your current knowledge of these structures in the exercise that follows.

4 The following sentences contain all the tenses of English. Underline the verbs and circle any time expressions. How many of the verb tenses can you identify?

Example: Animals communicate (present tense) through sounds, but only human beings are (present tense) able to speak.

A cuneiform tablet

1. How long have people been using language?
2. We don't know the exact date, but written language probably began in Sumeria.
3. Today, linguists are studying the ancient written language of Sumeria.
4. The Sumerians were writing at least 8,000 years ago.
5. However, people had learned to speak long before this.
6. In fact, humans had been speaking for thousands of years before starting to write.
7. Languages are so complex that pages of diagrams are necessary to explain a short simple sentence.
8. Yet, children have always learned their language simply by hearing it spoken.

9. When a child learns his native tongue, his life will change forever.
10. Soon he will be talking incessantly.
11. Before long, he will have begun to look at the world through his language.
12. However, he will have been speaking for several years before he learns to read and write well.

Using What You've Learned

5 Learning a second language can be frustrating, yet it can also be one of the most rewarding experiences of a lifetime. A second language may be important for your education or profession. But beyond this, it is a pass key that allows you to explore the world and its people in a way that no monolingual person can. In pairs or small groups, use English, *your* second language, to learn about the lives of your new classmates. Use the following words to form questions. Then add any additional questions that you may think of.

1. name
2. age
3. native country and language
4. length of time in the United States or Canada
5. reason for studying English
6. number of years of English study
7. major or job
8. family (single, married, children)
9. hobbies, interests, travels
10. other

After you've finished, take turns telling the class about each other.

Web Note

The Web has dozens of interesting sites for research on world languages. Here are a few sites to check. You'll find many others, too.
www.sil.org/ ethnologue (Site of *Ethnologue: Languages of the World*)
www.lingnet.org/ home.htm (Site of *LingNet*, U.S. Dept. of Defense)
www.june29.com/HLP/ *(The Human Languages Page)*

6 Find out more about the structure of your classmates' languages. Or, find out about another language your classmates have studied or have knowledge of. In pairs, ask and answer questions about the following. Then, using the same questions, compare your languages to English.

1. parts of speech
2. verb tense system (Does your language have a future tense? A past tense? Other tenses?)
3. the word order in sentences (How do you form questions? Would you say *house white* or *white house*?)
4. the use of special forms with certain groups of people (with older people, strangers, etc.)

7 Research the grammar of another language. Check your library or consult the Web. Find out information similar to that in Activity 6, and add any other interesting information you can find. Prepare a brief talk for your classmates.

8 What curious facts do you know about languages? Test your knowledge. Work in small groups and see if you know the answers to the following questions. Then, as a class, compare answers. Your teacher will verify them, or you can look at page 44.

1. How many languages can one individual learn to speak fluently?
2. If varieties of English worldwide are combined, the language has more than 610,000 vocabulary words with an additional 400,000 technical terms. How many words can the average native speaker with 16 years of education understand?
3. For native English speakers, how many words does someone with 16 years of schooling actually use in day-to-day conversation? In written language?
4. How many different vocabulary words did Shakespeare use in his works?
5. What is the oldest unchanged letter in the English alphabet?
6. What are the newest letters?
7. What are the most frequently used words in English?
8. Which word in English has the greatest number of different meanings?

PART 2

The Simple Tenses

Setting the Context

Prereading Questions. How do animals communicate with each other, and what do they communicate about? How is this different from human speech?

Humans Versus Animals

Several animals can stand upright like humans. Some use their hands in a similar way. A few know how to make and use tools. But only humans are able to speak.

When lions roar or monkeys hoot, they are indeed communicating, but only simple ideas and emotions such as "food" or "fear." A chimpanzee that happens upon a mango tree can use a call to alert his companions to his good luck. However, no chimpanzee (or any other animal) is able to discuss what he ate yesterday or what he will have tomorrow.

Human languages, on the other hand, allow us to talk about anything we think of. We can draw lessons from the distant past or speculate on the distant future; we can create mythical beings that have never existed; we can lie and deceive . . . all because of language.

Discussing Ideas. The passage seems to indicate that the greatest difference between humans and animals is language ability. Do you agree? Why or why not?

A. The Simple Tenses: An Overview

The simple present, past, and future are the most often used of the tenses and generally the easiest to understand. However, they are rather flexible and can sometimes be employed in unusual ways.

Tense	Examples	Time Frames
Simple Present	Dezen **studies** every day.	Extended present
Simple Past	She **studied** for three hours yesterday.	Past
Simple Future	She **will** probably **study** another three hours tomorrow.	Future

B. The Simple Present Tense

The simple present tense is used to describe habits or routines, to make general statements of fact, or to express opinions. The usual time frame of this tense is the extended present. Adverbs of frequency such as *always, seldom,* and *never* are often used with the simple present tense. They normally precede the main verb and follow auxiliary verbs or *be* as a main verb. Longer time expressions usually come at the beginning or end of the sentence.

	Examples	Time Expressions
Habits or Routines	I **study** English three hours a day.	*Adverbs of frequency: always, frequently, generally, never, often, seldom, sometimes, usually*
Facts **Opinions**	Learning English **is** not easy. I usually **enjoy** my classes very much.	*Other expressions: from time to time, in general, now and then, once in a while,* and so on.

Note: See Appendix 2 for spelling rules and Appendix 3 for pronunciation guidelines for *-s* endings.

C. Special Uses of the Simple Present Tense

The simple present tense can be used for specific future events, particularly when a schedule, itinerary, or travel plans are being discussed. In informal situations, it may be used to tell stories in the past. The simple present is also used with nonaction verbs—verbs that express feelings, thoughts, perceptions, or possession.

	Examples	Notes
Reference to the Future	I **leave** Canada in two weeks. I **go** to Cairo for a month. Then I **travel** to Beirut.	Verbs often used with this meaning include *arrive, leave, come, go, travel,* and so on. Time expressions used with this meaning include *last week (month), yesterday,* and so on.
Reference to the Past	Yesterday, Jack **walks** into the office and **tells** me he's quitting. So I **say** to him that if he **quits,** I **quit.**	
Nonaction Verbs	The ocean **looks** very cold today. The waves **seem** higher than normal. I **love** the sound of the waves. This beach **belongs to** the city.	Certain verbs of feeling, perception, and possession are almost always used in the simple tenses.

1 What is your daily schedule like? What do you do on weekends? First, complete the following chart and then work with a partner. Take turns telling about your schedules. Use complete sentences and include the appropriate adverbs of frequency.

	Something You Always Do	Something You Rarely Do	Something You Do from Time to Time	Something You Never Do
Weekdays A.M. P.M. Weekends A.M. P.M.				

2 Work in pairs. Use the present tense to tell each other your plans for this weekend or for another day in the near future.

Example: *Next month, I go to Paris. I arrive at the airport at 10:00 A.M. The plane leaves at 11:30.*

3 Working with a partner, add at least five sentences in the present tense to finish the story that follows.

Two months ago after a long day at work, I arrive home at my usual time, about 8:00 P.M. I say, "I'm home, Honey," but no one answers. Anyway, I get a bottle of soda and start walking to the TV. That's when I see the note taped to the kitchen table. It says . . .

D. *The Simple Future Tense and* Be Going To

Will is often used to express the future in written English. In spoken English, it is frequently used with predictions, promises, offers, and requests. *Be going to* is also used in conversational English. It implies more certainty than *will* and often involves actions that have been planned before the moment of speaking. Both *will* and *be going to* are followed by the simple form of a verb.

Simple Future	Examples	Time Expressions
Offers **Predictions** **Promises** **Requests**	You look cold. I'**ll get** you a sweater. The weather **will be** better tomorrow. I'**ll buy** you a new jacket soon. It's raining. **Will** you **give** me a ride?	*After a while, before long, in a few minutes, in a (little) while, later, sometime, soon, sooner or later,* and so on.

Be Going To	Examples	Time Expressions
Actions Planned for the Future	Kunio **is going to take** the TOEFL tomorrow. We'**re going to meet** him after the test.	*In ten minutes, later, this afternoon (weekend), tomorrow, tonight,* and so on.

4 Complete the following dialogue with *will* or *be going to*. In some cases, either is possible.

Example: *Will* you *have* (have) lunch with me tomorrow?

Sorry, I *'m not going to be* (not be) in town tomorrow.

Stan: I ________ (1) (have) a dinner party on Monday. ________ (2) you ________ (3) (come)?

Tess: You know I'm kind of shy. Who else ________ (4) (come)?

Stan: Actually, you are the only person that I ________ (5) (invite).

Tess: Really? Then, I'd be happy to come! Can I bring something?

Stan: How about a salad?

Tess: Sure, I ________ (6) (bring) a salad . . . and I ________ (7) (come) early and help if you like.

Stan: I'd love for you to come early, but I've already decided on a meal, so I ________ (8) (not need) much help.

5 Look at Activity 2 again. With a different partner, tell what you plan to do this weekend or another day in the near future. However, this time, use *will* and *be going to*.

Example: *Next month, I'm going to go to Paris. I'll arrive at the airport about 10:00 A.M. . . .*

E. The Simple Past Tense

The simple past tense describes actions or situations that began and ended in the past.

	Examples	Time Expressions
Actions or Situations Completed in the Past	Joe **came** to Canada three months ago. On August 20, he **entered** the English program. Later he **began** to study at a university.	*Ago, first, then, later, finally, last* (and other sequence expressions), *last week (month, year), from . . . to,* and so on.

Note: See Appendices 2 and 3 for spelling rules and pronunciation guidelines for *-ed* endings and Appendix 1 for a list of irregular past forms.

6 Helen Keller was a remarkable person who learned to communicate in several languages despite being completely deaf and blind. Complete the following sentences about her with the simple past form of the verbs in parentheses. Include adverbs when indicated, and pay close attention to the spelling of the past forms and the pronunciation of any *-ed* endings.

Helen Keller

1. Helen Keller ____________ (be) born a healthy child.
2. As a baby, she ____________ (like) to play.
3. Helen ____________ (develop) a fever at 19 months old.
4. This fever ____________ (leave) Helen permanently deaf and blind.
5. As a result, Helen ____________ (not learn) language as other children ____________ (do).
6. Helen ____________ (be) difficult.
7. She ____________ (ignore) everyone for hours at a time.
8. Helen ____________ (get/often) frustrated and ____________ (refuse) to cooperate.
9. Helen ____________ (have) a dog, and she ____________ (sit) for hours with her dog and ____________ (stare) into space.
10. She ____________ (refuse/frequently) to eat and ____________ (throw/sometimes) her food on the floor.
11. Her family ____________ (think) that Helen was going to grow up to be like an animal.
12. They ____________ (worry) that nothing could help her.

F. The Habitual Past: Would + *Simple Form and* Used To + *Simple Form*

Both *would* and *used to* may be used to describe actions in the past that were repeated on a regular basis. *Used to* may also refer to past situations, opinions, and general states of being that were continuous, not repetitive. *Would* does not give this continuous meaning. Notice the complete difference in meaning: ***I used to like** coffee. **I would like** coffee.*

	Examples	Notes
Repeated Past Actions	As a child, Helen Keller **used to (would) spend** all day with her tutor. They **would frequently take** walks. They frequently **used to take** walks.	Both *used to* and *would* can describe a repeated past action. Note the position of adverbs with these constructions.
Past Situations	Helen **used to love** to study languages. She **used to** study at a university.	*Used to,* not *would,* can describe situations that were continuous, not repetitive.

7 Reread your sentences from Activity 6. Which sentences refer to the habitual past? Which sentences can use *used to?* Which sentences can use *would?* Which sentences cannot use either? Rewrite the sentences that can be changed and pay attention to the placement of adverbs in your new sentences.

Examples: 1. Helen was born a healthy child.
This sentence cannot use would or used to.

2. As a baby, Helen liked to play. *Helen used to like to play. Would is not possible.*

8 Fill in the blanks with *used to* or *would* + verb. If neither *would* nor *used to* is possible, use the past-tense form of the verbs in parentheses. Remember not to "overuse" either *would* or *used to*.

Helen Keller with Anne Sullivan

Culture Note

The Miracle Worker, *by William Gibson, tells the story of Annie Sullivan's work with Helen Keller and the incredible breakthrough that allowed Helen Keller to learn to communicate with language. Gibson originally wrote the play for CBS in 1957; it was given as a live performance, starring Anne Bancroft as Annie Sullivan and Patty Duke as Helen Keller.* The Miracle Worker *went on to become one of the most beloved pieces of world literature of all time.*

Example: Alexander Graham Bell *advised* (advise) Helen's father to hire Anne Sullivan as a tutor.

The "Miracle Worker"

Anne Sullivan first *met* (1) (meet) Helen when Helen ________ (2) (be) seven years old. Sullivan ________ (3) (move) into the Keller house, and for the next several years, she ________ (4) (spend) long hours working with Helen almost every day. At first, Helen ________ (5) (try) to communicate with her tutor by using gestures and meaningless sounds. When Sullivan couldn't understand Helen, Helen ________ (6) (become / often) furious.

Web Note

You can learn more about Helen Keller, as well as work being done today with the blind, at the Website of the Helen Keller Foundation: *www.hkerf.org/*

or at the Website of the American Foundation for the Blind: *www.afb.org/default.asp.*

Sullivan ________ (decide) to teach Helen the finger patterns* of the alphabet. (7) During their lessons, Sullivan ________ (put) Helen's hand on different objects such (8) as a chair or a plate. Then, she ________ (spell) the name of the object in Helen's (9) hand. The great breakthrough for Helen ________ (come) one morning when Anne (10) ________ (hold) Helen's hand under some water and ________ (spell) w-a-t-e-r (11, 12) using the hand signals. Helen later ________ (write) that at that moment, "Somehow (13) the mystery of language ________ (be) revealed to me. I ________ (know) that (14, 15) w-a-t-e-r ________ (be) the wonderful cool something flowing over my hand." (16)

From then on, a new world ________ (open) to Helen. She ________ (become) fascinated with language and (17, 18) ________ (work/eagerly) with Sullivan for long (19) periods of time. Eventually, Keller ________ (go) on to attend Radcliffe College, (20) where she ________ (graduate) with honors. Before she ________ (die), she had (21, 22) learned six languages and had written 11 books.

9 **Error Analysis.** Each of the following sentences has an error in verb form or usage or in adverb placement. Find and correct the errors.

Example: Language learning never is easy, but it can be rewarding.

Correction: Language learning is never easy, but it can be rewarding.

1. I having a friend named Jack, who used to live a few houses away.
2. When I met him, Jack is determined to learn Spanish.
3. He was used to buy lots of language tapes.
4. He would live in Colombia.
5. Unfortunately, he practiced never speaking and listening to Spanish.
6. Now he reads and write Spanish well, but he isn't able to converse in it.
7. He will be going to speak Spanish well one day.
8. He is knowing lots of people from Spanish-speaking countries.

Using What You've Learned

10 Were you a difficult child? Or were you always obedient and cooperative? Of course, even the most cooperative children occasionally cause their parents problems. Use *would, used to,* and the simple past tense as you share memories about this aspect of

finger patterns System of spelling, developed for the blind, in which the fingers form the letters.

your childhood. You can tell your stories first and then write them, or vice versa. Work in small groups when you tell (not read) your stories.

PART 3

The Continuous Tenses

Setting the Context

Prereading Questions. What is grammar? Why is it important?

Creatively Speaking

The sentence you are reading now, the one you were reading a minute ago, and the one you will be reading in a moment may be completely original. Each may never have been written or spoken before. How is this possible?

People do not learn language by memorizing millions of sentences. Instead, they learn to attach meaning to particular words. Then, they begin to acquire a grammar, which can generate an infinite number of new sentences.

When people talk, they aren't just repeating sentences that they have already learned; they are organizing words into grammatical sentences. They are creating sentences, many of which they have never heard before.

Thus, when you understand the grammar of a language and you know enough vocabulary, you will be able to "say" the same thing in any number of ways—many of them quite original.

Discussing Ideas. When you speak, you often make sentences that you have never heard before and that have perhaps never been said by anyone. Use your own words to explain how knowledge of the grammar of a language makes that possible.

A. The Continuous Tenses: An Overview

These tenses generally describe actions that are in progress during another time or event. The second time or event must be given or (especially in the case of the present continuous) implied. Verbs that show no action are not used in the continuous tenses.

Tense	Examples	Time Frame
Present Continuous	Jane **is driving** to work now.	In progress now
Past Continuous	Jane **was driving** to work at 8:00 A.M.	In progress at 8:00 A.M.
Future Continuous	Jane **will be driving** home at 6:00 P.M.	In progress at 6:00 P.M.

1 Quickly reread the passage "Creatively Speaking." Which verb tenses are used in the first sentence? Give the tense and time frame of each.

B. The Present Continuous Tense

The present continuous tense is often used for activities or situations that are temporary rather than permanent. The usual time frames of this tense are the moment of speaking, a specific period of time including the present, and reference to the future.

	Examples	Time Expressions
At the Moment of Speaking	Martha **is studying** for her final exam in French now.	*Now, right now, at the moment,* and so on.
Over a Specific Period of Time	She **is studying** French composition this quarter.	*Today, this morning, this quarter, this year,* and so on.
Reference to the Future	She **is taking** a literature class next quarter.	*In a few minutes, at 9:00, tomorrow,* and so on.

Note: See Appendix 2 for spelling rules for *-ing* endings and Appendix 4 for a list of verbs not normally used in the continuous tenses.

2 Think of someone that you know well in your home country or in another country. Working with a partner, discuss what he or she is doing now. Try to include all three time frames of the present continuous tense.

Example: *It's 3:00 P.M. in Egypt, so my sister is probably in the chemistry lab. (moment of speaking)*
She's studying a lot this month. (a specific period of time)
She is taking exams in about six weeks. (reference to the future)

3 Complete the following with either the simple present or the present continuous tense. In some cases, both tenses are possible, but be ready to explain any differences in meaning that may occur.

Living in the U.S.A.

Hi! My name *is* (1) (be) Mohsen. I ________ (2) (come) from Egypt, but three weeks ago, I said good-bye to my family and got on a plane to the United States. Now I ________ (3) (study) at Cornell University in New York, and I ________ (4) (live) in the dorms.

How ________ (5) (be) dorm life? It ________ (6) (be) noisy and crowded, but it ________ (7) (be) also a lot of fun. I ________ (8) (meet) new people every day. It ________ (9) (be) a funny thing. Everyone ________ (10) (want) to ask me the same question: How ________ (11) you ________ (12) (like) it here? Well, it's not that I

__________ (not appreciate) the opportunity coming to the United States represents.
13

It's just that a lot of things __________ (seem) strange to me. For example, the lan-
14

guage __________ (sound) different from the English I learned at home. And every-
15

body __________ (talk) so fast. Sometimes I __________ (become) nervous and I
16 17

__________ (not understand) everything that people say to me. Worse, people
18

__________ (seem/never) to understand me. I __________ (have to/always) repeat
19 20

myself two or three times. Now, I __________ (work) on my pronunciation to improve
21

the situation, and I __________ (believe) that it __________ (begin) to get better. But,
22 23

to be truthful, at times, I get terribly embarrassed.

But it's not only the language that seems so different. There's much more. For instance, . . .

4 Imagine that you are Mohsen. Complete the passage by adding one or two additional examples and as many details as you can to explain what you mean. You can talk about the food, the weather, the people, or anything you can think of. Pay particular attention to the use of the present tense and the present continuous, but don't limit yourself to these two tenses.

C. The Past Continuous Tense

This tense describes actions in progress in the past. It is often used to "set the scene" in speaking or in writing by telling what was happening, what people were doing or wearing, how they were feeling, and so on, at a given time in the past. The "given" time may be in the recent past or it may be in the more distant past; in either case, the time is normally specified.

	Examples	**Time Expressions**
In the Recent Past	That truck almost hit me! I **was looking** at the traffic signal but not the traffic. Kurt **was sleeping** at 10:00.	*A moment (hour, week) ago, just,* and so on
At a Point of Time in the Past	He **was sleeping** when the phone rang. While he **was sleeping,** the phone rang. The phone rang as he **was sleeping.** We **were studying** while he **was sleeping.**	*At* + specific time *When* + simple past tense *As/while* + past continuous tense

Note: See Appendix 2 for spelling rules for *-ing* endings and Appendix 4 for a list of verbs not normally used in the continuous tenses. See Chapter 5 for more information on *when* and *while*.

5 Mohsen had a difficult first day at Cornell University. Complete the following exercise about Mohsen's experience. Use the simple past and past continuous tenses.

The First Day

Mohsen's first day at the university _was_ (1) (be) less than perfect. As he ________ (2) (walk) to his chemistry lecture, he ________ (3) (realize) that the walk ________ (4) (take) longer than he ________ (5) (think) it would. In fact, he ________ (6) (get) to the classroom just as the teacher ________ (7) (introduce) himself. This ________ (8) (upset) Mohsen a lot.

He ________ (9) (tiptoe) into the room and ________ (10) (try) to find a place to sit. While he ________ (11) (look) around, the professor ________ (12) (direct) a question to him. Mohsen could not understand what the professor ________ (13) (say), but he ________ (14) (be) too embarrassed to tell the professor that he ________ (15) (not understand). The professor ________ (16) (try) to help him find a seat. Finally, the professor ________ (17) (point) to an empty chair. Mohsen ________ (18) (understand) this form of communication and ________ (19) (sit) down quickly.

6 Read the following story and complete it by adding the appropriate form of the verb in simple past or past continuous form. (*Note:* You may find that one or two sentences can take the simple present tense as well.)

A Late Night Surprise

One night around 10:00 P.M., Charlie Scruggs _was reading_ (1) his newspaper in his favorite armchair. Everyone ________ (2) (be) asleep except for Charlie. Suddenly, there ________ (3) (be) a knock at the door. "Who ________ (4) (can) it be at this hour of the night?" he ___5___ (ask) himself. Charlie ___6___ (get up) and ___7___ (walk) to the front door. As he ___8___ (open) the door, he ___9___ (see) someone running away from his house. He ___10___ (be about) to run after the person when he ___11___ (feel) something at his feet. While ___12___ (bend down) to get a closer look, the thing at his feet ___13___ (let out) a tiny cry. "My goodness!" ___14___ (think) Charlie, "What ___15___ (can) this be?" Charlie ___16___ (kneel down) to get very close. Whatever it ___17___ (be) ___18___ (be wrapped) in a blanket. Charlie ___19___ (uncover) the blanket. He ___20___ (can not believe) what he ___21___ (see). It ___22___ (be) a baby!

7 Pretend you are detective who has come to Charlie Scruggs' home after Charlie reported finding a baby on his doorstep. You want to know exactly what happened, so you make a list of questions to ask Charlie. Work with a partner to make a list of ten questions to ask Charlie Scruggs. Then find another pair of students. Make a new pair with one student. Your partner can make a new pair with the other student. Take turns playing Charlie and the detective. When you are the detective, write down Charlie's answers to your questions. After you have finished the role play, write the answers into a report about the incident.

8 The following passage relates a funny story. Fill in the blanks with either the simple past or the past continuous. In some cases, either is possible, but be ready to explain any differences in meaning that may occur.

An "Embarrassing" Moment

About ten years ago, my boyfriend and I ___*were vacationing*___ 1 (vacation) in Mexico when we suddenly ___2___ (decide) to get married, right then and there! Neither of us ___3___ (can speak) much Spanish, but a hotel receptionist ___4___ (set up) a meeting with a priest for 1:00 P.M.

Unfortunately, we ___5___ (do) a million things that day, so we ___6___ (be) an hour late for our meeting. When we ___7___ (arrive), the priest ___8___ (wait/still) patiently. Of course, I ___9___ (be) embarrassed and ___10___ (want) to apologize for being late. While the priest ___11___ (introduce) himself,

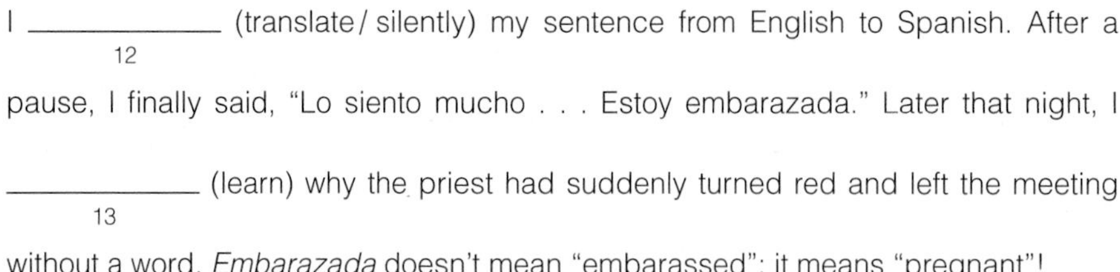

I ____________ (translate/ silently) my sentence from English to Spanish. After a
12

pause, I finally said, "Lo siento mucho . . . Estoy embarazada." Later that night, I

____________ (learn) why the priest had suddenly turned red and left the meeting
13

without a word. *Embarazada* doesn't mean "embarassed"; it means "pregnant"!

D. The Future Continuous Tense

This tense refers to actions that will be in progress in the future. It is commonly used within one of two time frames: at a point in time or during a period of time in the future. In some cases, both the simple future and the future continuous may be appropriate, but there is a difference in tone between the two tenses. Generally, the future continuous is friendlier and more conversational in tone. Compare: *When will you be going to Chicago?* (more conversational) *When will you go to Chicago?* (more formal)

	Examples	Time Expressions
A Point in Time in the Future	What **will** the senator **be doing** at 3:00? He**'ll be resting** then.	*At 3:00 (4:00), by (at) that time, next Monday, tomorrow night,* and so on.
A Period of Time in the Future	What **will** he **be doing** between 5:00 and 7:00? He**'ll be meeting** with the press.	*During the afternoon (evening), from 5:00 to 7:00, next week (month),* and so on.

Note: See Appendix 2 for spelling rules for *-ing* endings and Appendix 4 for a list of verbs not normally used in the continuous tenses.

9 You are a reporter trying to get an interview with the president. Your partner is the president's aide and has the schedule of the president's activities. This schedule is confidential and only he or she may look at it. Ask your partner at least ten questions about when you will be able to see the president. Your partner will answer your questions by referring to the schedule. Use the future continuous or the simple future in your questions and answers. In some cases, either tense is possible; however, be ready to explain any differences in meaning that might occur.

Example: *Reporter:* Will he be available at 8:00 A.M.?
Aide: Sorry, he'll be eating at 8:00.

The President's Schedule

8:00–9:00	Eat breakfast.
9:00–9:30	Read newspapers and mail.
9:30–10:00	Do exercises.
10:00–10:30	Swim.
10:30–12:00	Take nap.
12:00–1:00	Eat lunch.
1:00–5:00	Go horseback riding.
5:00–7:00	Attend cocktail party.
7:00–8:00	Prepare for speech.
8:00–9:00	Give speech.

10 What does the future hold for you? Use the following time expressions to make statements about your future. Make at least one statement in the simple future with *will* or *be going to,* one in the future continuous, and one in the present continuous for each time expression.

Examples: soon

I'm going to return to my country soon.
Noriko will be arriving soon.
David is leaving for South America soon.

1. tomorrow
2. tomorrow at 3:00 P.M.
3. before long
4. a month from now
5. next year
6. in 2001

11 **Error Analysis.** Most of the following sentences have one or more errors in the use of verbs. Find the errors and correct them. If a sentence has no error, make no changes.

Example: Mark is coming from the United States, but now he studies in Florence for the year.

Correction: Mark comes from the United States, but he is studying in Florence this year.

1. Mark is trying to learn Italian, but it isn't easy.
2. When he was arriving in Florence, he immediately enrolled in a language school.
3. It has been three months, but when people are speaking to him, he still isn't understanding them.
4. Yesterday Mark was going to the language lab.
5. When the class was over, Mark was waving "good-bye" to his teacher.
6. At the same time she motioned for him to come to the front of the class.
7. However, when Mark got to the front of the class, the teacher was looking confused.
8. She said that she was simply waved "good-bye" to Mark.
9. Mark suddenly realizes that the Italian "good-bye" gesture is very similar to the American "come here" gesture.
10. Mark will be study for the next year in Florence.
11. When Mark goes back to the United States next year, he will be speaking perfect Italian.
12. At least that is what he is wanting!

Using What You've Learned

12 Anyone who spends time in a new culture has some problems with miscommunication. It may involve misinterpreting language or not understanding an unfamiliar culture. In pairs or small groups, talk about one or more experiences that you have had with miscommunication. Start with setting the scene and then describe the incident itself.

Example: *The three of us arrived in the New York airport late in the afternoon. It was really busy. As we were going through customs . . .*

PART 4

The Perfect and Perfect Continuous Tenses and Verb Tense Review

Setting the Context

Prereading Questions. Do you know a religious explanation for why the world has so many languages?

The *Tower of Babel* by Pieter Bruegel (Elder)

Babel

All the world once spoke a single language, but this changed at Babel . . . Men had been journeying east for many months when they came upon the land of Shinar. "Come," they said. "We have been traveling days without end. Let us build ourselves a city and a tower with a top in the heavens, and make a name for ourselves."* But the Lord came down to see the city and tower which mortal men were building. And He said, "Here they are, one people with a single language, and now they have begun to do this. After this, nothing they want to do will be beyond their reach. Come, let us go down there and confuse their speech. When we finish, they will have lost their one language and in its place there will be many." So the Lord went down to the city. And after He had done this, the city was given the name "Babel" because there the Lord had made a babble of the language of the world.

**make a name for oneself* make oneself famous

Discussing Ideas. According to the story, why was the Lord angry when he saw the city? What did he do? Do you know any other explanations for why we have thousands of languages in the world?

A. The Perfect Tenses: An Overview

The perfect tenses generally refer to events that are completed before another time. The exact completion time is not stated, however.

	Examples	Time Frames
Present Perfect	Dale **has finished** the assignment.	Sometime before now
Past Perfect	He **had finished** by 6:00 yesterday.	Sometime before 6:00
Future Perfect	He **will have finished** by 6:00 tomorrow.	Sometime before 6:00

B. The Present Perfect Tense

The present perfect tense frequently refers to events that happened (or did not happen) at an *unstated* time in the past. It also refers to *repeated past* actions. If the specific past time is given, the simple past tense is used.

Following is a list of adverbs and other time expressions frequently used with this tense. In terms of placement, most adverbs come before the main verb. *Yet* usually goes at the end, and *still* goes before the auxiliary verb *have.*

	Examples	Time Expressions
Events at an Unstated Time in the Past	**Have** you ever **studied** Spanish? I'**ve** already **taken** two courses. **Has** Chuck **returned** from Spain yet? No, he still hasn't returned.	*Already, always, ever, just, lately, recently, still, yet, so far, up to now, once, twice, three (four, five) times, how many times* (with questions), and so on.
Repeated Past Actions at Unstated Times	Chuck **has visited** Spain twice. How many times **have** you **gone** there?	

Note: See Appendix 2 for spelling rules for *-ed* endings and Appendix 1 for a list of irregular past participles.

1 Go back to the passage "Babel" and underline the uses of the perfect (*have* + past participle) and perfect continuous (*have* + *been* + present participle) tenses. Then, answer the following questions.

1. How do the following sentences differ in meaning?
   Now they have begun to do this.
   Now they are beginning to do this.
2. What is the difference between the following sentences?
   When we finish, they will have lost their one language.
   When we finish, they will lose their one language.
3. Was the city given the name Babel before or after *the Lord had made a babble of the language of the world?* Which verb tense indicates which action came first?

2 Use the simple present, present perfect, or the simple past tense to complete these short passages. It will help you to try underlining the time expressions first.

Example: There _have been_ (be) many changes in linguistic theory in the last 50 years. For example, the idea that all languages share certain elements _became_ (become) popular in the 1960s.

1. For thousands of years, scientists ________ (wonder) how children learn languages. Recently, researchers ________ (make) a number of discoveries that help explain how language is acquired. We ________ (know / now) that all healthy children ________ (go) through the same steps while learning their native tongues. They ________ (do) this at approximately the same period no matter where they ________ (live).
2. Deaf children ________ (have / always) a difficult time learning language. However, over 100 years ago, teachers ________ (begin) using sign language with deaf children. This ________ (help) Helen Keller in the late 1800s, and it ________ (help) thousands since her time.
3. Linguist Noam Chomsky ________ (be) famous for several decades. He ________ (do) some of his greatest work in the 1960s. Since then, he ________ (continue) to make important discoveries about language.
4. Children ________ (be / always) able to learn two or three languages at the same time. Twenty-five years ago, most linguists ________ (believe) that being monolingual (learning only one language) was better for a child's intellectual development. A great deal of research in the last decades ________ (show) the opposite to be true. A famous research study on language learning ________ (be) conducted in Canada in the 1970s.

C. The Perfect Continuous Tenses: An Overview

The perfect continuous tenses refer to actions that *begin* before and *continue* up to another time or event. The duration of the first action is often given. The second time or event is either given or (especially in the case of the present perfect continuous) understood.

	Examples	Time Frame
Present Perfect Continuous	Jill **has been sleeping** for two hours.	The last two hours
Past Perfect Continuous	She **had been sleeping** for two hours by 5:00.	From 3:00 to 5:00
Future Perfect Continuous	She **will have been sleeping** for two hours by 5:00.	From 3:00 to 5:00

D. The Present Perfect Continuous and Present Perfect Tenses

The present perfect continuous tense can describe actions or situations that began in the past and continue to the moment of speaking. It often implies that the action or situation will continue in the future. This tense stresses the continuous nature of the activity; it is not normally used with expressions that indicate repeated action (*one time, two times,* and so on).

In some cases, the present perfect tense can have a past-to-present time frame. This meaning occurs most commonly with verbs such as *begin, expect, hope, live, study, teach, wait,* and *work.* In addition, this use of the present perfect tense occurs with verbs not normally used in the continuous tenses.

	Examples	Time Expressions
Actions or Situations That Began in the Past and Have Continued to the Present	Joe **has been studying (has studied)** here since March. He **has been living (has lived)** in Ottawa for three months. He **has been working (has worked)** hard all day.	*Since* + a point of time in the past, *for* + a period of time, *all* + a period of time, and so on.

Note: See Appendix 2 for spelling rules for *-ing* and *-ed* endings, Appendix 1 for a list of irregular past participles, and Appendix 4 for a list of verbs not normally used in the continuous tenses. See Chapter 5 for more information on *since.*

3 Fill in the correct forms of the verbs in parentheses. Use the present perfect continuous when it is possible. When this is not possible, use the present perfect.

Example: Beatrice and Allen Gardner *have decided* (decide) to teach a number of chimps Ameslan, a type of sign language.

Chimpanzee, Nim, learning to sign from his trainer

1. Deaf people ______________ (communicate) with Ameslan for decades.
2. The Gardners ______________ (teach) a small amount of Ameslan to a number of chimps since the 1960s; the most famous chimp is named Washoe.
3. Washoe ______________ (learn/already) to use 150 Ameslan signs.
4. Using these signs, Washoe ______________ (ask) for such things as food or games hundreds of times.
5. Another chimpanzee ______________ (practice) Ameslan for several years.
6. This chimp ______________ (master) almost 200 words.
7. He ______________ (combine) these words into short but grammatical sentences a number of times.
8. Still, even this chimpanzee ______________ (not learn) nearly as much as a three-year-old human.

E. The Past Perfect and Past Perfect Continuous Tenses

The past perfect tense refers to an activity or situation that had ended *before* another event or time in the past. The second event or time must be either mentioned or implied. The past perfect continuous tense describes an action that began before and continued up to another action or time in the past. The duration of the first action is normally given.

These tenses are somewhat formal and appear more often in written English than in spoken English. Both tenses are frequently used in complex sentences using more than one time in the past. This will be discussed in detail in Chapter 5.

	Examples	Time Expressions
Past Perfect	Joy **had finished** the article by 8:00 P.M. She **had** never **read** that author before last night. I tried to call her, but she **had** already **left.** After I **had phoned,** I went to a movie. When I phoned, she **had** just **left** to go to the theater.	*Before* or *by* + point in time, *after, before, until, when, by the time that* + clause, and adverbs of frequency such as *already, just, never, still, yet.* Note that adverbs of frequency have the same placement as with the present perfect tense.
Past Perfect Continuous	By midnight, Claudia **had** already **been working** for 12 hours. After she **had been working** for 16 hours, she fell asleep.	*For* + period of time *Since* + point in time

Note: See Appendix 2 for spelling rules for *-ed* and *-ing* endings, Appendix 1 for a list of irregular past participles, and Appendix 4 for a list of verbs not normally used in the continuous tenses.

4 Fill in the following blanks with the correct forms of the verbs in parentheses. Use the past perfect continuous wherever possible. Where this is not possible, use the past perfect.

Example: Claudia starts her day early. By 7:00 A.M. this morning, she had already gotten up (get up / already).

1. At 6:45, after she __________ (sleep) for eight hours, Claudia __________ (get up).
2. She __________ (finish) breakfast before the newspaper __________ (arrive).
3. By 8:00, she __________ (shower) and __________ (eat) breakfast.
4. At 8:15, she left the house. After she __________ (close) and __________ (lock) the door, she began walking to the bus stop.
5. On the way, she noticed that a man __________ (follow) her for several blocks.
6. When she reached the bus stop, she sat down. The man sat next to her. They __________ (sit) together for about five minutes when the bus arrived.
7. Claudia climbed on the bus and took a seat, but she __________ (begin / just) to relax when she realized her purse was missing.
8. She was sure that she __________ (not forget) to bring her purse that morning.

9. When she looked out the window, she saw that the man who __________ (follow) her was running down the street with her purse.
10. When Claudia went to the police station later that day, someone __________ (turn in / already) her purse; unfortunately, all the money __________ (be) removed.

5 Use either the past or the past perfect tense to complete the following passage.

Rip van Winkle

In the 18th century, Washington Irving wrote a famous tale about a man named Rip van Winkle. In the story, Rip drank a secret potion given to him by a wizard. Soon, Rip fell asleep under a tree and didn't awake for 20 years.

Example: When Rip finally woke up, everything *seemed* (seem) different. In fact, many things *had changed* (change).

1. His gun __________ (be / still) next to him, but it __________ (rust / completely).
2. He __________ (find) his house, but it __________ (be) empty because his wife __________ (pass away / already).

3. Rip ____________ (walk) to the center of his village, but no one ____________ (recognize) him. That is partly because nobody ____________ (see) him for over 20 years, and most of his friends ____________ (die) or ____________ (move) away from his village.
4. In addition, he ____________ (look) quite different. His hair ____________ (be) much longer and very dirty. His beard ____________ (grow) more than a foot. Also, his clothes ____________ (disintegrate / almost).
5. Luckily, Rip ____________ (find) his daughter, who was now an adult, and he ____________ (move) in with her family.

6 Imagine that you, too, drank the secret potion. Last year you woke up from your 20-year nap. Make at least six sentences (three with the past tense and three with the past perfect) describing the situation that you *found* and the changes *that had occurred.*

F. The Future Perfect and Future Perfect Continuous Tenses

These tenses refer to actions or situations that will have occurred before another event or time in the future. The second event or time must be either mentioned or implied. As with other continuous tenses, the future perfect continuous emphasizes an activity in progress. The future perfect emphasizes the completion of an activity.

	Examples	Time Expressions
Future Perfect	By next year, my daughter **will have started** elementary school. Also, she **will have begun** tennis lessons. She **will** already **have won** her first tournament when you see her.	*Before* or *by* + point in time, adverbs of frequency such as *already, just, recently,* and *yet.*
Future Perfect Continuous	She **will have been talking** for three years by her fifth birthday. She **will have been going** to school for 18 years by graduation day.	*For* + period of time *Since* + beginning time

Note: See Appendix 2 for spelling rules for *-ed* and *-ing* endings, Appendix 1 for a list of irregular past participles, and Appendix 4 for a list of verbs not normally used in the continuous tenses.

7 Rap (Rip van Winkle's grandson) has just been given a magic potion that will make him sleep for 20 years, also. Use either the future or the future perfect to talk about how things will be different when he wakes up.

Example: When Rap wakes up, everything *will seem* (seem) different. In fact, many things *will have changed* (change).

1. His gun ____________ (be / still) next to him, but it ____________ (rust / completely).
2. He ____________ (find) his house, but it ____________ (be) empty because his wife ____________ (pass away / already).
3. Rap ____________ (walk) to the center of his village, but no one ____________ (recognize) him. That is partly because nobody ____________ (see) him for over 20 years, and most of his friends ____________ (die) or ____________ (move) away from his village.
4. In addition, he ____________ (look) quite different. His hair ____________ (be) much longer and very dirty. His beard ____________ (grow) more than a foot. Also, his clothes ____________ (disintegrate / almost).
5. Luckily, Rap ____________ (find) his daughter, who ____________ (be / now) now an adult, and he ____________ (move) in with her family.

8 **Review.** Fill in the blanks with the verb *discuss.* Choose from all tenses. In many cases, more than one tense may be appropriate. However, be ready to describe any differences in meaning that might result.

Example: We __discussed__ this problem last year.

1. They ____________ the problem since 10:00 A.M.
2. Some students ____________ the problem when we came to class.
3. They ____________ (probably) the problem when class ends.
4. We ____________ it a number of times in the past.
5. I never ____________ this problem last year.
6. We ____________ this problem for two hours by the time he arrives.
7. College students ____________ this issue quite often these days.
8. Marion and Vittorio ____________ the problem right now.
9. After they ____________ it for three hours, they reached a decision.
10. They ____________ (never) this issue again.

9 **Review.** Create sentences using the following time expressions. Use as many different tenses as you can with each time expression, but be ready to explain the differences in meaning that may result.

1. for two hours last Thursday
2. for the past 15 minutes
3. when I saw the fire
4. in 1995
5. when we meet in 2010
6. tomorrow
7. every morning at 6:00
8. at the moment
9. when I was a child
10. since we last met

10 **Error Analysis.** Each of the following sentences contains an error related to verb tense. Identify the errors and correct them.

think

Example: I (am thinking) that English is impossible to learn.

1. Before I had studied English, I thought it was an easy language.
2. Now I am knowing that it isn't easy.
3. My language has had only a little slang.
4. I am studying English since April, and I only begin to learn some of the common slang words.
5. I have been tried to learn more of these words every day.
6. Last night, for example, I have studied from 9:00 P.M. to midnight.
7. I was studying for three hours when I finally quit.
8. I had gone to my teacher last Monday and she was telling me to see her after class.
9. But when I went to her classroom after school, she already left.
10. It's now May 15; by the middle of June, I will be studying English for three months.
11. On June 23, I am studying German.
12. On June 30, I will be studying German for one week.

11 **Review.** Fill in the blanks with appropriate forms of the verbs in parentheses. In some cases, more than one verb form may be appropriate. However, be ready to explain any differences in meaning that may occur.

Esperanto at a Glance

The grammar is based on 16 fundamental rules, which have no exceptions. Examples: All adjectives end in *-a*. All nouns end in *-o*. The simple verb has only six inflections:

Infinitive	Present	Past	Future	Conditional	Imperative
I	**As**	**Is**	**Os**	**Us**	**U**
Esti Studi Helpi	Estas Studas Helpas	Estis Studis Helpis	Estos Studos Helpos	Estus Studus Helpus	Estu Studu Helpu

Esperanto

The idea of a universal language ______ (1) (interest) people since the time of Babel. In the 1870s, a Polish teenager named Ludwik Zamenhof ______ (2) (begin) to develop such a language. He ______ (3) (call) his new language Esperanto, which ________ 4 (mean) "hope." At that time, he ________ 5 (live) in a Polish town where Poles, Russians, Germans, and Jews all ________ 6 (speak) their own languages. Zamenhof ________ 7 (believe) that language differences ________ 8 (be) the major cause of difficulties among different ethnic groups. By 1890, ________ 9 (publish) his first book on Esperanto, and within a short time, thousands of people ________ 10 (learn) this new language.

Esperanto ________ 11 (be) simple to learn and use. The grammar ________ 12 (be) based on 16 fundamental rules. There ________ 13 (be) no exceptions and no irregularities. In addition, the accent or stress always ________ 14 (fall) on the last syllable of a word, and every letter ________ 15 (have) one and only one sound.

At first, Esperanto ________ 16 (be) a great success. Within a few years, hundreds of thousands of people ________ 17 (speak) Esperanto. (In fact, people ________ 18 (write) over ten thousand books in Esperanto since 1900.) However, after a few decades, interest in the language ________ 19 (decline). Today, it ________ 20 (be) still popular among thousands of people, but few ________ 21 (think) that Esperanto ________ 22 (become) a universal language.

This ________ 23 (not mean), however, that there ________ 24 (be/never) a universal tongue. In fact, English ________ 25 (be/likely) to become just such a language. Unlike Esperanto, English ________ 26 (have) thousands of exceptions and irregularities. But it ________ 27 (have/also) the greatest number of speakers, and this number ________ 28 (grow/rapidly). Today, there ________ 29 (be) close to a billion speakers of English. By the year 2010, well over a billion and a half people ________ 30 (speak) English. Some experts ________ 31 (predict) that by 2100, English ________ 32 (become) the first truly universal language.

Using What You've Learned

12 The last 100 years have seen more change than any other period in the history of mankind. With a partner, make at least five sentences for each of the following:

1. changes that had taken place before you were born
2. changes that have taken place since you were born
3. changes that will have taken place before you die

Example: *Before I was born, humans had landed on the moon.*
Since I was born, computers have become very popular.
Before I die, we will have explored another solar system.

PART 5 Modal Auxiliaries

Setting the Context

Prereading Questions. In your language, how would you ask a close friend to lend you a book? Would you use different words to ask your boss the same thing?

Language and Politeness

Every language has certain forms that are used to show respect or politeness. For example, in English, "Would you please open the door?" is normally a more polite request than "Open the door, would you?" or simply "Open the door." Moreover, "You might see a doctor" is usually a more polite suggestion to someone who is sick than "You should (must) see a doctor."

In Japan, politeness is extremely important, and the Japanese language has many polite forms. In an informal situation, a Japanese can talk about a person's return to his house by simply saying, "He came home." However, a more formal situation may produce the sentence, "The fact of his return happened." And if local politicians are announcing the return of their leader, they might say softly, "He has become visible."

Discussing Ideas. Compared to English, does your language have many polite forms? How is politeness expressed in your language?

A. Introduction to Modal Auxiliaries

Modal auxiliaries form a special group because they have only one form for all persons of the verb and because they can have several meanings, depending on their context. Modal auxiliaries can be divided into two broad categories: modals of logical probability, which make inferences about actions, ideas, and people, and modals of social interaction, which indicate politeness in usage. Compare:

Judy's absent today. She *might be* sick. (logical probability)

Would you mind picking me up? (social interaction)

In this section, you will look at common uses of the modal auxiliaries and related structures. In Chapters 8 and 10, you will study further uses of these auxiliaries.

Forms of Modal Auxiliaries

	Formation	Examples
Simple	modal + verb	He **should arrive** at any moment.
Continuous	modal + *be* + present participle	He **may be arriving** soon.
Perfect	modal + *have* + past participle	He **must have had** a problem.
Perfect Continuous	modal + *have been* + present participle	He **might have been driving** that old car.

Related Structures

can, could	be able to	ought to,	be supposed to, had better
may, might	be allowed to	should	
must	have to, have got to	shall, will	be going to, be about to

Pronunciation of Reduced Forms

In rapid speech, many of these structures are not always pronounced clearly. Some are often reduced, as shown in the following:

Can	*/kin/*	You had better	*/ya bedder/*	Won't you?	*/woncha/*
Can you?	*/kinya/*	Ought to	*/otta/*	Would you?	*/wudja/*
Can he?	*/keni/*	Ought to have	*/ottuv/*	Would he?	*/wudi/*
Could you?	*/cudja/*	Should you?	*/shudja/*	Would have	*/wudduv/*
Could he?	*/cudi/*	Should he?	*/shudi/*		
Could have	*/cudda/*	Should have	*/shudduv/*		

1 Read the following sentences. Find another way to express the same idea.

Example: I may go tomorrow.

I might go tomorrow.

1. Deb can't go out because she must study for the test.
2. I am able to translate from Korean to English.
3. They should keep their promise.
4. You are going to enjoy that movie.
5. We weren't able to help her.
6. He has to take ten courses in Spanish in order to major in it.
7. I don't feel good; I might be getting a cold.
8. We are supposed to review this chapter for the test.

B. Modals of Logical Probability

When the speaker makes an inference about a situation or a prediction about it, he or she will usually use a modal (or an adverb or adjective). This usage of modals does not usually require being aware of politeness. Compare:

	Examples
Modal Auxiliary	It **should rain** very soon. The clouds are dark and low in the sky.
Adjective or Adverb	It is **probably** going to rain very soon. It is **most likely** going to rain shortly.

In making an inference, there is an order of certainty among the modals. Compare:

	Examples	
Present or Future Inference	There is a dog barking outside. That **must/has to** be Marty's dog. That **may/might** be Marty's dog. That **could be** Marty's dog.	More certain ↓ Less certain
Past Inference	There was a dog barking outside last night. That **must have been** Marty's dog. That **may/might/could have been** Marty's dog.	More certain ↓ Less certain

Note: Can is not used in making a positive inference. In negative inferences, *should* and *must* are not used.

2 Give at least two reactions to each of the following statements with *could*, *may*, *might*, or *must*.

Example: There's a light on in the house.

Somebody must be home. Someone must have forgotten to turn it off.

1. I hear a scratching noise.
2. The traffic is moving very slowly.

3. Jack didn't go home for Christmas.
4. Paula has gained weight all of a sudden.
5. The Browns aren't having their holiday party this year.
6. I didn't do well on the final exam.
7. He had only known her for two months before he proposed.
8. Thomas and his wife have not been at any of our meetings lately.

C. Expressing Predictions

In predicting what will happen, there is an order of definiteness (from more to less certain).
With negative predictions, the order is reversed.

	Examples	
Affirmative	How will the court rule? They **will decide** against the union. They **should decide** against the union. They **may decide** against the union. They **could/might decide** against the union.	Certain ↓ Less certain
Negative	How will the court rule? They **might not decide** against the union. They **may not decide** against the union. They **shouldn't decide** against the union. They **won't decide** against the union. They **can't/couldn't decide** against the union.	Less certain ↓ Certain

Web Note

For a more accurate (perhaps!) view of the future, consult the Website of the World Future Society. The World Future Society is a nonprofit educational and scientific organization for people interested in how social and technological developments are shaping the future.
www.wfs.org/index.htm

3 Read each of the following predictions of the famous astrologer and palm reader Madame DePriest. Then make an appropriate comment with a positive or negative modal.

Example: In 2010, we will discover little green men living under the earth.
That can't be possible.

1. The United States will revert to an English colony in 25 years.
2. In ten years, the CD will vanish like the vinyl record has.
3. Madonna will undergo plastic surgery that keeps her a constant 40 years old.
4. People will talk to their computers instead of using a keyboard.
5. The world will run out of drinkable water in our lifetime.
6. There will be a high-speed ship linking the Far East to the West Coast of the United States.
7. The nations of the world will do away with passports because all people on the earth will be entered into a worldwide computer network as soon as they are born.

8. In 100 years, there will be no paper or metal money.
9. Some sports stars will become rich enough to buy their own countries.
10. It will rain tomorrow.

D. Modals of Social Interaction

Modals of social interaction require the speaker to be aware of politeness, formality, and the relationship between the speaker and the person he / she is addressing.

	Examples	Notes
Making Requests	**Would** you mind helping me? **Would** you help me? **Could** **Can** **Will**	*Would* is a softer request than *will*, and *could* is softer than *can*. In general, formality is shown by using *would* and *could* rather than *can* and *will*.
Asking for Permission	**Might** I speak with Bruce? **May** **Could** **Can**	*May* and *might* are more formal than *can* and *could*.
Giving Advice	You **must** arrive on time. **Should** **Ought to** **Might** **Could**	While *must* has the feeling of a requirement or very strong advice, *might* and *could* make the advice seem more like a suggestion than a required action.

4 In English, commands and requests show varying degrees of politeness or formality. A list of commands follows. Suppose that you are speaking to each of these people. Change the commands to appropriate requests.

the president of your university	your son or daughter
a classmate	your students
your teacher	your best friend

Example: Open the door.

Speaking to the president of the university, you should use very formal language. It would be appropriate to say, for example,

Would you mind opening the door for me?

Speaking to your son or daughter, you could say

Open the door, please.

1. Pass the salt.
2. Give me the homework assignment.
3. Help me with this problem.
4. Stop talking and listen to me.
5. Turn off the lights before you leave.
6. Wait a minute.

5 First, complete the items in this activity with appropriate modal auxiliaries. After each, indicate wheather your sentence is formal or informal. Then, with a partner or as a class, compare your choices and discuss the level of formality of each item.

Example: *Will* you pass the mashed potatoes, please?

Informal (for example, as a request to a family member at the dinner table).

1. You ________ see a doctor. That lump looks suspicious. ________
2. ________ I shut the window? It's really cold in here. ________
3. ________ Billy come with us to the movie this afternoon? ________
4. Every citizen ________ to vote in a presidential election. ________
5. You ________ try meditating to lower your blood pressure. ________
6. I just loved San Francisco. You really ________ go there if you have the chance ________.
7. ________ I have this dance? ________
8. Mr. President, ________ I be permitted to say a few words? ________
9. If you don't like the color, you ________ always bring it back for another. ________
10. Reverend Weir, ________ you give me permission to ask for your daughter's hand in marriage? ________

E. Other Modals and Their Uses

	Examples	Notes
Expressing Abilities	I **can** count to ten in five languages: English, Spanish, Italian, Korean, and Japanese. When I was a boy, I **could** spend hours with my baseball card collection.	*Can* is often used to express an ability that we have. When we use *could* to express ability, it refers to an ability we no longer have.
Showing Preference	I **would rather spend** time in the mountains than at the seashore. I **would prefer** to have an aisle seat.	*Would rather* is used to show a preference. We can also use *would prefer* to show preference, but it sounds more formal.
Expressing Urgent Need	I **have to stop** smoking, or I'll have serious problems. You **must not smoke** in here.	*Must, must not, have to,* and *have got to* are used for situations or actions that are important and necessary.
Expressing Lack of Need	We **don't have to leave** until 10:30.	The negative, *not have to,* has a very different meaning. It shows that something is not necessary or important.

6 Complete the following with *must not* or *doesn't/don't have to.*

Example: A student <u>doesn't have to</u> do extra credit work if he chooses not to.

1. You ____________ use electrical appliances while you are in the bathtub.
2. This homework is optional; you ____________ do it.
3. Students ____________ go on the field trip to the art museum; they can go to the language lab instead.
4. You ____________ make a left turn if there are cars coming from the opposite direction.
5. You ____________ use a pen on standardized tests such as the TOEFL.
6. If you drop a class, you ____________ wait until late in the semester.
7. A student ____________ buy a gift for the teacher at the end of the course.
8. Students ____________ attend graduation, but most do.

7 In the United States, rules of politeness are strictest within certain institutions. A good example is the military. Restate the following sentences, using the affirmative or negative forms of these expressions of necessity: *must, have to, have got to, had to.*

Example: It is forbidden for a common soldier to yell at a superior.
A common soldier must not yell at a superior.

1. It's necessary for soldiers to call officers "sir."
2. It's forbidden to call officers by their first names.
3. It is not necessary to bow to officers.
4. It is necessary to salute officers.
5. Many years ago, it was necessary for soldiers to treat officers almost like gods.
6. Many years ago, it wasn't necessary for officers to give soldiers any rights at all.
7. Today, it is necessary for soldiers to respect their officers, but it isn't necessary for them to be afraid of their officers.

8 Complete the conversation below. Then practice it with a partner. Take turns playing both roles.

Jack: Are you really a good soccer player, Kate?

Kate: Well, perhaps I ______(1) play so well now, but when I was younger I really ______(2) play well.

Jack: I was never good at soccer. I ______(3) play basketball than soccer any day.

Kate: Not me. I dislike basketball. I ______(4) think of an excuse not to play each time my friends invite me to play basketball.

Jack: Well, we're certainly different as far as sports is concerned. You ______(5) play soccer, and I ______(6) basketball.

Kate: Yes, and we ______(7) like the same things. Sometimes it's good for friends to have different interests.

Jack: Yeah, you're right.

Kate: I know I am.

Using What You've Learned

9 Slogans are short, catchy phrases designed to get your attention. They are often used in advertising and in politics to tell you what to do, whom to vote for, or what to buy. With your classmates, look at the slogans from these advertisements. Try to figure out which product is being advertised. Then find the modal auxiliary in each and give both its function and time frame in the context of the ad.

Example: The competition is good. We <u>had to</u> do better.
function: need; time: past

Next, look through newspapers and magazines to find more advertisements containing modal auxiliaries. Bring the ads to class and show them to your classmates. Explain the slogan and how the modal is used within it. Finally, tell the class your opinion of the ad.

SCRABBLE® is the registered trademark of Selchow & Righter Co., Bay Shore, NY, for its line of word games and entertainment services.

Wouldn't you
really rather have a Buick?

This opportunity may never come again! We can make you an offer you *can't* refuse!

For quality and dependability, shouldn't you have a Quasar?

COULD I HAVE AVOIDED THIS DAMAGE TO MY DRIVEWAY? YOU COULD HAVE WITH SMITH'S PROTECTIVE PAINT!

10 With a partner, role-play the following short situations. Take turns making requests and either granting or denying them. Use language that is appropriate to the relationship between the two speakers.

1. You want to borrow your classmate's dictionary.
2. You want to use your friend's car.
3. You want to make a long-distance phone call on your neighbor's phone.
4. You want to meet your professor in his office at 1 P.M. today.
5. You want to borrow $1,000 from your father.
6. You want to borrow some lecture notes from a classmate whom you know casually.
7. You want your boss's permission to leave work early because you need to go to the dentist.

11 Nonverbal communication, which includes body movements and gestures, can be just as expressive as verbal language. Your teacher will give each of you a card with an occupation or activity on it. Use body language as you take turns pantomiming these "occupations" in front of the class. As each student performs, try to guess what he or she is doing by using modals of probability or possibility. When someone guesses correctly, the pantomime can stop. While pantomiming, you may make sounds but don't use words.

Example: Plumber

He couldn't be a dentist.
He may be a repairman.
He might be working in the bathroom.
He could be fixing the sink.
He must be a plumber.

12 Language is very complex, and although most people learn their first language easily, few people find learning a second language as easy. In small groups, use the following questions to discuss the process of learning another language. After you've finished, choose one member of the group to give a brief summary of your discussion for the entire class.

1. Why is it difficult to learn a second language?
2. How can people best learn another language? Give some specific suggestions or advice that has been helpful for you.
3. What roles do/might computers play in language learning? In communicating across cultures and language groups?
4. Linguists talk about interference (the problem caused by trying to apply the ideas or rules of your first language to the second language). What problems do you have because of interference?
5. How important is grammatical correctness? When is it most important? What about pronunciation? Is it possible to "lose" an accent?

Web Note

Bell Labs, at Lucent Technology, is doing very interesting work on speech recognition for computers. Learn more about this work and try some fun demonstrations at www.bell-labs.com/project/tts/.

13 The actress Meryl Streep is famous for her ability to learn new accents. For her various films, she's learned Danish, Irish, and Polish accents, among others. How do actresses and actors learn different accents? Do some research at your library or on the Web. Give a brief presentation of your information for the class, and try to apply any new "tricks" to your learning of English!

Video Activities: The School of Success

Before You Watch. Discuss these questions in small groups.

1. Which of these things do you think are most important for students' academic success? Why?

   a. their school b. their home life c. their parents

2. What can parents do to help their children be more successful in school?

Watch. Answer these questions in small groups.

1. What is the name of the school featured in the video?____________
2. Who takes classes at this school?____________
3. Which of these things does George Frasier think causes failure in schools?
   a. Children watch too much television.
   b. Schools don't have enough money.
   c. Parents are not paying enough attention to their children.
4. Circle the things that George Frasier says that parents must give their children.

   a. love b. attention c. discipline d. support e. values

Watch Again. Listen for these words and say what they mean.

1. *Link* means the same as __________.

   a. connect b. establish c. separate

2. *Maintain* means the same as __________.

   a. begin b. finish c. continue

3. *Nurturing* means __________.

   a. talking to b. taking care of c. leaning on

4. *Structured* means __________.

   a. having rules b. being free c. safe

After You Watch. Complete these sentences with the correct form of the verb in parentheses.

The "School of Success" ________ (base) on the ideas of George Frasier. Frasier ________ (say) that parents ________ (need) ________ (be) involved in their children's education. He ________ (believe) that parents should ________ (make) sure that their children ________ (give) the kind of attention they need. When a good home life ________ (combine) with a structured learning environment, all children ________ (succeed).

Focus on Testing

Introduction to Focus on Testing

Each chapter includes a short practice exam that is similar to a standardized test like the TOEFL. With these, you will also find reminders about common problems with the structures covered in the chapter. Most of the tests focus on the structures of the particular chapter. Chapters 4, 8, and 12 have practice exams that include a variety of structures covered in the book. Use the various exams to help you to clarify any areas that you don't understand well and to learn which structures you need to study more.

Verbs and Modal Auxiliaries

Problem areas with verb tenses and modal auxiliaries always appear on standardized tests of English proficiency. Check your understanding of these structures by completing the sample items.

Remember . . .

- Verb tenses can have a variety of uses. For example, the simple present tense is sometimes used for past or future situations.
- The continuous tenses are used for actions in progress at a certain time.
- The perfect tenses are used for actions completed before another point in time.
- Modal auxiliaries do not change form, but their meanings usually depend on the context.

Part 1. Circle the best completion for the following.

Example: By 9:00 Ned ____________ his breakfast.

a. has finished
b. finishing
(c.) had finished
d. had been finishing

1. When she was an adolescent, Kate ____________ in a small state in the northern Midwest.
   a. used to live
   b. would live
   c. has lived
   d. living

2. I still ____________ my job, but I wouldn't mind an extended vacation in a tropical paradise.
   a. am loving
   b. have been loving
   c. love
   d. have loved

3. Anyone who attains a library card __________ take materials out of the library for two weeks.
   a. should
   b. must
   c. may
   d. had better

4. Has she ________ in London?
   a. ever live
   b. been live
   c. lived ever
   d. ever lived

Part 2. Each sentence has one error. Circle the letter below the word(s) containing the error.

Example: Joe goes (A) to Paris next week, but when I saw (B) him, he hasn't (Ⓒ) bought (D) his ticket yet.

1. I am sure (A) that she is having (B) a rewarding experience, but I am wanting (C) her to return (D) home by tomorrow at noon.

2. Their guide suggested that the hikers must (A) to start (B) walking (C) back to camp before it became (D) too dark and windy.

3. In retrospect, he realizes (A) that he should have not (B) voiced (C) his opinion before verifying (D) all the facts.

4. Until last year, we hadn't been (A) camping there since we used to (B) going (C) as (D) small children.

ANSWERS FOR PART 1, ACTIVITY 8

1. In terms of living persons, Derick Herning of the Shetland Islands won the "Polyglots of Europe" prize in 1990. He speaks 22 languages.
2. approximately 60,000
3. approximately 5,000 in spoken English and 10,000 in written English
4. approximately 33,000
5. "O." It has not changed since it was used in cuneiform writing in Syria around 1450 B.C.
6. Until 1600 A.D., "I" and "J" were used interchangeably, and likewise "U" and "V." Around 1600, "I" and "U" became vowels and "J" and "V" became consonants. However, even during the 19th century, some dictionaries still did not show the difference.
7. In order of frequency (including both spoken and written English): *the, of, and, to, a, in, that, is, I, it, for,* and *as*. In spoken English, number 1 is *I*.
8. *Set:* Oxford University Press gives 58 uses as a noun, 126 as a verb, and 10 as an adverb.

Chapter 2

Danger and Daring

IN THIS CHAPTER

Part 1 Review of Nouns, Pronouns, and Possessive Adjectives

Part 2 Indefinite Articles and Quantifiers

Part 3 The Definite Article with Count and Noncount Nouns

Part 4 The Definite Article with Proper Nouns

Part 5 More on Nouns and Noun Modifiers

Introduction

In this chapter, you will review singular and plural forms of nouns, use of articles and adjectives, and subject/verb agreement. As much of this chapter is review, you may not need to study everything in detail.

The following passage introduces the chapter theme "Danger and Daring" and raises some topics and issues you will cover in the chapter.

The Challenge of Exploration

In the summer of 1275, Marco Polo reached Shangtu, China. It was the end of a grueling* three-year journey. During the journey, Marco Polo came close to losing his life more than a few times. Yet he persisted and finally succeeded in reaching his goal: the kingdom of Kublai Khan.

At about the same time, Polynesians were exploring the thousands of islands of the South Pacific. Despite the great dangers of sailing long distances in open canoes, the Polynesians managed to explore and populate all the major islands within the triangle formed by Hawaii, Easter Island, and New Zealand.

About 200 years later, on August 3, 1492, Christopher Columbus left Europe to explore the unknown reaches of the Atlantic Ocean. Believing the earth to be flat, many feared that Columbus would fall off the edge of the world. Yet Columbus persevered. He did not reach his goal, Asia. Instead, he opened up a vast new world, the Americas.

Every explorer needs a vision, a goal. What drives explorers to leave the security of the known world and to face the dangers of the unknown? For many, it is a restless spirit. For a few, it is purely the love of adventure. Perhaps a paraphrase from George Mallory expressed this best; when asked why he wanted to climb Mt. Everest, Mallory's answer boiled down to "because it is there."

Discussing Ideas. For some people, the unknown is something to be feared. For others, however, the unknown holds a tremendous attraction. Why do you think people throughout history have been willing to risk their lives exploring the unknown?

PART 1 Review of Nouns, Pronouns, and Possessive Adjectives

Setting the Context

Prereading Questions. When you hear the name Marco Polo, what comes to mind? Where was he from? Where did he travel? Why is he considered important?

**grueling* extremely difficult physically or psychologically

Marco Polo

In 1271, 17-year-old Marco Polo left Venice to begin one of the most amazing odysseys of all time. Marco, along with his father Nicolo and his uncle Maffeo, was about to enter Asia, a land completely unknown to Europe. The mysteries that Marco Polo saw and reported changed not only his life but also the lives of Europeans in general.

Marco Polo was amazed by the wonders and riches he saw. The sophistication of the Orient made Europe seem primitive. While the weavers of Venice were just learning to work with silk, Oriental weavers had been producing exquisite brocade* for centuries. In making porcelain,** Oriental craftsmen had long used techniques that were unknown in the West. Throughout the empire of Kublai Khan, money made of paper was used for business transactions, something unheard of in Europe. In all, Marco Polo spent 24 years exploring the Eastern world from Venice to Cathay. The diary of his travels remains a remarkable tale of adventure as well as a record of the Orient of the thirteenth century.

Discussing Ideas. After reading "Marco Polo," can you answer the preceding questions? Can you add any other information about Marco Polo or his journeys?

A. Introduction to Nouns

A noun may be a person, a place, an object, an activity, an idea or emotion, or a quantity. A noun may be concrete (physical or tangible) or abstract (nonphysical or intangible). Both abstract and concrete nouns can be classified into two types: count nouns and noncount nouns.

B. Count Nouns

Count nouns are nouns that can be counted: *cars, ideas, people, trucks.* They have both singular and plural forms. Most count nouns are concrete (tangible); they can be seen, heard, felt, and so on. Some count nouns are abstract, however: *emotions, ideas.*

	Examples	Notes
Singular	I have **a car.** **The car** is small but comfortable. I bought **my car** in 1998.	A singular count noun *must* be preceded by an article (*a, an,* or *the*) or by an adjective (*his, my, one, three,* etc.).
Plural	**Bicycles** are usually much less expensive than **cars.** **Some bicycles** are made for racing. **The bicycle that he bought for the race** was very expensive.	Most plural nouns are not preceded by an article. Adjectives *(many, most, some)* can precede plural count nouns. *The* is used only when the noun is specifically known or identified *(the car that Jack bought).* See Part 3.

Note: See Appendix 2 for spelling rules for *-s* endings and for a list of irregular noun plurals, and Appendix 3 for pronunciation guidelines for *-s* endings.

**brocade* silk woven in complicated patterns of flowers and so forth

***porcelain* "china"; finely made ceramic dishes and figures

1 Give the plural of the following words.

1. valley
2. mouse
3. index
4. table
5. church
6. child
7. deer
8. baby
9. crisis
10. curriculum
11. hero
12. analysis
13. belief
14. alumnus
15. mosquito
16. stimulus
17. series
18. play
19. tooth
20. knife
21. tomato
22. monarch

2 On his journey to the empire of Kublai Khan, Marco Polo encountered many exotic customs. Complete these sentences about his experiences. Write the plural forms of the nouns in parentheses. Then practice the pronunciation of each. Pay special attention to the pronunciation of the *-s* ending.

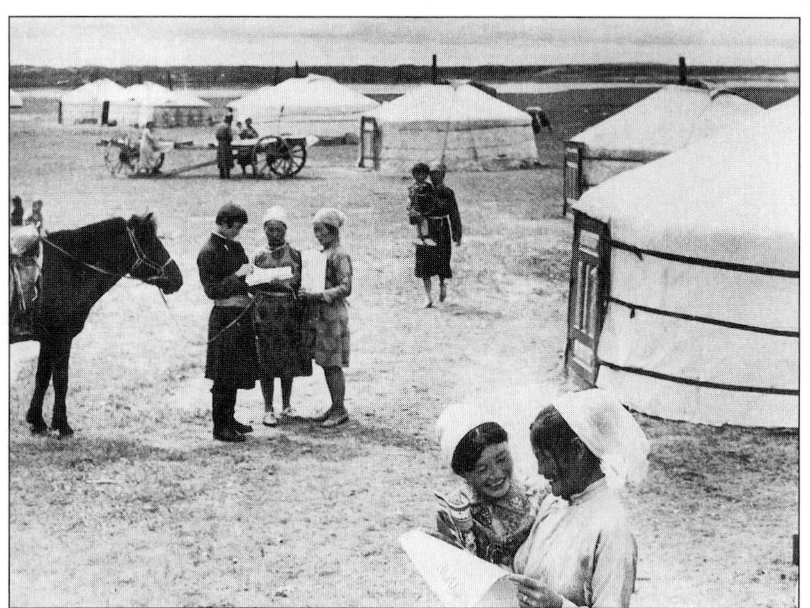

A modern Central Asian village with yurts

1. In India, Marco Polo found __________ (woman) who padded their __________ (hip) and who wore magnificent __________ (ruby).
2. The __________ (person) of the __________ (highland) of Kashmir hunted and herded giant __________ (sheep) still known today as "Marco Polo __________ (sheep)."

3. Before reaching the __________ (desert) of western China, Marco Polo found green __________ (oasis) and beautiful river __________ (valley) filled with __________ (gem) and __________ (mineral).
4. On the steppes of central Asia, Marco met the Tartars, nomadic __________ (horseman) who traveled constantly across the __________ (plain).
5. __________ (family) lived in __________ (yurt), wooden "__________" (tent) that had round __________ (roof) and that were easy to move.
6. The Tartar __________ (wife) decorated their __________ (home) with colorful __________ (tapestry*), hanging __________ (shelf), and beautiful __________ (dish).
7. Nomads whose __________ (journey) never ended, the Tartars used __________ (ox) to pull __________ (wagon) filled with their __________ (possession).
8. They carried their __________ (possession) from place to place in waterproof __________ (box).

C. Noncount Nouns

Noncount nouns are usually mass nouns *(butter, oil, water)* or abstract nouns *(honesty, love)* that we don't normally count. Noncount nouns are always singular.

	Examples	Notes
Mass Nouns	**Food, clothing,** and **shelter** are basic needs for all people. How much **water** do you drink daily? Humans need at least **a gallon of water** daily. **Air** is essential for most living things.	*A* and *an* are never used with noncount nouns. *The* may be used in specific cases (see p. 63). Units of measurement such as *gallon* and *pound* are often used with mass nouns (see p. 58). Adjectives *(any, our, some)* and other quantifiers *(a lot of, plenty of)* may be used with noncount nouns. Most activities and studies are noncount nouns, even though some end in *-s.* Gerunds (the *-ing* form of verbs) function as noncount nouns.
Abstract Nouns	Everyone hopes for **happiness.** We all need **a little love** and **consideration.** We appreciated **your consideration.** We also appreciated **your help** with **our math homework.** **Mathematics** is a difficult subject. **Your helping** me was very considerate.	

**tapestry* woven fabric for wall hangings or rugs

D. Nouns That Are Both Count and Noncount

Some nouns can be count or noncount, depending on the context. Compare:

	Examples	Notes
Noncount Noun	**Experience** is a good teacher.	*Experience* = an idea with no specific limits
Count Noun	She's had many good **experiences** and some bad ones.	*Experiences* = specific actions or situations
Noncount Noun	I had **turkey** for lunch.	*Turkey* = a type of food
Count Noun	Have you ever seen **a** wild **turkey?**	*A turkey* = a bird

3 For each sentence, indicate whether the noun(s) in italics are count or noncount.

Example: N His *work* is restoring old paintings.
C He restores *works* of art.

1. ______ We've traveled to Italy many *times.*
2. ______ I had a wonderful *experience* on my last trip.
3. ______ Do you have *time* to tell us about your trip to Rome?
4. ______ What are your *thoughts* about a trip to Venice?
5. ______ I have to consider my *finances* before planning a trip.
6. ______ Current *thought* holds that many Europeans traveled to China both before and after Marco Polo.
7. ______ At the time of Marco Polo, Venice was a center of *business* for all of Europe.
8. ______ Venice is a city surrounded by *water.*
9. ______ The *waters* of several rivers flow towards Venice.
10. ______ In Marco Polo's time, a wide variety of *businesses* flourished in Venice.
11. ______ Venice was a center of *finance.*
12. ______ Venice was also the center of ship *building* in Europe.
13. ______ In today's Venice, few *buildings* remain from pre-medieval times.
14. ______ Venice was and still is a center for the *arts.*
15. ______ Students from all over the world study *art* in Venice.
16. ______ Venice is famous for *artwork* made of *glass.*
17. ______ For centuries, artisans in Venice have crafted beautiful *glasses* and *bowls.*
18. ______ It takes many years of *experience* to become a master glassblower.

4 Quickly reread the passage "Marco Polo" on page 47. Then, underline all the common nouns in the second paragraph (not the proper names). Indicate which are noncount and which are count. For the count nouns, if the noun is singular, also give the plural form. If the noun is plural, also give the singular form.

5 Form complete sentences from the following cues. Make all count nouns plural. Use *was* or *were* + *being* + the past participle as in the example.

The Orient of the thirteenth century was much more advanced than the medieval cultures Marco Polo had left in Europe. His diary serves as a record of all the amazing things he encountered. He wrote that . . .

Examples: ruby / mine throughout Asia

He wrote that rubies were being mined throughout Asia.

Oil / use for heating and lighting in Persia

Oil was being used for heating and lighting in Persia.

1. milk / dehydrate into powder
2. jewel / trade throughout Asia
3. sophisticated city / construct
4. canal / build
5. weather / study
6. star / map
7. paper money / use throughout the empire
8. eye glasses / develop
9. ice cream / perfect
10. spaghetti / make
11. silk / weave into beautiful brocade
12. gunpowder / use
13. highway / build
14. plumbing system / develop
15. astrology / practice

E. Personal Pronouns and Possessive Adjectives

Pronouns take the place of nouns. Possessive adjectives come before nouns or noun forms such as gerunds (see Chapter 9).

	Singular					Plural	
Subject	I	You	He	She	It	We	They
Object	Me	You	Him	Her	It	Us	Them
Possessive Adjective	My	Your	His	Her	Its	Our	Their
Possessive Pronoun	Mine	Yours	His	Hers	Its	Ours	Theirs
Reflexive	Myself	Yourself	Himself	Herself	Itself	Ourselves Yourselves	Themselves

6 Fill in each blank with an appropriate pronoun. Use arrows to indicate which noun each pronoun refers to.

Example: Marco Polo traveled with <u>his</u> father and <u>his</u> uncle.

1. The three Polos financed the trip ________.
2. The Polos left ________ home in Venice, Italy, in 1272.
3. In 1275, the Polos ended ________ journey when ________ reached Shangtu.
4. The great Chinese emperor Kublai Khan had built ________ summer palace in Shangtu.
5. The summer palace was magnificent with ________ walls of marble and ________ 16 square miles of parks.
6. Soon after the Polos' arrival, Marco was added to the Khan's household, and during ________ 17 years of service, ________ made ________ so useful that ________ became the Khan's personal representative throughout the empire.
7. We owe much of ________ knowledge of thirteenth-century China to Marco Polo.
8. The diary of Marco Polo, with ________ tales of danger and daring, is fascinating to read even today.

Web Note

For further information on Marco Polo, consult your library or the Web. A good source on the Web is the Fordham University Center for Medieval Studies, which offers its Internet Medieval Sourcebook *at www.fordham.edu/halsall/sbook.html.*

Using What You've Learned

7 Many people dream of traveling to exotic places in search of unusual experiences. Others can find the unusual close to home. What unusual experiences have you had? What unusual sights have you seen? In a five-minute presentation, describe one particularly unusual place that you have visited. Try to mention as many of the different things that you saw as possible and tell about experiences that you had.

Focus on Testing

Pronoun and Adjective Usage

Pronouns and possessive adjectives are frequently tested on standardized English proficiency exams. Check your understanding of these structures by completing the sample items that follow.

Remember that . . .

- Singular pronouns are used to refer to singular nouns.
- Plural pronouns are used to refer to plural nouns.
- Subject (not object) pronouns are used as complements of linking verbs.
- Object (not subject) pronouns are used as direct or indirect objects of verbs and as objects of prepositions.
- Possessive adjectives *(her, my)* are used with body parts.

Part 1. Circle the best completion for the following.

Example: By 9:00 Ned ____________ his breakfast.

a. has finished
b. finishing
(c.) had finished
d. had been finishing

1. John ____________ went to the concert.
   a. and I
   b. and me
   c. and myself
   d. along with I

2. Kublai Khan failed in ____________ to conquer Japan in 1281.
   a. he attempted
   b. him attempt
   c. his attempt
   d. he attempting

3. The Jacksons invited ____________ to dinner.
   a. Steven and I
   b. Steven and myself
   c. Steven and me
   d. Steven along with I

4. The silkworm moth produces the basis for silk when weaving ____________ cocoon.
   a. it's
   b. their
   c. theirs
   d. its

Part 2. Each sentence has one error. Circle the letter below the word(s) containing the error.

Example: He wrote (A) that rubies were being (B) mine (Ⓒ) throught (D) Asia.

1. Long before (A) elaborate water systems were used (B) in Europe, the Chinese had developed them (C) for his (D) major cities.
2. A craftsman (A) may spend years studying the making of (B) porcelain before they become (C) true masters of their (D) art.
3. According (A) to psychologist Frank Farley (B), risk takers are people who (C) need a high level of stimulation in his (D) day-to-day life.
4. During his journeys (A), Marco Polo encountered groups of (B) nomads in Central Asia who wore colorful clothing and wrapped embroidered (C) cloth around the legs (D).

PART 2 Indefinite Articles and Quantifiers

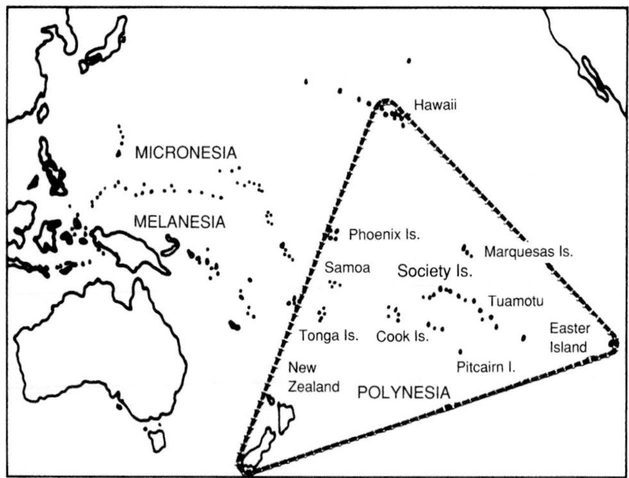

Setting the Context

Prereading Questions. Where is Polynesia? How large is the area that it includes?

Web Note

An interesting Website on explorations, including information on the Polynesians, is 1492, *an exhibit of the U.S. Library of Congress, found at www.ibiblio.org/expo/1492.exhibit.*

The Polynesians

The people of Oceania were an extremely adventurous group. As a distinct population with common origins, the Polynesians were the most widely spread people on earth before 1500 A.D. Few other groups in history have traveled so much while taking so few material possessions with them. The Polynesians settled the islands of the vast triangle formed by the Hawaiian Islands, Easter Island, and New Zealand. With sides approximately 6,500 kilometers in length, this triangle covers almost twice the area of the United States. The Polynesians began their expansion through the South Pacific around 2000 B.C., and by the time of Marco Polo's visit to China, they had settled all of its major islands.

Discussing Ideas. Have you visited Polynesia? What do you know about the ancient Polynesians? How were they able to navigate the large distances between the islands?

A. Indefinite Articles

A or *an* is used before a singular count noun. The indefinite article may mean *one,* or it may mean an unspecified person or thing. A singular count noun always takes an article (*a, an,* or *the*) or an adjective *(one, another). A* or *an* is not used with a noncount noun or with a plural count noun.

	Examples	Notes
a	**a** sailor **a** house **a** European	*A* is used before a singular count noun that begins with a consonant sound.
an	**an** island **an** hour	*An* is used before a singular count noun that begins with a vowel sound.

1 Complete the following passage by using *a, an,* or *X* (to indicate that no article is necessary).

Voyages to the Unknown

___X___ (1) Polynesian travelers underwent ________ (2) hardships that are difficult for ________ (3) modern people to imagine. The 4,000 kilometer voyage from the Society Islands to the Hawaiian Islands may cover only inches on ________ (4) map, but in ________ (5) open canoe loaded with ________ (6) men, ________ (7) women, ________ (8) children, ________ (9) animals, and ________ (10) precious seed plants, the voyage must surely have been ________ (11) incredible ordeal. Still, the Polynesians reached virtually every island within the huge Polynesian triangle—________ (12) amazing accomplishment!

2 Try to imagine what the first voyage to Hawaii was like. Complete the following by using *a, an*, or *X* (to indicate that no article is necessary).

On the High Seas

For ___X___ (1) centuries, the people of the Marquesas Islands had noticed that ______ (2) birds flew north from the islands in the fall and returned in the spring. The islanders knew that the birds must be flying to ______ (3) piece of land where they spent the winter.

Finally, in about 500 A.D., ______ (4) young chief decided to search for the land to the north. He recruited both ______ (5) men and ______ (6) women for the journey. He also recruited ______ (7) experienced navigator who knew how to follow ______ (8) steady course even though the Polynesians didn't have ______ (9) compasses or ______ (10) other equipment. For ______ (11) centuries, ______ (12) Polynesian navigators had been using ______ (13) birds, ______ (14) cloud formations, ______ (15) stars, ______ (16) wave patterns, and the sun to guide them in their ocean voyages.

As the explorers made ______ (17) preparations for this voyage northward, ______ (18) food and ______ (19) water were ______ (20) major problems. They knew that they would be able to catch ______ (21) fish along the way. But they would need ______ (22) fresh water supply that would last throughout the trip. In addition, they prepared ______ (23) dried bananas, ______ (24) coconut, ______ (25) fish, ______ (26) large bag of taro root,* and ______ (27) cooked breadfruit* for each canoe.

Finally, ______ (28) dozens of ______ (29) double canoes were packed and ready to begin this voyage. After at least ______ (30) month on the open ocean, these

---

**taro root, breadfruit* Polynesian staple foods

explorers spotted ________ (31) land birds, ________ (32) signal to any navigator that ________ (33) island or other landmass was near. They had completed ________ (34) voyage of over 1,500 miles and had discovered the Hawaiian Islands.

3 Change the words in italics from singular to plural or from plural to singular. Add or delete *a* or *an* when appropriate, and make all necessary changes in verbs or pronouns.

Example: Polynesian *navigators* had to be very skillful.
A Polynesian navigator had to be very skillful.

1. *Navigators* had to notice and understand particular movements of waves.
2. An ocean *wave* near an *island* has a particular appearance and "feeling" from the inside of a canoe.
3. A good *navigator* could tell the difference between one type of wave and another.
4. Polynesian *navigators* could also use *stars* to guide them during *voyages.*
5. A *navigator* watched a *star* that rose or set over a particular *island.*
6. *He* would only use a *star* that was near the horizon.
7. To plan the course or direction, *they* would use zenith *stars.*
8. Zenith *stars* point down to specific *islands,* and they helped *navigators* determine location.
9. By the mid 1700s, a *sextant* was generally used to determine the location of a *ship.*
10. *Sextants* can determine latitude and longitude.

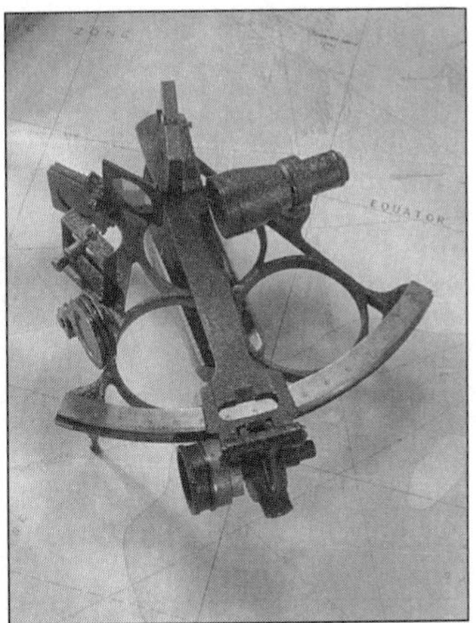
Sextants were used for navigation.

4 In pairs, test your knowledge of the equipment used in different occupations. Ask and answer questions from the following cues. Then add at least five of your own.

Example: a pilot
What equipment does a pilot use?
A pilot uses a compass.

1. radiologist
2. secretary
3. gardener
4. cowboy
5. hunter

B. Units of Measurement

Units of measurement are used with both count and noncount nouns. With noncount nouns, they allow us to count or measure quantities *(rice/one cup of rice, gas/one gallon of gas).* Units of measurement are commonly used in this pattern: number or percent + unit + *of* + name of item. *Dozen* does not follow this pattern, however; see the example that follows.

Examples	Common Units of Measurement			
I'd like **a box of cookies.**	bag	carton	loaf	six-pack
Please get **a gallon of milk.**	bottle	dozen	piece	twelve-pack
Could you also get **two pounds of Swiss cheese?**	box	gallon, etc.	package	tube
We need **a dozen eggs,** too.	bunch	head	pound, etc.	
	can	jar	roll	

5 Look at the picture. Then use units of measurement to complete the following list of provisions.

1. ______ bread
2. ______ oranges
3. ______ jam
4. ______ water
5. ______ soap
6. ______ bananas
7. ______ eggs
8. ______ rice
9. ______ toothpaste
10. ______ soda pop
11. ______ chips
12. ______ paper towels

C. Indefinite Adjectives and Pronouns

Indefinite expressions of quantity such as *some, many,* and *little* can be used as adjectives when they are combined with nouns. (Do you want *some coffee?*) Or they can be used as pronouns when they replace nouns. (No, I've already had *some*.) The type of noun (count or noncount) determines which adjective or pronoun may be used.

	Examples	Notes
Noncount Nouns	How **much** (time) do you have? I have **a little** (time). I have **only a little** (time). I have **very little** (time). I have **less** (time) than I'd thought.	*Much, quite a little, a little, only a little, not much, little, very little, less,* and *the least* are used as adjectives with noncount nouns. They also may be used without the noun.
Count Nouns	How **many** (trips) do you have to take this year? I have to take **several (a few, a couple)** (trips).	*Many, quite a few, several, a couple (of), a few, only a few, not many, few, fewer,* and *the fewest* are used with count nouns. They may also be used without the noun.
Both Count and Noncount Nouns	Do you have **some** money? Do you have **some** one-dollar bills? Do you have **any** money? Do you have **any** one-dollar bills? I have **lots of** money, but I have **no** one-dollar bills. I have **none.**	*(The) most, a lot (of), lots (of), plenty (of), some,* and *no* are used with both count and noncount nouns. *None* is a singular pronoun. *Any* is used in questions and negatives with both count and noncount nouns.

Note: A few and *a little* mean "some." *Few* and *little* mean "almost no": *I have a few (some) friends. I have few (almost no) friends.*

6 Work in a chain. One student begins by making a question with *some* or *any* from the first item. A classmate will answer it using *not much* or *not many.* He or she will then make a question. Another classmate will answer that question using *not much* or *not many,* and then ask the next question.

Example: money

A. **Do you have any money?**

B. **I don't have much money.**

one-dollar bills

B. **Do you have some one-dollar bills?**

C. **I don't have many one-dollar bills.**

1. free time
2. homework
3. e-mail messages to send
4. quarters

5. good food at home
6. snacks with you
7. homework assignments
8. blank paper
9. good magazines
10. gas in your car
11. change
12. good advice for me
13. news from home
14. information about good Websites
15. time for a cup of coffee

7 Repeat Activity 6, this time giving answers with *a little* or *a few.*

Example: money

A. **Do you have any money?**

B. **Sure, I have a little money.**

one-dollar bills

B. **Do you have some one-dollar bills?**

C. **Sure, I have a few one-dollar bills.**

8 Imagine that you are about to leave for a four-week sailing trip. You will be on the open ocean for almost a month, so you need to plan carefully which supplies to take. In pairs, ask and answer questions from the following cues. Use *how much* or *how many* in the questions and indefinite pronouns or adjectives in the answers. When you finish with the cues, add some of your own from each category or add some new categories.

Example: fruit

A. **How much fruit should we bring?**

B. **I love fruit! Let's buy a lot.**

or A. **How many mangoes should we buy?**

B. **Let's buy only a few mangoes. They spoil easily.**

1. meat (hot dogs, steak, etc.)
2. dairy products (milk, yogurt, etc.)
3. water
4. vegetables (carrots, potatoes, lettuce, etc.)
5. staples (flour, rice, corn, beans, etc.)
6. vices (cigarettes, beer, games, etc.)

9 You are nearing the end of the four-week sailing trip. It has been three weeks since you last saw land, and supplies are beginning to run short. Complete the following conversations with *(only a) few, a few, (only a) little,* and *a little.*

Example: Could I have *a little* coffee with breakfast?

1. A. I'd like to have ______ sugar with my coffee.
   B. There is some sugar, but we have ______ fresh water. Maybe you should forget about the coffee.
2. A. What are we going to eat for dinner?
   B. We still have ______ rice left. Let's have that.
3. A. I'm tired of rice. Let's eat ______ hamburgers instead.
   B. Sorry, there is ______ hamburger meat left. But we do have ______ hot dogs. Shall we try those?
4. A. This trip is boring. Do you want to play ______ poker?
   B. Sure, but I should warn you that ______ cards are missing.
5. A. I hope we reach land soon. Then we can have ______ fun.
   B. There'll be ______ time for fun when we reach shore. We'll be too busy eating.

Using What You've Learned

10 Have you gone grocery shopping lately? Will you go soon? In pairs, take turns telling what you bought or what you are going to buy. Be sure to use specific units of measurement.

Example: *I'm going to the store tonight, and I need to buy a lot of things. I need two or three bars of soap, a bottle of dishwashing soap, a bottle of shampoo. . . .*

11 In small groups, imagine that you are making plans for a space voyage to a distant planet. There may or may not be fresh water and/or food available when you arrive. Also, the chances are that you will never be able to return to earth. Make a list of items for each of the following categories. Then choose a total of ten things that you will take. Don't choose more than three items from one category, and be sure to specify how much or how many of each item you are planning to take. Your spaceship is quite small, so space and weight are important considerations. When you are finished, report your selections to the class. Be ready to give explanations for your choices.

foods	animals	tools
plants	liquids	educational materials
weapons		

PART 3

The Definite Article with Count and Noncount Nouns

Setting the Context

Prereading Questions. What period was called the "Age of Discovery"? What were Europeans searching for? How did this lead to the discovery of the Americas?

Trade Routes to the East

By the first part of the fifteenth century, Europe was beginning the most dramatic period of change in its history. Economics, together with politics and religion, was changing the societies of Europe. The recent, tremendous growth in the population of Europe had brought the cultivation of new land, the demand for new products, and a new class of merchants to trade in these products. The merchants were interested in trading in Asia. However, Asia was still a mystery to them, for most of their knowledge of the East was based on Marco Polo's hundred-year-old diary. Its tales were fresh and enticing enough, though, to spark the search for new sea routes to Asia. The European search for new trade markets and products led to discoveries that radically changed the course of history. This search eventually led to the discovery of the "New World."

Columbus's ships on the open sea

Discussing Ideas. What was happening in Europe at the beginning of the 1400s? Why were Europeans so interested in trading with Asia?

A. The Definite Article with Count Nouns

The is used before a singular or plural count noun when that noun is specifically identified: *They bought a boat, but* ***the*** *boat sank;* or its identity is already understood: *the beautiful new boat that Nick bought. The* is often used when a noun is identified by a prepositional phrase or an adjective clause: *the man in the hallway; the man who came to dinner.*

However, if the noun is used in a more general way, *the* is not used: *Cars can be more convenient than bicycles; faith, hope, and courage are important virtues.*

	Examples	Notes
Nonspecific	**Merchants** had been interested in a new trade route for years. **A merchant** always needs new markets.	No article is used with nonspecific plural nouns. *A* or *an* is used with nonspecific singular nouns.
Specific	**The merchants** of Spain were particularly interested in a new route. **The merchants** that paid for explorations wanted to become rich. **The most dramatic period** of change in the history of Europe was beginning.	The prepositional phrase tells *which* merchants. *Note: The + noun + of* is a frequent combination in English. The adjective clause tells *which merchants.* Note that no commas are used with this clause. See Chapter 4 for more information. *The* is almost always used with superlatives.

B. The Definite Article with Noncount Nouns

Articles are not normally used with noncount nouns. However, noncount nouns, like count nouns, may be preceded by *the* when the noun is *specifically* identified.

	Examples	Notes
Nonspecific	**Pepper** was very important to Europeans.	No articles are used with unspecified noncount nouns.
Specific	**The pepper** from India was treasured. **The pepper** that was sold in European markets was often more valuable than gold. At that time, India produced **the most pepper** in the world.	*The* is often used with a noncount noun when the noun is identified by a phrase or clause. *The* is almost always used with superlatives.

1 Quickly reread the passage "Trade Routes to the East" on page 62. Then do the following:

1. Underline all examples of identifying phrases that follow this pattern: *the* + noun 1 + *of* + noun 2. Then, identify each noun 1 as count or noncount.
2. Now underline any other examples of identifying phrases that follow this pattern: *the* + noun 1 + preposition + noun 2. Then, identify each noun 1 as count or noncount.

2 Work in a chain and add identifying phrases or clauses to the following count nouns. Choose any noun on the list or add some count nouns of your own.

Example: A. book
B. **the book on the table**
B. boat
C. **the boat that I want to buy**

apple	camera	computer	month	stereo
boat	car	egg	painting	sweater
book	class	exam	party	vacation
businessperson	clothes	house	problem	yacht

3 Now, do the same with noncount nouns. Work in a chain and add identifying phrases or clauses to the following noncount nouns. Choose any noun on the list or add some of your own.

Example: A. sugar
B. **the sugar in the sugar bowl**
B. oil
C. **the oil that Kuwait exports**

advice	energy	gas	oil	tea
anger	fish	love	studying	time
chicken	furniture	money	sugar	traffic
coffee	jewelry	news	sunlight	water

4 Complete the following by using *the* or *X* (to indicate that no article is necessary). In some cases, either may be appropriate. Be prepared to explain your choices.

A caravan makes its way across the desert.

Culture Note

For a long time, pepper was one of the few ways available for preserving food. Today, however, numerous preservatives are used in the United States and other countries. Growing numbers of Americans are concerned about this issue and try to learn more about what is added during the processing of food. If you are concerned, you can consult this Website from the U.S. Food and Drug Administration: www.vm.cfsan.fda.gov/~lrd/foodadd.

Example: Fifteenth-century Europe needed _X_ precious metals.

1. Europeans wanted ________ metals so that they could make ________ coins for use in trading.
2. Of course, ________ most valuable metal was ________ gold.
3. ________ Europeans wanted to control ________ gold that ________ Arab traders were bringing from the East.
4. ________ Arab merchants in the Middle East were also dealing in ________ emeralds, ________ rubies, ________ sapphires, and ________ silk.
5. ________ silk from China was far superior to ________ silk from Europe.
6. Above all, ________ Europe wanted ________ spices.
7. ________ Europeans used these spices from Asia to preserve and season ________ meat.
8. ________ pepper grew far away in India and Sumatra, and it was outrageously expensive.

C. The with Quantifiers

Quantifiers such as *all, most, some,* and *enough* can be used as pronouns followed by prepositional phrases. These phrases use *the* or another determiner such as *these* or *those*. When the quantifier is used as an adjective, *the* is omitted in most cases.

	With *the* (pronoun quantifier + phrase)	**Without *the* (adjective quantifier)**
Count Nouns	**All of the passengers** are on board.	**All passengers** are on board.
Noncount Nouns	**Most of the luggage** is now on board.	**Most luggage** is now on board.

Note: In conversational English, *the* is sometimes used after *all*. Compare: *All of the passengers are on board. All passengers are on board. All the passengers are on board.*

5 **Error Analysis.** Many of the following sentences have errors in the use of *the* with expressions of quantity. Find and correct each error.

Example: All of money for Columbus's voyage came from Spain.
Correction: All money for Columbus's voyage came from Spain.
All of the money for Columbus's voyage came from Spain.

Web Note

See a great article about the medieval spice trade from a 1998 Economist *at www.economist.com/displayStory.cfm?Story_ID=179810*

1. Some of world's greatest explorers lived during the fifteenth century.
2. All of these explorers were hoping to find a short route to "the Indies."
3. Some explorers were financed by merchants.
4. Many of explorers were financed by monarchs of different European kingdoms.
5. Most of exploring was in search of faster routes to bring pepper and other spices to Europe.
6. Enough pepper eventually reached Europe that ways of cooking and preserving meat actually changed because of this exotic spice.
7. The most of pepper came from India.
8. Some of other spices valuable in 15th century Europe were anise, cinnamon, coriander, and marjoram.

D. Quantifiers and Subject/Verb Agreement

Many pronoun quantifiers can be followed by phrases with either count or noncount nouns. The noun in the prepositional phrase determines whether the verb is singular or plural. When count nouns are used, plural verbs follow. When noncount nouns are used, singular verbs follow.

	Examples	**Notes**
All, Most, Some, Enough Fractions and Percentages	**All** of the **money was** from Spain. **Most** of his **ideas were** wrong. **Half** of the **food has** been eaten. **The rest** of the **food has** spoiled. About **75 percent** of the **sailors were** sick. **The majority** of the crew **members were** sick.	A variety of quantifiers may be used as pronouns and followed by *of the* (or *of* + a demonstrative or possessive) + noun. They may also be used as adjectives with either count or noncount nouns *(all money, enough people)*. With these expressions a singular verb follows a noncount noun, and a plural verb follows a count noun.
None	**None** of the **sailors was** experienced.	In formal English, *none* is always followed by a singular verb.

6 Complete the sentences by using the singular or plural forms of the nouns and verbs in parentheses. Use the past tense.

Example: All of the great fifteenth-century European _explorers were_ (explorer / be) trying to find a short route to "the Indies."

1. All of their early ____________ (exploring / be) directed toward eastward routes.
2. At that time, most ____________ (person / be) convinced that the earth was flat and that a westward voyage would be impossible.
3. In the late 1400s, some of the important ____________ (ruler) of Europe ____________ (be) interested in trying a westward route.
4. Two of these ____________ (leader / be) told of a young man named Christopher Columbus.
5. Most of Columbus's ____________ (knowledge) of the earth ____________ (be) based on incorrect theories.
6. Many of his ____________ (calculation) of distance ____________ (be) wrong.
7. Enough of his ____________ (guess / be) correct, however, and he accurately calculated the 2,500-mile width of the Atlantic Ocean.
8. At first, none of the ____________ (monarch) of Europe ____________ (be) interested in financing Columbus.
9. Finally, enough of the necessary ____________ (money / be) gathered for Columbus to set sail on August 3, 1492.

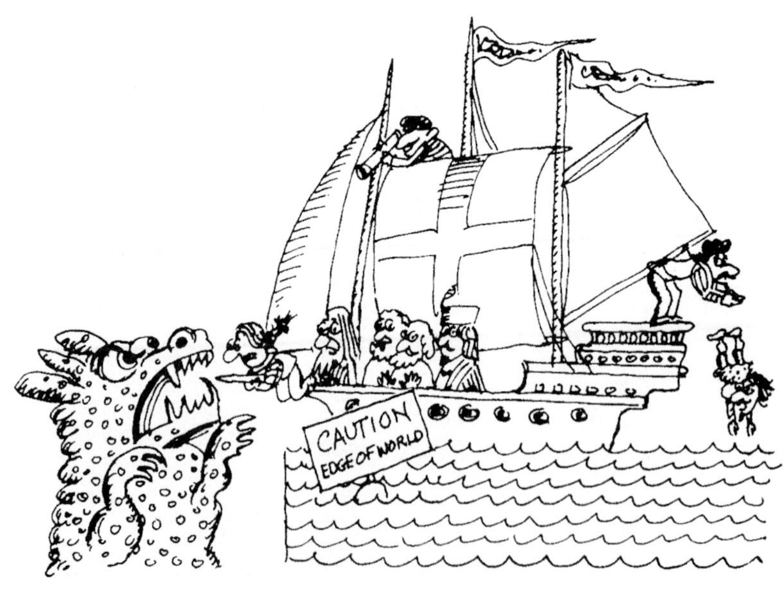

10. The majority of the ____________ (crew) with Columbus ____________ (be) trustworthy.
11. Many of the ____________ (sailor) ____________ (be) ready to turn back at times during the long and arduous voyage, but eventually they reached land—"the New World"—on October 12, 1492.
12. Because of Columbus's voyage, all of the existing ____________ (idea) about the shape and size of the earth ____________ (be) eventually proven wrong. Unfortunately, however, Columbus never knew the incredible impact of his explorations.

E. The Number of *Versus* A Number of: *Subject/Verb Agreement*

Both *a number of* and *the number of* are followed by plural nouns. However, the use of *a* or *the* affects both the meaning of the phrase and the form of the verb that follows.

	Examples	Notes
a Number of	**A number of** ships **were** built.	*A number of* means "many." The verb must be plural.
the Number of	**The number of** ships **was** quite high.	*The number of* refers to a specific quantity. It must be followed by a singular verb.

7 Choose the correct verb form to complete the sentences on the following page.

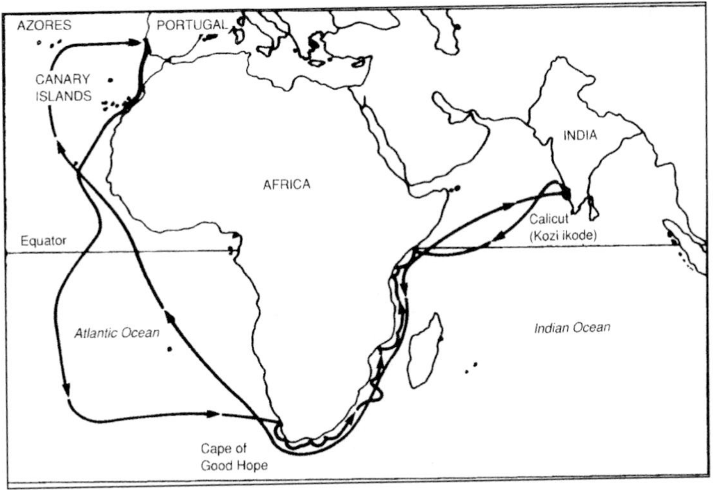

1. By the mid-1400s, a number of European monarchs (was / were) paying for explorations in search of a new route to India.
2. A number of unsuccessful attempts to circle Africa (was / were) financed by the Portuguese king, Manuel I.
3. In 1497, Manuel I chose Vasco da Gama to make another attempt to circle Africa. The number of sailors (was / were) determined by da Gama.
4. A number of his sailors (was / were) veterans of many voyages.
5. Three long months on the open ocean passed before a number of land birds (was / were) spotted.
6. Because of da Gama's "fearfully violent" character, the number of attempted mutinies on the voyage (was / were) low.

F. Two-Part Subjects: Subject / Verb Agreement

When there is more than one noun before the verb, there may be confusion about whether the verb should be singular or plural.

	Examples	Notes
both . . . and	**Both** the sailors **and** Columbus **were** considered mad.	A plural verb always follows subjects with *both . . . and.*
either . . . or neither . . . nor not only . . . but also	**Neither** Columbus **nor** his aides **were** Spanish. **Neither** his aides **nor** Columbus **was** Spanish.	The verb is singular or plural, depending on the subject closest to the verb when *either . . . or, neither . . . nor,* or *not only . . . but also* is used.
along with as well as in addition to together with	**Columbus, together with** his men, **was** ready to set sail on August 3, 1492. **The sailors, as well as** their captain, **were** on the open seas a few days later.	The nouns that follow these expressions do not affect the verb. The subject alone determines whether the verb is singular or plural. *Note:* Phrases with these expressions are normally set off by commas.

8 Complete the following by choosing the appropriate verb form in parentheses.

1. Both the loyalty and ability of the Portuguese sailor Ferdinand Magellan (was / were) well known by King Manuel I.
2. However, neither King Manuel I nor his advisers (was / were) interested in Magellan's plan to reach the East by sailing west.
3. Neither his pleas for money nor his request for a ship (was / were) granted by the Portuguese king.
4. However, King Carlos I of Spain, as well as several rich and influential Spaniards, (was / were) willing to pay for Magellan's new voyage.
5. Magellan's flagship *The Trinidad,* along with four other ships, (was / were) ready to sail for "the Indies" by September 1519.
6. Not only Spaniards and Portuguese but also one Englishman (was / were) in Magellan's crew.
7. Magellan set sail with 250 sailors, but either battles or sickness (was / were) going to kill 232 of the crew.

8. On September 8, 1522, Juan Sebastian del Cano (who commanded after Magellan's death), along with 18 survivors, (was / were) welcomed back to the Spanish harbor of Seville.
9. Neither Magellan nor many of his crew members (was / were) able to survive.
10. The survivors, as well as their dead captain, (was / were) heroes, for they had participated in the first trip around the world.

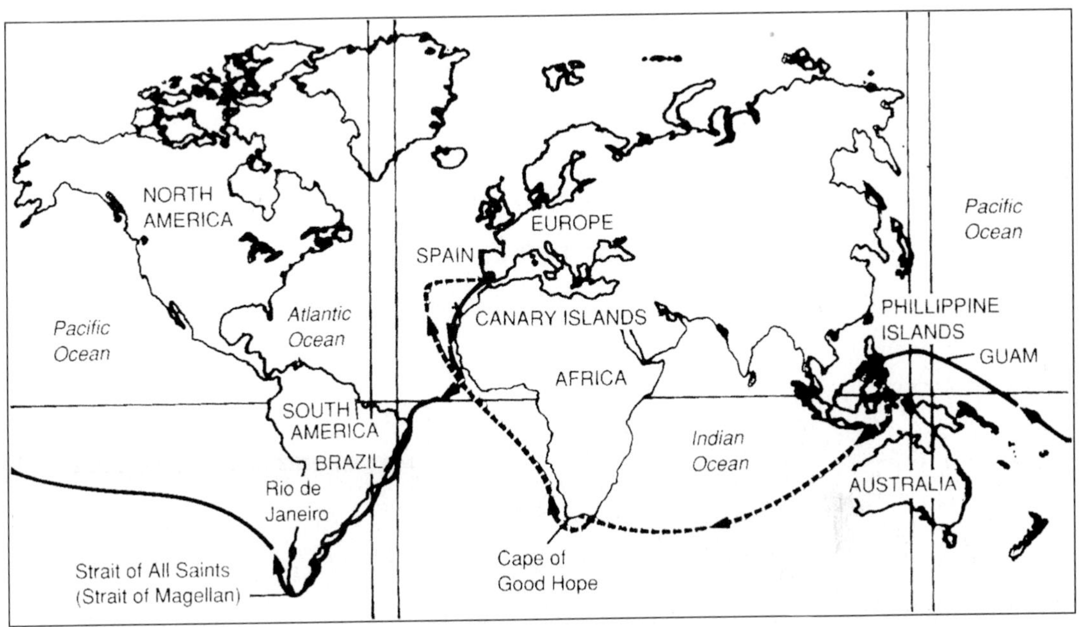

The first voyage around the world. Solid lines indicate Magellan in command; dotted lines indicate del Cano in command.

Using What You've Learned

9 Natural resources are an essential part of every economy. Different countries have resources such as oil, minerals, water, and good soil. What are the primary resources in your area or native country? Work in pairs or small groups, and take turns telling about resources. Make a general statement about one of these resources. Then follow this with a more specific remark.

Example: Oil is one of our most important natural resources.

Most of the oil is in the northwestern part of the country.

or

The oil from the southern part is very heavy.

10 Use your knowledge of products and resources worldwide to organize a trivia game. Separate into two groups and prepare a brief list (ten to fifteen words) of products (watches, golf clubs, cars, chocolate, etc.) or resources (oil, diamonds, uranium, etc.) to use in the game. Then, write at least two questions for each item. The questions may ask for any type of information, but someone on your team must know the answer. Write the answers to give to your teacher.

Example: Question: *Which country produces most of the world's diamonds?*
Answer: *South Africa.*

To play the game, take turns asking and answering each other's questions about the different items. A different student must answer each item until everyone on the team has participated. Score five points for acceptable answers; your teacher will be the judge of the answers.

PART 4

The Definite Article with Proper Nouns

Setting the Context

Prereading Questions. What is the Arctic? Where is it? When did the Europeans begin to explore this region?

The Polar Regions

In the 16th century, Spain and Portugal controlled the only known sea routes to Asia. As a result, the northern nations of Europe began to explore the Arctic for a passage to China. Their voyages took them to the icy edges of Siberia and into the unknown northern tip of North America. During the following two centuries, Britain and Russia, in particular, sent numerous expeditions into the North Atlantic and the North Pacific oceans.

The 18th century's greatest explorer, the British commander James Cook, traveled far into both the frigid north and the icy south. In 1773, Cook made the first known crossing of the Antarctic Circle, and in 1778, he sailed through the Bering Strait. Cook was looking for an ice-free passage east or west, but he failed to find one.

Discussing Ideas. According to the reading, what was the purpose of exploring the Arctic? Why were Britain and Russia so interested in finding a "Northwest Passage"?

A. The *with Proper Nouns and Other Expressions*

The is frequently used with proper nouns, especially with geographical locations and other landmarks. This is because proper nouns identify specific places. *The* is also used with nouns and with adjectives used as nouns when they identify specific groups of people, periods of time, and so on. For a detailed summary of these special uses of *the* with certain grouping of nouns and adjectives, see Appendix 3.

1 Quickly reread the passage "The Polar Regions" and then answer the following questions.

1. Underline the proper nouns in the passage. Which are preceded by *the* and which are not?
2. Are names of countries usually preceded by *the?* Can you give any examples?
3. Are names of oceans and seas usually preceded by *the?*

2 Complete the following by using *the* or *X* (to indicate that no article is necessary).

1. ______ Africa
2. ______ continent of Africa
3. ______ Santa Barbara
4. ______ Park Avenue
5. ______ Hawaiian Islands
6. ______ Madagascar
7. ______ Lake Tahoe
8. ______ Sahara Desert
9. ______ Black Sea
10. ______ England
11. ______ Panama Canal
12. ______ Stanford University
13. ______ University of Connecticut
14. ______ Washington Monument
15. ______ General Ripper
16. ______ Dr. Strangelove
17. ______ president
18. ______ April 27th
19. ______ 1600s
20. ______ Queen of England

3 The following exercise concerns the voyages of Captain James Cook. Fill in the blanks with *the* or *X* (to indicate that no article is necessary).

Example: Since __the__ time of __the__ ancient Greeks, __X__ some geographers had believed that a great unknown southern continent was balancing __the__ land masses of __the__ northern hemisphere.

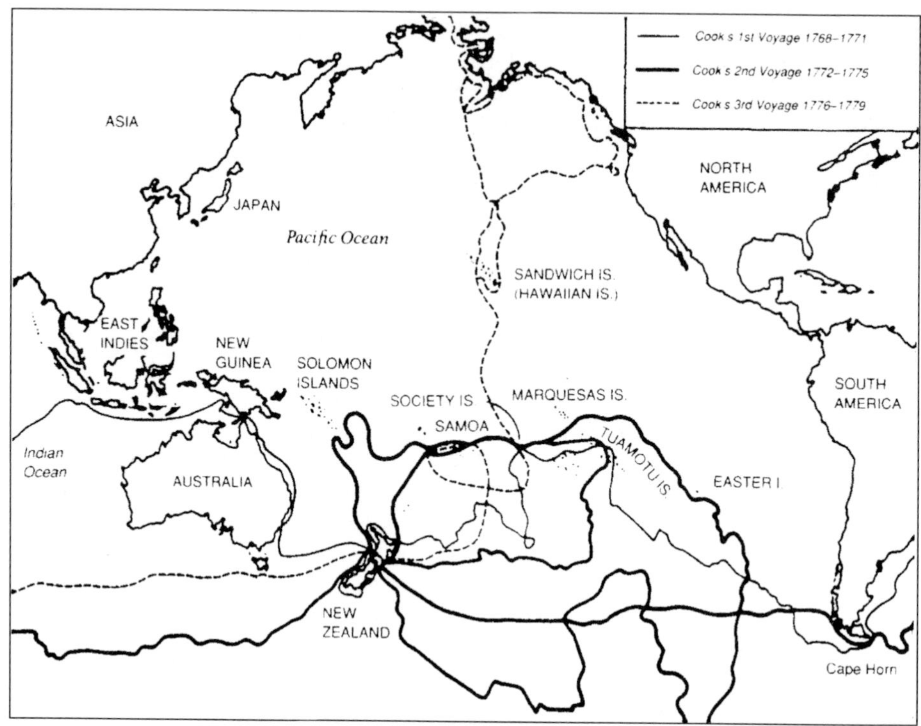

The voyages of Captain Cook

1. In 1768, the British Navy commissioned _______ Captain James Cook to explore _______ South Pacific in search of this unknown continent.
2. On _______ August 25, 1768, _______ Captain Cook's ship, _______ *Endeavor,* set sail, leaving _______ English Channel to cross _______ Atlantic Ocean.
3. After a brief stop in _______ Madeira Islands, Cook headed _______ south to _______ South America, _______ Pacific Ocean, and up to _______ Tahiti.
4. After a stay on _______ island of _______ Tahiti, which is part of _______ Society Islands, Cook sailed to _______ New Zealand.
5. Cook then crossed _______ Tasman Sea, and on April 28, 1770, he came to _______ Australia, docking in _______ Botany Bay (which he named for _______ great number of _______ new plants he found there).
6. Cook claimed all of _______ east coast of _______ Australia for _______ British, naming it _______ New South Wales.
7. On his return to _______ England, Cook continued westward, following _______ treacherous Great Barrier Reef, stopping in _______ Indonesia, crossing _______ Indian Ocean, and finally reaching _______ home on _______ 31st of _______ July, 1771.
8. On his second voyage, Cook left _______ Great Britain on July _______ 13, 1772, to attempt an exploration of _______ Antarctica.

9. On January 17, 1773, his ship, _______ *Resolution,* became _______ first ship in _______ history to enter _______ Antarctic Circle.
10. On this voyage, Cook continued eastward, still searching for _______ unknown southern continent, and finally arrived at _______ Spitshead, England on July 30, 1775, having covered a total distance of 70,000 miles (equal to almost three full navigations around the earth).
11. Cook left for his third and final voyage in _______ 1776 to explore _______ Northern Hemisphere in search of the "Northwest Passage," a mythical northern link between _______ Atlantic and Pacific Oceans.
12. Sailing _______ north from _______ New Zealand, Cook and his crew became _______ first Europeans to visit _______ Hawaiian Islands (Cook called them _______ Sandwich Islands).
13. Stepping ashore on _______ island of Kauai, Cook found himself being honored as a god by _______ native Hawaiians.
14. From _______ Hawaii, Cook went northward, sailing along _______ coast of _______ Alaska, crossing _______ Bering Strait, and even entering _______ Arctic Circle, until he was finally stopped by _______ walls of _______ ice.
15. He returned to _______ Hawaii, where he was killed on February _______ 14, 1779.

Captain James Cook, the English explorer, 1728–1779

4 Complete the following by using *a, an, the,* or *X* (to indicate that no article is necessary).

1. The Arctic is the northernmost ocean; _______ two-thirds of it is covered by _______ ice.
2. _______ outer limits of _______ Arctic are surrounded by _______ coasts of _______ northern continents.
3. _______ Antarctica, in contrast, is _______ continent larger than _______ Australia.
4. In _______ years after _______ Cook's voyages, only _______ few ships attempted to explore _______ northern and _______ southern extremes of _______ earth.
5. It wasn't until _______ late 1800s that _______ explorers were successful in reaching _______ polar regions.
6. In _______ 1893, Norwegian Fridtjof Nansen, with _______ crew of 13 sailors and scientists, headed for _______ Arctic Ocean.
7. _______ Norwegians turned back before they reached _______ pole. However, they had come _______ closest in _______ history: 224 miles from _______ pole.
8. _______ years later, in 1909, after _______ number of _______ attempts, _______ American explorer, Robert Peary, reached _______ northernmost point of _______ world, _______ North Pole.
9. In _______ 1911, _______ expedition led by _______ Norwegian Roald Amundsen and _______ expedition led by _______ American Robert Scott began _______ exploration of _______ Antarctica at approximately _______ same time.
10. _______ Scott's expedition came to _______ tragic end, but _______ Amundsen's expedition became _______ first in _______ history to reach _______ South Pole.

Culture Note

The Antarctica Treaty, signed by 12 nations in 1959, established a legal framework for governing Antarctica. The continent is to be used for peaceful purposes only, and military activity is prohibited. Today, 18 countries maintain over 40 research stations in Antarctica. The United States maintains a station at the Scott-Amundsen station at the South Pole, and it can be reached through quest.arc.nasa.gov/antarctica/.

5 Complete the following by using *a, an, the,* or *X* (to indicate that no article is necessary).

Shackleton's Incredible Voyage

The story of X Ernerst Shackleton and _______ (1) crews of _______ (2) British ships _______ (3) *Endurance* and _______ (4) *Aurora* is one of _______ (5) most remarkable stories of

Shackleton's ship, *Endurance* was destroyed by ice.

______(6) adventure, ______(7) courage, ______(8) endurance, ______(9) heartbreak, and ______(10) stamina ever told. ______(11) goal of ______(12) Shackleton expedition was to cross ______(13) Antarctica on ______(14) foot and ______(15) dogsled. Their goal was never reached, but their story is perhaps ______(16) greatest adventure story ever told.

In ______(17) December 1914, Shackleton and ______(18) his crew left ______(19) island of ______(20) South Georgia on board ______(21) ship ______(22) *Endurance.* ______(23) another ship, ______(24) *Aurora,* left ______(25) port of ______(26) Sydney, Australia. ______(27) *Endurance* would head for ______(28) Weddell Sea, in ______(29) western hemisphere, and the *Aurora* would head for ______(30) Ross Sea, on ______(31) other side of ______(32) continent. ______(33) winter of 1915 was ______(34) early winter. ______(35) both ships encountered ______(36) high winds and ______(37) heavy ice much sooner than expected.

Despite horrific conditions, ______(38) crew of ______(39) *Aurora* completed ______(40) its duty of leaving food supplies for ______(41) Shackleton expedition overland. Shackleton's overland expedition never took place, as ______(42) ice of ______(43) Weddell Sea trapped ______(44) boat. ______(45) fierce storm destroyed ______(46) *Aurora,* and ______(47) ice pulled and then crushed ______(48) *Endurance.* Eventually, ______(49) both ships were lost, and ______(50) both parties had to face ______(51) tremendous hardships in order to survive. ______(52) entire crew of ______(53) *Endurance* survived, but ______(54) three members of ______(55) crew of ______(56) *Aurora* died. All of these men, those who died and those who lived, will be remembered in ______(57) history for their incredible bravery and fortitude.

Culture Note

For more information on this expedition, you can read Endurance, *by Alfred Lansing, and* Shackleton's Forgotten Men, *by Lennard Bickel.*

Web Note

For more information on Shackleton and his voyages, visit the Web. Shackleton's decendants have a Website, and Kodak has a Website with magnificent photos of the Endurance *expedition at www.kodak.com.*

Using What You've Learned

6 Everyone has one special place where he or she feels most comfortable. For some, this is a city; for others, a park. Still others find that one room or even one particular chair provides an atmosphere that allows them to relax. At the end of a long and difficult day, where do you most like to go? Give a brief presentation describing a place that is special for you. Tell why it is special, why it helps you relax. Paint a verbal portrait, giving so much detail that other students will be able to picture your special place and to share in its serenity.

PART 5 More on Nouns and Noun Modifiers

Setting the Context

Prereading Questions. What is the highest mountain on earth? Where is it located?

Mt. Everest

Other mountains share with Everest a history of adventure, glory, and tragedy, but Everest is unique in that it is the highest mountain on earth. More than two-thirds of the earth's atmosphere lies below its summit, and for an unacclimatized* person without oxygen, the top of the mountain is endurable for only two or three minutes. The primitive, often brutal, struggle to reach the top is an irresistible challenge to the human need for adventure. But more than this, Everest has become, since the first attempt to climb it, a universal symbol of human courage and endurance.

*_unacclimatized_ not accustomed, physically, to high altitudes

Discussing Ideas. What do you know about attempts to climb Mt. Everest? Why do you think so many people have attempted this dangerous feat?

A. Word Order with Noun Modifers

When a noun has several modifiers, the modifiers are generally used in a set order.

Articles, Demonstratives, Possessives	**Numbers**	**Descriptive Words** 1. changing qualities or characteristics 2. date 3. shape or size 4. color 5. unchanging qualities or characteristics	**Other Nouns**	**Noun**	**Phrases, Clauses, Appositives**	**Predicate**
The		long, winding		path	to the house	was very dark.
These	two	red	paper	clips		are from Japan.
His father's		beautiful 1990		Porsche,	which is outside,	has a dent in it.
That		nice new		student,	Kunio,	is coming for dinner.

1 Complete the following sentences by adding the information in parentheses. Pay careful attention to word order as you complete each. Add punctuation where necessary. Some sentences may have more than one possible answer.

Example: In 1852, calculations revealed data. (exciting / routine / very / survey / of the Himalaya Mountains / new)

In 1852, routine survey calculations of the Himalaya Mountains revealed very exciting new data.

1. The Himalayas are the highest range. (of mountains / in the world)
2. According to a clerk, Peak XV was the mountain. (highest / at the Trigonometric Survey of India / in the world)
3. This peak, Peak XV, was the highest peak. (that had ever been recorded)
4. A check confirmed his claim. (of his calculations / careful)
5. The elevation was set at 29,002 feet. (of Peak XV / of the top)
6. Observations have established an elevation. (modern / of 29,028 / careful / more)
7. Early surveyors did not know that Tibetans had long ago recognized Peak XV. (as the mountain / greatest / world's)
8. For centuries, the Tibetans had called it Chomolongma. (which means mother goddess of the world / many)

B. Collective Nouns: Agreement with Verbs and Pronouns

Collective nouns are nouns that refer to a group of people, animals, things, and so on *as a unit.* Collective nouns can use either singular or plural verbs, depending on the context. In American English, collective nouns generally use singular verbs; however,

British English uses plural verbs more frequently. In American English, both singular and plural pronouns are used to refer to the nouns, although singular pronouns are preferred in standard written English.

	Examples	Common Collective Nouns	
Singular	The **team** of climbers **hasn't arrived** yet. **It is** expected soon.	army audience	furniture gang
Plural	The **team** of climbers **haven't arrived** yet. (more common in British English) **They are** expected soon. (common in spoken American English)	class committee community company couple crew crowd data department family food	generation government group jury majority pair population public staff team union

2 In each of the following sentences, choose the form(s) that would be most acceptable in written American English.

1. The Tibetan government (was / were) unwilling to give permission for explorers to visit the Himalayas. (It / They) did not allow foreigners to enter the mountain range until 1921.
2. In 1921, after years of negotiation, the British government (was / were) given permission to enter Tibet, and the first British climbing expedition (was / were) organized.
3. The first group explored various climbing routes on Mt. Everest, but (it / they) did not even come close to the summit.
4. In 1922, an exploratory team located the northeast route up Mt. Everest, but (it / they) (was / were) unable to reach the summit.
5. The third Everest expedition (was / were) to have a tragic ending, as (its / their) most famous member, George Mallory, would disappear while trying to reach the summit.
6. After Mallory disappeared in 1924, a number of expeditions (was / were) launched from Tibet in the attempt to climb the northeast route.
7. In 1949, the government of Nepal finally gave (its / their) permission for foreigners to enter the territory, and several teams tried to climb the mountain from the south.
8. In 1953, a British team (was / were) successful in (its / their) attempt.
9. The 1953 group (was / were) composed of ten climbers, including Edmund Hillary (age 33), a beekeeper from New Zealand, and Tenzing Norkay (age 39), a Sherpa guide from India.
10. At 11:30 on May 29, 1953, this pair of climbers—Edmund Hillary and Tenzing Norkay—(was / were) standing on the highest place in the world, the summit of Everest.

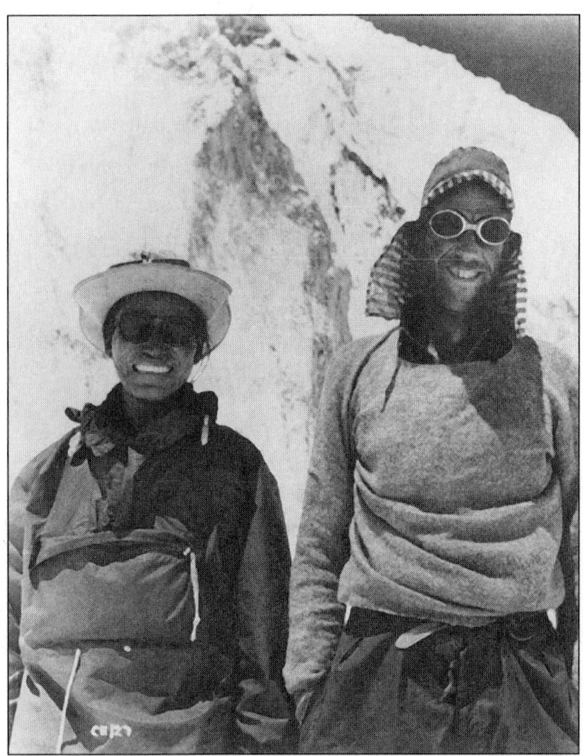

Tenzing Norkay (left) and Edmund Hillary celebrate the day after they reached the summit of Mt. Everest.

C. Subject/Verb Word Order with "Negative" Adverbs

When a "negative" adverb precedes the subject of a sentence, the auxiliary verb or the verb *be* is placed before the subject, just as it is in most questions. When these adverbs occur after the subject, no inversion takes place.

Standard Word Order	Inverted Word Order	Notes
He was **scarcely** able to breathe. He **never** considered quitting.	**Scarcely was he** able to breathe. **Never did he consider** quitting.	Inverted word order is used with *barely, hardly, hardly ever, never, no sooner, rarely,* and *seldom.*

3 Restate each of the sentences in italics in two ways. First, add the adverb in parentheses to the beginning of the sentence; second, add it to the middle of the sentence. Make all necessary changes.

Example: In 1953, a group of climbers was organized for another attempt at Mt. Everest. *The climbers had been chosen when they left for Nepal.* (scarcely)

Scarcely had the climbers been chosen when they left for Nepal.

The climbers had scarcely been chosen when they left for Nepal.

1. *A man had succeeded in reaching the summit.* (never)
2. Ten climbers were chosen, including a doctor. *Men had climbed to such heights without needing medical assistance.* (seldom)

3. On May 29th, the day of Hillary's and Norkay's final climb, the wind was calm. *There are calm days on Mt. Everest.* (rarely)
4. After several hours of extremely dangerous climbing, Hillary and Norkay arrived at the top of the world. *They had reached the summit when they embraced and Hillary took Norkay's picture.* (barely)
5. *Human beings endure so much hardship and yet succeed.* (rarely)

D. Parallel Structure with Nouns and Noun Modifiers

When a noun has two or more modifiers, parallel structures should be used. That is, the same grammatical form should be used whenever possible: Words, phrases, and clauses should not be mixed. While a sentence with mixed forms may be grammatically correct, the mixed forms are considered incorrect usage.

Correct Usage	Incorrect Usage	Notes
The **cold, tired climbers** returned to their camp. Both **Swiss** and **British climbers** reached the top of the mountain.	The tired climbers, who were also cold, returned to their camp. Both Swiss climbers and climbers from Britain reached the top.	Parallel forms should be used in series of words, phrases, and clauses. Parallel forms must also be used with these connectors: *and, but, or, both . . . and, not only . . . but also, either . . . or,* and *neither . . . nor.* See Chapter 3 for more information on these structures.

4 **Error Analysis.** Study the following sentences. Then correct those that have errors in parallelism. If a sentence contains no error, write "correct" after it.

Example: By the time the Americans arrived, both a British expedition and an expedition that was Swiss had already climbed Mt. Everest.

Correction: *By the time the Americans arrived, both a British (expedition) and a Swiss expedition had already climbed Mt. Everest.*

1. After 1953, different climbing teams established routes on the northeast ridge and the ridge on the south side of Mt. Everest.
2. None of these expeditions attempted the west ridge, which was considered to be an extremely difficult route, and it was dangerous.
3. Between 1953 and 1963, only a British expedition and a Swiss expedition succeeded in reaching the summit of Mt. Everest.
4. In 1963, an American group planned to climb Everest from not only the south ridge but also the west ridge.
5. The south ridge of the mountain was quite well known to the climbers, but the west ridge of the mountain was something that was completely unknown.
6. On February 20, 1963, an army of a thousand, including people who climbed, Sherpas, and porters, began the 185-mile hike to Mt. Everest.
7. On May 1, James Whittaker, an American from Washington, and Nawang Gombu, a nephew of Tenzing Norkay, reached the summit of Everest.
8. Three weeks later, on May 22, Luther Jerstad and Barry Bishop, climbing the south ridge, and Thomas Hornbein and William Unsoeld, who were climbing the west ridge, reached the top of Mt. Everest.

Using What You've Learned

5 George Mallory was the most famous of the early climbers who attempted to reach the summit of Mt. Everest. His death was a tragedy to all who knew him. Yet like many before and after him, Mallory died attempting to attain a personal goal.

In small groups, read the following quotation from Mallory. Consider Mallory's goal and his outlook on life. Then discuss other occupations or hobbies that require the bravery, determination, and drive that Mallory had. As a group, try to answer the question that Mallory was so often asked, "Why?"

The first question which you will ask and which I must try to answer is this, "What is the use of climbing Mount Everest?" and my answer must at once be, "It is no use." There is not the slightest prospect of any gain whatsoever. Oh, we may learn a little about the behavior of the human body at high altitude, where there is only a third of an atmosphere, and possibly medical men may turn our observation to some account for the purposes of aviation. But otherwise nothing will come of it. We shall not bring back a single bit of gold or silver, not a gem, nor any coal or iron. We shall not find a foot of earth that can be planted with crops to raise food. It's no use.

So, if you cannot understand that there is something in man which responds to the challenge of this mountain and goes out to meet it, that the struggle is the struggle of life itself upward and forever upward, then you won't see why we go. What we get from this adventure is just sheer joy. And joy is, after all, the end of life. We do not live to eat and make money. We eat and make money to be able to enjoy life. That is what life means and what life is for.

George Leigh Mallory, Lt. Col. C. K. Howard-Bury's *Mount Everest, the Reconnaisance,* 1921, Longmans, Green, and Company

This Nova sponsored expedition found George Mallory's body in 1999. The world will never know if Mallory reached the top of Mt. Everest before he died. For more information, transcripts, and photos, see *www.pbs.org/wgbh/nova/everest/lost/*.

Video Activities: Extreme Sports

Before You Watch. Discuss these questions in small groups.

1. What is the most dangerous sport you have tried? Why did you try a dangerous sport?
2. What do you know about hang gliding and paragliding? Describe these sports.
3. Have you ever meditated? What was it like?

Watch. Complete these sentences.

1. People enjoy hang gliding and paragliding because they are ______________.
   a. peaceful b. good exercise c. safe
2. Hang gliding and paragliding are similar to ______________________.
   a. riding in a plane
   b. going up in a rocket ship
   c. flying like a bird
3. Tandem rides are for ______________________.
   a. one person b. two people c. three people

Watch Again. Answer these questions in small groups.

1. What is the name of the place that many people go to hang glide? __________
2. The narrator says, "To you and me it might be intimidating; to the veteran, it's blissful."
   a. What is *it?*
   b. Who are the veterans?
   c. What are other words for *intimidating?*
   d. What are other words for *blissful?*
3. Circle the words that are used to describe hang gliding.
   a. spiritual b. holy c. dreamlike d. natural e. ethereal

After You Watch. Circle *a/an* or *the* in each sentence.

1. I took a/the hang gliding flight yesterday.
2. I went with an/the experienced hang glider.
3. The/A flight was fantastic.
4. It was one of a/the most amazing experiences I have ever had.
5. A/The sky was bright blue and a/the sun was shining.
6. While we were flying, a/the bird flew very close to us.
7. A/The bird looked surprised to see us.

Focus on Testing

Noun and Article Usage

Problem areas with nouns and articles are frequently tested on standardized English proficiency exams. Check your understanding of these structures by completing the sample items that follow.

Remember that . . .

- A singular noun takes a singular verb, while plural nouns take plural verbs.
- An article or adjective is always used before a singular count noun.
- *The* is used with many proper nouns, names of landmarks, superlatives, and many expressions of quantity.
- Modifiers of nouns have a set word order.
- Collective nouns are generally singular in formal American English, and singular pronouns are used to refer to them.
- Subjects and verbs are inverted when "negative" adverbs are used at the beginning of sentences.
- Parallel structures should be used with groups of nouns and noun modifiers.

Part 1. Circle the best completion for the following.

Example: By 9:00, Ned __________ his breakfast.

a. has finished
b. finishing
(c.) had finished
d. had been finishing

1. He enjoys traveling on __________.

   a. airplane b. airplanes c. an airplanes d. a airplane

2. Brocade is __________________ fabric with raised designs.

   a. an Oriental rich silk
   b. an Oriental silk rich
   c. a rich silk Oriental
   d. a rich Oriental silk

3. __________________________ when the phone rang.

   a. Scarcely I had walked in the door
   b. Scarcely had I walked in the door
   c. I had walked scarcely in the door
   d. I had walked in the door scarcely

4. ______________ most beautiful pre-Columbian artwork can be seen in Bogotá's Gold Museum.

   a. Much of the
   b. Much of
   c. Many of
   d. Many of the

Part 2. Each sentence has one error. Circle the letter below the word(s) containing the error.

Example: By the time the Americans arrived, (A) both (B) a British and a Swiss expedition already had (Ⓒ) climbed (D) Mt. Everest.

1. The (A) Norwegians spent many months assembling (B) its team, (C) which included a number of (D) scientists.
2. The (A) Arctic is a frozen ocean surrounded by land, while Antarctica (B) is a landmass that is frozen (C) surrounded (D) by ocean.
3. In the 1400s, (A) a number of unsuccessful (B) voyages around the horn of Africa was financed (C) by the (D) king of Portugal, Manuel I.
4. Highest mountain (A) in the world, Mt. Everest was named after (B) George Everest, the (C) first surveyor-general of India (D).

Chapter 3

Sex and Gender

IN THIS CHAPTER

Part 1 Commands and Exclamations

Part 2 Compound Sentences

Part 3 Transitions

Part 4 Complex Sentences

Part 5 Sentence Problems

Introduction

In this chapter, you will review the various types of sentences in English, and you will study problems with incorrect punctuation or sentence structure.

The following passage introduces the chapter theme "Sex and Gender" and raises some topics and issues you will cover in the chapter.

The Sexes

How different we all are from each other! Take a moment to study the people around you, and you'll undoubtedly be struck with this fact. Features such as height, weight, skin color, and hair texture vary markedly from individual to individual and from race to race.

These characteristics, however, are not what we notice first about any other human being. Regardless of how tall, dark, or heavy another person is, it is his or her gender that first catches our attention. In fact, no matter how different two people are, we view them as fundamentally similar if they are of the same sex. Thus, the most basic division among human beings is that between male and female.

Because of this division, special roles for each sex have developed. Obviously, males and females perform different functions in reproduction, but the distinction goes far beyond that. In fact, it enters into every area of our lives.

Discussing Ideas. In your opinion, are there differences between the way males and females act in the workplace, at home, at sporting events? Give specific examples.

PART 1

Commands and Exclamations

Setting the Context

Culture Note

The Human Genome Project, the mapping of DNA, is giving us a tremendous amount of new information about heredity versus environment. For example, some personality traits, such as shyness, seem to be inherited. For more information on human differences and similarities—in personality or in gender—consult your library or the Web.

Prereading Questions. Do you think that parents treat boys differently than they treat girls? If so, why do they do this? What effect can this have on children as they grow up?

A Traditional Nursery Rhyme

What are little girls made of?
Sugar and spice and everything nice.
What are little boys made of?
Snakes and snails and puppy dog tails.

Conditioning

Society "teaches" children to act like males or females at a young age. In fact, the lifelong process of conditioning the infant to fit his or her sex role begins at birth. Pink or blue clothing is purchased, a name is chosen from the appropriate category, and the pronoun "he"or "she" is used. Even before the child can talk, he or she is told such things as, "What a handsome boy you are!" or "How pretty you look!" Later come the constant reminders from parents, relatives, and teachers: "Be a brave boy; don't cry" or "Be a nice girl and help Mother with the dishes."

Discussing Ideas. In your opinion, how much of male and female behavior is natural or innate and how much is learned?

A. Commands

Affirmative	Negative	Notes
Wait a minute. **Stop** it! **Listen** to me. Please **be** quiet.	Please **don't go.** **Don't do** that! **Don't talk** so much. **Don't raise** your voice.	Commands are the simplest complete sentences in English. Commands in the second person consist of the simple form of the verb with or without modifiers. The subject *you* is not stated.

1 Quickly reread the passage "Conditioning." Then underline the commands at the end of the passage. What is the verb for each of these commands? What is the subject?

2 Make the following six statements and requests into commands. Some of these represent stereotypes that have been changing worldwide in recent years. According to the stereotypes, which of these commands would most likely be directed toward a boy and which toward a girl?

Example: You can cry if it makes you feel better.
Cry if it makes you feel better.

1. You need to get some exercise.
2. You should go on a diet.
3. You should eat all your food so you can be strong.
4. You shouldn't go around with those types of people.
5. You need to think about your reputation.
6. You should have a good time before you're too old.

3 Fill in the blanks with affirmative or negative commands.

Example: ___*Don't go*___ to the show before your homework is done.

1. ______________ so much or you'll get fat.
2. ______________ your hair. You look like a girl!
3. ______________ your hair. It's a mess.
4. ______________ this perfume. It will drive men crazy.
5. ______________ this cologne. No woman will be able to resist you.
6. ______________ your hands. They're filthy!

B. Exclamations

Exclamations are used for emphasis and in emotional statements. *How* or *what* begins the exclamation, and the subject and verb follow in normal word order. In conversational English, the subject and verb are often omitted, however.

Examples	Notes
ADJECTIVES AND ADVERBS	
How quickly he works!	Adjectives and adverbs follow *how.*
NOUNS	
What a terrible job he is doing. **What** a terrible job!	Nouns follow *what* or *what a(n).*

4 Look at the passage "Conditioning" once again. This time, underline the exclamations that compliment the appearance of a boy or a girl. Why is what used in the first case and how used in the second?

5 Form exclamations from these statements. Use either *how* or *what*.

Example: Jane's baby is cute.
How cute Jane's baby is!
Jane has a cute baby.
What a cute baby Jane has!

1. Bill looks tired.
2. Bill has a tired expression.
3. Pinocchio had a large nose.
4. Pinocchio's nose was large.
5. Mary has a warm smile.
6. Mary is smiling warmly.
7. Tim is incredibly rich.
8. Tim has an awful lot of money.

Using What You've Learned

6 Work in pairs for a role play. Pretend you are talking to your 12-year-old son or daughter. "Lay down the law," telling your "child" what to do and what not to do. Make at least three affirmative commands and three negative commands.

7 Give a short description of another member of your class without giving his or her name. Use exclamations when possible. When you are finished, the other members in the group will try to guess whom you were describing.

Example: *How beautiful her hair is! What lovely brown eyes she has! But what terrible handwriting she has.*

What bushy eyebrows he has! What curly hair he has! How warm his smile is! What a lazy student he is! How little work he does! But what good grades he gets!

8 Are any of you good actresses or actors? Imagine yourselves acting in a melodramatic soap opera, and pretend you and your partner are boyfriend and girlfriend. Gaze into each other's eyes and exchange compliments (or insults) using exclamations! As this is melodrama, be sure to exaggerate! (And please avoid doing this in real life. . .)

Example: *Jack:* **What beautiful brown eyes you have!**
Jill: **How charming you are!**

9 Read the fairy tale "Little Red Riding Hood" and then, in groups, prepare a skit of the story. As you act out the skit, be sure to emphasize Little Red Riding Hood's exclamations, "What big ears you have! What big eyes you have! What a big mouth you have!"

PART 2 Compound Sentences

Setting the Context

Prereading Questions. Do you believe there are differences in intelligence between women and men? Are there differences in achievement levels?

Wasted Potential?

In neither primitive nor modern societies do the achievements of women even approach those of men. Yet the reason for this gap apparently has little to do with natural ability. It is obvious that women are at least as intelligent as men, for girls consistently perform better on IQ tests than boys do. Still, studies of gifted children of both sexes have shown that boys with high IQ scores almost always achieve success as adults, but high-scoring girls often do not.

Discussing Ideas. Why do you think that women have traditionally tested as well or better than men but have not achieved as much? Is this changing?

A. Coordinating Conjunctions with Clauses

Coordinating conjunctions (*and, but, for, or, so, yet,* and *nor*) are used to join two independent clauses of roughly equal importance into one *compound sentence.* The specific coordinating conjunction chosen highlights the logical relationship between the clauses. When a coordinating conjunction joins two clauses, it is normally preceded by a comma. However, with two short clauses, the comma can be omitted.

And, But, For, Or, So, Yet		
	Examples	**Notes**
Fred is antisocial,	**and** he can be quite rude. **but** he has a few friends. **for** he is very insecure. **or** at least he seems that way. **so** many people don't like him. **yet** he loves to go to parties.	*and* = addition *but* = contrast *for* = reason *or* = choice *so* = result *yet* = contrast

Nor		
Simple Sentences	**Compound Sentences**	**Notes**
Fred is not very sociable. He is not very polite. Patty doesn't stay out late. She doesn't gamble. May hasn't read the chapter. She hasn't written her essay.	Fred is not very sociable, **nor is he** very polite. Patty doesn't stay out late, **nor does she** gamble. May hasn't read the chapter, **nor has she** written her essay.	*Nor* is used to join two negative clauses. When *nor* begins the second clause, the auxiliary or the verb *be* is placed before the subject and the negative in the second clause is omitted.

1 Quickly reread the passage "Wasted Potential?" Underline the connecting words *for* and *but.* What type of relationship does each express? Are the sentences punctuated in the same way?

2 Combine these sentences with coordinating conjunctions, making necessary changes in punctuation and capitalization. Use each conjunction once.

Example: In rural areas of developing nations, women are often underfed. They are also overworked.

In rural areas of developing nations, women are often underfed, and they are also overworked.

1. Men are more muscular than women. Women often do the hardest physical labor.
2. Male infants receive better treatment in many countries. They are more highly prized than female babies.
3. Often, baby girls are not fed as much as their brothers. The girls don't get as much attention.
4. In rural Guatemala, female infants are less valued than males. Female babies are breast-fed for a much shorter period than male babies.
5. In 1970, during the Biafran War, Nigerian girls often suffered from severe malnutrition. Their brothers did not.
6. Female babies may be treated better in the future. Their situation may worsen.

3 Complete the following sentences with a clause. Use students in your class for the subjects.

Example: *Francesca* loves to dance, but. . . .

Francesca loves to dance, but she rarely goes out at night.

1. Last Friday, ______________ asked me to go to a movie, but. . . .
2. ______________ is engaged to be married, so. . . .
3. ______________ may never get married, for. . . .
4. ______________ will never get married, nor. . . .
5. ______________ is in love with one of his/her teachers, yet. . . .
6. ______________ doesn't have a new car, nor. . . .

7. _____________ has several boyfriends, and. . . .
8. After dinner, _____________ does the dishes, or. . . .

4 Some people have strong opinions about the roles of men and women, but other people are more flexible. How flexible are you about what you believe men and women should and shouldn't do? Give your opinions. Choose the word that best expresses your own opinion and then finish each sentence by adding a complete clause. Use the connecting words that are provided.

Depending on your class, you may choose to discuss your opinions in small or large groups. You can also discuss your opinions in groups of all women and all men.

Example: Men are (stronger) / weaker than women, so men should make all the decisions.

Men are (stronger) / weaker than women, but women are more intelligent.

1. Men are mentally stronger / weaker than women, yet. . . .
   Men are mentally stronger / weaker than women, so. . . .
2. Women / Men should never have to do any housework, nor. . . .
   Women / Men should never have to do any housework, but. . . .
3. A woman's / man's place is at home with the children, yet. . . .
   A woman's / man's place is at home with the children, or. . . .
4. Men / Women are more important in the world, so. . . .
   Men / Women are more important in the world, and. . . .

B. Coordinating Conjunctions with Words and Phrases

The coordinating conjunctions *so* and *for* can join clauses only. *Nor* usually joins clauses. However, *and, but, yet,* and *or* are often used to join units smaller than clauses. For example, they can join two or more nouns, adjectives, verbs, adverbs, or phrases. Of course, the structures must be parallel (noun . . . noun, adjective . . . adjective).

	Examples
Nouns	**Khalil** and **Tasir** met us at the airport.
Adjectives	We were **tired** but **happy.**
Verb Phrases	They **took** us to the hotel and **arranged** for a room.
Adverbs	The clerk spoke **rapidly** yet **clearly.**
Prepositional Phrases	We will return **in August** or **at the end of the year.**

5 Combine each group of sentences that follow into one sentence, using *and, or, nor, for, so, but,* or *yet*. Don't use the same connecting word more than once within each set. Make these sentences as short as possible by omitting all unnecessary words.

Julie

Some women have decided that their place is not at home even if they have children. This is the story of such a woman, Julie.

Example: In class, Julie's eyes are always sparkling with attention.
In class, Julie's eyes are always sparkling with joy.
In class, Julie's eyes hold a deep sadness.
In class, Julie's eyes are always sparkling with attention and joy, but they hold a deep sadness.

1. Julie's face seemed, at times, childlike.
Her face on closer inspection was wizened.*
She had been through a lot in her life.

2. Julie was born in the Philippines.
She grew up in China during the ten-year Cultural Revolution.
She is no stranger to hard times.

3. Some of her family starved during the Cultural Revolution.
There was no food to buy.
There was no food to borrow.

4. Julie was able to stay alive by moving to a communal farm.
She became ill with hepatitis** there.
She almost died.

5. Eventually, the situation in China improved.
Julie moved back to the city.
She got married.

6. She had a husband.
She had a child.
She had a relatively well-paying job.
She left them all to come to the United States.

7. She worked in Santa Barbara, California.
She studied in Santa Barbara.
She didn't see her son for several years.
She didn't see her husband for several years.

8. Leaving China was a big sacrifice for her.
Leaving China was a big sacrifice for her family.
It was an opportunity that comes once in a lifetime.

9. Julie finally left California for China.
She wanted to see her son.
She wanted to see her husband.
She planned to return to Santa Barbara someday to finish her degree.

**wizened* wrinkled, with lines in the skin
***hepatitis* a disease of the liver

10. Life gave Julie an opportunity.
    The opportunity was very special.
    Life also forced Julie to make choices.
    The choices were difficult.
    The choices were between family and education.

C. Correlative Conjunctions

Correlatives are conjunctions that have two parts: *either . . . or, not only . . . but (also), neither . . . nor, both . . . and.* They can connect either clauses or smaller grammatical units, but the structures must always be parallel. For example, if a clause follows *either,* a clause must follow *or;* if a noun follows *either,* a noun must follow *or.*

	Examples	Notes
Clauses **Nouns**	**Either** we should give Ann a raise **or** we should give her a vacation. We should give her **either** a raise **or** a vacation. (Incorrect: *Either we should give Ann a raise or a vacation.)	*Either . . . or* = choice
Clauses **Adjectives**	**Not only** is her boss dishonest **but (also)** he is temperamental. Her boss is **not only** dishonest **but (also)** temperamental. (Incorrect: *Not only is her boss dishonest but also temperamental. Her boss is not only dishonest, but also he is temperamental.)	*Not only . . . but (also)* = addition When *not only . . . but (also)* joins two clauses, the auxiliary is placed before the subject in the first clause only.
Verb Phrases **Nouns**	She **neither** got a raise **nor** took a vacation. She got **neither** a raise **nor** a vacation. (Incorrect: *She neither got a raise nor did she take a vacation. Neither did she get a raise nor a vacation.)	*Neither . . . nor* = negative addition *Neither . . . nor* is often used to join smaller units. It is usually not used to join clauses.
Adverbs **Nouns**	He works **both** quickly **and** carelessly. **Both** Ann **and** her boss are stubborn. (Incorrect: *He works both quickly and he works carelessly. Both Ann is stubborn and her boss is stubborn.)	*Both . . . and* = addition *Both . . . and* is not used to join clauses.

Note: In writing, it is considered better style to combine the smallest possible grammatical units with correlative conjunctions. Thus, while the first sentence below is perfectly grammatical, the second sentence is preferred.

Not only have I written the president, but I have also talked to my congressman.
I have not only written the president but also talked to my congressman.

6 Combine the following sentences using correlative conjunctions. In 1 and 2, combine the sentences in two ways. Combine the two clauses; then remove all repetition. In 3 and 4, remove all repetition.

Jassem

In 1993, Jassem Al Khadher learned that his company in Kuwait was willing to sponsor him to do graduate study in the United States.

Example: He could study in the United States.
He could stay at his present job in Kuwait. (either . . . or)

a. Either he could study in the United States, or he could stay at his present job in Kuwait.

b. He could either study in the United States or stay at his present job in Kuwait.

1. Jassem loved the idea of studying in the United States.
He wanted a break from his job. (not only . . . but also)

a.

b.

2. He could study at Columbia University.
He could study at Michigan State University. (either . . . or)

a.

b.

3. His colleagues encouraged him to go.
His family encouraged him to go. (both . . . and)

a.

4. However, his wife couldn't accompany him for at least six months. She couldn't visit him for at least six months. (neither . . . nor)

a.

7 Underline the repetitive parts within the following sets of sentences. Then combine each of the sets, using a logical correlative conjunction. Remove all repetition.

Example: After arriving in New York, Jassem was impressed. He was frightened.
After arriving in New York, Jassem was both impressed and frightened.

1. He had never been far away from his family. He had never been outside of Kuwait.
2. The language was new to him. The food, climate, and culture were new to him.
3. His fellow students couldn't help him. His friends from Kuwait couldn't help him.
4. In the following months, Jassem's homesickness grew. His telephone bill grew. (It was $1,000 one month.)
5. He would call his wife every morning and afternoon. She would think that something was wrong. (If he didn't call his wife, she would think something was wrong.)

8 After a few months, Jassem went to his consulate to complain. Complete the following sentences.

Example: I will either stay in the United States. . . .
I will either stay in the United States or return to Kuwait.

1. I want to see both my wife. . . .
2. Either send my family to the United States. . . .
3. I am not only bored. . . .
4. Living alone is neither convenient. . . .
5. I wish I knew someone who was both rich. . . .
6. Neither my son. . . .
7. Not only are my children intelligent. . . .
8. Either my children will study at Berkeley. . . .

Unfortunately for the phone company, Jassem's wife and children joined him after six months.

9 **Error Analysis.** Most of the following sentences have errors. Find each error and correct it. If the sentence is correct, do not change it.

Example: Julie ~~both~~ was *both* sick and hungry.

1. Julie not only survived the Cultural Revolution but also life without her mother and father.
2. She didn't stop neither working nor studying.
3. Both Julie and her husband hope she will graduate soon.
4. Either Jassem had to pay the phone bill or lose his phone.
5. Not only was Jassem unhappy, but also was his wife unhappy.
6. Neither Jassem nor Julie still live in Santa Barbara.

Using What You've Learned

10 Marriage customs differ from one culture to another. Think about marriage customs in a culture you know, or research marriage customs in a culture of your choice. Does the married couple usually live alone, or do relatives live with them? Do both the husband and wife work outside the home? Which person does which household chores?

In a five-minute presentation, discuss these and any other points about marriage customs in the culture you chose. You may give your presentations individually or in groups.

PART 3 Transitions

Setting the Context

Prereading Questions. What are genes? What are chromosomes? Does the mother or the father determine the sex of a child?

Biological Differences

The sex of a child is determined at conception through the parents' chromosomes. Each human cell contains 23 chromosome pairs. (One of each pair is from the mother and one from the father.) However, the sex of the child is determined by only one of these chromosome pairs, the so-called sex chromosomes.

There are two types of sex chromosomes: X and Y. The mother always contributes an X. The father, on the other hand, may contribute either an X or a Y. Therefore, when united, the chromosomes from the mother and father form one of two patterns: an XX—a baby girl, or an XY—a baby boy.

Interestingly, the XY combination is more likely. In fact, some 20 percent more males than females are conceived. Nature soon changes this ratio, however. Many more males die during pregnancy; moreover, more baby boys die at birth. As a result, only 4 percent more males are born than females.

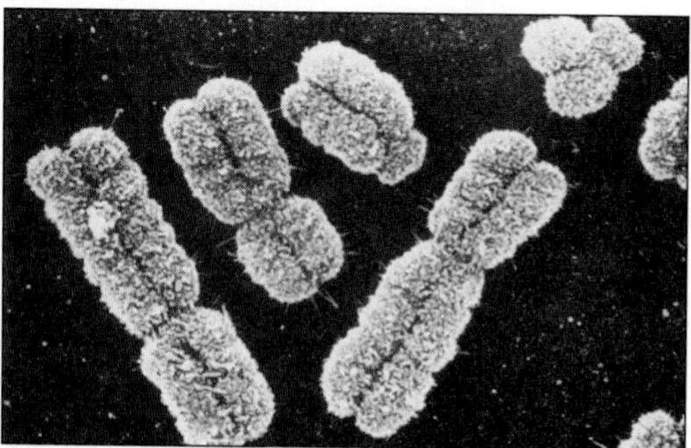

Human chromosomes

Discussing Ideas. According to the passage, which chromosome combination is more probable? Does the ratio of XX to XY change during pregnancy or birth? How?

A. Transitions

Transitions are words or phrases that link two related ideas. They may be used in a series of simple sentences, or they may be used with a conjunction or semicolon to join two sentences. Transitions are particularly common in formal situations and in writing.

	Examples	**Notes**
A Series of Sentences	The dinner was delicious. **Nevertheless,** we felt that it was overpriced.	Transitions may begin sentences; they are normally followed by commas.
Compound Sentences	The main course was superb; **however,** none of us liked the dessert. The meal was expensive; **as a result,** we decided not to return there. **However,** we enjoyed ourselves very much. The Smiths, **however,** enjoyed themselves very much. The Smiths enjoyed themselves very much, **however.**	In written English, a semicolon and a transition are often used to form compound sentences. Some transitions (particularly *however*) may be used at various points within a sentence. In these cases, commas precede and/or follow the transition.

1 Link the following sentences with the transitions indicated. Add all necessary punctuation. The transitions within each group are interchangeable.

Additional Information

moreover, furthermore, in addition, also

Example: More baby boys die in childbirth. More males die in each succeeding year of life.

More baby boys die in childbirth; moreover, more males die in each succeeding year of life.

Additional Information

moreover, furthermore, in addition, also

1. At birth, boys are, on average, one-half inch taller than girls. Boys weigh slightly more.
2. Girls develop faster physically than boys. Girls mature more quickly intellectually.
3. Female babies suffer from fewer birth defects. As they mature, women contract fewer diseases.
4. Later in life, men are more prone to hepatitis. They are more susceptible to heart disease, tuberculosis, and asthma.

Contrast

however, nevertheless

5. The Y chromosome brings more males into the world. It does not make things easier for them when they arrive.
6. By the age of 20, the number of surviving males and females is about equal. By the age of 30, women are clearly ahead.
7. A great number of diseases are more likely to trouble men. Only genital cancer and diabetes more often strike women.
8. Women have a higher rate of genital cancer. When all types of cancer are included, men suffer in greater numbers.

Result

thus, therefore, hence, consequently, as a result

9. Men's bodies are generally bigger than women's. Men have heavier brains and hearts.
10. A man's lungs are larger than a woman's. He takes four to six fewer breaths per minute.
11. Women's hips are larger than men's. When women walk, their hips sway, and they run more slowly.
12. Women have less water in their bodies. Women become drunk more quickly.

Negative Condition

otherwise

13. Scientists have done a great deal of genetic research. We wouldn't know the role of genes and chromosomes in reproduction and illness.
14. The Y chromosome weakens males. Men would live as long as women.

15. Men have more water in their bodies. They would get drunk just as easily as women.
16. Women have larger hips. They might be able to run faster than men.

Added Comment or Clarification

in fact, as a matter of fact

17. Women are stronger than most people think. A woman can often lift and carry a larger percentage of her body weight than a man can of his.
18. Women float in water more easily than men. Women are on average 10 percent more buoyant.
19. Women often have a great endurance for extremely low temperatures. They can survive in very cold conditions much longer than men can.
20. Men tend to have a lower percentage of fat than women. Adult males average 20 percent fat, whereas adult women commonly have over 25 percent.

2 The following paragraphs are missing necessary capital letters and punctuation. Read the paragraphs carefully. Then underline all transitions and make changes in punctuation and capitalization. Finally, suggest one or more alternatives for as many of the transitions as you can.

Male or Female?

The sex of a child is determined at conception however no differences begin to show in the fetus* until six to eight weeks later. At that point, androgens, the male hormones, come into play. Interestingly, these male hormones (or their absence) affect both sexes. Androgens are produced within the XY fetus as a result a boy begins to develop. These androgens are absent in the XX fetus thus the latter starts to take on female characteristics.

How important are these androgens to the development of the male child? As a matter of fact they are essential. For the boy to develop, the male hormones must be present otherwise "he" will be born with the anatomy of a girl.

---

3 How well did you understand the ideas presented in Activity 2? Close your book and work in pairs to summarize (in your own words) the major ideas in the exercise. Refer back to the book only if really necessary. When you are finished, write your summary, adding transitions where appropriate.

4 Read the following paragraphs carefully. Then fill in the blanks with the transition that best shows the logical relationship between the sentences. Don't use any transition more than one time in each paragraph. Be sure to add all necessary punctuation.

■ Men are bigger and stronger than women. ____Thus,____ (1) they tend to do better in athletics. In 1911, a British magazine found that men were about 50 percent better in

---

**fetus* unborn child

sports than women ________ (2) in recent years, the gap has been shrinking. For example, in javelin, the men's record of about 325 feet is only about 60 feet ahead of the women's record ________ (3) in the high jump women now reach heights of almost 7 feet—less than 14 inches below the men's record.

- Women are still about 10 percent slower than men in some long-distance swimming events ________ (4) they are swimming faster today than many of the men's champions of the past. In the 1924 Olympics, Johnny Weissmuller, who later played Tarzan in movies, gained world fame by winning the 400-meter freestyle event ________ (5) today there are thousands of women who have beaten Weissmuller's Olympic time. ________ (6) if a world-class female swimmer could be transported back to 1924, she would beat Weissmuller by an embarrassing 80 meters!
- Women can be much stronger than they appear ________ (7) under certain circumstances women have shown incredible strength. Florence Rogers of Tampa, Florida, provides a good example. When a jack* collapsed, pinning her son under the car, she knew she had to lift the car ________ (8) he would die. This, of course, seems impossible even for a man ________ (9) in the desperation of the moment, Florence raised one end of the 3,600-pound car ________ (10) her son was able to escape.

5 Complete the following sentences, using all of the transitions provided. Add appropriate punctuation.

Example: Women are smaller than men; furthermore, *they weigh less even at birth.*

1. Women are smaller than men nevertheless
2. In the past, women rarely exercised consequently
3. Women suffer from fewer diseases as a result
4. Men have historically dominated women in fact
5. Boys are believed to be better at math however
6. We should finish this exercise otherwise

**jack* device used to lift a car when, for example, a tire is being changed

Using What You've Learned

6 What was the strongest position that you took in Activity 5? Could you defend that position? Choose a partner of the opposite sex. Find one issue from Activity 5 about which you are in total disagreement. Then take turns explaining your position and summarizing your partner's. Begin by stating your opinion in no more than two minutes. Your partner must then summarize what you have said to your satisfaction. Only then can your partner state his or her opinion. Continue this process for several rounds or until you and your partner understand each other's positions completely.

PART 4 Complex Sentences

Setting the Context

Prereading Questions. Are the differences between men and women reflected in their speech? How do men and women talk differently?

Language Differences

Throughout history, the most important distinction between human beings has been their sex. Linguists have found that this distinction between males and females even affects people's speech.

Among some peoples, differences in the way men and women speak are apparent in pronunciation. In the Chukchi society of Siberia, men pronounce the word that means "people" *ramkichnin.* Women, on the other hand, pronounce it *tsamkitstsin.* Women of the Yana Indian tribe in California say *au* ("fire") and *ya* ("people"), whereas men say *auna* and *yana.*

In many other cultures, certain words are used by one sex but not the other. In Madagascar, women use more direct language and harsher words. If a confrontation between males is necessary, the men often have their female relatives say the harsh words for them. Later, the men patch up any hurt feelings that may have resulted.

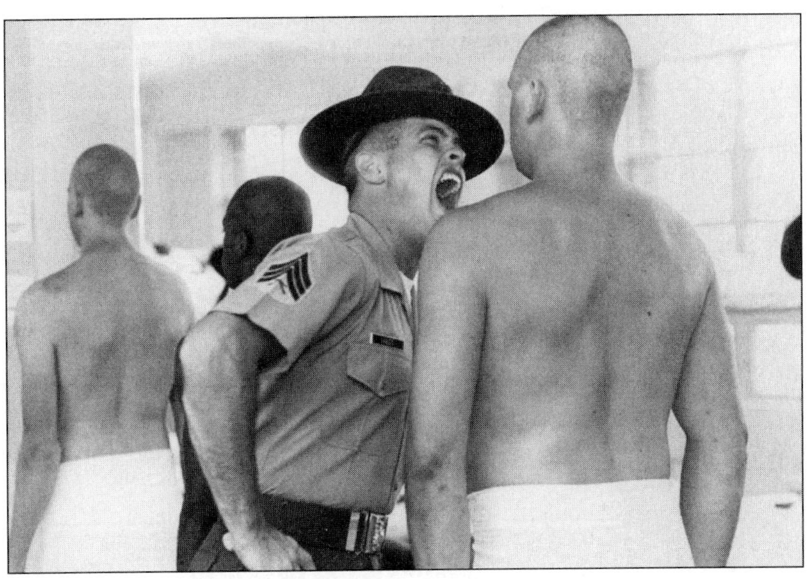

Discussing Ideas. What differences in men's and women's speech exist in your culture? Do men pronounce certain words differently than women? Do men and women use different vocabulary?

A. Complex Sentences: An Overview

A variety of connecting words may be used to join clauses of unequal importance. These sentences are called complex, and each includes at least one *main (independent) clause* and one *dependent clause*. There are three basic types of dependent clauses:

Adjective	MAIN CLAUSE: Everyone ... needs a vacation. DEPENDENT CLAUSE: who worked on this Everyone who worked on this needs a vacation.
Adverb	DEPENDENT CLAUSE: After we have finished, MAIN CLAUSE: we'll take a long vacation. After we have finished, we'll take a long vacation.
Noun	MAIN CLAUSE: Phil said DEPENDENT CLAUSE: that we should all go to a movie. Phil said that we should all go to a movie.

Connecting Words Used in Adjective Clauses (Relative Pronouns)

	Examples
Animals and Things	which, that
People	who, whom, that
Place	where
Possessives	whose
Reason	why, that
Time	when

Common Connecting Words Used in Adverb Clauses (Subordinating Conjunctions)

	Examples
Comparison Condition	more (less, -er) . . . than, as . . . as if, unless as long as, provided that, whether or not
Contrast: Concession	although, even though, though despite (in spite of) the fact that
Contrast: Opposition	while, where, whereas
Manner	as, as if, as though
Place	where, wherever
Purpose	so that, in order that
Reason	as, because, since
Result	so . . . that, such . . . that
Time	after, as long as, as soon as, before, once, since, until, when, whenever, while

Common Connecting Words Used in Noun Clauses (Subordinating Conjunctions)

	Examples
Reported Speech	that (or no conjunction)
Embedded Questions	how, if, when, whether, why, and all other question words.

1 Quickly reread the passage "Language Differences." Then look at the sentences in lines 2 to 3, 7 to 8, and 10 to 12, and answer these questions for each sentence.

1. How many clauses are there in the sentence?
2. What connecting word is used?
3. Which is the main clause?
4. Which is the dependent clause?
5. Where does the dependent clause come in relation to the main clause?
6. What punctuation (if any) is used?

2 Underline the dependent clauses and circle the connecting words in each of these sentences. Then identify the type of dependent clause: adverb, adjective, or noun. In some cases, there may be more than one dependent clause; in others, there may be none.

Example: In Madagascar, women use more direct language than men (because) women are in charge of situations of confrontation. *adverb clause*

1. Researchers in Madagascar have found that the most aggressive buyers and sellers are women. ____________
2. Although women often bargain in the marketplace, men only buy and sell goods that have a fixed price. ____________
3. Social scientists who have studied Madagascar aren't sure why the women dominate confrontations. ____________

A marketplace in Madagascar

4. In most other cultures, the men control situations of confrontation. ____________

5. Any Japanese speaker can add *yo* at the end of a sentence, but the meaning changes somewhat, depending on the sex of the speaker. ____________

6. When a male uses *yo,* it means something similar to, "You had better believe me!" ____________

7. If a female says *yo,* it often has a softer meaning. ____________

8. Sex differences in the English language were much greater in the past because men and women socialized together very little. ____________

9. In Victorian England (1837–1901), the difference between male and female language was so great that women couldn't use or listen to a large number of "male" words. ____________

10. For example, leg was considered such an offensive word that it was never used in the presence of a woman. ____________

11. Even the legs of furniture were covered so that women would not be shocked. ____________

3 Fill in each blank with a connecting word from the category in parentheses. Then underline the dependent clause(s).

Culture Note

Deborah Tannen, Ph.D., is an American scholar and author who has researched and written extensively about differences in male and female speech and behavior. If you are interested in learning more about these differences, look for some of her books: You Just Don't Understand: Women and Men in Conversation; That's Not What I Meant!: How Conversation Style Makes or Breaks Relationships; Talking from 9 to 5: Women and Men in the Workplace.

Example: The reason __that/why__ (adjective clause) men don't use "refined" English is __that__ (noun clause) they admire the rougher qualities of the working class.

1. ______________ (adverb clause: time) Victoria ruled Britain, the language of males and females has become quite similar.
2. Linguists have proved ______________ (noun clause) differences still exist in the way men and women speak English.
3. The differences ______________ (adjective clause) remain are more subtle, however.
4. ______________ (adverb clause: contrast) some "offensive words" are more common among males, women are using these words more and more.
5. Still, women tend to speak a more refined form of the language than men ______________ (adjective clause) are in the same social class.
6. In most languages, the voice quality of males and females is ______________ different ______________ (adverb clause: result) the sex of a speaker is recognized immediately.
7. In fact, there is ______________ a big difference ______________ (adverb clause: result) one sex has trouble imitating the other.
8. ______________ (adverb clause: time) an American woman imitates a man, she separates the syllables more clearly and lowers the pitch.
9. However, ______________ (adverb clause: condition) an American male wants to sound like a female, he uses more "breathiness" in his voice, blends the stressed syllables, and raises the pitch.
10. By contrast, a male Mohave Indian needs only to use words typical of a woman ______________ (adverb clause: purpose) he can sound like one.

B. Complex Sentences: Focus

In a complex sentence (a sentence with both a main clause and a dependent clause), the information that the speaker or writer wants to emphasize is usually placed within the main clause. The main clause is, therefore, the focus of most complex sentences; it gives the topic or "main" idea. In contrast, clauses in compound sentences (sentences with two independent clauses) generally have equal importance. Compare:

Complex Sentences	Focus
In England, sex differences in language were greater in the past because men and women rarely socialized together.	Sex differences in language were greater in the past.
In England's past, men and women rarely socialized together, which created greater sex differences in language than exist today.	In the past, men and women in England rarely socialized together.
During England's past, men and women had so little social contact that sex differences in language developed.	In the past, men and women had very little social contact.

Compound Sentences	Focus
During England's past, men and women had very little social contact; as a result, sex differences in language developed.	In the past, men and women did not socialize. Because of this, sex differences in language developed.

4 Study the following sets of sentences and underline the main clause in each. Discuss the differences in focus in each set. In some cases, there may be only main clauses.

Example: The word *matriarchy*, which appears in all dictionaries, is usually defined as a society dominated by females.

The word *matriarchy* appears in all dictionaries, where it is usually defined as a society dominated by females.

In sentence 1, the focus is on the meaning of the word matriarchy. *The clause* which appears in all dictionaries *is extra information; it doesn't give information necessary to the main idea of the sentence.*

In sentence 2, the focus is on dictionaries and the fact that matriarchy appears *in them. The clause* where it is usually defined as a society dominated by females *gives additional information. It reinforces the main idea of the main clause: dictionary definitions.*

1. The Iroquois Indians, who probably came as close to having a matriarchal society as any people, lived in North America.

   The Iroquois Indians, who lived in North America, probably came as close to having a matriarchal society as any people.
2. In this society, even though the women played a central role in the election of new leaders, these leaders were always men.

   In this society, even though the leaders were always men, women played a central role in the elections of these leaders.
3. In the last century, Great Britain and the Philippines each gave the highest governmental position to a woman; thus, these might at first glance appear to have been matriarchal societies.

   Because Great Britain and the Philippines each gave the highest governmental position to a woman, they might appear at first glance to have been matriarchal societies.

4. While the leaders of both countries were female, the governments actually were dominated by males.

   The leaders of both countries were female in spite of the fact that the governments actually were dominated by males.*

5. Margaret Thatcher became Prime Minister of Great Britain when her Conservative Party defeated the Labor Party in 1979.

   When Margaret Thatcher became Prime Minister of Great Britain in 1979, it was due to the victory of the Conservative Party over the Labor Party.

6. It was a revolution in 1985 that brought Corazon Aquino to power in the Philippines.

   Corazon Aquino came to power in the Philippines because of the revolution that broke out in 1985.

5 Reread the sentences in Activity 4 and then try to create a third possibility for each set. Do this by omitting the connecting word and replacing it with either a transition (*however, therefore,* and so forth) or a coordinating conjunction (*and, or,* and so forth). Finally, discuss the difference in focus between the old and new sentences.

Using What You've Learned

6 Beyond physical differences, how do men and women differ? Should men and women share household duties? Should both have equal opportunities in the business world? Should boys and girls be raised in the same way?

The roles of men and women differ from culture to culture. Interview a classmate from a different cultural background than yours and learn his or her opinions about sex roles. Ask the preceding questions and others that you may think of. Then write a short summary of your partner's opinions, using as many connecting words as possible.

PART 5 Sentence Problems

Setting the Context

Prereading Questions In your culture, do fathers often stay at home and raise the children while mothers work outside the home?

Variations on a Theme

Karen and Bob Maness. They were married about 15 years ago; she was 16 and he was 21. Eventually, one of them became a police officer; the other got a part-time job and took care of the house and the children. Even though this family seems quite ordinary, it was not. It was Karen who was the police officer and Bob who raised the couple's two daughters.

*In Great Britain, in the late 1980s, for example, every one of Prime Minister Margaret Thatcher's ministers were male.

The couple seemed quite satisfied with the unconventional marriage. "I could never go back to doing all the housework," Karen told an interviewer while Bob nodded his head in agreement. Unfortunately (some might say inevitably), the strains of this lifestyle were greater than the couple was willing to admit. Karen and Bob filed for divorce only one month after their interview.

Peter Swerdloff

Discussing Ideas. What do you think happened to Bob and Karen's marriage?

A. Comma Splices and Run-On Sentences

There are three ways to join two clauses correctly.

	Examples of Correct Sentences
Coordinating Conjunction	Bob got married in June, **but** he was divorced by July.
Semicolon	Bob got married in June**;** he was divorced by July.
Subordinating Conjunction or Relative Pronoun	**Although** Bob got married in June, he was divorced by July. Bob, **who** had gotten married in June, was divorced by July.

Two clauses cannot be joined correctly without one of the preceding. Therefore, the following sentences are incorrect:

	Examples of Incorrect Sentences
Comma Splice	*Bob got married in June, he was divorced by July.
Run-On	*Bob got married in June he was divorced by July.

1 **Error Analysis.** Identify the run-on sentences in the following exercise. Then correct them by adding a connecting word, a semicolon, or a period. Make all necessary changes in punctuation and capitalization. If a sentence has no mistake, do not change it.

Example: A number of couples have changed their husband/wife roles⊙
Many
(many) have been more successful than Karen and Bob Maness.

1. They live in a traditional society Jean and Françoise have a "modern marriage."
2. Jean is a well-known political cartoonist and works at home his wife, on the other hand, teaches linguistics at a university and spends most of her day on campus.
3. Since Jean is at home more, he does more of the housework and helps care for the children, Françoise does the rest of the cleaning and all of the sewing.
4. Whereas Françoise fills out the tax forms, Jean does the shopping and most of the cooking the relationship is not perfect but it works.
5. They are delighted to have three daughters each of the marriage partners disciplines the children, but Jean is more successful at it.
6. The whole family spends as much time together as possible, for they want their modern family to have old-fashioned love and warmth.

B. Fragments

Fragments are incomplete sentences; thus, they are also incorrect. There are two common types of fragments:

Incomplete Clauses

Every clause must have at least one subject and one verb.

Fragment	Problem	Correction
*Helen, Harry, and the rest of the family.	No verb	Helen, Harry, and the rest of the family are in China.
*In the middle of July began work.	No subject	In the middle of July, Ellen began work.

Dependent Clauses

A dependent clause cannot be a sentence by itself. It must be accompanied by a complete main clause.

Fragment	Problem	Correction
*Although they had been married for years.	No main clause	Although they had been married for years, they were quite unhappy.
*The couple that lived next to us.	No verb in main clause	The couple that lived next to us had a perfect marriage.

2 **Error Analysis.** Underline the fragments in the following sentences. Identify the problem in each, then correct the problem.

Example: Monogamy* is practiced by a majority of people in all societies. Thus, making it the most popular form of marriages.

Correction: Thus, it is the most popular form of marriage.

1. Many other types of marriage have been tried in different cultures. For example, polygamy.**
2. Polygamy, which is another marital variation. It involves the marriage of several women to one man.
3. Polygamy is still practiced in several societies. Particularly where there are large numbers of Muslims.
4. Although most Muslims have monogamous marriages. The Koran, the holy book of Islam, allows a man to be married to four wives at one time.
5. Ibn Saud, who founded the Kingdom of Saudi Arabia, had hundreds of wives in his lifetime. But never more than four at one time.
6. The marriage of several men to one woman. This is called polyandry.
7. Polyandry is uncommon today. Despite the fact that it was practiced in India, Ceylon, Tibet, and the South Pacific.

**monogamy* the practice of having only one husband or wife at one time

***polygamy* the practice of having more than one wife at one time

3 **Error Analysis.** Find the fragments and run-on sentences in the following paragraph. Then make necessary corrections.

Web Note

For more information on the Oneida Community, see: xroads.virginia.edu/~HYPER/HNS/cities/oneida.htm/.

The Oneida Community

The marriage of one group of males to another group of females is not practiced today, however, "group marriage" has been tried at different times in the past. The Oneida community in upstate New York was the most successful of these efforts. Oneida, which was founded in 1848 with some 58 adults and their children. It was perhaps the most radical social experiment in the history of the United States.

Oneidans believed that romantic love produced selfishness and jealousy, in its place, the members adopted a policy of "free love." Under this policy, all adults were considered married to all adults of the opposite sex. Any male could mate with any female. Though both parties had to agree. Later, in 1869, Oneida began the world's first large-scale experiments in eugenics.* At that time, a special committee selected certain males and females to be mates. So that the strongest and most intelligent children would be born.

Using What You've Learned

4 Poets try to express a great deal in as few words as possible, often ignoring many of the rules of grammar. In pairs or in small groups, read and discuss the following poem. Then try to find all the rules of grammar and punctuation the author has broken. Finally, change the lines of this poem into grammatical sentences, adding subjects, verbs, conjunctions, and punctuation.

She

Mischievous eyes peeping from tiny windows
Sweet smiles flowing from rosy lips
Peaceful expression rendering endless affection
Long black eye-lashes in a continuous dance
Resembling a frail shining hummingbird
Not only is she beautiful but shy,
She wanders about the most splendid gardens
Darting between green leaf and silver blossom
Whenever you are down and needing warmth
Lie on your garden and raise your eyes
Search among the flowers, scan the clouds,
She will be there, she is part of the sky

JOHN BENITES

**eugenics* the science of improving the inherited traits of human beings

Video Activities: Seeking Love

Before You Watch. Discuss these questions in small groups.

1. What are some ways to meet people?
2. Which ways are the most effective?
3. What is the most important quality to seek in a boyfriend or a girlfriend?

Watch. Answer these questions in small groups.

1. What does the narrator say is probably what most of us want and need the most? ________________________
2. Check the ways of finding a mate that are mentioned in this video segment.
   a. ____ using a dating service
   b. ____ placing personal advertisements
   c. ____ getting involved in activities that you enjoy
   d. ____ asking friends to help you meet someone
3. Put a check (✓) next to things that you should do and an (x) next to things that you shouldn't do on a first date.
   a. ____ Ask creative questions.
   b. ____ Dress well.
   c. ____ Be someone that you're not.
   d. ____ Ask questions to find out about your date's financial status.

Watch Again. Circle the correct answers.

1. What does Dr. Jim Soulis say you should do before you start looking for a mate?
   a. look into yourself
   b. lose weight and buy new clothes
   c. read books about relationships
2. Dr. Jim Soulis says that the most important quality you must have to find love is ____________.
   a. good looks b. money c. intelligence d. confidence
3. Which three things does Victoria Parker tell her clients to do?
   a. meditate
   b. think positively
   c. study themselves
   d. listen to a tape recorder
   e. become active in things they enjoy
4. Judy Knoll says that ____________ personal ads are not effective.
   a. imaginative b. negative c. boastful

5. Men should never ______________________.
   a. pay for a woman's friends
   b. compliment a woman on a part of her body
   c. call a woman when they said that they would

6. Men don't like women who ______________________.
   a. become attached too quickly
   b. ask them a lot of questions
   c. make a lot of money

After You Watch. Complete the following sentences.

1. I want to have both a career . . .
2. Either call me on Tuesday . . .
3. I am not only lonely . . .
4. Living alone is neither economical . . .
5. I wish I could meet a person who was both intelligent . . .
6. Neither my friends . . .

Focus on Testing

Compound and Complex Sentences

Problem areas with compound and complex sentences are frequently tested on standardized English proficiency exams. Check your understanding of these structures by completing the sample items that follow.

Remember that . . .

- Every sentence must have at least one subject-verb combination.
- Compound sentences are formed by joining sentences with a comma and a coordinating conjunction, with a semicolon, or with a semicolon and a transition.
- Compound sentences with *nor* use special word order.
- Correlative conjunctions such as *either . . . or* connect parallel structures.
- Complex sentences are formed by joining sentences with a subordinating conjunction.

Part 1. Circle the best completion for the following.

Example: Although people are similar, ______ are still divided by their sex.
a. always b. but (c.) they d. we

1. The child appears healthy; ______, it's a good idea for her to have a check up soon.
   a. otherwise c. nevertheless
   b. therefore d. always

2. We had wanted to go for a walk, ______ it was raining.
   a. furthermore
   b. but
   c. but however
   d. so

3. To lead a peaceful life, women should not try to do too much, nor ______ do too little.
   a. should they
   b. they
   c. women should
   d. they should

4. Human beings are divided by sex; ______ we view all people as fundamentally similar.
   a. on the contrary,
   b. however,
   c. moreover,
   d. but,

Part 2. Each sentence has one error. Circle the letter below the word(s) containing the error.

Example: During England's past, men and women had (A) very little contact; but, (B — circled) sex differences in the language (C) developed (D).

1. Sometimes (A) a man takes care of the children because (B) his wife has a job outside the home; but (C) however, (D) this arrangement may not work well for every couple.

2. Even though (A) the men were the leaders in the (B) society; nevertheless, (C) within the family, they were subordinate to (D) the women.

3. In Madagascar, the women are such (A) aggressive buyers and sellers so (B) that (C) they dominate the (D) marketplace.

4. Although (A) the Weikers live in a relatively (B) traditional society, and (C) the couple has (D) a modern marriage.

Chapter 4

Mysteries Past and Present

IN THIS CHAPTER

Part 1 Adjective Clauses: Restrictive Versus Nonrestrictive

Part 2 Adjective Clauses: Replacement of Subjects

Part 3 Adjective Clauses: Replacement of Objects

Part 4 Other Adjective Clause Constructions

Part 5 Review of Chapters 1 to 4

Introduction

In this chapter, you will study a variety of adjective clauses. As you study, pay careful attention to the use of or the lack of commas with these clauses.

The following passage introduces the chapter theme "Mysteries Past and Present" and raises some issues that you will cover in the chapter.

Knowledge of the Ancients

Until recently, anthropologists believed human history to be a steady line of progress that stretched from the Stone Age to the present day. Consequently, today's humans were seen as far more advanced than their ancestors.

Nevertheless, our knowledge is quite limited of the truly ancient civilizations, some of which existed up to 100,000 years ago. In fact, written history reaches back only a few thousands of years. Even in Egypt, where the documents go back the furthest, we have only the vaguest ideas of history before 1600 B.C. Thus, on the scale of our time on earth, it is as if we had written records of only three years out of a thousand.

This lack of concrete knowledge, along with some fascinating evidence, has led a number of scientists to change their view of human development. They now believe that thousands of years ago there were certain societies whose accomplishments rival our own. In fact, modern findings suggest that certain ancient cultures had an advanced knowledge of mathematics, astronomy, and geography that we have gained only recently.

Discussing Ideas. How many ancient societies can you name? In what areas (architecture, mathematics, etc.) did these societies have advanced knowledge? Explain what the last sentence in paragraph 2 means. Why is this significant?

PART 1 Adjective Clauses: Restrictive Versus Nonrestrictive

Setting the Context

Prereading Questions. What do you know about the Egyptian pyramids? What is the name of the largest?

Enigma

The Great Pyramid of Cheops, which is the last remaining of the Seven Wonders of the World, has been a puzzle to scientists and laymen for thousands of years. Is an advanced science that has been lost over time hidden within the pyramid? Or is this huge, incredibly precise structure simply a tomb that ancients built to commemorate a pharaoh?

For centuries, scholars have been asking questions such as these. All agree that the Great Pyramid, which is at least 4,000 years old, is among the most important historical structures on earth. However, none can say for certain just how, when, or—perhaps most importantly—why it was built.

The Great Pyramid of Cheops

Discussing Ideas. Approximately when was the Great Pyramid built? Why do you think it was built?

A. Introduction to Adjective Clauses

An adjective (or relative) clause is one type of dependent clause. It modifies a noun or pronoun or occasionally a whole sentence. An adjective clause usually comes immediately after the word(s) that it modifies; however, in some cases, a prepositional phrase may come between the (pro)noun and the clause. There are several types of adjective clause constructions, as shown in the following. Each one will be examined in detail in this chapter.

	Examples
Subject Clauses: ***That, Which, Who***	Archeology is a subject **that is very interesting.**
Object Clauses: ***That, Which, Who(m)***	It is a subject **which I would like to study.**
Possessive Clauses: *Whose*	Dr. Jenkins, **whose class meets today,** is an expert.
Time and Place Clauses: ***When, Where***	Does the class meet at a time **when you can attend?**
Quantity Clauses: ***Quantity + Of + Which/Whom***	I saw three classes, **one of which was boring.**

B. Restrictive Versus Nonrestrictive Adjective Clauses

Adjective clauses are divided into two basic types: restrictive and nonrestrictive. Restrictive clauses identify or limit the word(s) they modify. In contrast, nonrestrictive clauses *do not* define or identify the word(s) they describe. Rather, these clauses give extra information. The type of clause determines whether or not commas are used. Compare the following examples.

Restrictive Clauses	Notes
Many of the men **who (that) broke into the tombs** died suddenly. Most of the tombs **which (that) they opened** had already been robbed. Imhotep, **who built Joser's Pyramid,** was worshipped after his death. The pyramid, **which is located near Cairo,** is in ruins. The sun, **which appears in many ancient drawings,** was an important symbol.	A restrictive adjective clause explains *which* people, places, things, or ideas: not everyone or everything. It limits the (pro)noun that it modifies to only what is described in the clause. No commas are used. A nonrestrictive adjective clause adds information about the (pro)noun. It does *not* explain *which* people, places, etc. Clauses that modify proper names, entire groups, nouns that are unique (the sun, etc.) and nouns preceded by demonstratives (*this, these,* etc.) are generally nonrestrictive. Commas are used to set off these clauses. *That* may *not* be used.

In some cases, a particular adjective clause can either identify or give extra information. It depends on the context or the writer's point of view. Compare the following sentences:

Restrictive Clauses	Meaning	Notes
My sister **who lives in Bishop** teaches high school.	I have several sisters. I am talking about one in particular.	This clause identifies *which* sister. No commas are used. In spoken English, no pause comes before the clause.

Nonrestrictive Clauses	Meaning	Notes
My sister**, who lives in Bishop,** teaches high school.	I have only one sister. By the way, she lives in Bishop.	This clause gives extra information. Commas are used. In spoken English, pauses are likely before and after the clause.

1 Underline the adjective clauses in the following sentences and circle the nouns that they modify. Add commas where necessary.

Example: Ten miles west of Cairo stands the man-made (plateau of Giza,) <u>which overlooks the Nile Valley from a height of 130 feet.</u>

1. In all, ten pyramids of varying sizes stand on Giza, but the one which archeologists have studied the most is the Great Pyramid.
2. This pyramid was named after the pharaoh Cheops who supposedly ordered it built.
3. The Great Pyramid which is as tall as a 40-story modern skyscraper is made up of more than two and a half million blocks of limestone and granite.
4. These blocks which came from an area about 20 miles to the east weigh from 2 to 20 tons apiece.

5. The Great Pyramid contains more stone than all the cathedrals, churches, and chapels that have been built in England since the time of Christ.
6. The Great Pyramid's base which is perhaps the most impressive feature would cover 13 acres or seven blocks in New York City.
7. The huge piece of land on which the pyramid sits was made level to within a fraction of an inch.
8. Modern engineers who have studied the structure are astounded by the problems which were involved in building the pyramid.

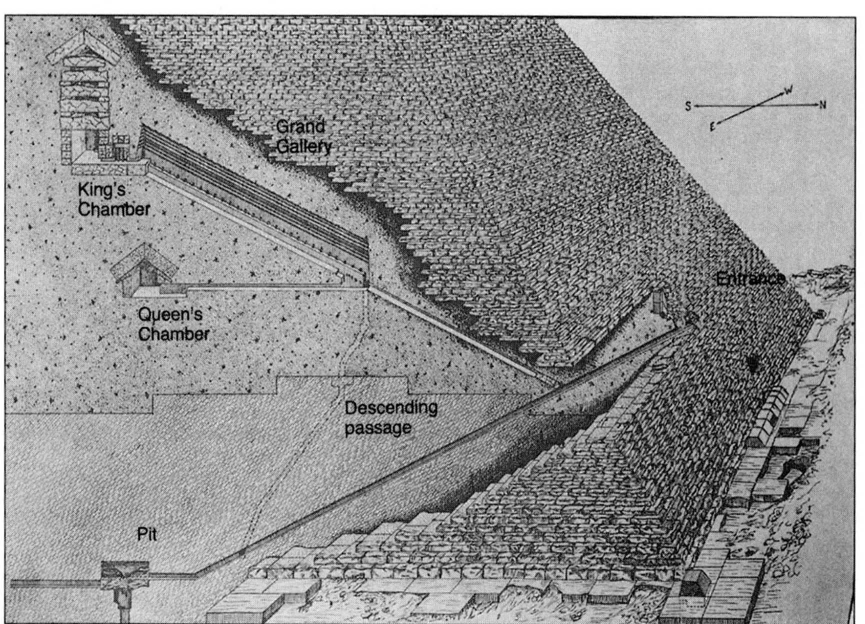

2 Add the adjective clause to each sentence that follows. If the clause is nonrestrictive (only gives extra information), add punctuation. If the clause is restrictive (defines or identifies the noun it follows), do not add punctuation.

Example: which are located near Cairo

There are thousands of pyramids in the world, but the pyramids *which are located near Cairo* are perhaps the most famous monuments in the world.

The pyramids of Giza, *which are located near Cairo,* are perhaps the most famous monuments in the world.

1. where the pyramid stands

   The place ______________________ is almost perfectly level.

   The plateau of Giza ______________________ is almost perfectly level.

2. who majored in Egyptian architecture in college

   My brother ______________________________________ visited Giza in 1985. (I have only one brother.)

My brother ______________________________ visited Giza in 1985. (I have three brothers.)

3. whose ancient name was Thebes

   The famous Temple of Karnak is located near a town ____________________ ____________________.

   The famous Temple of Karnak is located in Luxor ____________________ ____________________.

4. who was to become the world's most famous archeologist

   In 1922, Howard Carter ______________________________ uncovered the tomb of Tutankhamen across the Nile from Karnak.

   In 1922, the man ______________________________ uncovered the tomb of Tutankhamen across the Nile from Karnak.

5. which warned "Death will slay with his wings anyone disturbing the pharaoh"

   While Carter and his men were opening this tomb, they came upon a curse ______________________________.

   While Carter and his men were opening this tomb, they came upon the curse of Tutankhamen ______________________________.

Web Note

For a very interesting interactive Website on King Tut and the treasures of his tomb, see the 1923 National Geographic *that reported the findings at www.nationalgeographic.com/egypt/.*

King Tutankhamen's death mask

6. who were present at the tomb's opening

   Not one of Carter's 20 men ______________________________ believed that his life was in danger.

   Not one of the 20 men believed that his life was in danger.* ______________________________

3 The following passage has many adjective clauses, but it does not include commas with the nonrestrictive clauses. First, read the paragraph silently. Underline the adjective clauses. Add commas around adjective clauses when you feel they are necessary. Then, read the passage aloud or listen as your teacher reads it aloud. Does the oral reading of the paragraph match your punctuation of it? *Remember:* In spoken English, a pause is likely before (and after) a nonrestrictive clause. The first adjective clause is done as an example.

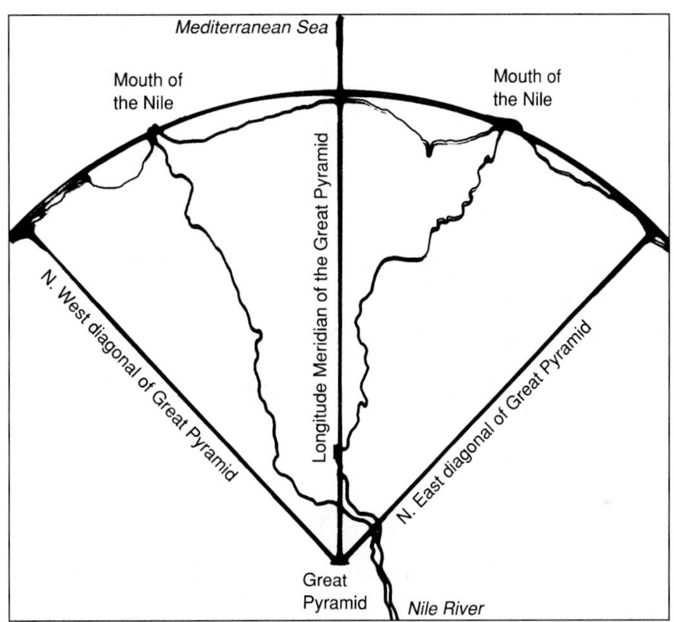

The diagonals from the Great Pyramid create a concise border for the delta of the Nile.

The Knowledge of the Ancients

In 1798, Egypt was invaded by Napoleon, who wanted to cut off the British trade route to India. With him, Napoleon brought 35,000 troops and a collection of "savants"** whose job was to gather knowledge about Egyptian artifacts.† The French advanced to Giza where they were confronted by the Mamluks who ruled Egypt in the name of the Ottoman Empire.

*Within five years, 13 of these men, none of whom was over 50 years old, had died suddenly of either an unidentified virus or heart failure.

***savant* person having great knowledge about some subject

†*artifact* object made by humans

In the Battle of the Pyramids, the Mamluks who fought with swords and knives were easily defeated. Napoleon's troops whose weapons included cannons and rifles killed 2,000 Mamluks while losing only 40 of their own. Soon afterward, the Mamluks surrendered to Napoleon whose savants were then free to explore the pyramids in great detail.

Napoleon's savants who surveyed the pyramid were astonished at the geological positioning of the pyramid. First, they discovered that the pyramid was precisely aligned north, south, east, and west. Even more amazing, diagonals that were drawn through the pyramid at right angles outlined the entire Delta of the Nile. Obviously, the structure whose orientation is a perfect geographic marker, could not have been located at random. And just as surely, the ancient Egyptians who built the pyramid had a knowledge of astronomy and geography that was not equaled for thousands of years.

Using What You've Learned

4 Do you believe that the Egyptian curse could have caused the death of the men who opened the tomb? Do you have any superstitious beliefs? (For instance, in the United States and Canada, many people believe that black cats can cause bad luck.) What are some of the superstitious beliefs in your culture? In small groups, share information about things in your culture that are associated with good and bad luck. Be sure to include information about colors, numbers, and animals. After you've finished your discussion, choose one member of the group to give a summary to the entire class.

PART 2

Adjective Clauses: Replacement of Subjects

Setting the Context

Prereading Questions. What do you know about the Mayans of the past? Of today's Mayans?

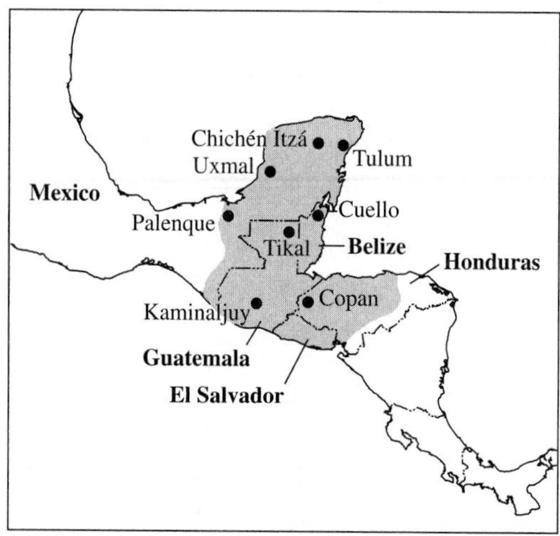

The Mayans

Who were the Mayans, the people who built such complex cities and majestic temples? What happened to this amazing civilization, whose total collapse came suddenly around 900 A.D.?

Earliest evidence of the Mayan civilization dates to over 4,000 years ago. The Mayan culture developed in independent but loosely linked city-states and then flourished during its classic period, which spanned about 700 years. The classic period was the glory period of the Mayans, whose accomplishments included a highly complex writing system, advanced mathematics and the concept of zero, astrological calendars of astonishing accuracy, and massive constructions all over Central America, from Yucatan to modern Honduras.

Then came the collapse. It was around 900 A.D. that the southern Mayans abandoned their cities. The northern Mayans were absorbed by another society, the Toltec, by 1200 A.D., and the Mayan dynasty ended, although some outlying city-states continued until the Spanish Conquest in the 1500s.

Today, over 1 million Mayans live in Chiapas, which is a state in southern Mexico, and about 5 million are spread throughout Belize, Guatemala, Honduras, El Salvador, and the Yucatan Peninsula of Mexico.

Will we ever understand what happened to the early civilization? Was it drought or war that caused the Mayans to abandon their cities abruptly? Was it disease or overpopulation that led to the collapse of this great civilization? Perhaps new ruins that have been found in the jungles of Belize may give us better clues to the events that led to its disintegration.

Discussing Ideas. Civilizations seem to go in cycles of growth and development and then disintegration and decline. Can you name other great civilizations that eventually collapsed? What caused their collapse?

A. Clauses with Who, Which, *or* That

The relative pronouns *who, which,* and *that* may replace the subject of a simple sentence in order to form an adjective clause. In restrictive clauses, *who* or *that* can refer to people, but *who* is preferred. *Which* or *that* can refer to animals or things, but *that* is preferred. In nonrestrictive clauses, only *who* or *which* can be used (*that* is *not* possible).

	Examples
Simple Sentences	**The man** was named Stephens. **He** found the ruins.
Complex Sentence with *Who* or *That* (Restrictive)	The man **who (that) found the ruins** was named Stephens.
Simple Sentences	I read about **Stephens. He** was a very interesting character.
Complex Sentence with *Who* (Nonrestrictive)	I read about Stephens**, who was a very interesting character.**
Simple Sentences	The **pyramid** is El Castillo. **It** is the most famous.
Complex Sentence with *That* or *Which* (Restrictive)	The pyramid **that (which) is the most famous** is El Castillo.
Simple Sentences	We visited **El Castillo. It** is at Chichen Itza.
Complex Sentence with *Which* (Nonrestrictive)	We visited El Castillo**, which is at Chichen Itza.**

1 Make the second sentence in each pair of sentences that follow into an adjective clause using *who, that*, or *which* to combine it with the first. Add commas where necessary.

Example: Mayan ruins can be found from southern Mexico to Honduras. These Mayan ruins range from crumbling walls of temples to full cities.

Mayan ruins that (which) range from crumbling walls of temples to full cities can be found from southern Mexico to Honduras. (no commas)

1. John Lloyd Stephens was an American lawyer and explorer. He came across the ruins of Copan in the 1840s.
2. The famous Pyramid of Kukulcan is located at Chichén Itzá. Chichén Itzá was the capital of the Mayas of the Yucatan.
3. Palenque was built as a gateway to the Underworld. Palenque is in the Chiapas highlands of southern Mexico.
4. Small windows in the observatory tower at Palenque frame the rising of the planet Venus. The planet Venus was used to determine when to begin war.
5. War was declared by the kings. The kings used the stars and planets such as Venus to decide when to fight.
6. Tikal is located in the Tikal National Park. This park is a 575-square-kilometer preserve with thousands of ruins.
7. The central city of Tikal had about 3,000 buildings. The central city was about 16 square kilometers.
8. Tikal was first explored in 1881 by Alfred Maudslay. Maudslay was an English archeologist.
9. Tulum was a fortresslike port. This port was established by the Maya for its vast trading network.
10. The temple at Tulum has a small arch. This arch frames the rising sun at dawn on the winter solstice.

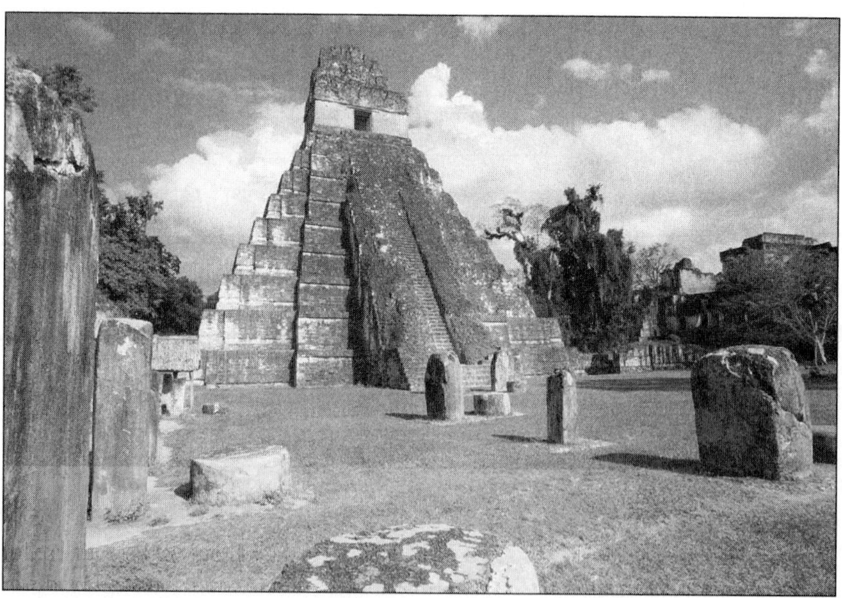

Ruins in Tikal National Park

11. Copan has the best-preserved court of the ancient ball courts. Copan was one of the largest Mayan cities.
12. Copan has amazing examples of Mayan hieroglyphs. These hieroglyphs include the longest stone inscription in the Western Hemisphere.

B. Clauses with Whose

Whose may replace a possessive noun, pronoun, or adjective in the subject of a simple sentence in order to form an adjective clause. It may be used to refer to people, animals, or things, and it may be used in both restrictive and nonrestrictive clauses.

	Examples
Simple Sentences	Kings employed **priests. Their** job was to keep written records.
Complex Sentence with *Whose* (Restrictive)	Kings employed priests **whose job was to keep written records.**
Simple Sentences	We read about **John Stephens. His** book on the ruins became famous.
Complex Sentence with *Whose* (Nonrestrictive)	We read about John Stephens**, whose book on the ruins became famous.**

2 Make the second sentence into an adjective clause and use *whose* to combine it with the first. Add commas when necessary.

Example: The Mayan writing was in the form of hieroglyphs. Their inscriptions were made on stone and wood.

The Mayan writing was in the form of hieroglyphs whose inscriptions were made on stone and wood.

Mayan hieroglyphs

1. A great accomplishment of the Mayans was their writing system. Its inscriptions were in the form of hieroglyphics.
2. The Mayans developed a complex system of books. Their primary purpose was to record the transition of power from king to king.
3. Archeologists found several "codexes" of the Mayans. Their history was recorded in these books.
4. Many Mayan books did not survive the Spanish Conquest. Its goal was to convert native populations to Christianity.
5. Many of the books were destroyed by the Spanish. Their priests burned the books.
6. Explorers found four books. Their names are the Dresden Codex, the Madud Codex, the Paris Codex, and the Grolier Codex.
7. The bark of fig trees was used to make these books. Their pages were inscribed and then folded together and placed in royal tombs.
8. Today many of the Mayan pyramids are still covered by the jungle. Its humid climate continues to deteriorate the ruins.

3 Make adjective clauses from the sentences in column 2. Combine these with the cues from column 1 to form definitions.

Example: The boa constrictor is a snake whose size and ability to crush its prey makes it a dangerous predator.

1. The Mayans of the Yucatan had to be cautious of many dangerous animals in the region. Here are some of those animals.

a. Boa constrictor/snake	1. Its size and ability to crush its prey make it a dangerous predator.
b. Caiman/fierce crocodile	2. It lives in tropical areas in the Americas.
c. Coral snake/reptile	3. It is small and highly poisonous.
d. Jaguar/spotted feline	4. Its size and ferocity make it feared throughout the region.
e. Ocelot/spotted leopardlike cat	5. Its habitat extends from Texas through South America.

2. Other animals had to be cautious of the Mayans, as the Mayans hunted them for food.

a. Agouti/rodent	1. It is short haired, short eared, and similar to a rabbit.
b. Peccary/hoofed mammal	2. It looks somewhat like a pig.
c. Rabbit/small, long-eared rodent	3. It lives in burrows.
d. Tapir/large, stout mammal	4. Its snout is flexible.

3. Other birds and animals shared jungle habitats with the Mayans.

a. Black howler/monkey	1. It is one of the largest primates in the Americas.
b. Spider monkey/golden brown monkey	2. Its tail is often longer than its body.
c. Quetzal/large tropical bird	3. Its bright red, green, and white feathers gave Mexico its national colors.

Web Note

Visit Black Howler Monkeys in the Belize zoo. See its Website for photos, a video, and even sounds: www.belizezoo.org/zoo/zoo/mammals/how/how1.html.

The quetzal is a bright, tropical bird.

C. Anticipatory It *with Adjective Clauses*

Anticipatory *it* is often used with adjectives to place more emphasis on the word or phrase modified by the adjective clause. Compare:

> Hernando Cortez led the Spanish Conquest of Central America.
> *It* was Hernando Cortez *who led the Spanish conquest of Central America.*
>
> Did an environmental catastrophe cause the end of the Mayan empire?
> Was *it* an environmental catastrophe *that caused the end of the Mayan empire?*

4 Rephrase the following sentences to begin with *It* and to include adjective clauses.

Example: Cortez conquered much of Central America.
It was Cortez who conquered much of Central America.

1. Disease killed thousands of Mayans.
2. Catholic missionaries prohibited the Maya religion.
3. Catholic missionaries burned all but four of the sacred Maya bark-paper books.
4. Did drought or overpopulation cause the collapse of this civilization?
5. John Lloyd Stephens published *Incidents of Travel in Central America, Chiapas, and Yucatan* in 1841.
6. The English artist Frederick Catherwood drew amazing pictures of the ruins covered by jungle growth.
7. The Mayans created the Sun Stone, an elaborate calendar.
8. The Mayans invented the concept of zero.
9. Mayan geometric architecture amazed archeologists.
10. The famous conductor Leopold Stokowski spent four days trying to understand the acoustics of the Great Ball Court at Chichén Itzá.

The Ball Court at Chichén Itzá is 545 feet long and 225 feet wide. Its acoustics are such that a whisper from one end can be heard clearly at the other end, 500 feet away, and through the length and breadth of the court. The sound waves are unaffected by wind direction or time of day.

5 Rewrite the paragraph by changing some sentences into adjective clauses and combining them with other sentences. Do not try to combine every sentence. Sometimes more than one adjective clause can be added to one sentence. Add all necessary punctuation.

Chichén Itzá

The Yucatan is a peninsula. It juts into the western Caribbean Sea. The Yucatan is the site of many impressive Mayan ruins. Many of the ruins are amazing, but it is Chichén Itzá. Chichén Itzá is perhaps the most amazing. Chichén Itzá was the most important city in the peninsula from the 10th to the 12th century.

Chichén Itzá is filled with structures. These structures are enormous and awe inspiring. For example, at Chichén Itzá is an impressive Ball Court. Its acoustics are phenomenal. In fact, the accoustics of the Ball Court still baffle scientists and musicians. Scientists and musicians have spent long hours analyzing its construction. Dominating the ruins is the famous 98-foot-tall El Castillo pyramid. El Castillo is the most impressive monument in Chichén Itzá. El Castillo is a masterpiece of Toltec-Maya architectural design and genius.

Using What You've Learned

6 With a partner, write definitions for three of the following terms. Then add three more interesting words and write definitions for them. Make the definitions as clear and thorough as possible. Finally, write a couple of your best definitions (not the words) on the board. See if the class can guess which words you are defining.

Example: pyramid *a four-sided figure whose sides slope upward and meet at their uppermost point*

architecture	justice	solstice
art	knowledge	rectangle
astrologer	predator	square
astronomer	prey	
habitat	priest	

7 Think of five important or unusual animals from your region or country. Name them and describe them with adjective clauses. You can look back at Activity 3 for ideas and examples.

PART 3

Adjective Clauses: Replacement of Objects

Setting the Context

Prereading Questions. Where was the Inca Empire located? Do you know of any other advanced Indian culture from this region?

Aerial view of some Nazca lines in Peru.

The Lines of Nazca

Perhaps 300 miles south of Lima, the capital city of Peru, lies the elevated plateau of Nazca. At ground level, there is little one can see to arouse interest. It's a flat, arid plain on which animal and plant life seem not to exist. As one rises above the bleak landscape in an airplane, however, a strange sight is revealed. Carved in the soil of the plateau are mysterious lines forming hundreds of shapes about which archeologists have speculated for decades.

There is general agreement that the lines date back to 1000 B.C. and were drawn by the native population, the Nazca Indians. But many questions remain. How did Indians living 3,000 years ago manage the complex set of huge figures drawn to scale? How did they create the perfectly straight lines extending miles into the desert? Even more puzzling, why should a society undertake such a monumental set of drawings when they could be appreciated only from the air?

Discussing Ideas. What does *drawn to scale* mean? Why could these drawings be appreciated only from the air? Can you think of other examples of "art" that were not created so that people could appreciate them?

A. Clauses with Whom, Which, *or* That *(1)*

The relative pronouns *whom, which,* or *that* may replace the object of a simple sentence in order to form an adjective clause. In restrictive clauses that refer to people, *who(m)* or *that* can be used, or the relative pronoun can be omitted. *Whom* is preferred in formal English, however. In restrictive clauses that refer to animals or things, *which* or *that* can be used, or the relative pronoun can be omitted. In nonrestrictive clauses, only *who(m)* or *which* are possible, and they cannot be omitted. The examples are in order of most to least formal.

	Examples
Simple Sentences	The **Nazca Indians** lived some 3,000 years ago. Scientists credit **them** with drawing the lines.
Complex Sentence with *Whom* (Nonrestrictive)	The Nazca Indians**, whom scientists credit with drawing the lines,** lived some 3,000 years ago.
Simple Sentences	The **Nazca figures** must be protected. Tourists visit **them** daily.
Complex Sentence with *Which* (Nonrestrictive)	The Nazca figures**, which tourists visit daily,** must be protected.
Simple Sentences	The **artists** lived centuries ago. Scientists credit **them** for the lines.
Complex Sentence with *Who(m)* or *That* (Restrictive)	The artists **whom scientists credit for the lines** lived centuries ago. (formal) The artists **who scientists credit for the lines** lived centuries ago. The artists **that scientists credit for the lines** lived centuries ago. The artists **scientists credit for the lines** lived centuries ago.
Simple Sentences	The **figure** is of a hummingbird. I like **this figure** the most.
Complex Sentence with *Which* or *That* (Restrictive)	The figure **which I like the most** is of a hummingbird. The figure **that I like the most** is of a hummingbird. The figure **I like the most** is of a hummingbird.

1 In these sentences, change the italicized word(s) to *who(m), which,* or *that*. Then make the second sentence into an adjective clause and combine it with the first. Give all possible combinations and add commas when necessary. Finally, indicate any sentence in which the relative pronoun may be omitted.

Example: What could have inspired the drawings? Nazca artists fashioned *these drawings* some 3,000 years ago.

What could have inspired the drawings that Nazca artists fashioned some 3,000 years ago?

What could have inspired the drawings which Nazca artists fashioned some 3,000 years ago?

The relative pronoun can be omitted: *What could have inspired the drawings Nazca artists fashioned some 3,000 years ago?*

1. Why did the Indians make designs and figures? They could not appreciate *these designs and figures* from the ground.
2. Some argue that the Nazca figures were created by extraterrestrials.* The Indians might have treated *these extraterrestrials* as gods.

**extraterrestrial* being from outer space

3. A more conventional theory holds that the Nazca figures were dedicated to the mountain gods. The Indians worshipped *these gods*.
4. Newer evidence suggests some of the designs acted as solar calendars. The Indians used *these calendars* to determine when to plant new crops.
5. In fact, some of the lines point directly to the places where the sun sets on winter and summer solstice days. The Indians drew *these lines*.

B. *Clauses with* Whom, Which, *or* That *(2)*

The relative pronouns *whom, which,* or *that* may replace the object of a preposition in a simple sentence in order to form an adjective clause. In formal English, the preposition is sometimes placed before the relative pronoun. In this case, only *whom* or *which* can be used. If the preposition is placed at the end of a restrictive clause, *that* can also be used, or the relative pronoun can be omitted. In nonrestrictive clauses, *whom* or *which* must be used. The following examples are in order of most to least formal.

	Examples
Simple Sentences	**The gods** are not depicted in the lines. The Indians believed **in them.**
Complex Sentence with *Who(m)* or *That*	The gods **in whom the Indians believed** are not depicted in the lines. The gods **whom the Indians believed in** are not depicted in the lines. The gods **who the Indians believed in** are not depicted in the lines. The gods **that the Indians believed in** are not depicted in the lines. The gods **the Indians believed in** are not depicted in the lines.
Simple Sentences	Recent books suggest fanciful **theories.** Few scientists have faith **in them.**
Complex Sentence with *Which* or *That*	Recent books suggest fanciful theories **in which few scientists have faith.** Recent books suggest fanciful theories **which few scientists have faith in.** Recent books suggest fanciful theories **that few scientists have faith in.** Recent books suggest fanciful theories **few scientists have faith in.**

2 In these sentences, change the italicized word(s) to *who(m), which,* or *that*. Then make the second sentence into an adjective clause and combine it with the first. Give all possible combinations and add commas when necessary. Indicate any sentence in which the relative pronoun may be omitted. Finally, tell which possibility is most formal.

Example: Perhaps the lines formed ceremonial pathways. The Indians held processions on *these pathways*.

Perhaps the lines formed ceremonial pathways on which the Indians held processions. **(most formal)**

Perhaps the lines formed ceremonial pathways that the Indians held processions on.

Perhaps the lines formed ceremonial pathways which the Indians held processions on.

The relative pronoun can be omitted: *Perhaps the lines formed ceremonial pathways the Indians held processions on.*

1. The Nazca figures are at least 3,000 years old. So much has been written about *these figures*.
2. The plateau is about 20 miles wide. The figures are located on *this plateau.*
3. The gods were thought to reside in distant mountains. The Indians probably drew the lines for *these gods.*
4. A German named Maria Reiche is responsible for preventing the destruction of the figures. The world owes a great debt to *Maria Reiche.*

C. Clauses with Whose

The relative pronoun *whose* may replace a possessive in the object or the object of a preposition in a simple sentence in order to form an adjective clause. It can refer to people, animals, or things in both restrictive and nonrestrictive clauses. *Whose* may not be omitted.

	Examples
Simple Sentences	Little is known about **these Indians.** Scientists have studied **their drawings** for decades.
Complex Sentence with *Whose*	Little is known about these Indians, **whose drawings scientists have studied for decades.**

3 Change the italicized word to *whose*. Then change the second sentence into an adjective clause and combine it with the first. Add all necessary punctuation.

Example: There are several theories about the lines of Nazca. We may never discover *their* true purpose.

There are several theories about the lines of Nazca, whose true purpose we may never discover.

1. Some lines extend for miles and are almost perfectly straight. Scientists still argue about *their* function.
2. The geometrical designs range from rectangles and triangles to spirals. The Nazca Indians drew *their* lines with astounding accuracy.
3. How could a society from 1000 B.C. construct figures and lines? It would be difficult to duplicate *their* precision today.
4. Maria Reiche has spent 40 years studying the lines. We are about to examine *her* life.

4 The following has been adapted from an account written by an archeologist who met Maria Reiche in 1984. Read it carefully. Then combine as many sentences as you can by changing the italicized words to *who(m), which, that,* or *whose* and forming adjective clauses. Don't try to combine every sentence. Add all necessary punctuation.

Lady of the Lines

Maria Reiche slowly made her way to the terrace. A group of tourists had gathered to hear her speak on *this terrace*. Though trembling from Parkinson's disease and nearly blind, this 84-year-old ex-mathematics teacher had a commanding presence. Using one of her five languages, Maria Reiche spoke to the audience for over an hour of the abiding passion. She has devoted four decades to *this passion*.

If Maria is a celebrity today, it has not always been so for this ex-school teacher from Germany. Local people now call *her* "Santa Maróa." In fact, the admiration is relatively new. She is now held in *this admiration*. When she began to study and protect the lines of Nazca over 40 years ago, few outsiders knew of her work, and most of the people of the region thought she was mad.

At the end of the talk, Maria's listeners were invited to buy copies of her book Mystery on the Desert. She uses the book's proceeds to pay the salaries of the guards. Maria employs *these guards* to protect the ancient lines.

Evan Hadingham

Using What You've Learned

5 Ancient cities have fascinated historians and archeologists for hundreds of years. Choose one of the cities listed below (or any other that you are interested in) as the subject for some library research. Use the Internet, encyclopedias, or other sources to gather information. Then in a one-page paper, summarize what you have found.

Ankor Wat	Tikal
Babylon	Troy
Persepolis	

PART 4 Other Adjective Clause Constructions

Setting the Context

Prereading Questions. Where is Easter Island? What is it famous for?

Easter Island

Easter Island is one of hundreds of Pacific islands that were formed from volcanic eruptions thousands of years ago. It is, however, the only one of these islands that carries its own mystique. First, it is isolated: It lies 2,000 miles from the South American coast and 1,400 miles from the nearest inhabited islands. But more importantly, it is a place where a mysterious civilization once flourished, leaving behind more than a thousand huge stone statues as testimony to its greatness.

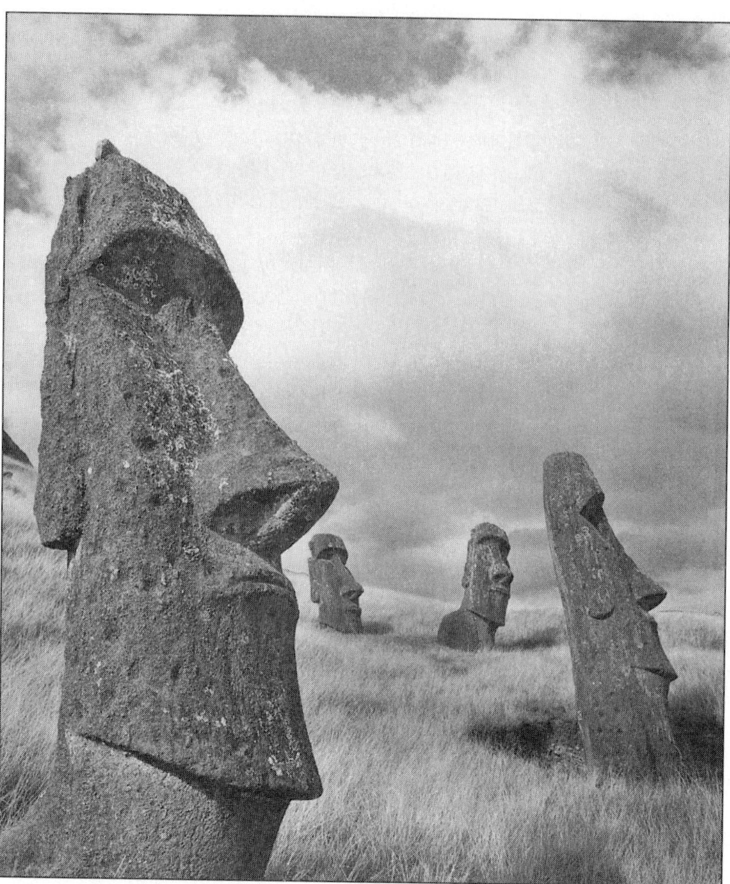

Easter Island Statues

The first Europeans came to the island in 1722, when three Dutch ships landed on Easter Sunday. Since that time, thousands of archeologists have come to Easter Island to study the great stone statues, some of which weigh over a hundred tons. The archeologists' work has yielded many answers, but we may never understand all of the history behind these haunting stone faces. Even after a century of study, the written language found on the island has not been deciphered. In addition, no one knows for certain how the stone statues were transported or even why they were built.

Discussing Ideas. To create and transport these statues must have been extremely expensive in terms of workers and planning. What could lead people to make such a tremendous effort to produce statues? In modern society, are we willing to make such efforts? Can you give any examples?

A. Clauses with When *and* Where

When and *where* may be used to form adjective clauses. In nonrestrictive clauses, only *when, where,* or *which* + preposition is possible. In restrictive clauses, *that* or *that* + preposition is also used, or the relative pronoun is omitted. A variety of possibilities exist, as shown in the following.

	Examples
Simple Sentences	**At the time,** the statues were standing. The Dutch arrived **then.**
Complex Sentence with *When* or *That* (Restrictive)	At the time **when (that) the Dutch arrived,** the statues were still standing. At the time **the Dutch arrived,** the statues were still standing.
Simple Sentences	**In 1722,** the statues were standing. The Dutch arrived **then.**
Complex Sentence with *When* (Nonrestrictive)	In 1722, **when the Dutch arrived,** the statues were still standing.
Simple Sentences	This is **an island.** An advanced society had flourished **here.**
Complex Sentence with *Where, Which,* or *That* (Restrictive)	This is an island **where an advanced society had flourished.** This is an island **on which an advanced society had flourished.** This is an island **which an advanced society had flourished on.** This is an island **that an advanced society had flourished on.** This is an island **an advanced society had flourished on.**
Simple Sentences	This is **Easter Island.** An advanced society had flourished **here.**
Complex Sentence with *Where* or *Which* (Nonrestrictive)	This is Easter Island, **where an advanced society had flourished.** This is Easter Island, **on which an advanced society had flourished.** This is Easter Island, **which an advanced society had flourished on.**

1 Make the second sentence into an adjective clause and combine it with the first. Use *when* or *where* and add commas when necessary.

Example: The statues were built at a time. A mysterious society ruled the island then.

The statues were built at a time when a mysterious society ruled the island.

The relative pronoun can also be omitted: *The statues were built at a time a mysterious society ruled the island.*

1. The statues were built during the sixteenth and seventeenth centuries. A mysterious society ruled the island then.
2. By 1722, the society that made the statues had vanished. The Dutch visited the island in 1722.
3. On this island, there were only 4,000 inhabitants. The Dutch had gone there in search of supplies.
4. The Dutch left a few days later, recording that the island was a place. Tremendous stone figures stood facing the ocean there.

5. Fifty years later, all the statues were lying face down. Captain James Cook visited Easter Island at this time.
6. Recently, archeologists have gone to Easter Island. They have used modern machinery there to stand some of the statues upright.

B. Nonrestrictive Adjective Clauses and Expressions of Quantity

Expressions such as *one of, all of, none of,* and *the rest of* may be used to begin nonrestrictive adjective clauses. These clauses must include *whom* or *which,* and they must be preceded and/or followed by commas. Note that *either of* and *neither of* may also be used in this pattern: a singular verb is used in adjective clauses that follow them.

Simple Sentences	Complex Sentences
Sailors attacked **the islanders.** **Three of the islanders** were killed.	Sailors attacked the islanders, **three of whom** were killed.
These statues are world famous. **Many of them** weigh over 20 tons.	These statues, **many of which** weigh over 20 tons, are world famous.
They sailed **two ships.** **Neither of the ships (neither ship)** was safe.	They sailed two ships, **neither of which** was safe.

2 In these sentences, change the italicized words to *whom* or *which.* Then change the second sentence into an adjective clause and add it to the first. Add all necessary punctuation.

Example: No one knows for certain how the islanders transported the statues. Most of *them* are located miles from the quarry.*

No one knows for certain how the islanders transported the statues, most of which are located miles from the quarry.

1. These huge stones certainly could not have been carried. Several of *them* weigh 20 tons or more.
2. It seems unlikely that they were dragged over the land. Much of *the land* is extremely rough.
3. Some archeologists think that the islanders used huge wooden platforms. They have never found the remains of *these platforms.*
4. The wood for these platforms would have had to come from large forests. None of *these forests* existed on the island.
5. A number of authors suggest that extraterrestrials moved the statues. Archeologists totally disregard most of *these authors.*
6. According to the islanders, the finished statues were transported by the island's kings. All of *the kings* had magical powers.

**quarry* place from which stone is taken

C. Adjective Clauses and Subject/Verb Agreement

In adjective clauses where the subject has been replaced, the form of the verb depends on the noun(s) being modified.

	Examples	Notes
Singular	The **islander** who **was** kidnapped later died.	Use a singular verb in an adjective clause that modifies a singular noun and a plural verb in an adjective clause that modifies a plural noun.
Plural	The **islanders** who **were** kidnapped later died.	
Singular	It was **the only one of the islands** that **was** formed by volcanoes.	Use a singular verb with *the only one* (even though a plural noun follows in the prepositional phrase).
Plural	It is **one of the islands** that **were** formed by volcanoes.	A plural verb is used in an adjective clause that follows *one of the* + plural noun because the clause modifies the plural noun in the prepositional phrase.

3 Select the singular or plural form of the verbs in parentheses.

Example: The famous Norwegian Thor Heyerdahl is one of the many archeologists who (has/(have)) studied Easter Island.

1. Heyerdahl is one of the few archeologists who (believes/believe) that the first people on Easter Island came from South America.
2. He is the only one of his colleagues who (has/have) made the 4,000-mile journey from Peru to Easter Island on a primitive raft.
3. Erich von Daniken is one of the scientists who (has/have) proposed theories about Easter Island's statues.
4. Van Daniken's book *Chariots of the Gods* is one of a few books that (suggests/suggest) that extraterrestrials built the statues.
5. *Chariots of the Gods* is the only one of these books that (has/have) sold over a million copies.

4 In the following passage, select the correct form of the verbs in parentheses.

The Tablets from Easter Island

Written languages originate only in large, complex societies that (has/(have))[1] a great deal of information that (needs/need)[2] to be stored. Even the Incas, who (was/were)[3] very advanced, never developed a writing system. It is, therefore, astounding that wooden tablets that (contain/contains)[4] writing (was/were)[5] discovered on tiny

These hieroglyphs on a wooden tablet are believed to have been used by priests on Easter Island to recite ritual chants. The only writing of the Polynesians, these tablets remain undeciphered.

Easter Island in the 19th century. The writing was in hieroglyphics, and among the characters (was/were)[6] figures of animals that (was/were)[7] unknown on the island.

For over a hundred years, scientists worldwide (has/have)[8] tried to decipher the writing. However, any hope of doing this (was/were)[9] probably lost in 1862, when one-fifth of the island's population (was/were)[10] carried off to slavery in Peru. Among the unlucky (was/were)[11] King Mauratu and his family, who (was/were)[12] the last of the learned* on Easter Island.

Political pressure, which (was/were)[13] supplied by France and England, eventually brought the release of the captives. Unfortunately, by that time, over 80 percent (was/were)[14] dead. And the survivors who (was/were)[15] returned to the island brought smallpox, which ravaged the natives. Thus, by 1875, the population, which in 1860 (was/were)[16] about 5,000, had shrunk to 600.

Of course, these victims did not die alone. With them died knowledge of the oral history and written language that (has/have)[17] not been and perhaps will never be recovered. Today only a few of the tablets (remains/remain)[18]; the rest (has/have)[19] vanished.

**learned* a person (people) having great knowledge. Note that in the adjective form, the word has two syllables and the *-ed* ending is clearly pronounced.

5 **Review of Adjective Clauses.** Complete the following sentences with adjective clauses. Add commas when necessary.

Example. My favorite ocean is the Pacific which. . . . *has thousands of islands with beautiful beaches.*

1. Easter Island is the place where. . . .
2. It had a small population that. . . .
3. We visited the island in the summer when. . . .
4. We arrived in a large boat which. . . .
5. We were traveling with several people most of whom. . . .
6. Our group had five children three of whom. . . .
7. I was talking with one young man whose father. . . .
8. Our group also included an archeologist whom. . . .
9. He explained many things that. . . .
10. The island is filled with beautiful statues many of which. . . .

Using What You've Learned

6 Including one adjective clause in a sentence may now be easy for you. But could you include ten? In pairs, test your grammatical skill and creative genius by writing a sentence with one main clause and ten or more adjective clauses. When you are finished, put your sentence on the board and read it to your classmates. Be sure to use each of the following connecting words at least once and add commas where necessary: *who, whom, that, which, on which, whose, some of whom, where, when, most of which.*

Example: *There was an old woman who lived in a house that was on a hill which. . . .*

Warning: This is a once-in-a-lifetime opportunity. Don't ever create a sentence like this again, especially not in a composition. It could jeopardize the mental health of your writing teacher!

7 Test your memory of information from this chapter. Separate into three or four small groups and write ten to fifteen questions about people, places, or things discussed in this chapter. Then exchange quizzes with another group. As a group, complete your quiz. To get "credit," your answers must include adjective clauses. Return your quiz to the original group for grading.

Examples: *Question:* Who was John Stephens?

Answer: John Stephens was the American explorer who first wrote about the Mayan ruins in 1841.

Question: Who were the savants?

Answer: The savants were experts that Napoleon took with him to Egypt.

Focus on Testing

Adjective Clauses

Problem areas with adjective clauses and phrases are frequently tested on standardized English proficiency exams. Check your understanding of these structures by completing the sample items that follow.

Remember that . . .

- Adjective clauses are generally placed immediately after the word(s) they modify.
- Subjects and verbs must agree in number.
- *That* may not be used in nonrestrictive clauses.
- In formal English, *whom* (not *who*) must be used in object clauses.

Part 1. Circle the best completion for the following.

Example: The people ________ scientists credit for the work lived centuries ago.

a. that
b. whose
(c.) who
d. they

1. Our friend Mary, ________ was recently promoted, really likes her new position.
   a. whom
   b. who
   c. that
   d. who she
2. The ruby-throated hummingbird, ________ the most common variety in North America, beats its wings about 50 times per second when flying.
   a. who
   b. which
   c. which is
   d. that
3. Today, the Egyptian pyramids are endangered by pollution, ____________ may destroy them completely.
   a. the effect of whose
   b. whose its effect
   c. whose effect
   d. which its effect
4. Dr. Jones, ____________ at the party, will teach History 225 next semester.
   a. who we met her
   b. whom we met
   c. whom we met her
   d. we met

Part 2. Each sentence has one error. Circle the letter below the word(s) containing the error.

Example: <u>This is</u> (A) Easter Island, <u>where</u> (B) an advanced society <u>had flourished</u> (C) <u>here.</u> (Ⓓ)

1. A variety of <u>economic</u> (A) indicators, <u>some</u> (B) <u>of which</u> (C) is the consumer price index, <u>are used</u> (D) to calculate the rate of inflation.

2. In 1923, Howard Carter, who he was to become the world's most famous
A B
archeologist, uncovered the tomb of the pharaoh Tutankhamen.
C D
3. One of the strongest fibers that it exists on earth is the silk that spiders use to
A B C D
create their webs.
4. Paul Cézanne was one of the painters who was part of the 1874 exhibition
A B
that would mark the beginnings of Impressionism.
C D

PART 5

Review of Chapters 1 to 4

1 **Review.** Complete the following with an appropriate form of the verb in parentheses. In some cases more than one verb form may be appropriate.

Mysteries of Stonehenge

Stonehenge ______1______ (be) a fascinating archaeological site in southwestern England. It ______2______ (consist) of a small but impressive set of structures arranged in concentric circles of earth and stonework. Its rings of stones, ditches, pits, and banks ______3______ (interest) people for hundreds of years. Who ______4______ (build) Stonehenge? When ______5______ construction ______6______ (take) place? Why ______7______ (be) it built?

Through the centuries, people ______8______ (speculate) about these questions. Today this much ______9______ (be) known. Stonehenge ______10______ (be) built in three phrases over several centuries, and the building ______11______ (be) done by different groups of people. Archaeologists ______12______ (argue/still) about exactly when construction ______13______ (begin). However, most believe that the first phase of construction ______14______ (start) about 2800 B.C. and that the third and last phase ______15______ (end) by

1500 B.C. Thus, the builders of Stonehenge ______ (work/probably) on the site for over a thousand years.
16

Scientists ______ (study) Stonehenge for hundreds of years, but there ______ (be/still) much disagreement about many aspects. For example, theories about why Stonehenge was built ______ (be) numerous. Perhaps we ______ (know/never) all its purposes. However, many scientists ______ (believe/now) that in ancient times Stonehenge ______ (serve) as an astronomical observatory and a calendar.
17, 18, 19, 20, 21, 22

The structures at Stonehenge remain a mystery.

2 **Review.** Complete the following with *a, an, the,* or *X* (to indicate that no article is necessary).

The Construction of Stonehenge

______ Stonehenge was built over ______ several centuries in three phases. It's outer and second circles were completed in ______ first phase, about ______ 2800 B.C. In ______ second phase, ______ innermost circle was constructed. Inside this circle, ______ series of 80 pillars was placed in ______ two rows to form ______ half circle. Each of ______ pillars weighed as much as ______ four tons. ______ third phase created ______ most famous features of Stonehenge, its
1, 2, 3, 4, 5, 6, 7, 8, 9, 10, 11, 12, 13

great stone posts and arches. ______ (14) arches form ______ (15) horseshoe shape that points to ______ (16) summer solstice sunrise on ______ (17) June 21 of each year.

3 **Review.** Complete the following sentences. Be sure to add capital letters and/or punctuation.

Example: Archaeology is an interesting subject, but *I'd rather talk about Andy.*

1. Andy stayed out very late last night therefore ______.
2. Andy stayed out very late last night yet ______.
3. Andy stayed out very late last night in fact ______.
4. Andy stayed out very late last night for ______.
5. Andy didn't get to work on time so ______.
6. Andy didn't get to work on time in addition ______.
7. Andy didn't get to work on time nor ______.
8. Andy didn't get to work on time nevertheless ______.
9. Andy is now looking for a new job however ______.
10. Andy is now looking for a new job and ______.
11. Andy is now looking for a new job otherwise ______.
12. Andy is now looking for a new job as a matter of fact ______.

4 **Review.** Make the second sentence into an adjective clause and add it to the first. Be sure to include commas where they are appropriate.

Example: South America has many areas. These areas have archaeological wonders.
South America has many areas that have archaeological wonders.

1. Machu Picchu is now very popular with tourists. It is a famous archaeological site in Peru.

Machu Picchu, Peru

2. It's a place. Its history is fascinating.
3. It's located above a river valley in the Andes Mountains. The Inca Indians fled there from the Spanish conquerors.
4. Tourist trains take most foreigners to Machu Picchu. All of these trains are rather expensive.
5. It is also possible to walk to Machu Picchu on a trail. The Incas built this trail hundreds of years ago.
6. I arrived on the train one morning. It was raining then.
7. I climbed the adjacent mountain called Huayna Picchu. Many photographers have captured its beauty.
8. The view of the ruins is spectacular. Climbers have this view of the ruins.
9. Our guide had a bachelor's degree in antiquities. We hiked with him for several hours.
10. Next to the archaeological site there is a hotel. We found the hotel very comfortable.

Video Activities: Abduction by Aliens

Before You Watch. Discuss these questions in small groups.

1. Do you think that people from other planets have visited Earth? Have you ever seen a UFO? (Unidentified Flying Object)
2. *Abduct* means the same as ________________.

   a. borrow   b. kidnap   c. visit

Watch. Answer these questions in small groups.

1. Ruth Foley says that she ____________________.
   a. has been abducted by people from outer space
   b. was born in outer space
   c. has visited other planets
2. What do the abductors look like? Write a description.

   ____

   ____

   ____
3. According to Ruth, what is the abductors' purpose?
   a. to perform medical tests
   b. to ask people about life on Earth
   c. to tell people about their planet
4. People in Indiana say that ____________ burned the ground near a house in Indiana.

   a. an abductor   b. a light   c. a spaceship
5. The author of *Secret Life* ________________ abductions really happen.

   a. isn't sure if   b. is positive that   c. doesn't believe that

Watch Again. Write answers to these questions.

1. How old was Ruth Foley when she was first abducted? ______________
2. Who once saw Ruth being abducted? ______________
3. What was the year of the abduction in Indiana? ______________
4. How long did it take for the grass to grow on the burned spot? ______________
5. Who is John Mack and what did he write? ______________
6. What does John Mack believe? ______________

After You Watch. Combine these sentences with relative pronouns.

1. Ruth Foley is about 45 years old. She was first abducted when she was four.
2. Her sister saw a beam of light. The beam of light took Ruth to the spaceship.
3. Ruth doesn't remember the spaceship. They took her to a spaceship.
4. Many people have reported abductions. The purpose of these abductions is not known.

Focus on Testing

Review of Problem Areas from Chapters 1 to 4

A variety of problem areas are included in this test. Check your understanding by completing the sample items that follow.

Part 1. Circle the best completion for the following.

Example: By 9:00 Ned ______________ his breakfast.

a. has finished   (c.) had finished
b. finishing   d. had been finishing

1. Anne Sullivan ______________ Helen Keller when Helen was about seven years old.
   a. first met   b. was first meeting   c. had first met   d. met first
2. Before going into the meeting, he stopped to have __________ coffee.
   a. little   b. a little   c. some of   d. a few
3. The traditional yurt is a wooden tent __________ has a round roof and is covered with animal skins.
   a. what   b. what it   c. which it   d. that
4. It's late. We ______________ now.
   a. should be leave   c. should left
   b. should be leaving   d. should have left
5. George Mallory, __________ had been a member of the 1921 and 1922 Everest expeditions, disappeared on the mountain in 1924.
   a. who   b. whom   c. that   d. who he

6. During the Middle Ages, spices, ________________ did not grow in Europe, had to be imported from Asia.
   a. most of which   c. most of them
   b. most of which they   d. most of what

7. Molly and Richard ____________ lost.
   a. looking   b. looks   c. look   d. has looked

8. Mark Twain felt that using humor was a good way to change minds; ______, he made great use of humor when he wrote about slavery in *Huckleberry Finn.*
   a. neither   b. unless   c. thus   d. on the other hand

Part 2. Each sentence has one error. Circle the letter below the word(s) containing the error.

Example: Joe goes (A) to Paris next week, but when I saw (B) him, he hasn't (C — circled) bought (D) his ticket yet.

1. Marco Polo was the first European (A) explorer to enter, live in (B), and write about Asia, a land (C) completely unknown to Europe in thirteen century (D).

2. Gold (A) has been one of the (B) most prized metal (C) throughout history (D).

3. Social scientists who have studied (A) Madagascar has found (B) that women tend to be (C) the most aggressive buyers and sellers in marketplaces (D).

4. Oceania (A) is an area in Pacific Ocean (B) that (C) is bounded by (D) Hawaii, New Zealand, and Easter Island.

5. The Arandan people, that live (A) in the (B) Australian desert, have a verb system with approximately (C) 1,000 different endings, all of which (D) can change the meaning of a verb.

6. Beginning (A) in Arabia in the (B) 600s, the religion we (C) now call it (D) Islam spread quickly throughout Asia.

7. Ms. Jones would like (A) to interview the (B) woman from who (C) we received a resume early (D) last week.

8. English is one of the (A) richest languages in the world, for (B) it is having (C) over 400,000 vocabulary words (D).

Chapter 5

Transitions

IN THIS CHAPTER

Part 1 Clauses and Related Structures of Time: Future Time

Part 2 Clauses and Related Structures of Time: Present and Unspecified Time

Part 3 Clauses and Related Structures of Cause and Result

Part 4 Clauses and Related Structures of Time: Past Time

Introduction

In this chapter, you will study adverb clauses and related structures that show relationships by time, cause, and result. As you study these structures, pay attention to how the focus or main idea of a sentence can change, depending on the choice of connecting word.

The following passage introduces the chapter theme "Transitions" and raises some topics and issues you will cover in the chapter.

Transitions: Evolutionary and Revolutionary Changes

Change, movement, and transition characterize our lives as we grow and age. In addition to our own personal growth and change, we are frequently faced with global changes in technology, culture, religion, economics, and politics.

Some of these changes are radical. And occasionally, the shock waves of their impact are felt globally, as in the case of political revolution. For example, when the American colonies successfully revolted against the British, a wave of revolutions began. Shortly after the American Revolution had ended, the French Revolution erupted. Within less than 25 years, most of Latin America had begun to rebel. These revolutions, in turn, have sparked others.

Not all change is dramatic, however. Most changes are more subtle. Just as we don't notice ourselves aging day to day, it is difficult to notice the evolution of our societies. Yet human history has been a constant progression of development from primitive hunting tribes to sophisticated postindustrial nations. Since our ancestors first organized villages and towns, we have been developing social structures to give solidity to our lives.

Today's world is unique in human history because both primitive and highly developed societies live within a few hundred miles of each other. We can actually see revolution and evolution in politics and economics as different countries and cultures experiment with new forms of government, ownership, and production. Changes in family and social structures surround us. Today, change is virtually unavoidable. The world is in a state of continuous transition.

Discussing Ideas. Can you give some specific examples of important changes that occurred during the twentieth century? Now that we have entered the twenty-first century, what further changes can you foresee or imagine?

PART 1 Clauses and Related Structures of Time: Future Time

Setting the Context

Prereading Questions. What are some of the physical and mental changes that people go through during their lives, from infancy to old age?

Personal Transitions: The Stages of Life

At certain times in life, we all face changes that many social scientists consider to be natural stages. Let us take a newborn, Alex, as an example. The first few months of his life will be spent in a limited environment. In fact, he won't develop an awareness of his surroundings or truly enter the world until he's begun to walk and talk. Alex will be spending the next few years discovering the world around him. Later, as he approaches adolescence, his ideas and feelings, as well as his body, will begin to change. His outlook on the world will broaden. When he has passed through his teenage years, he'll face the choices of young adulthood: marriage, family, career. Through the thirties, his life may go smoothly, but yet another "passage" will approach near "midlife," as he reaches his forties. At that point, time will "speed up," and suddenly, he will find himself in his sixties or seventies, fast approaching the end of his life.

BLOOM COUNTY **by Berke Breathed**

Discussing Ideas. What are some specific changes that occur to all of us as we go through childhood? What is adolescence? At what age do children become adults? At what age do adults become middle-aged? Elderly?

A. Transitions of Sequence

Transitions of sequence may be used to relate a series of events or situations by order of occurrence. For example, they are commonly used in descriptions of processes. Transitions of sequence may be used with any verb tense. They are generally followed by a comma.

Examples	Notes
First, a child will start smiling at its mother. **Later,** it will learn to tell the difference between people. **After that,** the child will begin to imitate its parents' actions.	Many transitions of sequence are used in English, but some of the most common are *first, second* (etc.), *now, then, after that, afterward, earlier, later, meanwhile, at the same time, then,* and *finally.*

1 The following are steps in a child's process in learning to talk. Form complete sentences from the cues and put them in order using transitions of sequence (*first, second,* etc.). Then check the correct order.*

Example: First, *the child will respond when talked to.*

1. uses his or her first words
2. begins to use tenses
3. makes sounds such as *ma, mu, dar,* and *di*
4. understands and uses up to 50 words
5. responds when talked to
6. puts two words together

2 How does a child first begin to walk? How does a child learn to read? Think of these or other processes related to a child's development. Briefly describe the steps involved. Create at least six sentences for one or more of the following processes. Or, choose one or more of your own. Use transitions in your description.

1. learning to walk
2. learning to climb stairs
3. learning to eat by oneself
4. learning to read
5. learning to write
6. learning to ride a bicycle
7. learning to swim
8. learning to skip

B. Time Clauses with the Present, Present Perfect, and Future Tenses

Time clauses may be used to relate actions or situations that will occur at the same time or in a sequence in the future. In general, the focus of these sentences will be on the main clause.

*Answers: 5, 3, 1, 4, 6, 2

	Examples	Notes
after as soon as before once until when	**After** the baby finishes eating, we'll put her to bed. I'm going to bathe her **as soon as** she's finished eating. I'll give her a bath just **before** I put her to bed. **Once** she goes to bed, we may be able to relax a little. You shouldn't put her to bed **until** her hair has dried. **When** her hair has dried, you can put her to bed.	In sentences referring to the future, the verb in the dependent clause can be in the simple present or the present perfect (*not* the future). The present perfect emphasizes the completion of the first action. The verb in the main clause uses a future form (*will* or *be going to* + verb) or a modal auxiliary (*can, may, should,* etc.). The expressions *as soon as* and *just* + conjunction (*just before, just after*) give the strongest sense of immediacy. *Once* emphasizes the idea of *not before.*
as while	I might read her a story **while** I am waiting for her hair to dry.	The present continuous is often used in dependent clauses with *while* or *as.* It emphasizes an action in progress.

Note: See Chapter 11 for information on how these adverb clauses can be reduced to phrases. See Chapter 3 for more information on sentence focus.

C. Time Clauses with the Simple Present and Future Perfect (Continuous) Tenses

	Examples	Notes
To Introduce Clauses when by the time (that)	**When (By the time)** she gets up, she will have slept for ten hours.	The future perfect (continuous) is sometimes used to emphasize that an action or situation will be completed before a certain time in the future. It is most often used in sentences with *by* or *when.* In general, the focus of the sentence is on the main clause.
To Introduce Phrases by + time	She will be awake **by** about 9:00. **By** 9:30, she will have finished her breakfast.	

D. Placement and Punctuation of Adverb Clauses and Phrases

Most adverb clauses and phrases come either before or after the main clause in a sentence. Phrases can also come at different points within the sentence, depending on the meaning and the length of the phrase. Commas are generally used after introductory phrases and clauses, but in the case of short phrases, the comma is frequently omitted. Other time expressions, such as adverbs of frequency, often come between a subject and verb or between verbs, but they almost never come between a verb and its direct object.

Clauses of Time	
Placement	**Punctuation**
When the baby wakes up, we'll leave. We'll leave **when the baby wakes up.** (no comma)	Connecting word + clause _____, _____ main clause _____ _____ main clause _____ connecting word + clause _____ (no comma)

Phrases of Time	
Placement	**Punctuation**
After the baby's nap, we'll leave. We'll leave **after the baby's nap.** (no comma)	Connecting word + phrase _____, _____ main clause _____ _____ main clause _____ connecting word + phrase _____ (no comma)

Other Time Expressions	
Placement	**Punctuation**
Before the baby's nap, we **almost always** feed him. **Before the baby takes a nap,** we **almost always** feed him.	Connecting word + phrase or clause _____, _____ main clause _____
We **almost always** feed the baby **before his nap.** (no comma) We **almost always** feed the baby **before he takes his nap.** (no comma)	_____ main clause _____ connecting word + phrase or clause _____ (no commas)

Culture Note

Jean Piaget was a pioneer in our understanding of personal development. Other psychologists, like Howard Gardner of Harvard University, have expanded on Piaget's work, looking not only at cognition but also other areas, such as emotional, artistic, and spatial development. Consult your library or the Web for more information.

3 Imagine that you are taking a course in child development. You are listening to a lecture about Jean Piaget. Complete the lecture by using the present continuous, simple present, present perfect, future continuous, or simple future form of the verbs in parentheses. When more than one tense is appropriate, show all possibilities.

Jean Piaget

Today's lecture is on Jean Piaget, a French-Swiss child psychologist who developed detailed theories on children's intellectual growth. I *will begin* (1) (begin) by giving you a brief overview of Piaget's theories. To do so, I _______ (2) (follow) the probable development of my newborn niece Molly. After I _______ (3) (give) you the overview, we _______ (4) (look) at each stage in more detail.

What changes _______ (5) Molly _______ (6) (go through) during the next few years? According to Piaget, Molly _______ (7) (start) to recognize and organize her environment while she _______ (8) (be/still) an infant. During her first 18 months, she _______ (9) (develop) a basic model of her world.

Child psychologist Jean Piaget

By the time Molly ________ (10) (be) 18 months old, she ________ (11) (begin/actively) to expand, organize, and reorganize her view of the world. She ________ (12) (do) this through play and through exploring and experimenting. However, she ________ (13) (not be) able to understand things beyond present situations until she ________ (14) (reach) age four or five.

Within another year or two, a notable change ________ (15) (take) place. Molly ________ (16) (start) to understand the basic concepts of distance, length, number, speed, mass, and groupings. By the time that Molly ________ (17) (turn) seven or eight, she ________ (18) (enter) Piaget's stage of "concrete operations": Her thinking ________ (19) (develop) structured patterns. At the same time, she ________ (20) (prepare) for the final development: abstract thought. For Molly, like other children, thinking abstractly ________ (21) (involve) the ability to imagine and hypothesize. As Molly ________ (22) (go) through this stage, she ________ (23) (develop) all the basic skills for adult thinking.

4 Following are notes taken during a child development class. Use the notes to help you form sentences with the cues. Use appropriate verb tenses and be sure to add articles, pronouns, and so forth.

Examples: when / be born

When a baby is born, it cannot move by itself.

When a baby is born, it will have reflexes. . . .

by the time / two months

By the time the baby is two months old, it should be able to focus its eyes. . . .

1. by the time / two months
2. before / four months
3. when / 20 weeks
4. until / 24 weeks
5. before / eight months
6. by the time / eight months
7. after / ten months
8. when / 12 months

Child Development 210—Monday lecture
Physical Development, First Year

1. *At birth*
   a. *is immobile*
   b. *has reflexes like sucking, finger grasping*
2. *Up to 2 months*
   a. *is able to focus eyes and coordinate stares*
   b. *begins to lift head*
3. *By 4 months*
   a. *can raise head*
   b. *can turn head and eyes to speaker*
4. *4–6 months*
   a. *20 weeks: opens hand to grasp an object*
   b. *24 weeks: grasps objects with palm and fingers but not thumb*
5. *6–8 months*
   a. *7 months: sits alone without support for a short time*
   b. *8 months: stands with minimum help; grasps objects using thumb and index finger*
6. *10–12 months*
   a. *walks with help*
   b. *stops putting objects in mouth*

Web Note

If you are interested in more information on cognitive development or developmental psychology in general, consult your library or the Website of the American Psychological Association: www.apa.org/. This site also offers links to other Websites.

5 Use your own knowledge and experience to follow an infant through its life. Name the child and then, use *when, before, after, until,* or *by the time that* and a variety of present and future verb tenses. Write at least eight sentences describing his or her development. Be sure to include emotional, educational, and physical factors.

Example: *When she's 13, she'll be entering high school. By age 16, she'll have finished two years of high school.*

1. age 6
2. age 13
3. age 16
4. age 25
5. age 40
6. age 65

Using What You've Learned

6 Visit your resident "fortune-teller." In groups or as a class, take turns role-playing a fortune-teller and telling the secrets of the future to your classmates. Ask and answer questions using time clauses.

Example: A. **Will I be married by the time I am 25?**
B. **By the time you're 25, you will have been married three times!**
A. **How many children will I have?**

7 Much of our development centers on our outlook for the future and the goals that we set. Take a more serious look at your own future and your own goals. In pairs or in groups, discuss your futures. You can use the following ideas to help you.

1. What are your immediate plans for the future (educationally, etc.)?
   a. Before I. . . .
   b. I'll . . . until. . . .
   c. Once I have. . . .
2. What are your long-term goals (lifestyle, career, etc.)?
   a. When I. . . .
   b. After I. . . .
   c. By (the time that). . . .

PART 2 Clauses and Related Structures of Time: Present and Unspecified Time

Setting the Context

Prereading Questions. What is the theory of evolution? Does it apply only to biological development, or do societies evolve just like plants and animals?

Social Transitions: The Evolution of Societies

Evolution is not only a biological theory but a social phenomenon as well. Whenever living things exist in groups, their societies tend to become more complex and specialized. Human societies are no exception. Although some groups develop more slowly than others, all human societies follow the same basic pattern. After a hunting society has established a permanent base in one area, its people begin to use agriculture for their food needs. When surpluses of food develop, the population grows and commerce begins. As villages grow into towns and cities, technological innovation is introduced. This pattern is true of almost every time and place in history.

Discussing Ideas. According to the passage, what is the basic pattern of development in human societies?

A. Time Clauses with the Simple Present, Present Continuous, and Present Perfect Tenses

Time clauses can relate situations or actions that occur at the same time or in a sequence. These activities may occur habitually, or they may be occurring at the moment of speaking. A present form of the verb is used in each clause. In general, the focus of these sentences will be on the main clause.

	Examples	Notes
when whenever	**When(ever)** people work together, they can accomplish much more.	*When(ever)* means "any time." *When(ever)* joins two actions that happen one immediately after the other. *When(ever)* comes before the earlier action.
after as soon as before once until up to the time (that)	People settle in one area **before** they develop agriculture. **Once** more people have begun to farm, a food surplus often develops There is very little commerce **until** the village grows.	*After, as soon as, before, once,* and *until* join actions that occur in sequence. Either the simple present or the present perfect may be used in the dependent clause. The present perfect emphasizes the completion of the action.
as while	**As** the population increases, a need for technology develops. **While** villages are growing, their societies become more complex. In some societies, **while** men are hunting, women are working in the fields.	*As* and *while* join two actions that happen at about the same time. The present continuous can be used in the dependent clause to emphasize the continuous nature of the activity. It may also be used in the main clause.
since	Societies have been developing **since** the first humans walked on the earth. Commerce has increased steadily ever **since** people have lived in communities.	*Since* joins a previous action or situation to an action or situation in progress. The main clause is in the present perfect (continuous). The dependent clause may be in the simple past or the present perfect. When both clauses are in the present perfect, both activities are still in progress.

1 Complete the following by using appropriate forms of the verbs in parentheses. Choose between the simple present, simple past, and present perfect tenses or add the modal auxiliaries *can* or *must*.

The Evolution of Communities

Whenever living things _work_ (1) (work) in groups, they ______ (2) (have) a better chance for survival. When life forms ______ (3) (cooperate) for defense and for labor, they ______ (4) (be) much more successful than life forms working independently. In fact, since life ______ (5) (begin) as single, independent cells, it ______ (6) (evolve / steadily) into more and more complex communities. This ______ (7) (be) true of the tiniest cells as well as the most complicated humans.

Before living things ______ (8) (function) successfully in groups, they ______ (9) (develop) systems for communication. Interestingly, even communities made up of the most primitive organisms ______ (10) (have) communication systems. For example, microscopic plants and animals ______ (11) (communicate) by chemical signals. Insects, birds, and animals ______ (12) (use) a variety of sounds and movements when they ______ (13) (need) to communicate. However, no group ______ (14) (develop / ever) a communication system comparable to human language.

2 Combine the following pairs of sentences using the connecting words in parentheses. Change or omit words and add punctuation when necessary. When you have finished, discuss any difference in meaning or focus in each pair of sentences.

Example: Communities can develop. Living things have a form of communication. (whenever, when)

Communities can develop whenever living things have a form of communication.

Communities can develop when living things have a form of communication.

Focus: The focus of both sentences is "The development of communities."

Meaning: The meaning is basically the same, but whenever gives more emphasis to the idea of "anytime."

1. People must have a way of producing a steady supply of food. They can build settled communities. (before, after)
2. People build villages. Large marketplaces develop. (after, when)
3. Commerce expands. Cities develop. (as, as soon as)
4. The social structure of a village remains generally constant. The population reaches 500 to 1,000. (until, up to the time that)

5. Towns grow in size. Their character changes drastically. (when, once)
6. The population grows to several thousand. The impersonal nature of a city begins to develop. (after, as soon as)

3 According to anthropologist Robert Redfield, there is a continuum of community development ranging from the village at one extreme to the full-fledged city at the other, and certain characteristics are typical of these communities in every part of the world.

Use information from Charts 1 and 2 to form at least eight sentences with *as, once, when,* and *whenever.* Add *more* or *less* when necessary.

Examples: diversified

Whenever towns grow in size, they become more diversified.

heterogeneous

As more and more people move to a city, the city becomes more heterogeneous.

religious

When the population increases, it becomes less religious.

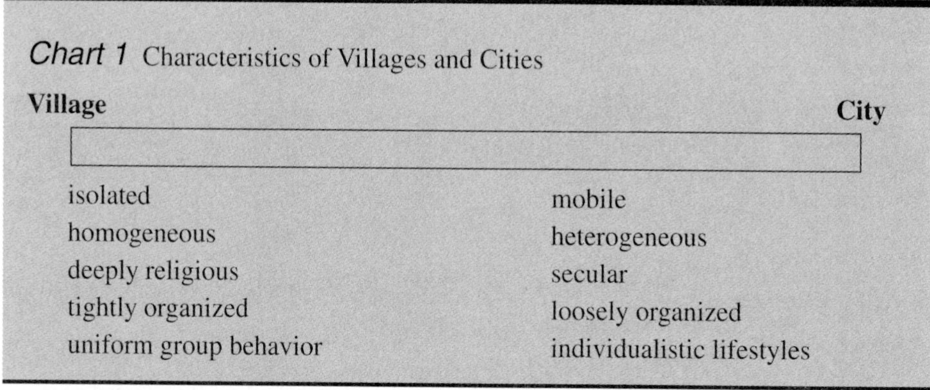

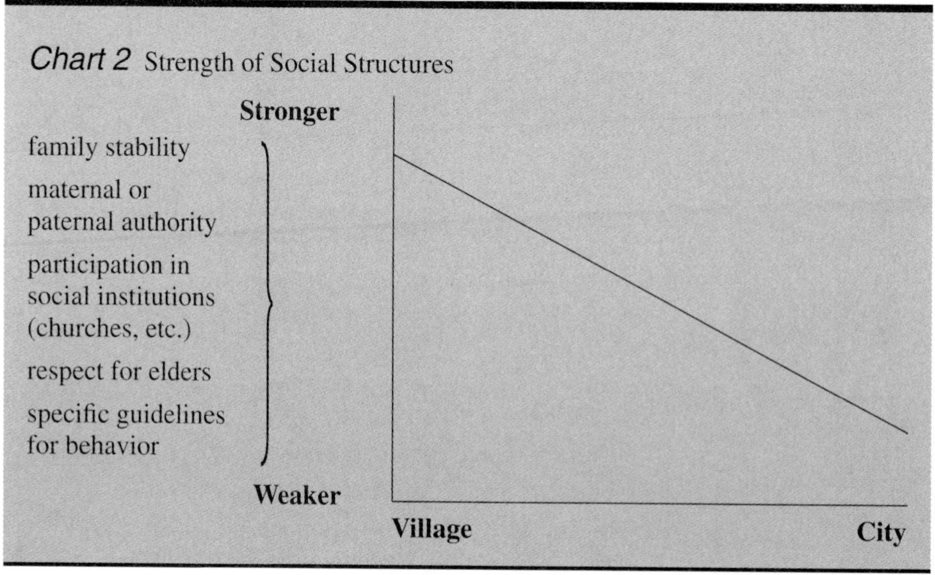

4 Jacob Bronowski wrote *The Ascent of Man,* an account of human development. In his book, he emphasized the fundamental role of settled community life in the development of civilization. He said, "Settled agriculture creates a technology from which . . . all science takes off. [It began] . . . when man first harnessed a power greater than his own, the power of animals. Every machine is a kind of draft animal—even the nuclear reactor."*

Consider the following developments in human history. What have these inventions or discoveries led to? Use the following list and add your own information to form at least five sentences with *since.*

Example: steam engine / railroads

Since the steam engine was invented, we've developed trains and built railroads throughout the world.

Beginning Point	Further Developments
invention of lenses and mirrors	eyeglasses, contact lenses, cameras, microscopes, telescopes
invention of the steam engine	railroads, turbines, steamboats, internal combustion engine, cars, airplanes, rockets
discovery of electricity	batteries, lights, telegraphs, radios, telephones, televisions, computers
splitting of the atom	atom bomb, nuclear reactors
invention of the silicon chip	smaller micro-, mini-, and main-frame computers, handheld organizers, microelectronic devices

Using What You've Learned

5 Most observers agree that people living in large cities are somehow different from their counterparts in less crowded areas. From your experience, what seems to happen to people when they leave the countryside and move to the city? What happens when cities become overcrowded? Write a brief essay about population movement and growth. Write from a general standpoint, but be sure to add specific examples from your own experience, too.

6 Look at Activity 4 again. Can you think of other landmark discoveries or inventions? Can you tell what changes or breakthroughs have occurred since that invention or discovery was made? Try to create a chart similar to the one in Activity 4, using information from your own field or from another area that interests you. Then, in pairs or small groups, take turns explaining the ramifications of the discoveries or inventions that you've listed.

7 Rube Goldberg was an American artist who created some of the most amazing inventions possible (at least on paper!). In small groups, look at the following example of his inventiveness and follow it step by step.

*Jacob Bronowski, *The Ascent of Man* (Boston and Toronto: Little, Brown, 1973), p. 74.

FLAME FROM LAMP (A) CATCHES ON CURTAIN (B) AND FIRE DEPARTMENT SENDS STREAM OF WATER (C) THROUGH WINDOW-DWARF (D) THINKS IT IS RAINING AND REACHES FOR UMBRELLA (E), PULLING STRING (F) AND LIFTING END OF PLATFORM (G) - IRON BALL (H) FALLS AND PULLS STRING (I), CAUSING HAMMER (J) TO HIT PLATE OF GLASS (K) - CRASH OF GLASS WAKES UP PUP (L) AND MOTHER DOG (M) ROCKS HIM TO SLEEP IN CRADLE (N), CAUSING ATTACHED WOODEN HAND (O) TO MOVE UP AND DOWN ALONG YOUR BACK.

Example: *After the lamp has set the curtains on fire, the firefighters arrive. . . .*

Now, as a group, try to come up with your own invention! Make a drawing of it and explain it in writing using a variety of time clauses and transitions. You might invent a machine to do your homework, wake you up in the morning, etc. Finally, present your inventions to your classmates.

PART 3 Clauses and Related Structures of Cause and Result

Setting the Context

Prereading Questions. What is charisma? In your opinion, who are some of the most charismatic individuals alive today? What is the source of their charisma?

Martin Luther King, Jr., delivers his famous speech, "I Have a Dream," Washington, D.C., 1963.

Transitions: The Role of Leaders

Every movement needs a leader if it is to be truly successful. At various times and places, people have risen up to demand political, social, economic, or religious change. Yet, because of human nature, most of these movements have died as soon as a few of the demands have been met. To unite people in a long-term struggle toward a goal, charismatic leadership is necessary. Because people are usually more willing to fight or die for a leader than an idea, the success of a movement often depends on the personality of one individual.

Discussing Ideas. What charismatic leaders do you know of from the past? What social, political, economic, or military movements did they lead? Were they successful?

A. Adverb Clauses and Related Structures of Cause and Result

Both phrases and clauses may be used to relate ideas and to show cause and result. Transitions may also be used to relate effects or results to their causes. In general, the focus of the sentence will be on the main clause(s). See Chapter 3 for more information on compound and complex sentences.

	Examples	Notes
To Introduce Clauses because due to the fact (that) since	**Because** he was a dynamic speaker, crowds always gathered to hear Martin Luther King, Jr.	*Because* is used in both spoken and written English. *Due to the fact (that)* is more formal, while *since* is less formal.
To Introduce Phrases as a result of because of due to owing to	**Because of** his dynamism, crowds always gathered to hear Martin Luther King, Jr. People still admire Dr. King **due to** his amazing accomplishments.	These expressions are followed by a noun (phrase) or a gerund. They may *not* be followed by a subject and verb.
Transitions as a consequence as a result consequently hence therefore thus	Gandhi was respected throughout India; **as a result,** he was given the name *Mahatma,* meaning "Great Lord." Gandhi was respected throughout India. **Thus,** he was given the name *Mahatma,* meaning "Great Lord."	Like other transitions, these may begin sentences, or they may be used with a semicolon to join two clauses. In either case, a comma is used after the transition. Note that *hence* and *thus* are used primarily in formal English. The other transitions, especially *as a result,* are used in both formal and informal language.

Note: Traditionally, *due to*/ *due to the fact* were used only adjectivally, to refer to nouns, not actions. They were used to show cause, not reason. Today *due to*/ *due to the fact* are widely used to show either cause or reason. Compare:

The violence at the demonstration was *due to* (caused by) the police.

The police at the demonstration started the fight *due to* (because of) their frustration.

1 Quickly reread the passage "Transitions: The Role of Leaders." Then answer these questions.

1. Underline *because of* and *because* in the passage. What follows *because of?* What follows *because?*
2. What words or phrases could be used instead of *because of* and *because?*

2 Change the following sentences from compound to complex or from complex to compound. Use appropriate connecting words or transitions. Pay close attention to the punctuation. Then compare each original and new sentence. What is the focus of the original sentence? What is the focus of the new sentence?

Simón Bolívar, known as "the Liberator"

Example: Because Spain was taken over by France in 1808, a crisis of authority developed in Spanish lands in South America.

Spain was taken over by France in 1808; as a result, a crisis of authority developed in Spanish lands in South America.

Original focus: the crisis of authority in Spanish lands

New focus: on both the French takeover of Spain and the crisis of authority in Spanish lands

1. Because many South Americans had resented Spanish rule for years, they were prepared to revolt.
2. South America had a mixture of races and interest groups; therefore, it was difficult to unite all the people.
3. Since the various colonial groups disagreed with each other, one leader was needed to unite all of these groups.

4. Simón Bolívar ultimately became the political and military leader of the South Americans because he was able to appeal to a wide variety of people.
5. Bolívar could see beyond immediate problems and conflicts; thus, he was able to develop long-term military and political goals.
6. Bolívar directed the war for independence throughout much of South America; as a result, he is known today as "the Liberator."
7. Bolívar believed in a united South America; hence, he struggled to unite the region into one nation—"Grand Colombia."
8. Because individual groups and regions had their own interests in mind, most leaders resisted the idea of one nation in South America.
9. Even without political or cultural differences, South America would be difficult to unite since most areas are separated into distinct regions by major geographic boundaries such as the Amazon and the Andes Mountains.
10. Many geographical, political, and cultural differences exist among regions in South America; for this reason, perhaps, one united country has never been achieved.

3 Complete the following with *because, since, because of, due to*, or *as a result of.*

Example: Because his brother was killed by the tsar's* government, Lenin decided to become a professional revolutionary.

Removing Lenin's statue in Moscow.

1. ______________ his personal strength and dedication, Lenin succeeded in shaping a new Russia.
2. ______________ Lenin was totally dedicated, he risked his life to overthrow the tsar.
3. ______________ his political position, Lenin went into exile.
4. ______________ he needed a way to send information back into Russia, Lenin established the newspaper *Iskra* ("the spark").
5. ______________ his power of persuasion, various groups began to support Lenin and his party, the Bolsheviks.
6. ______________ Lenin believed that only violent revolution could succeed, he fought against more moderate groups.
7. ______________ careful planning and the economic and political confusion in Russia, Lenin and the Bolsheviks took control of the government in October of 1917.
8. ______________ his role in shaping post-tsarist Russia, Lenin still "sparks" strong feelings—both negative and positive—even 80 years after his death.

**tsar* king, male ruler of Russia before 1917.

4 Rephrase each pair of sentences in italics three different ways, using the connecting words indicated. Then explain the focus of each new sentence.

Example: *Some leaders are very charismatic. They are able to unite large, diverse groups of people.*

therefore

Some leaders are very charismatic; therefore, they are able to unite large, diverse groups of people.

Focus: equal focus on both clauses

because

Because some leaders are so charismatic, they are able to unite large, diverse groups of people.

Focus: ability to unite large, diverse groups

because of

Because of their charisma, some leaders are able to unite large, diverse groups of people.

Focus: ability to unite large, diverse groups

1. Mustafa Kemal (Ataturk) led the four-year revolution that formed Turkey in 1923. He then devoted his last 16 years to religious, economic, and educational reform.

   Kemal dreamed of modernizing Turkey. He toured every part of his country to learn the conditions and needs of the people.

   therefore because because of

2. Martin Luther King, Jr. was a black minister who fought segregation* through nonviolent protests.

   Martin Luther King, Jr. was successful in uniting people in nonviolent protest. He attracted worldwide attention and was awarded the 1964 Nobel Peace Prize.

   thus since as a result of

3. A missionary born in Yugoslavia, Mother Teresa devoted much of her life to helping the desperately poor in the slums of Calcutta. In later years, she extended her work to help the poor in many countries worldwide.

   Mother Teresa worked tirelessly for the hungry, the homeless, and the sick. She was awarded the Nobel Peace Prize in 1979.

   because owing to thus

5 Combine each of the following sets of sentences in at least two ways. Use connecting words such as *as a result, because, because of, consequently, due to, since, that, therefore, which, who,* or any others that are appropriate. You may also reword some of your sentences to eliminate the connecting word(s). After you have finished, discuss the focus or main idea of each sentence. Explain how the focus may change when a different connecting word is used (or when it is eliminated).

Example: In the early 20th century, Great Britain ruled an enormous empire. This empire included India.

In the early 20th century, Great Britain ruled an enormous empire that (which) included India.

**segregation* forced separation of people based on race

Focus: Great Britain and its empire

In the early 20th century, India was part of an enormous empire (that was) ruled by Great Britain.

Focus: India as part of the British empire

Mohandas Gandhi at his spinning wheel.

1. Mohandas K. Gandhi was an Indian. This man worked for change through nonviolent means.
2. Gandhi believed that violence only produced more violence. Gandhi devoted his life to the idea of nonviolent resistance.
3. Gandhi developed numerous techniques for nonviolent disobedience of the British. These techniques included economic boycotts, national strikes, and refusal to pay taxes.
4. Most governments expect revolutionaries to be violent. Gandhi's nonviolent techniques confused the British.
5. Gandhi and his followers had incredible inner strength. They were able to protest nonviolently.
6. Many Indians didn't understand the idea of nonviolent resistance. These Indians found it difficult to follow Gandhi's example.
7. Nonviolent protests required tremendous self-control (which many protesters didn't have). Many large demonstrations became violent.
8. Gandhi persevered in his struggle against British rule. He became a worldwide symbol of nonviolent resistance.

Using What You've Learned

6 What charismatic leaders have led movements in your country or culture? What movements did they lead and why? What were the results of their efforts?

Choose a leader from your culture and write a brief composition about this individual. If necessary, do some research at the library in order to complete your composition. As you write, try to include as many of the following connecting words as possible: *as a result, because, because of, consequently, due to, therefore,* and *thus.*

7 Most charismatic individuals are very persuasive. They can influence others easily. Some people seem to be born with this ability, whereas others cultivate it.

One way to cultivate your powers of persuasion is through learning to debate. A formal debate has specific rules of order, including the order of speakers, time limits, and types of responses. Judges determine whether the rules have been followed and points can be scored.

Separate into two or more groups to prepare a debate on one of the following issues or on a topic of your choice. Your teacher may be the judge, or you may choose one or more classmates to be judges.

Possible Topics

1. Religious cults are dangerous and should be prohibited by law.
2. Capital punishment is necessary to stop violent crime.
3. The United Nations should have a permanent army to settle all global disputes.
4. All drugs should be legalized.

Guidelines for a Debate

1. Time limit for answers: three minutes.
2. To gain points, you must first respond to the opposing team's statement before you make a new statement of your own.
3. Each person on the team must have a turn to respond.

PART 4 Clauses and Related Structures of Time: Past Time

Setting the Context

Prereading Questions. Which occurred first, the French or the American Revolution? What were some of the causes of these revolutions?

Countries in Transition: Revolution

March 5, 1770, "Boston Massacre": British soldiers attack an angry crowd of American Colonists. One of the first to be killed was a black man named Crispus Attucks, shown in the center.

Change comes in many forms, but perhaps the most radical form is revolution. While many causes underlie revolutions, economics is a factor in virtually every one. The world's first two political revolutions, the American and the French, illustrate the role of economics in political uprisings and demands for social change.

In the case of the American Revolution, the main issue was taxation. In 1763, Great Britain completed a series of expensive wars against France that had lasted for 70 years. Soon after peace had been declared, the British Parliament instituted a number of taxes to make the American colonists help pay for these wars. The reaction in America against the new taxes led to the war for independence and the founding of the first free nation in the New World.

While the American Revolution was taking place, the forces behind the French Revolution were building. France in the 1700s was sharply divided along class lines. The wealth and power of the upper class were increasing steadily.

At the same time, the middle class was paying most of the taxes, and the large peasant population was becoming desperately poor. The economic situation worsened in the 1780s, and in 1789, revolution erupted. When it ended some six years later, over 40,000 people had been executed, and a new social order was in place.

Discussing Ideas. Since these two major revolutions, what other revolutions have taken place around the world? Have the causes always been similar?

A. Time Clauses and Phrases with the Simple Past and Past Perfect Tenses

Phrases and clauses may be used to relate an earlier time or event to a later one. The past perfect (continuous) is generally used for the earlier event; it can never be used for the later event.

Note that in conversational English, the simple past is often substituted for the past perfect in sentences with *before, after,* or *until.* In written English, writers sometimes change to the simple past after the time frame has been established by the past perfect (continuous). In clauses with *when,* however, the past perfect must be used if there is a distinct difference in time. Compare: *It began to rain when I went outside. (The rain began at that time.) It had begun to rain when I went outside. (The rain had begun earlier.)*

	Examples	Notes
To Introduce Clauses		
before	**Before** the war began, American colonists had already been rebelling for several years.	*Before, by the time (that),* and *until* + the simple past are used with the later event.
by the time (that)	**By the time (that)** the British brought more troops to the colonies, the rebellion had already spread.	Adverbs such as *already, just, hardly, recently,* and *scarcely* are frequently used with the past perfect tense.
until	**Until** the British instituted these taxes, most colonists had been loyal to England.	
after	Fights broke out **after** the British had passed a series of taxes.	*After* + the past perfect is used with the earlier event.
when	The rebellion had already started **when** the British passed new taxes.	In some cases, *when* can be used with either the earlier or later event. In sentences with the past perfect and simple past tenses, *when* + the simple past is usually used with the later event.
To Introduce Phrases		
by	**By** 1776, colonists had already been rebelling for several years.	Remember that phrases do not include a subject/verb combination.
up to	**Up to** 1776, they had not officially declared war.	
within	**Within** seven years, the Americans had gained independence.	

B. Time Clauses and Phrases with the Simple Past and Past Continuous Tenses

Clauses and phrases can be used to relate actions or situations that happened at approximately the same time.

	Examples	Notes
To Introduce Clauses with the Simple Past		
when (whenever) as soon as	Fighting began **when** the British tried to collect more taxes. **As soon as** colonists learned of the fighting, rebellion spread rapidly.	*When* and *as soon as* express a direct connection in the time of occurrence of the two events. *Whenever* may be used to describe habitual occurrences.
To Introduce Clauses with the Past Continuous (and Simple Past)		
as while when	**While (As)** colonists in Boston were fighting the British, colonists in the South were organizing an army. Colonists in Virginia were planning their own revolt **when** they received news of the fighting in Boston.	The past continuous is often used with *while* or *as* to describe past actions in progress. *When* may be used with a clause in the simple past to describe an event that occurred while another event was in progress.
To Introduce Phrases		
during	They received news of the fighting in Boston **during** a meeting of anti-British colonists.	Remember that phrases do not include a subject/verb combination.

1 **Review.** Complete the following sentences by using the simple past, past continuous, or past perfect forms of the verbs in parentheses.

Example: In 1620, after they *had spent* (spend) five months on the Atlantic Ocean, 143 British colonists, or "Pilgrims," *landed* (land) in Massachusetts.

1. While these Pilgrims ______________ (settle) in Massachusetts, they ______________ (face) many problems.
2. There ______________ (be) unfriendly Indians; the winter ______________ (be) severe; there ______________ (not be) enough food.
3. During the first year, many of the Pilgrims ______________ (die).
4. However, before the year ______________ (be) over, the Pilgrims ______________ (sign) a treaty with the local Indians.
5. After a few years, they ______________ (produce) more food than they could eat.

6. In the years after the Pilgrims _______________ (arrive), the population _______________ (grow) steadily.
7. In 1650, 52,000 colonists _______________ (live) in North America.
8. By 1759, the population _______________ (increase) to over 1 million.
9. Colonial development _______________ (continue) until the revolution _______________ (start).
10. When the American Revolution _______________ (begin), there _______________ (be) 13 colonies.

2 Quickly reread the passage "Countries in Transition: Revolution" on page 164. Then analyze paragraph 2. In each complex sentence, tell which action came first and which came second.

3 The information that follows is listed in chronological order. Combine each pair of sentences using the connecting words in parentheses. Change the verb tense to the past perfect in one of the clauses in each new sentence. Note any cases where the simple past may be used instead of the past perfect without any change in meaning. Remember to omit any repetitious information.

Example: The British completed a series of wars against France. The British increased taxes in the American colonies. (soon after)

Soon after the British had completed a series of wars against France, they increased taxes in the American colonies. (The simple past may also be used.)

1. Most of the colonists felt loyal to Britain. The British started taxing the colonies. (until)
2. The British Parliament increased import taxes. American merchants began to rebel. (after)
3. The British started to collect the new import taxes. The colonists began to organize a rebellion. (by the time)
4. Boston was already a center of rebellion for years. The first armed conflict occurred there in March of 1770. (by the time)
5. The fighting around Boston stopped. The British Parliament passed the Tea Act of 1773, another new set of import taxes. (soon after)
6. British soldiers started enforcing the Tea Act. Boston merchants disguised as Indians attacked a British ship. (after)
7. These merchants secretly boarded the British ship. They dumped over 300 chests of British tea into the ocean.* (when)
8. The British learned of the dumping of their tea. British soldiers closed Boston Harbor to all trade. (after)

---

*This event is known as the Boston Tea Party

The Boston Tea Party

9. Only a few people were killed or injured in the rebellion. The British closed Boston Harbor. (before)
10. The rebellion continued to grow. The first real battles were fought at Lexington and Concord on April 19, 1775. (until)

4 Combine the following sentences using *while* or *as*. Change at least one of the verbs in each pair to the past continuous.

Example: Louis XVI ruled France. The French Revolution began.
While Louis XVI was ruling France, the French Revolution began.
or
The French Revolution began while Louis XVI was ruling France.

1. Louis XVI ruled France. He did little to help the poor.
2. France suffered an economic crisis. Louis XVI nearly bankrupted the country by sending large sums of money to the American revolutionaries.
3. French incomes fell dramatically. Prices seemed to rise daily.
4. Shortages of bread occurred regularly. The price of bread skyrocketed.*
5. The wealth of the upper class increased. The life of peasants became steadily worse.
6. Thousands of Parisians searched for work. Unemployed peasants looking for jobs flooded Paris.
7. His people lost their jobs and their homes. Louis XVI relaxed in his palace at Versailles, 30 miles from Paris.
8. Louis XVI stayed in Versailles. He had virtually no contact with the French people.

**skyrocket* to go up suddenly and sharply

5 Rephrase Sentences 1, 2, 4, and 8 from Activity 4. Use *during* and the nouns from the following list. Since you will be forming a phrase, remember to omit the verb.

Example: rule
During Louis XVI's rule, the French Revolution began.

1. rule
2. economic crisis
4. bread shortages
8. stay

6 Imagine that you have a series of Parisian newspapers from 1770 to 1790. The following might have been some of the headlines. Use the information, listed in chronological order, to form at least ten sentences in the simple past tense with *when.* Because headlines often leave out words, you may have to add articles or other words, in addition to changing the verbs.

Example: AMERICAN COLONIES DECLARE WAR ON BRITAIN!
FRANCE'S KING LOUIS XVI SUPPORTS COLONIES!
When the American colonies declared war on Britain, France's King Louis XVI supported the colonies.

1. COST OF SUPPORTING AMERICANS IS TOO HIGH
2. LOUIS XVI MUST INSTITUTE NEW TAXES
3. UPPER CLASSES REFUSE TO PAY!
4. LOUIS XVI IS FORCED TO CALL MEETING OF ESTATES GENERAL*
5. MEETING BEGINS MAY 5, 1789
6. FIRST MEETING IN 174 YEARS!
7. DELEGATES OF THIRD ESTATE DEMAND DISCUSSION OF GOVERNMENT REFORM
8. FIRST AND SECOND ESTATES REFUSE TO DISCUSS CHANGES
9. THIRD ESTATE DECLARES ITSELF THE NATIONAL ASSEMBLY!**
10. LOUIS XVI RECEIVES NEWS OF NEW NATIONAL ASSEMBLY
11. KING FORBIDS NATIONAL ASSEMBLY TO MEET
12. NATIONAL ASSEMBLY IGNORES KING!
13. KING ORDERS TROOPS TO PARIS
14. SOLDIERS SURROUND CITY!
15. RIOTS BREAK OUT IN PARIS AND THE PROVINCES

7 Complete the following paragraph with connecting words such as *after, as, by the time (that), because, because of, before, due to, since, when, while,* or any others that are appropriate. Do not use any connecting word more than twice.

**Estates General* legislative body that served the king. It had three branches: The First Estate, representing the nobles; the Second Estate, representing the church; the Third Estate, representing everyone else.

***National Assembly* legislative body with powers superceding the king's

The Storming of the Bastille

French crowds storm the Bastille, 1789.

___*When*___ (1) Louis XVI ordered troops to Paris, the working class organized protests, and the middle-class radicals formed a militia. ________ (2) workers were protesting in the streets, intellectuals were making plans for action. ________ (3) tensions had built up for several weeks, Paris exploded on July 14, 1789, with the storming of the Bastille.

The Bastille was a 14th-century fortress and prison. ________ (4) political prisoners were usually held there, it was a symbol of royal oppression. ________ (5) Parisian crowds attacked the Bastille, only a few political prisoners were actually being held. However, ________ (6) the military also stationed soldiers at the Bastille, a large amount of gunpowder was stored there. ________ (7) the crowds gathered outside the walls of the prison on July 14, they demanded gunpowder.

________ (8) the governor of the Bastille had refused to give up the gunpowder, the protestors forced their way into the prison. ________ (9) the crowd entered the courtyard, the governor ordered his soldiers to shoot. ________ (10) the shooting stopped, 98 had been killed and 73 wounded. Finally, the governor surrendered. ________ (11) the Bastille's importance as a revolutionary symbol, news of its fall sped through France. Today, Bastille Day, July 14, is an important French holiday.

8 Write a paragraph from the information that follows. Combine the sentences, using connecting words and transitions and omitting repetitious information. You may want to include some additional information covered in the previous exercises. Try not to use the same connecting word or phrase twice.

Example: May 5, 1789: The Estates General met. It was their first meeting in over a century. France was near financial disaster.

When the Estates General met on May 5, 1789, it was the first meeting in over a century, and France was near financial disaster. Two months later. . . .

July 12, 1789: Riots broke out throughout Paris. Louis XVI ordered new troops to Paris.

July 14, 1789: Angry crowds stormed the Bastille.

October 5, 1789: Over 10,000 Parisians marched to the Palace of Versailles. The crowds demanded bread. The crowds forced the royal family to return to Paris with them.

June 20, 1791: King Louis XVI and his family tried to escape to Germany. King Louis XVI and his family were captured at Varennes. The king and queen were forced to return to Paris.

April 20, 1792: France declared war on Austria. Austria declared war on France. Prussia declared war on France.

August 17, 1792: Parisians marched to the Tuileries. Louis XVI lived in the Tuileries then. The Tuileries was the royal palace in Paris. Parisians believed Louis XVI was a traitor. Louis's wife, Marie Antoinette, was Austrian. Parisians believed Louis was helping the Austrians in the war.

August 19, 1792: The revolutionary government took control.

September 20, 1792: The National Convention was formed to replace the Assembly.

September 21, 1792: The monarchy was abolished.

January 21, 1793: King Louis XVI was executed.

October 16, 1793: Queen Marie Antoinette was executed.

9 Think of an important time of change in your country or culture. You may choose a time of political change or a period of social, religious, cultural, or economic change. Answer the following questions about that particular time and the events that occurred then.

1. What had the general situation been before the period of change? Give a two- to three-sentence description.
2. What particular events led to the change?
3. What changes took place?
4. How did people react while the change was occurring?
5. How have these changes affected your area or culture since then? Give a brief (two- to three-sentence) description.

Example: *American music was beginning to change in the 1950s. Elvis Presley and many others had already created rock and roll. Then, in the early 1960s, the Beatles arrived in the United States. The country went wild when they arrived, and American music has never been the same.*

Using What You've Learned

1 Major political events often become national holidays. Bastille Day, July 14, is a national holiday in France. July 4 is celebrated in the United States. September 16 is celebrated in Mexico. Do you have a special holiday that commemorates a major political event in your country or culture? How do people celebrate this holiday? Are there parades? Do people wear special clothing? Is there special food or music to celebrate the day?

Individually or in small groups, prepare a brief presentation on an important holiday in your culture. Give some background information on its origins and explain how it is celebrated.

Video Activities: College Graduation

Before You Watch. Discuss these questions in small groups.

1. Have you ever attended a graduation ceremony? What happened at the ceremony?
2. How many years do people usually have to study to become doctors?

Watch. Circle the correct answers to the following questions.

1. Why is Mrs. Christianson so happy?
   a. She's graduating from college.
   b. Her son is becoming a doctor.
   c. She has just immigrated to the United States.
2. Louis Christianson says that his mother gave him a love of ____________.
   a. education b. medicine c. Mexico
3. Louis decided to become a doctor ____________.
   a. when he was young b. in high school c. after high school

Watch Again. Match the speaker to the quotations.

Quotations		Speakers
______	1. I'd love to share with you some stories about the medical students soon to be physicians before you.	a. narrator
______	2. I did a major in philosophy, so I had no plans to go to medical school.	b. graduation speaker
______	3. Nine years ago Christianson was graduating from Madison High School.	c. Mr. Christianson
______	4. I still see him as my baby.	d. Louis Christianson
______	5. We are delighted.	e. Mrs. Christianson

After You Watch. Complete the following with *because, since, because of, due to,* or *as a result of.*

1. ____________ his hard work, Louis graduated first in his class.
2. ____________ he hadn't taken pre-med courses in college, he had to take some courses before he applied to medical school.
3. His mother places great value on education ____________ she is an immigrant.
4. ____________ a sudden illness, his grandmother was unable to attend the ceremony.
5. Louis' parents are very proud of him ____________ of his hard work.

Focus on Testing

Connecting Words and Use of Tenses

Problem areas with connecting words are frequently tested on standardized English proficiency exams. Check your understanding of these structures by completing the sample items that follow.

Remember that . . .

- Clauses must be complete; that is, every clause must have a subject and verb.
- Phrases do not contain subject/verb combinations.
- Connecting words often determine which verb tense should be used.

Part 1. Circle the best completion for the following.

Example: The French Revolution began ________ Louis XVI was ruling.

a. because of
b. since
(c.) while
d. after

1. After Jack and I had gone to the concert, we ________ for dinner.
   a. was going c. went
   b. were going d. had gone

2. Mohandas Gandhi did not believe in violence; therefore, he ________ his life to change through nonviolent means.
   a. devoting c. devote
   b. was devoting d. devoted

3. After Edison ________ the first commercial light bulb, he went on to create the mimeograph, an early motion-picture camera, and a battery, along with many other inventions.
   a. develops c. had been developing
   b. developed d. was developing

4. Due to ________, Mr. Gonzalez is frequently out of town.
   a. his work c. he working
   b. he was working d. he works

Part 2. Each sentence has one error. Circle the letter below the word(s) containing the error.

Example: After they <u>had spent</u> (A) five months <u>on the ocean</u> (B), the British colonists <u>were landing</u> (Ⓒ) <u>in Massachusetts</u> (D).

1. Soon after peace had been declared, Parliament had levied heavy taxes
   A B C
because of heavy war expenses.
   D

2. The American cartoonist and sculptor Rube Goldberg grew tremendously
   A B
famous because of he diagrammed incredible contraptions to carry out
   C D
simple tasks.

3. As a result the invention of the steam engine, a number of major
   A B
technological breakthroughs became possible.
   C D

4. Whenever towns will increase in size, they become more heterogeneous,
   A B C
more secular, and less tightly organized.
   D

Chapter 6

The Mind

IN THIS CHAPTER

Part 1 Clauses and Related Structures of Contrast: Concession

Part 2 Clauses and Related Structures of Contrast: Opposition

Part 3 Clauses and Phrases of Purpose

Part 4 Clauses and Related Structures of Comparison

Part 5 Clauses of Result

Introduction

In this chapter, you will study adverb clauses and related structures that show contrast, purpose, and result. As you study the chapter, pay attention not only to the meanings of the connecting words but also to several other important factors in usage: what punctuation is used with each, where each can be placed in a sentence, and how the focus of a sentence can change according to the choice and placement of the connecting word.

The following passage introduces the chapter theme "The Mind" and raises some of the topics and issues you will cover in the chapter.

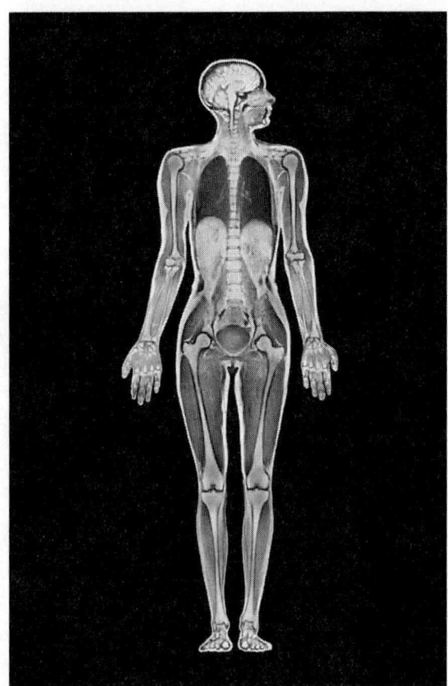

The central nervous system

The Mysteries of the Mind

Although the mind has always fascinated people, its workings were an almost complete mystery until recently. In the last several decades, however, researchers have been so active in this area that we understand more about the mind today than we ever imagined possible.

We now know that the brain controls the nervous system, which, in turn, directs all muscular and mental activity. In addition, we know that certain functions are carried out by specific parts of the brain. We have even come to realize that the brain must forget some pieces of information so that it can remember others.

But in spite of all the recent scientific advances, we continue to ask the most basic question: What *is* the mind? Is the mind merely an electrochemical operation, or is it much more? We are beginning to understand the complexities of the nervous system, but is the mind something that we will never completely understand?

Discussing Ideas. What else do we currently know about the functioning of the brain? What is some of the research that is being done to learn more? What about the mind?

PART 1

Clauses and Related Structures of Contrast: Concession

Setting the Context

Prereading Questions. What is the central nervous system? Which organ controls it? What are some examples of the central nervous system at work?

Nerve cells from the human brain

The Central Nervous System

At the sound of a horn, a child jumps back to the safety of the sidewalk even though he never saw the truck that almost hit him. A mother sleeps undisturbed in spite of the noise of her neighbor's television set yet wakes immediately at the first cry from her baby in the next room. Although a businessman worries about a problem for days, the answer comes to him out of the blue while he is busy thinking about something entirely different.

These are just three examples of the routine functioning of the human nervous system. A thousand examples, however, could only begin to describe the capabilities of this incredible system of nerves that leads throughout the body to the center of control, the brain.

Discussing Ideas. Can you give more information about the functioning of the central nervous system? Can you explain how the brain sends and receives messages?

A. Adverb Clauses and Related Structures of Contrast: Concession

The following clauses, phrases, and transitions are used to express ideas or information that is different from our expectations. In a sentence with an adverb clause or phrase, the focus is on the main clause. If a transition is used and there are two main clauses, each clause has equal focus. Note that a comma normally follows introductory clauses and phrases. Commas are also used occasionally with *although, even though, though, in spite of the fact that,* and *despite the fact that* when they appear in the middle of a sentence. Transitions are normally followed by commas. See Chapter 3 for more information on punctuation, sentence focus, and alternative positions for transitions.

	Examples
To Introduce Clauses although even though though in spite of the fact (that) despite the fact (that)	The child managed to avoid the truck **although** he hadn't seen it. **Even though** the child hadn't seen the truck, he managed to avoid it. The child managed to avoid the truck **in spite of the fact that** he hadn't seen it.
To Introduce Phrases in spite of despite regardless of	She was able to sleep **in spite of** the noise. **Despite** living next to a freeway, she was always able to sleep. She always sleeps well **regardless of** the noise.
Transitions* nevertheless still however even so all the same	Weeb took two sleeping pills; **however,** he couldn't fall asleep. His doctor had warned him not to take more than two. **Nevertheless,** he took four. Weeb took four pills altogether; **even so,** he didn't sleep well.

*These transitions are listed from more formal to less formal. All of them are used in both speaking and writing, however. Remember that transitions may be placed within a second sentence, but the punctuation changes: *The left hemisphere allows us to analyze. The right, however, provides us with our artistic ability.*

1 Quickly reread the passage "The Central Nervous System" on page 177. Then do the following:

1. Circle the following connecting words: *even though, in spite of, but, although,* and *however.*
2. What kind of relationship do these connecting words express?
3. Underline the subject(s) and verb(s) in the sentences with these connecting words. What structures does each connect (for example, phrases, clauses)?
4. What punctuation is used with each?

2 Our brains interpret our perceptions and often adjust them to our view of reality. As a result, we sometimes see, hear, or feel what we expect instead of what is really there. Change the following sentences from compound to complex or from complex to compound. Rewrite the sentence, using the connecting word in parentheses and omitting the connecting word already there. Change or add punctuation when necessary.

Example: Although the word *bear* can be written in a sentence about breweries, a person will usually misread the word as *beer.* (however)

The word "bear" can be written in a sentence about breweries; however, a person will usually misread the word as "beer."

1. Even though a large and a small box may be exactly the same weight, the large box will feel heavier. (however)
2. A person wearing blue-tinted glasses sees a blue world at first; nevertheless, the blue effect soon disappears, and the world looks normal again. (although)
3. The sound of the phone does not change although the phone appears to ring much louder when we are expecting a call. (still)
4. Despite the fact that five people may witness the same accident, each person will remember the accident differently. (nevertheless)
5. The air seems damper on a cloudy day than on a sunny day; however, the humidity level may be exactly the same. (in spite of the fact that)
6. Time seems to pass quickly on some days; nevertheless, it goes slowly on others. (even though)

3 Use *in spite of the fact that, despite the fact that, in spite of,* or *despite* to complete the following sets of sentences.

Examples: *Despite the fact that* we spend about one-third of our lives sleeping, we know relatively little about sleep.

Despite spending about one-third of our lives sleeping, we know relatively little about sleep.

1. ______________ years of study, no one knows for certain why humans and animals sleep.

   ______________ scientists have been studying sleep for years, no one knows for certain why humans and animals sleep.

2. ______________ the body seems to rest during sleep, the brain remains quite active.

   ______________ the rest that the body gets during sleep, the brain remains quite active.

Culture Note

Nobody knows for certain why we sleep. However, we now know that sleep has many phases, from light sleep to deep sleep or REM (rapid eye movement). REM sleep often takes place during dreams. Researchers report that if a person is not allowed to have any deep sleep (REM), the person will experience irritability and even hallucinations.

3. ______________ most adults like to sleep approximately eight hours a day, some people can survive comfortably on half that much.

   ______________ the desire that most adults have for about eight hours of sleep a day, some people can survive comfortably on half that much.

4. Some insomniacs* lead happy, productive lives, ______________ they sleep only one or two hours a night.

   Some insomniacs lead happy, productive lives, ______________ sleeping only one or two hours a night.

4 Provide an appropriate connecting word of contrast in each of the blanks that follow. Include all necessary punctuation.

Example: *Although* researchers used to think the brain was similar to a telephone switchboard, they now suggest the brain is more like a computer. *However,* even a supercomputer is not nearly as complicated as the brain.

1. Memories come from the sights and sounds of the world. __________ the eye may see an image for less than one second this image can be stored for a lifetime.
2. Scientists realized years ago that memories were saved through the use of electrical impulses. __________ today they know that chemicals also play an important role.
3. How exactly does memory work? __________ the question cannot be answered this much is known. The memory image moves from the eye to the brain in electrical form. This __________ provides for only short-term memory and the image may be forgotten within moments.
4. __________ many parts of the brain are involved in memory certain types of memory are controlled by specific areas. This has been shown in the case of a young man (H.M.), who was suffering from extreme epilepsy.** __________ many treatments had been tried none had been successful. In 1953, H.M. came to a group of neurosurgeons.† These doctors removed a small part of his brain, and his epilepsy was cured. __________ this operation left him with a permanent memory disability. __________ he was able to remember things that happened before the operation he could not form a single lasting new memory. "Every day is alone in itself," H.M. said. "Whatever enjoyment I've had, whatever sorrow I've had."

**insomniacs* people who have trouble falling or staying asleep

***epilepsy* disease of the brain that causes sudden uncontrolled movement and loss of consciousness

†*neurosurgeons* doctors who operate on the brain

5 Combine the following sentences by using *although, though, even though, even so, however, nevertheless, still, despite,* or *in spite of (the fact that).* Substitute pronouns for nouns to avoid repetition. Do not use any of these connecting words more than once.

Example: The brain controls all of our body movements. The brain itself never moves.

Even though it controls all of our body movements, the brain itself never moves.

1. The adult brain uses up to 25 percent of the blood's oxygen supply. The adult brain does not perform physical work.
2. The brain comprises only 2 percent of the body's weight. The brain receives 20 percent of all the blood pumped from the heart.
3. All parts of the brain receive blood. Areas that control intellectual activity have the most blood vessels.
4. Blood pressure often changes in other parts of the body. Blood pressure stays relatively constant in the brain.
5. Great amounts of energy are consumed in the production of thought. The exact process is still not understood.
6. A loss of blood in a body part only causes numbness. A 15-second interruption in the blood flow to the brain results in unconsciousness.

6 Use your knowledge and imagination to complete the following sentences. Be sure to add capital letters and appropriate punctuation.

Example: Although I usually get 8 hours of sleep, *last night I slept for only 3 hours.*

1. Even though time usually passes very quickly in this class
2. I have a headache today however
3. Molly couldn't get to sleep last night despite the fact that
4. Kate studied for the test all last night nevertheless
5. I stayed up until 4 A.M. even so
6. Jack finished all of the work despite
7. In spite of the fact that Mark has lost all of his hair
8. Jorge was fired last week in spite of

Web Note

For a very interesting interactive site on optical illusions, consult "The Exploratorium" on the Web at www.exploratorium.edu/exhibits/f_exhibits.html. You might also look for Websites on the artist Max Escher and his works.

Now go back and suggest a different connector for each of the sentences that you have created.

Using What You've Learned

7 Use sentences from Activity 5 and other information from this section to write a short paragraph on the working of the brain. Rephrase sentences to use a variety of connecting words and be sure to include both compound and complex sentences.

8 In normal vision, our eyes actually receive a distorted view of the world. The image on our retina is upside down and reversed left to right. Straight lines curve and colors form a fringe around the edge of the image.

The brain, however, takes over and adapts the information it receives from our eyes. It matches the new information with what it already knows about the world in order to give us a true picture.

Because the brain insists on correcting new information, it also corrects optical illusions. What we believe we see at first may not be the true image at all.

In pairs or in small groups, look carefully at the following pictures and share your first impressions. Then look more carefully and compare what you now see with what you thought you saw.

What's wrong with this phrase?
(a)

What kind of animal is this?
(b)

Who or what is this?
(c)

Is this woman young or old?
(d)

9 Think about the experiences mentioned in Activity 8. Then work in small groups and discuss the following. Add ideas of your own, too.

Have you ever had experiences similar to those mentioned in Activity 8?

Think about your perception of time. When does time seem to pass quickly? When does it pass slowly?

Think about your perception of temperature. Do clouds or sunshine affect whether you feel hotter or colder?

Think about your hearing. When you're in a dark room, can you hear things more clearly? Do sounds seem louder? What about when you're in a strange place?

10 When you move to a new place, and especially when you live in a new culture and speak a new language daily, your perceptions are often much more acute than they would be in a familiar place. You may notice many things that others don't because they are completely accustomed to them, while you are not.

Think about some of your perceptions in recent months: the sights, the sounds, the smells, the textures surrounding you. Write a short paragraph describing something that has struck you in particular. This perception may involve one sense or a variety of senses.

Then work in small groups and share your observations. Tell about them, but don't read them!

Example: *One of the most interesting things for me here has been the smells, or rather, the lack of smells, especially in the markets. In my own country, food smells are a very common part of everyday life, but here, nothing smells. Everything seems to be antiseptic!*

PART 2

Clauses and Related Structures of Contrast: Opposition

Setting the Context

Prereading Questions. Do certain parts of the brain have specific functions, or does the entire brain function as one unit? Questions like these are frequently debated as research reveals new information on the brain. The following is one current viewpoint.

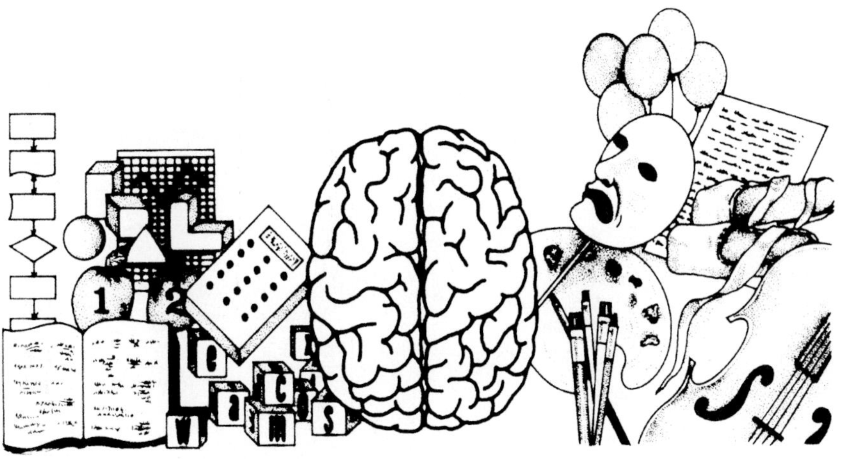

The Two Hemispheres of the Brain

The cortex of the brain is divided into two hemispheres. The right hemisphere mainly controls the left side of the body, whereas the left hemisphere directs the body's right side.

While both hemispheres can potentially perform many of the same functions, each of the hemispheres tends to specialize. The left hemisphere seems to control most analytic, logical thinking. It appears to process information in sequential order, handling logical thought, language, and mathematics. The right hemisphere, on the other hand, is limited in language ability, but it appears to process different kinds of information simultaneously. It specializes in spatial orientation, artistic endeavors, crafts, body image, and recognition of faces. Thus, where the left hemisphere is more analytic and sequential, the right is more holistic and relational.

Discussing Ideas. This passage presents one theory that says the brain is highly specialized for certain types of tasks. Do you know of other theories that currently exist?

A. Adverb Clauses and Related Structures of Contrast: Opposition

The following clauses, phrases, and transitions are used to express opposite views about a subject or subjects. Note that a comma normally follows an introductory phrase or clause or a transition. Commas may also be used with *while, where,* and *whereas* when they appear in the middle of a sentence. See Chapter 3 for more information on punctuation and sentence focus.

	Examples	Time Expressions
To Introduce Clauses		
whereas where while	**Whereas** the right hemisphere of the brain is much older in terms of human evolution, the left hemisphere is more highly developed.	*Whereas, where,* and *while* are often used to contrast direct opposites. *Whereas* is used in formal English.
To Introduce Phrases		
similar to different from	The right side of the brain seems quite **different from** the left side. The right side is apparently not very **similar to** the left.	*Different from, unlike,* and *instead of* contrast opposites. *Similar to* and *like* compare related ideas. Noun or gerund phrases normally follow these expressions.
like unlike	**Unlike** the left hemisphere, which is responsible for language, the right hemisphere specializes in body image and recognition of faces.	
instead of	The right hemisphere tends to process a variety of information simultaneously **instead of** sequentially.	*Instead of* can be followed by a variety of forms: adjectives, adverbs, noun phrases, or gerunds.
Transitions		
in contrast on the other hand	The left hemisphere seems to process information in sequential order; **in contrast,** the right hemisphere handles different types of data simultaneously.	*In contrast* and *on the other hand* relate different points that are not necessarily directly opposite.
on the contrary	The right side of the brain is not primarily analytical; **on the contrary,** it is responsible for the artistic aspects of the mind. Is the right side of the brain responsible for analyzing information? **On the contrary,** it is responsible for the artistic aspects of the mind.	*On the contrary* is used differently from other transitions of contrast. It indicates that the *opposite* of some idea is true. It often reinforces the negative idea in the preceding sentence or can be used to answer a question.

Note: Remember that transitions may be placed within a second sentence, but the punctuation changes: *The left hemisphere allows us to analyze. The right, however, provides us with our artistic ability.*

1 Quickly reread the passage "The Two Hemispheres of the Brain" on page 183. Then do the following:

1. Circle the connecting words that express contrast. For each case, find the subject(s) and verb(s) of the sentence. What structures do these words connect (for example, phrases, clauses)?
2. What punctuation is used with the various connecting words? Compare this to the punctuation used with connecting words in "The Central Nervous System" on page 177. Do you notice any differences in punctuation?

3. Look again at the second sentence and the last sentence in "The Two Hemispheres of the Brain" on page 183. What is the primary focus of each sentence? Now, rephrase the two sentences, using the connecting word at the beginning of the other clause. Does the focus change in the new sentences?

2 Rewrite the following sentences, using the connecting word in parentheses and omitting the connecting word already there. Give all possibilities. Change or add punctuation where necessary. Then tell the primary focus of both the original and the new sentences.

Example: A child's brain is one mass; in contrast, the brain of an adult is separated into two hemispheres.

Focus: Both a child's brain and an adult's brain

(whereas)

Whereas a child's brain is one mass, the brain of an adult is separated into two hemispheres.

Focus: An adult's brain

or

A child's brain is one mass, whereas the brain of an adult is separated into two hemispheres.

Focus: A child's brain

1. An adult brain is more specialized; on the other hand, a child's brain has large areas that are uncommitted. (while)
2. While children can learn many things easily, adults often have a much harder time. (in contrast)
3. Few adults can learn to use a new language without mistakes or accent; on the other hand, children frequently become completely fluent in new languages. (whereas)
4. Whereas most children do not favor either hand until they are about five years old, most adults are either right-handed or left-handed. (in contrast)
5. Some functions, such as smell, are located in specific areas in the brain, while others are handled throughout the brain. (on the other hand)
6. Considerable research is being done on the "geography" of the brain; however, only a few areas have actually been "mapped." (while)

3 Show the contrast in the following sentences by filling in *while, where, whereas, on the other hand,* or *in contrast.* Add *all* necessary punctuation.

Brains and Computers

The human brain is often compared with a computer. ___*While*___ (1) they may have a number of things in common, they are actually quite different. First, they differ physically. The brain is made up of soft tissue. A computer __________ (2) is composed of electrical circuits. In addition, the difference in capabilities is immense. __________ (3)

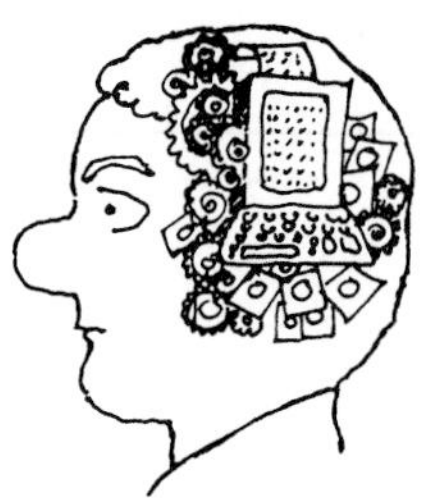

computers are complex a brain is a million times more intricate. The brain constantly gathers information from its five sophisticated senses. The computer ______ (4) receives its data from a keyboard. The brain can simultaneously process tremendous amounts of information; the computer ______ (5) must proceed one step at a time. But perhaps most significant of all, ______ (6) a brain is conscious of its own existence a computer is not.

4 Combine the following sets of sentences in two ways. First, use *unlike;* then, use *instead of.* Add necessary punctuation.

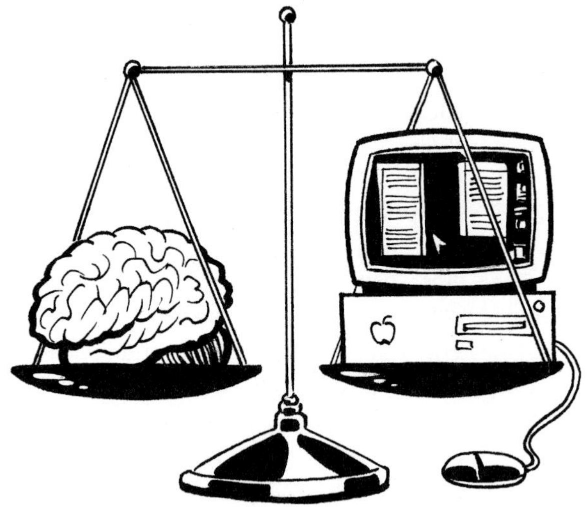

Example: A brain has thousands of neurons. A computer is made up of circuits.

Unlike a brain, which has thousands of neurons, a computer is made up of circuits.

Instead of having thousands of neurons like a brain, a computer is made up of circuits.

1. A brain is capable of emotions and dreams. A computer only processes information.
2. A computer may weigh hundreds of pounds. A brain weighs only about three pounds.
3. A computer can cover a desk. A brain fits neatly into the top of the skull.
4. A brain is aware of its own existence. A computer has no such sense of "being."

5 Complete the sentences that follow by using either *on the contrary* or *on the other hand.* Add punctuation when necessary.

1. The brain is not very much like a computer. ________ the two are quite different.
2. The brain is not very much like a computer. ____________ there are a few similarities between the two.
3. Some people believe computers will soon rule our lives. ____________ most think that this will never happen.
4. Some people believe computers will soon rule our lives. I don't believe it. ____________ in my opinion, this could never happen.
5. A. Do you think computers will ever take control of the world?
   B. I can't say. ____________ Frank is sure they will.
6. A. What about you? Do you think computers could take control of the world?
   B. ____________ computers are simply machines and always will be.

Web Note

Very interesting research is currently being done on how children learn foreign languages. For more information, you can consult these sites on the Web: wwwrcf.usc.edu/~cmmr/ (from the University of Southern California), http://carla.acad.umn.edu/NLRC.html (from the University of Minnesota), and http://polyglot.lss.wisc.edu/lss/lang/langlink.html (from the University of Wisconsin, Madison).

6 Use your own ideas to complete the following sentences.

Example: Some people believe we now know virtually everything about the brain. On the contrary, *we have only begun to understand its workings.*

1. Is there a difference between the brain and the mind?
   On the contrary, . . .
2. Children learn foreign languages with considerable ease.
   On the other hand, . . .
3. Adults rarely find it easy to learn a second language.
   On the contrary, . . .
4. John has had a difficult time learning Spanish.
   On the other hand, . . .
5. Artists often have trouble with analytical thinking.
   In contrast, . . .
6. Is mathematics done primarily by using the right side of the brain?
   On the contrary, . . .
7. Mathematics is done primarily by using the left side of the brain.
   In contrast, . . .
8. Are we getting tired of this exercise?
   On the contrary, . . .

7 Use your imagination to complete the following sentences. Be sure to add capital letters if needed and appropriate punctuation.

Example: Whereas some researchers believe the right and left sides of the brain have distinct functions *, others think this idea is nonsense.*

1. While Jamie loves to use computers
2. Children learn languages easily on the other hand

3. I had a fascinating dream last night in contrast
4. Where some people have no trouble sleeping
5. Unlike Molly, who sleeps 12 hours a night,
6. Whereas I take a nap every afternoon
7. A. Do you take a nap every afternoon?
   B. On the contrary,
8. My children are bilingual in contrast

Web Note

If you have access to the Internet, go to http://web-us.com/brain/LRBrain.html#Reality and take a test to see which side of your brain is more active.

8 Using a variety of phrases, connecting words, and transitions of contrast, combine the following into one paragraph. You may leave out some of the information or add information of your own to make the new paragraph read smoothly. Begin the paragraph with a general statement such as, *If recent research is correct, the left and right sides of the brain differ in a number of ways.*

The Right Brain

The right hemisphere of the brain probably dates back millions of years in our evolution. All mammals have right-hemisphere thinking. Right-hemisphere thinking provides us with instinct, feeling, and intuition. The right brain appreciates music, allows for three-dimensional vision, recognizes faces, and gets jokes. In short, the right hemisphere helps us feel where we belong in the world.

The Left Brain

The left hemisphere of the brain is relatively young in terms of evolution. The development of left-hemisphere thinking within the human species accounts for the fundamental differences between human and animal thought. The left hemisphere controls rational, verbal, and analytical thinking. It specializes in language, logic, long-term memory, reading and writing, and critical thinking. The left hemisphere is the business part of our brain organizing, analyzing, and choosing.

9 **Error Analysis.** Each of the following sentences contains an error concerning the connecting words from Parts 1 and 2. The error may involve the connecting word, the punctuation, or the need for a capital letter. Find and correct all errors.

Example: The right side of the brain seems quite different ‸(*from*) the left side.

1. Whereas the right brain processes information sequentially, on the other hand, the left brain handles information simultaneously.
2. Keesia studied left-brain functions last semester, in contrast Miki focused on the right.
3. Unlike the left brain is responsible for language, the right brain specializes in recognition of faces.
4. Where I love studying the brain, Shirley thinks it is fascinating.

5. Though I have spent nine months in China I still cannot communicate in Chinese.
6. Even though Chinese is very difficult, however, it is possible to learn it.
7. Artists tend to use the right side of the brain more. On the contrary, accountants rely more on the left.
8. Although, migraine headaches are associated with women millions of men have the same problem.
9. Despite Mary has taken four aspirin, she still has a terrible headache.
10. In spite the fact that Mary has seen several doctors, none has been able to help her.

Using What You've Learned

10 It is probable that no one is completely "right-" or "left-brained." However, many people seem to be influenced by one side more than the other. What about you? Review the information in Activity 8 and other information you can find. Then, write a short paragraph about yourself describing whether you are "right-" or "left-brained." Be sure to provide several examples to support your point of view. Finally, share your ideas with your classmates, in small groups or as a class.

11 No matter how good our vision is or how carefully we pay attention, we all overlook details. In pairs or in small groups, study the two pictures below. At first glance, the pictures may appear identical; on closer examination, however, you will discover numerous differences. Find all the differences and describe them using contrast words.

Mark

Vern

PART 3 Clauses and Phrases of Purpose

Setting the Context

Prereading Questions. Who was Dr. Alois Alzheimer? Which disease did he identify?

Alzheimer's Disease

"My mother always had such a sharp mind. Then, in her mid-seventies, she began to become forgetful. She would be halfway through a sentence and stop because she couldn't remember a word. Today, three years later, she can no longer carry on a conversation. Worse, most of the time, she doesn't even recognize me."

In 1906, Dr. Alois Alzheimer, a German doctor, decided to do an autopsy* on a woman so that he could better understand the strange mental illness that she had died of. The clumps of tissue and tangled bundles of fiber that he found in the woman's brain are now recognized as hallmarks** of the most common brain dysfunction in older people, Alzheimer's disease (AD).

Today we know a great deal about Alzheimer's disease. AD disrupts the way we think by causing physical changes in the brain. It affects the parts of the brain that control thought, memory, and language. While younger people may have AD, the disease normally attacks the elderly. Only about 3 percent of people are affected by AD before age 74. However, nearly one-half of those over 85 may have the disease.

For decades, scientists around the world have been doing research to find a cure for AD. Recently there have been promising developments, including a vaccine now being tested on mice and hormone therapy. In ten years, it is likely that we will have found a treatment to prevent the disease or at least to soften its effects.

Discussing Ideas. Do you know anyone who suffers from AD?

**autopsy* examination of a body after death to determine the cause of death or the extent of changes produced by disease

***hallmarks* distinguishing features, traits, or characteristics

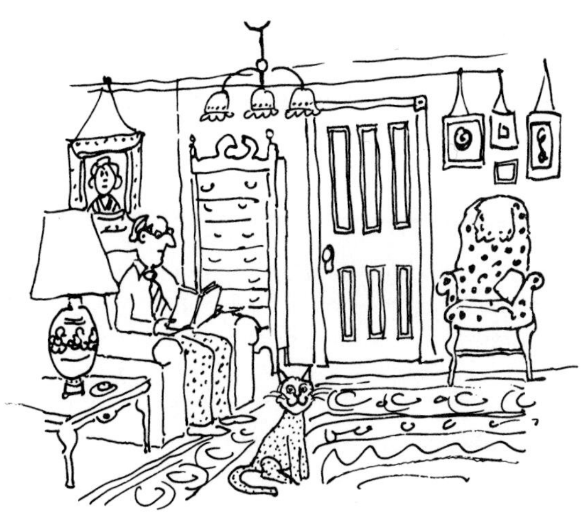

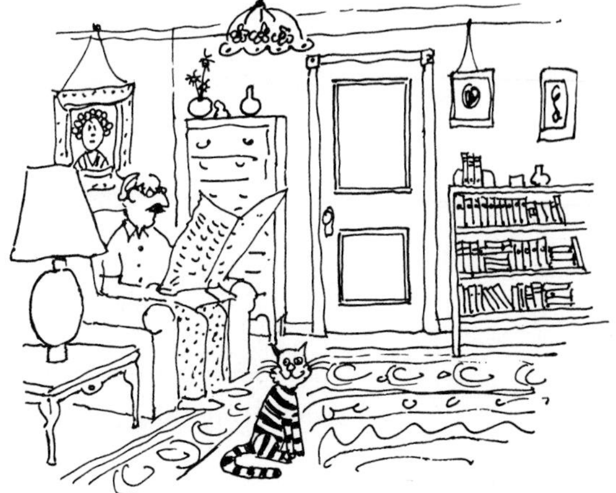

A. Adverb Clauses and Phrases of Purpose

Clauses with *so that* and *in order that* and phrases with *in order to* are used to show the intention or purpose of an action. Note that *in order that* and *so that* do not begin sentences and that commas are not normally used with either. Commas are used with *In order to* when it begins a sentence.

	Examples	**Notes**
To Introduce Clauses in order that so (that)	Scientists are studying the brain **so (that)** they can understand more about learning.	*So (that)* and *in order that* are usually used between two clauses. A modal auxiliary (can, will: present/future; could, would: past) is normally used in the dependent clause.
To Introduce Phrases in order to	Scientists are studying the brain **in order to** understand more about learning.	In written English, *in order to* is used more frequently than *so that*. *In order to* + verb and *to* + verb are considered better stylistically.

Note: That (in *so that*) is sometimes omitted. Do not confuse *so (that)* (expressing purpose) with the conjunction *so* (expressing result). The use of a modal auxiliary in the dependent clause signals "purpose" as opposed to "result." Compare: *Result: I wanted a college education, so I enrolled at the university. Purpose: I wanted a college education so (that) I could get a good job.*

1 Combine the sentences by using *so that* or *in order that.* You will need to omit some words from the second sentence and add a modal auxiliary.

Example: Dr. Alzheimer conducted an autopsy. He wanted to understand an unusual mental illness.

Dr. Alzheimer conducted an autopsy so that he could understand an unusual mental illness.

Web Note

For more information on Alzheimer's disease or other diseases, the Mayo Clinic offers an excellent Website at www.mayohealth.org/home.

1. Tests are being developed. We want to diagnose AD easily.
2. Researchers are working on a vaccine. They want to eliminate the disease.
3. Mice were used in experiments. Researchers wanted to see how effective the vaccine was.
4. Information on the research is posted on Websites. People want to know the latest developments.
5. The disease was named Alzheimer's. Everyone was able to recognize who discovered it.
6. I hope the vaccine is successful. I want Alzheimer's disease to disappear.

2 Western medicine has traditionally tried to treat illnesses through drug therapy. The Eastern approach is sometimes quite different. Substitute *in order to* for *so that* in the following sentences. Include all necessary changes.

Example: Today, doctors are developing biofeedback* techniques so that they can teach patients to heal themselves.

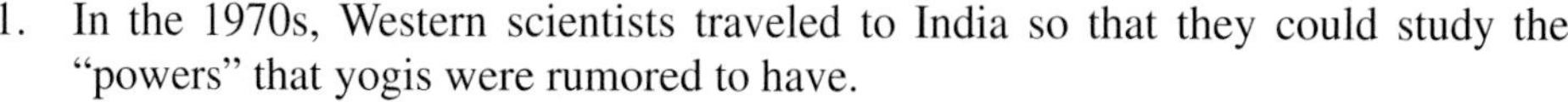
Today, doctors are developing biofeedback techniques in order to teach patients to heal themselves.

1. In the 1970s, Western scientists traveled to India so that they could study the "powers" that yogis were rumored to have.
2. The scientists used electronic instruments so that they could test yogis' ability to control "involuntary" body functions such as heartbeat and reaction to pain.
3. In one experiment, a yogi pushed a rusty needle completely through his arm so that he could demonstrate his ability to block all pain.
4. He used meditation** so that he could ignore this pain.
5. Yogis undergo years of training so that they can control their bodily functions through meditation.
6. Now some patients in the West are using biofeedback so that they can control their involuntary nervous system like yogis.
7. The patients use machines so that they can "see" and "hear" a problem and then consciously solve it.
8. Other people practice Transcendental Meditation† so that they can control their nervous system without the help of machines.

Culture Note

Transcendental Meditation, or TM, first introduced in the United States in 1957, involves a series of techniques that allow people to begin meditating after only a few training sessions. TM researchers report improved physical and mental coordination, lower blood pressure, reduced stress, and a reduction in crime in cities where it is practiced by at least 1 percent of inhabitants. The most famous advocate of TM in the West was Maharishi Mahesh Yogi, who brought TM to hundreds of thousands in the United States and Europe.

A yogi sitting on a bed of nails.

---

*_biofeedback_ technique of making certain bodily processes (such as the heartbeat or brain waves) perceptible to the senses in order to mentally control them

**_meditation_ At the heart of Eastern religions such as Hinduism and Buddhism, meditation is a method practiced in order to become pure consciousness, to transcend body and mind

†*Transcendental Meditation* See the above Culture Note

Maharishi Mahesh Yogi and followers

3 Use your knowledge and imagination to answer the following questions. Include *so that, in order that,* or *in order to* in your answers. Try to come up with at least three answers for each question.

Example: Why did you take a sleeping pill last night? *I took a sleeping pill so that I could get a good night's rest.*

1. Why do you have a physical checkup every year?
2. Why did you shave your head?
3. Why do you study so much?
4. Why didn't you go to the party last weekend?
5. Why don't you eat meat?
6. Why do you sing in the shower?
7. Why didn't you go to the movies with me last weekend?

Using What You've Learned

4 Scientists have been intrigued by the mind for thousands of years. The following is a list of five scientists and a brief summary of some of their work. Choose one of these scientists (or any other that you are interested in) as the subject for some research. Use encyclopedias, the Internet, or other sources to gather information on this person and his or her work. Then, in a one-page paper, summarize what you have found. Be sure to include information on the exact focus of the scientist's research and the purpose for doing this research.

Aristotle (384–322 B.C.) did research on animals to learn more about anatomy and to classify similarities and differences; he also studied dreams, memory, and the senses to create a theory about thought processes.

René Descartes (1596–1650) applied concepts of mathematics to psychology in order to develop a scientific method for the study of human behavior.

Sigmund Freud (1856–1939) studied hysteria to determine psychological factors that produce physical problems and used hypnosis to probe the subconscious mind.

Carl Jung (1875–1961) worked with dreams, mythology, Buddhism, and astrology to learn about the "unconscious."

Roger Sperry (1913–1994) received the 1981 Nobel Prize in Medicine for his discoveries concerning the specialized functions of the hemispheres of the brain.

Arvid Carlsson (1923–) was a 2000 Nobel Prize winner for discoveries concerning the transmission of signals in the nervous system.

Robert Ornstein (1942–) suggested that the two halves of the brain deal with different mental functions.

Maharishi Mahesh Yogi (1911–) influenced many in the West to begin meditation.

Richard Seed (1930–) is a geneticist who has gained notoriety for pledging to clone the first human being.

PART 4 Clauses and Related Structures of Comparison

Setting the Context

Prereading Questions. Name some animals that are approximately the same size as human beings. Now name some physical advantages human beings have over these animals.

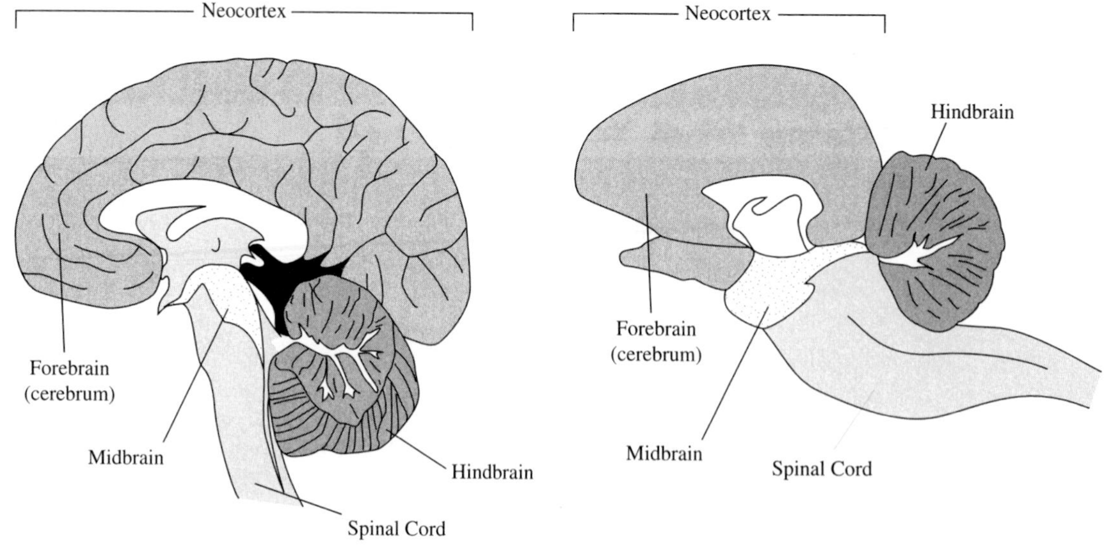

Man and Animals

Physically speaking, humans are rather unimpressive. We are not as strong as most other animals our size. We walk much more awkwardly, for example, than cats do. We cannot run as fast as dogs or deer can. In vision, hearing, and in the sense of smell, we are inferior to many other animals. When we think in evolutionary terms of the beautiful efficiency of fish for swimming or of birds for flying, we seem to be more clumsily and poorly designed than most creatures. In fact, we have come to dominate all other animals only because of one rather important specialization—our brain.

Discussing Ideas. Use your own words to explain the first sentence in the passage. In what way(s) are human beings superior to animals?

A. Comparative and Superlative Forms of Adjectives and Adverbs

The positive forms of adjectives and adverbs are used in expressions with *(not) as . . . as (as slow as, not as slowly as).* Comparative forms are used to compare two things. Superlative forms are used to discuss three or more things. *The* is normally used with superlative forms. Note that spelling rules for adding *-er* and *-est* are the same as for adding *-ed* (see Appendix 2).

	Positive	**Comparative**	**Superlative**
Add *-er* and *-est* to:			
One-Syllable Adjectives	nice	nicer	the nicest
	young	younger	the youngest
Adjectives and Adverbs That Have the Same Form	early	earlier	the earliest
	fast	faster	the fastest
	hard	harder	the hardest
	late	later	the latest
Add *-er* and *-est* OR Use *More, Less, the Most, the Least* with:			
Most Two-Syllable Adjectives	clever	cleverer	the cleverest
		more clever	the most clever
	funny	funnier	the funniest
		more funny	the most funny
	shallow	shallower	the shallowest
		more shallow	the most shallow
	simple	simpler	the simplest
		more simple	the most simple

Note: With words ending in *-y* and *-le*, the *-er* and *-est* forms are more common, although both forms may be used.

	Positive	Comparative	Superlative
Use *More, Less, the Most, the Least* with:			
Two-Syllable Adjectives That End in *-ed, -ful, -ing, -ish, -ous, -st,* and *-x*	worried	more worried	the most worried
	harmful	more harmful	the most harmful
	caring	more caring	the most caring
	selfish	more selfish	the most selfish
	joyous	more joyous	the most joyous
	robust	more robust	the most robust
	complex	more complex	the most complex
Longer Adjectives and Most *-ly* Adverbs	difficult	more difficult	the most difficult
	quickly	more quickly	the most quickly
	slowly	more slowly	the most slowly

Irregular Adjectives and Adverbs			
Adjectives	**Adverbs**	**Comparative**	**Superlative**
bad	badly	worse	the worst
good	—	better	the best
well	well	better	the best
far	far	farther	the farthest (distance)
		further	the furthest
little	little	less	the least
many	—	more	the most
much	much	more	the most

B. Clauses and Phrases Showing Comparison

Clauses of comparison can be formed with *than* or *as*. However, in speaking and sometimes in writing, the verb in the dependent clause is often changed to the corresponding auxiliary or omitted entirely. Compare:

> Susan runs fast, but Marina runs faster than Susan **runs.**
> Susan runs fast, but Marina runs faster than Susan **does.**
> Susan runs fast, but Marina runs faster.

In informal conversation, a subject pronoun is often replaced by an object pronoun, although it is grammatically incorrect. Compare:

> More formal: She runs as fast as **I.**
> She runs as fast as **I do.**
> Conversational: She runs as fast as **me.**

	Examples	Notes
To Introduce Clauses		
as . . . as	We cannot run **as fast as** many animals can.	Positive adjectives and adverbs are used with *as . . . as.*
the same . . . as	A lion cannot run **the same** distance **as** a cheetah can in the same time.	Nouns are used with *the same . . . as.*
more / less / *-er* . . . than	Cheetahs are **faster than** lions are. Lions run **more slowly than** cheetahs do.	Comparative adjectives and adverbs are used before clauses or phrases with *than.*
To Introduce Phrases		
as well as	Gorillas, **as well as** people, walk on their hind legs.	
both . . . and	**Both** chimpanzees **and** gorillas live in the jungle.	
similar to	**Similar to** chimpanzees, humans are omnivores.*	
Transitions		
similarly	Many birds have developed extraordinary eyesight. **Similarly,** the eyesight of humans has improved greatly through the ages.	
likewise	Lions are carnivores; **likewise,** cheetahs have a diet that consists mainly of meat.	

**omnivores* animals whose diet includes vegetables and meat

1 Give the affirmative (+) or negative (−) comparative and superlative of the following words.

Examples: (+) lazy *lazier, the laziest*
(−) bright *less bright, the least bright*

1. (+) tall
2. (+) stocky
3. (+) quickly
4. (−) interesting
5. (+) slowly

6. (+) bad
7. (+) good
8. (−) tired

2 Use the following model to make sentences from the words in Activity 1. Describe your friends, roommates, or classmates.

Examples: *Laura is lazier than Jane, but Nancy is the laziest person I have ever seen.*

Martha runs less than Susan, but Kathy runs the least of the three.

3 Fill in appropriate comparative or superlative forms of the adjectives and adverbs in parentheses.

Humans Versus Animals

In all animals—from the ______(1) (− developed) vertebrates, such as fish and reptiles, to humans—the brain is divided into three parts: the forebrain, the midbrain, and the hindbrain. The forebrain, or cerebrum, becomes ______(2) (+ developed) in ______(3) (+ high) animals until, in human beings, the cerebrum and its covering, the neocortex, dominate brain functions.

The neocortex plays an important role even in ______(4) (+ primitive) mammals. For example, although a horse's neocortex is ______(5) (+ small) and ______(6) (+ smooth) than that in ______(7) (+ high) mammals, it still oversees brain functioning.

In ______(8) (+ advanced) mammals, the neocortex becomes so much ______(9) (+ large) than the cerebrum that it is bent into folds or "convolutions". This folding makes possible the ______(10) (+ great) complexity of the brain of the primate—most notably that of humans.

4 Circle the correct answers. Then, add any appropriate punctuation and capital letters.

Example: Gorillas, ((as well as) / likewise) people, walk on their hind legs.

1. Gorillas walk on their hind legs (as well as / likewise) people stand upright on two legs.
2. Gorillas don't live to (the same age as / as old as) people.
3. Elephants can live past 60 (similarly / the same) dolphins survive six decades or more.

4. (Both Anne and Harry / Anne likewise Harry) are fascinated by various types of snakes.
5. At the zoo, Anne devotes most of her time to watching snakes (the same as / likewise) Harry can spend hours at the snake exhibit.
6. A worm isn't (as developed / more developed) as a crab.

5 Fill in the correct forms of the words on the left. Add any necessary words. Then try to answer the question.*

1. (fast) Lions can't run as *fast* as cheetahs. In fact, cheetahs run much ____________ than lions. Are cheetahs the ____________ animal on earth?
2. (far) Cheetahs can rarely run as ____________ as lions. In fact, lions can run a great deal ____________ than cheetahs. Do you know which predator can run the ____________?
3. (good) Humans can't see as ____________ as many birds. In fact, birds of prey have sight many times ____________ than people. Which bird, do you think, has the ____________ eyesight?
4. (tall) Elephants aren't as ____________ as giraffes. In fact, an adult giraffe is on average nine feet ____________ than a mature elephant. Is the giraffe the ____________ animal on earth?

6 Make at least three sets of sentences similar to those in Activity 5. You may write about animals, places, people, or things. Choose from the following list of adjectives or use some of your own: beautiful, striking, impressive, strong, healthy, careful, reckless, tiring, boring, enervating.

Example: *Houston isn't as beautiful as Austin. In fact, Austin is much more beautiful. Many people consider Austin to be the most beautiful city in Texas.*

7 **Error Analysis.** Each of the following sentences contains an error. Find the error and correct it.

Example: The cat that you have as a pet is, in some ways, similar ~~than~~ *to* a lion.

1. Humans are not more stronger than most other animals the same size.
2. We cannot run as quick as dogs or deer can.
3. We seem to be more clumsily than most creatures.
4. Horses are herbivores, likewise, cows eat only vegetation.
5. Many animals are less cleverer than chimpanzees.
6. Orangutans eat a mixed diet of seeds, nuts, fruit, and a little meat. Similarly, tigers are carnivores.
7. To some people, the coat of a leopard looks the same than the coat of a tiger.
8. Both sheep and deer provides meat to predators, including humans.

*Answers: 1. yes 2. the wolf 3. the eagle 4. The blue whale is more than four times taller (longer) than the giraffe.

Using What You've Learned

8 In pairs, use the following information comparing humans and various animals to write a true/false quiz for your classmates. Include at least ten statements with comparisons. Be sure to use *both and, as well as, more/er than, the most/est, the same . . . as, similarly,* and *likewise* at least once. When you have finished, exchange your quiz with another pair. Then, take the quiz without referring to the book. Finally, return the quiz to be graded.

Human Life Expectancies: Male and Female

Country	Male	Female	Country	Male	Female
Sweden	75	81	Uruguay	67	74
Japan	75	80	Nicaragua	67	74
Soviet Union	73	78	Cambodia	42	45
United States	72	76	Angola	41	43

Size: Mammals

blue whale	90 feet long	rhinoceros	6 1/2 feet at shoulder
giraffe	19 feet tall (full length)	cow	5 feet at shoulder
African elephant	10 1/2 feet at shoulder	cat	9 inches at shoulder
brown bear	8 feet when standing erect	shrew	1.7 inches long
camel	7 feet to top of humps		

Life Expectancies: Animals

mayfly	1 day	owl	24 years
mouse	1 year	lion	25 years
trout	5–10 years	horse	30 years
sheep	10–15 years	ostrich	50 years
squirrel	11 years	African elephant	60 years
rabbit	12 years	dolphin	65 years
cat	13–17 years	tortoise	100 years

Examples: (T) F An elephant lives much longer than a lion.

T (F) Lions, as well as rabbits, live over 20 years.

Web Note

Check the Guinness Book for all kinds of records at www.guinnessworldrecords.com/home.asp.

PART 5 Clauses of Result

Setting the Context

Prereading Questions. What percentage of the things that you saw, heard, felt, tasted, or smelled yesterday do you remember today? Why do you think the brain does not remember most of these things?

It's Important to Forget

For decades, scientists have been interested in how the brain stores and recalls memories. In fact, this has proved such an interesting topic that they have by and large ignored an area of equal importance—how the brain forgets.

Through the five senses, the brain receives the impressions from *everything* we see, hear, touch, taste, and smell. This amounts to so much information that it is impossible for the brain to commit more than a small percentage to permanent memory. If the brain held on to everything that it received, it would have so many memories that it would soon run out of room and could accept no more. As a result, the brain filters out or forgets millions of pieces of information every minute. This type of forgetting is so important that without it, the effcient use of memory would be impossible.

Discussing Ideas. When you consciously decide to remember something, are you always successful? Can you forget something if you want to?

A. Adverb Clauses of Result

Clauses with *so* or *such . . . that* may be used with adjectives, adverbs, or nouns to show the result or effect of a situation. In informal English, *that* is sometimes omitted.

	Examples	**Notes**
so . . . that	The idea was **so** complicated **that** no one could understand it.	Adjectives and adverbs are used with *so . . . that.*
so much . . . that	The speaker gave **so much** information **that** no one could understand the talk easily.	Noncount nouns are used with *so much . . . that.*
so many . . . that	He talked about **so many** ideas **that** we became confused.	Plural count nouns are used with *so many . . . that.*
such . . . that	He was **such** a poor speaker **that** we fell asleep. They were **such** good speakers **that** they influenced all of us. The speakers had **such** extensive knowledge **that** we were all impressed.	*Such . . . that* can be used with *a*(*n*) + adjective + singular count noun *or* adjective + plural noun *or* adjective + noncount noun.

Note: In conversational English, *so, such,* and *so many/much* are commonly used in simple (one-clause) sentences: *It's so hot today.* However, in formal English, these conjunctions are used in complex sentences with two or more clauses: *It's so hot today that I'm not going to go outside.*

1 **Review.** Complete the following passages by adding *much* or *many.*

1. The brain receives so ______ perceptions that it cannot begin to store all of them in the memory. Imagine yourself, for example, at a crowded party. There is so ______ input—so ______ colors, odors, and tastes, so ______ noise, so ______ shapes and sizes—that it must be selective. While you are enjoying yourself, your brain is hard at work deciding what you will or will not remember.
2. All memory experts agree that you will remember ______ more if you concentrate and practice. If you pay close attention and repeat a piece of information several times, you will remember ______ more details. In fact, ______ people have developed systems for repeating details.
3. We constantly receive ______ more information than we can remember, and we can remember some things ______ more easily than others. Memories are triggered by ______ things, including sight, sound, smell, and taste. However, there are only two basic types of memory: short-term memory and long-term memory.
4. ______ scientists believe that short-term memory, lasting only one-half hour or so, is only an electrical activity. Long-term memory, however, seems to be ______ more complicated. It involves ______ electrical and chemical processes, and it appears to actually change the brain physically.

5. Currently, _______ research is being conducted on the process of long-term storage of memories. _______ of these experiments are being directed toward dreams and their role in the process. Some scientists suggest that dreams are a review of _______ of the day's activities to determine which ones are important enough to remember.

2 Complete each sentence by using *so, such,* or *such a(n)* and adding an ending.

Example: I was ___so___ cold ___that I couldn't sleep___.

It was ___such a___ cold day ___that I couldn't get my car started___.

1. The weather was _________ beautiful. . . .

   It was _________ beautiful weather. . . .
2. They sang _________ wonderfully. . . .

   They have _________ wonderful voices. . . .
3. It was _________ loud noise. . . .

   The noise was _________ loud. . . .
4. The article was _________ interesting. . . .

   It was _________ interesting article. . . .
5. She got _________ bad sunburn. . . .

   She got _________ badly sunburned. . . .
6. The race was _________ exciting. . . .

   It was _________ exciting race. . . .

3 Complete the following on a separate piece of paper. Use *so, so much/many, such,* or *such a(n)* and add an ending to each sentence.

Example: Fresh-baked bread has ___such a___ wonderful smell that ___it makes my month water___. I put ___so much___ butter on it that ___it's very fattening___. It tastes ___so___ good that ___I can eat a whole loaf___.

A new city or country has ___________ (1) new sights, sounds, tastes, and smells that. . . . When I first arrived here, I had ___________ (2) difficult time adjusting that. . . . The people were ___________ (3) (adjective) that. . . . The food was ___________ (4) (adjective) that. . . . And there was ___________ (5) noise that. . . . The neighbors had

__________ violent arguments last night that. . . . Their voices were __________
6 7
(adjective) that. . . . They seem to have __________ problems that. . . . They are
8
both __________ aggressive people that. . . .
9

When I was younger, I used to have __________ nightmares that. . . . Some of
10
them were __________ vivid that. . . . In fact, one was __________ realistic night-
11 12
mare that. . . .

4 **Review.** In pairs or in small groups, combine the following ten sentences. Use a variety of connecting words, phrases, or transitions. These may include *that, which, when, so that, in order to, because, however, more than,* and so on. Many combinations are possible, but be prepared to discuss differences in meaning and/or focus as you try different possibilities. Omit unnecessary words.

1. Psychoanalysis involves remembering dreams. Psychoanalysis involves analyzing dreams. Psychoanalysis is a type of therapy. Psychoanalysis was developed by Sigmund Freud.
2. Freudian analysts use dreams. These analysts want to unlock the secrets of their patients' minds.
3. According to psychoanalysts, our dreams represent ideas. Our dreams represent emotions. We are trying to suppress these ideas or emotions.
4. We suppress these ideas. We suppress these emotions. Then we cannot resolve conflicts. Ideas or emotions create conflicts.

5. Many current brain researchers disagree with psychoanalysis. These researchers believe dreams have a different purpose.
6. According to them, the brain collects too much information. The brain cannot store all of this information.
7. The brain may use dreaming. In this way, it can forget incorrect information. It can forget useless information.
8. Attempting to remember dreams may not be helpful. Attempting to remember dreams may interfere with the brain's housecleaning.
9. Brain researchers and psychoanalysts do not agree. Both are attempting to unlock secrets. Our minds hold these secrets.
10. Both groups continue to search for answers. One day we may understand the mysteries of the mind.

5 **Error Analysis.** The following sentences all have one or more errors in connecting words or comparisons. Find the errors and try to correct each sentence in at least two different ways.

Example: In 1778, Franz Anton Mesmer went to Paris so that he demonstrated animal magnetism, better known today as hypnotism.

Correction: *In 1778, Franz Anton Mesmer went to Paris so that he could demonstrate animal magnetism, better known today as hypnotism.*

or

In 1778, Franz Anton Mesmer went to Paris to demonstrate animal magnetism, better known today as hypnotism.

1. Despite he had been unknown in the French capital, Mesmer soon became a celebrity.
2. Thousands flocked to his salon in order that be cured of every illness imaginable.
3. In fact, many patients came for help so that Mesmer had to turn large numbers of them away.
4. Mesmer's treatment gained popularity that crowds gathered outside his salon demanding treatment.
5. At one point, the crowds became such an uncontrollable that he devised a special treatment.
6. Mesmer "magnetized" a tree and had these people hang from ropes in order cure them.
7. However, Dr. Mesmer developed a large group of supporters, others were more skepticaler of the doctor and his treatments.
8. In particular, government officials in Paris were so unimpressed by animal magnetism. In spite Mesmer's loyal followers, a French Royal Commission declared animal magnetism dangerous.
9. This was so important judgment that Mesmer was forced to leave Paris in disgrace.
10. Mesmer was discredited. Therefore, hypnotism eventually became a respected treatment.*

---

*Today, hypnotism is used in fields such as psychiatry, medicine, sports, and entertainment. As for Dr. Mesmer, he has become immortalized in language. The verb *mesmerize* and its derivatives are found in English, French, and several other European languages.

Using What You've Learned

6 In groups of two or more, discuss the meanings of the following adjectives. Then try to use as many of them as possible in a two-minute conversation. You may want to discuss the weather, your apartment, a place near your home, various types of food, and so forth. Use the example as a model.

Example: cold

It's so cold today that there is ice on the road.

or

We're having such cold weather that I hate to go outside.

or

We've had so much cold weather lately that my tan has totally faded.

or

We've had so many cold days that the river may freeze.

soft	humid	foggy	hot	exhilarating
slippery	rough	tart	dreary	pungent
harsh	bitter	fragrant	acrid	nauseating
tense	painful	shrill	bumpy	frightening
sweet	repulsive	bright	ice	salty

Video Activities: Social Phobia

Before You Watch. Answer these questions in small groups.

1. A phobia is ___________.
   a. a need   b. a fear   c. an idea
2. What kinds of phobias do you know of?

Watch. Answer these questions in small groups.

1. What kind of phobia does Katherine Whizmore suffer from? ___________
2. Circle the things that people with this disorder believe.
   a. People are judging them all of the time.
   b. People want to physically hurt them.
   c. People are unfair to them.
3. Which kinds of treatments help these people?
   a. education about their illness
   b. antidepressant drugs and behavioral therapy
   c. surgery

Watch Again. Choose the correct answers.

1. By the age of 20, Katherine Whizmore was afraid to ___________.
   a. go to work   b. cross the street   c. go shopping alone

2. How many Americans suffer from this disease?
   a. 100 million b. 1 million c. 10 million
3. This disease usually begins in ______________.
   a. college b. high school c. junior high school
4. *Panicked* means ______________.
   a. confident b. very frightened c. sick
5. *Impaired* means ______________.
   a. afraid b. extraordinary c. injured
6. *Scrutiny* means ______________.
   a. correction b. inspection c. destruction
7. *Harshly* means ______________.
   a. fairly b. kindly c. cruelly
8. *Struggle* means to ______________.
   a. fight b. give up c. win

After You Watch. Rewrite the following sentences with the transition word or phrase in parentheses.

1. Even though she struggled for many years, Katherine Whizmore only recently overcame her phobia. (despite)
2. People with phobias usually understand that their fears are groundless; even so it is very difficult for them to defeat them. (nevertheless)
3. Despite the fact that millions of Americans suffer from social phobia, many doctors do not understand this disease. (in spite of)
4. Hundreds of millions of dollars are spent every year on research into physical illnesses whereas relatively little is spent on mental illnesses. (in contrast)

Focus on Testing

Adverb Clauses and Related Structures

Problem areas with adverb clauses often appear on standardized English proficiency exams. Check your understanding of these structures by completing the sample items that follow.

Remember that . . .

- Connecting words must link ideas grammatically and logically.
- Concession and opposition express different types of contrast.
- *So that* indicates purpose while *so* shows result.
- Modal verbs generally appear in clauses with *so that* or *in order that*.

Part 1. Circle the best completion for the following.

Example: She was able to sleep ______________ the noise.

a. although
b. even though
(c.) in spite of
d. however

1. Rex was exhausted and unsettled, ______________.
   a. he insisted on starting a new project
   b. he slept for the remainder of the day
   c. but he insisted on starting a new project
   d. and wanted to go to bed
2. Mike seemed optimistic and well-rested even though ______________.
   a. he was in the midst of an extended vacation
   b. he had been struggling with a tremendous task
   c. he had just returned from a month of vacation in Hawaii
   d. he appeared depressed and exhausted
3. Despite ______________, we decided against canceling the match.
   a. the impending bad weather
   b. the beautiful weather
   c. the fact that the weather was supposed to be acceptable
   d. of the bad weather which was forecast
4. Los Angeles is an enormous city. In contrast, ______________.
   a. it has intractable traffic problems
   b. Monterey is rather small
   c. San Francisco
   d. I adore large cities

Part 2. Each sentence has one error. Circle the letter below the word(s) containing the error.

Example: They were (A) such (B) good speakers so (C, circled) they influenced all of us. (D)

1. Jane tends to dominate (A) at all meetings. On the contrary (B), George prefers (C) to let others be (D) in charge.
2. Last night Jack stayed out very late and didn't get much (A) sleep, so (B) that (C) he feels awful (D) today.
3. The keynote (A) speaker at the campaign (B) luncheon was such (C) good that (D) almost the entire audience pledged to support him.
4. Robert has finally reached the (A) conclusion that he had better (B) give up his position in order that he returns (C) to school to earn a (D) Ph.D.

Chapter 7

Working

IN THIS CHAPTER

Part 1 Clauses with *That;* Reported Speech

Part 2 Clauses with Embedded Questions

Part 3 Statements and Requests of Urgency

Part 4 Clauses as Subjects of Sentences

Part 5 Reduction of Noun Clauses to Infinitive Phrases

Introduction

In this chapter, you will study ways of replacing words and phrases with noun clauses. As you study the chapter, notice any changes in emphasis when noun clauses are used. Also, pay attention to changes in verb tenses and position in noun clauses.

The following passage introduces the chapter theme "Working" and raises some topics and issues you will cover in the chapter.

The U.S. Workforce

The U.S. Census gathers much more information than simply the number of people living in the United States. The census tells us about population growth, life expectancy, housing, crime, eating and drinking habits, immigration and migration, and ethnic backgrounds of Americans. Some of the most interesting statistics, however, concern the work habits of Americans. The census gathers detailed information on who is or isn't working, what kinds of jobs people hold, where they find the jobs, how much money they make, how they spend their earnings, how often they change jobs, how many people are injured on the job, and when men and women retire.

What recent census information has shown is that a definite shift in employment is occurring. America is moving from goods-producing industries to service-sector jobs. That Americans are better educated, healthier, and more mature by the time they enter the labor force is also significant. What the statistics do not show, unfortunately, is a significant narrowing in the gap between the earnings of men and women or between the opportunities available for whites and for minorities. Even more troubling, the gap between rich and poor is widening.

Discussing Ideas. Do you think the information gathered from the census is important? What do you think about the changes shown by recent census information? Why do you think some things are changing? Why do you think some things aren't changing?

PART 1 Clauses with *That*; Reported Speech

Setting the Context

Prereading Questions. In the United States, which occupations are growing the fastest? Which are declining?

The Changing U.S. Job Market

Which fields offer the best opportunities for a job? This is a question millions of people in the United States ask daily and one of particular relevance given the dramatic change the economy is undergoing.

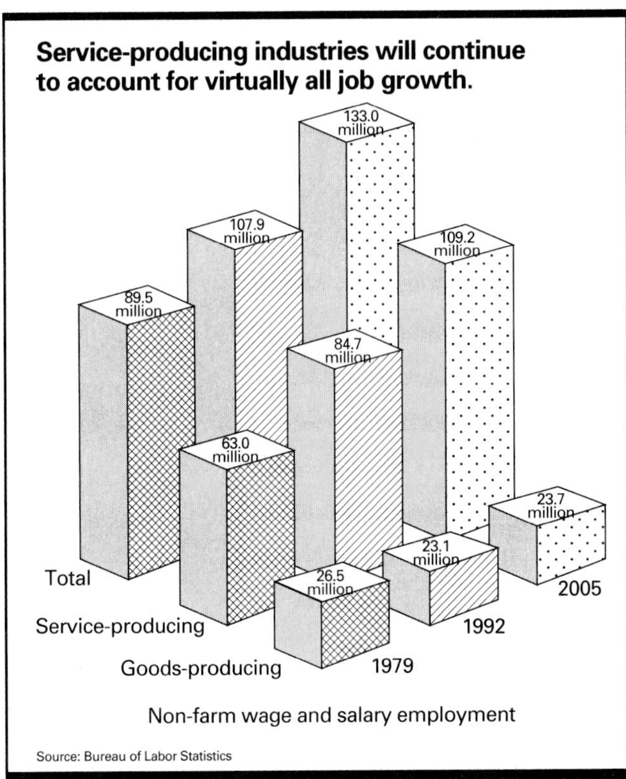

According to a report released by the Bureau of Labor Statistics (BLS), the transformation from a manufacturing to a service-based economy that began some 30 years ago is continuing at a rapid pace. The report indicated that the fastest-growing occupations were connected to areas such as computer systems support, medicine, and finances and that these trends would continue at least until 2008. It also noted that the educational level of workers had risen dramatically and speculated that those without a college education would find it increasingly difficult to find well-paying jobs.

Finally, the report showed that a population migration was taking place within the United States, with the West and the South experiencing huge population gains. According to the BLS, these two regions already have over 50 percent of the population and this will rise in the next ten years. Not surprisingly, job opportunities will increase in the West and the South but generally decline elsewhere in the country.

Discussing Ideas. How many service industries can you list? How many manufacturing industries can you list? What trend has been occurring in the U.S. economy during the past 30 years? Is this likely to stop soon?

A. Introduction to Noun Clauses

A noun clause functions as a noun in a sentence. Noun clauses may be used as subjects, objects of verbs or prepositions, and complements.

	Examples	Notes
Subject	**That the job market is changing** is obvious.	Noun clauses are often used after these verbs: *say, tell, ask, add, believe, conclude, estimate, exclaim, explain, find, hope, illustrate, indicate, mention, note, remark, show, think,* and *wish.*
Complement	A major concern is **how fast these changes are taking place.**	
Object of Preposition	We are concerned about **how fast these changes are taking place.**	
Object of Verb	Statistics show **(that) white-collar jobs are increasing.**	

Note: The verbs *say* and *tell* are often confusing. In general, *tell* is used when a person is referred to. Compare: *He told me he was leaving. He said he was leaving.* Not: **He said me he was leaving.*

1 Using the accompanying charts of changes in employment in the United States, form at least six sentences with noun clauses. Begin your sentences with *This chart shows* (*says, tells us, indicates, illustrates*, etc.). In your sentences, use adverbs (*slightly, moderately, substantially, tremendously,* etc.) or comparatives and superlatives to indicate the extent of the increase or decrease in jobs.

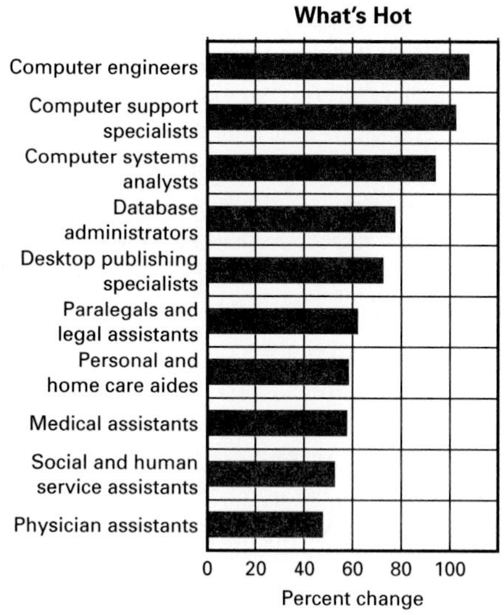

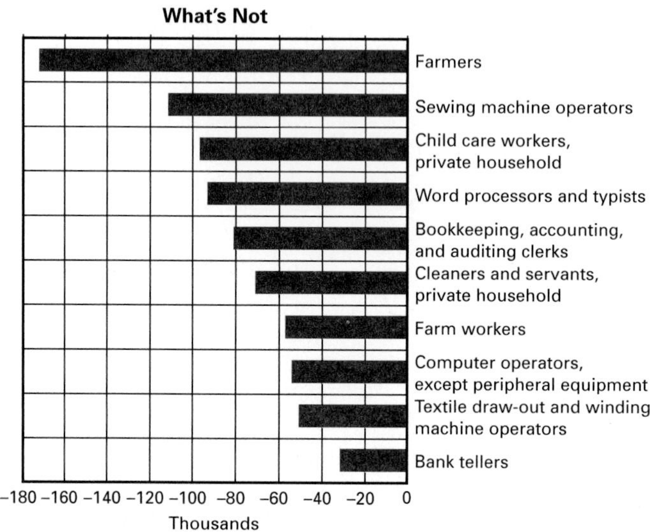

Example: farmers

This chart shows (indicates, tells us) that the number of farmers will decline by 180,000.

B. Quotations Versus Reported Speech

Quotations are the exact words that a person has used to state something. A quotation appears within quotation marks, and a comma normally precedes or follows it.

> Someone once said, "Work is what you do until you go home at night."

Reported speech tells the ideas, but not necessarily the exact words, of the original speaker. Reported speech does not normally require commas or quotation marks.

> Someone once said that work is (was) what we all do (did) until we go (went) home at night.

C. Changes in Verb Tense with Reported Speech

In reported speech, when the verb in the main clause (*Susan said,* etc.) is in the past, the verb in the noun clause is often shifted to one of the past tenses. In some cases, the shifts can be optional, especially if the information is still true at the moment of speaking. However, the changes must be consistent. The use of *that* is also optional in these sentences.

Quotations	Reported Speech
"Chris is at work."	Susan said that Chris **was** at work.
"Chris is finishing lunch."	She mentioned that Chris **was finishing** lunch.
"He is going to stay until he finishes."	She added he **was going to stay** until he **finished.**
"Chris hasn't finished yet."	Susan told me that Chris **hadn't finished** yet.
"He was working all day."	She remarked that he **had been working** all day.
"He came home very late."	She said that he **had come** home very late.

Note: When the noun clause gives "timeless" factual information, either present or past forms can be used: *Susan said that Chris always works (worked) on Saturdays.* The present is generally used when scientific or technical information is given: *The professor stated that water freezes at 32 degrees Fahrenheit.*

Culture Note

The last ten years has seen amazing growth in computer-related business in the United States. Software manufacturers say that they can not find enough qualified programmers even though they offer very high salaries. As a result, the government is allowing thousands more foreign programmers into the country each year.

D. Changes in Modal Auxiliaries with Reported Speech

In reported speech, the modal auxiliaries *can, may, must* (referring to need), and *will* also shift to past forms. When *must* expresses probability, it does not change. *Could, might, ought to, should, would,* and all perfect modals do not change.

Quotations with Modal Auxiliaries	Reported Speech
"Ann can help Chris."	Susan said that Ann **could help** Chris.
"John may help, too."	She added John **might help,** too.
"We all must help Chris."	She repeated that we all **had to help** Chris.
"Jami will also help."	She mentioned Jami **would** also **help.**

2 The Bureau of Labor Statistics compiles numerous statistics on jobs in the United States. The following information comes from a recent study. Change the information from direct statements to reported speech, making necessary changes in tenses. Begin with *This study showed* (*found, noted,* and so forth).

Example: "White-collar jobs are increasing faster than blue-collar occupations."
This study showed that white-collar jobs were increasing faster than blue-collar jobs.

1. "The trend will continue indefinitely."
2. "Computer-related jobs are becoming more and more popular."
3. "The number of teaching jobs has begun to increase."
4. "Many bank tellers have lost their jobs."
5. "Many clerical workers may be replaced by new office machines."
6. "Some fields of medicine are already overstaffed."
7. "The job market in other areas of medicine, such as nursing and physical therapy, should grow."
8. "A higher percentage of older people are going to work."
9. "A good education has become more important in finding a well-paying job."
10. "Most areas of computer work continue to offer opportunities."

Web Note

For more information on trends in employment, consult the U.S. Bureau of Labor Statistics at http://stats.bls.gov/.

E. Changes in Pronouns, Adjectives, and Adverbials with Reported Speech

Pronouns, time and place expressions, and certain verbs are often changed in reported speech. The changes are made to show the correct relationship between the original information and the reported information. All of these changes must be made consistently.

Quotations	Reported Speech
"I would like you to help us."	Susan said that **she** would like **me** to help **them.**
"These pages need to be corrected."	She said that **those** pages needed to be corrected.
"We need the work now."	She said that they needed the work **then.**
"We will need other pages tomorrow."	She added that they would need the other pages **the following day.**
"You should bring them here when you come to work."	She said that I should **take** them **there** when I **went** to work.

F. Changing Commands to Reported Speech

Commands are often changed into noun clauses in reported speech. To do this, an appropriate subject and a modal verb must be added to the command. *Should* is often used in reported commands, but *must, need to, have to,* and *ought to* can also be added, depending on the strength of the command.

Commands	Reported Speech
"Finish your report by 10:00."	My manager told me that I **should finish** my report by 10:00.
"Get it to me by 10:05."	He said that I **had to give** it to him by 10:05.

Note: Commands can also be reduced to infinitive phrases. This is discussed in detail in Part 5.

3 Part of a boss's job is to tell new employees what they have to do. Imagine that you are beginning a job. Your new boss told you many of the following things. Change the commands to reported speech. Use *said* or *told* and a variety of modals in your new sentences.

Example: Be on time every day.
My boss told me that I had to be on time every day.

1. Be at your desk by 9:00.
2. Do not take more than 15 minutes for your breaks.
3. Leave for lunch at the scheduled time.
4. Do not make personal phone calls while you are working.
5. Call as early as possible if you are sick.
6. Schedule your vacations as far in advance as possible.

4 Like work, school is often a world of rules and regulations. Teachers often tell students what they have to, should, shouldn't, must not, or can do. Make at least six sentences beginning with *Teachers tell students (us) that . . .* or *Teachers say that . . .*

Example: *Teachers say that we must not chew gum in class.*

5 Change the following quotations to reported speech. Pay close attention to changes in verb tenses and in pronouns. Remember to add a reporting clause (*He said . . . , She added . . .*) before each sentence.

Example: *Molly told me that she was a computer programmer around San Francisco but had grown up in India. She said that she had helped design several new Websites. She added that . . .*

1. "I'm a computer programmer around San Francisco. I grew up in India. I helped design several new Websites. There's a lot of pressure in this type of work. Shopping and playing golf seem to relieve some of the tension."

2. "I've been moving furniture for five years. Yesterday we made a local delivery. Tonight we'll be working on a job about 20 miles from here. Next week I might be halfway across the country. I don't think I could ever sit at a desk all day."

3. "I started delivering newspapers when I was seven. The work was hard and I didn't make very much money. Now I work in a coal mine, and my wife works, too. We still don't make enough money. The more things change, the more they stay the same."

4. "I'm a tennis instructor, and I love my job. I can really help people play better when they listen to me. I may do something else in a few years. Maybe I should join an organization and do some volunteer work."

Using What You've Learned

6 In pairs, take turns asking each other the following questions and add some of your own. Then report briefly to the class on the information your partner gave you. Begin each sentence of your report with *X said . . . , X told me . . . , X remarked . . . , X mentioned . . .*, etc.

1. Have you ever had a job?
2. If so, what kinds of jobs have you had? What were your duties, your hours, and so forth?
3. Did you enjoy your work?
4. What was the most unusual thing that ever happened to you while you were working?
5. If you haven't worked, what jobs would you be interested in trying?
6. Are you preparing for a career now? What will your duties be in that type of job?

7 Interview a friend, roommate, or someone in your community who is working full time. Ask them what they do, what their job is like, and what they like and dislike about it. Then report the information to the class.

PART 2 Clauses with Embedded Questions

Setting the Context

Prereading Questions. Have you ever interviewed for a job? What types of questions did the interviewer ask you?

Job Interviewing

Susan: Hi, Ellen. How was the job interview? How did it go?

Ellen: I think that it went well, but I'm not sure whether I've got the job. They're still interviewing a few more candidates. There are so many people looking for jobs these days.

Susan: Well, tell me about the interview. Who did you talk to? What kinds of questions did they ask?

Ellen: I talked with Mrs. Harris. Of course, she asked me how much experience I'd had and why I wanted to work there. I told her about my work in Boston and Toronto. Then she wanted to know why I was quitting my job in Toronto.

Susan: What did you tell her?

Ellen: I didn't know what to say. I finally said that I was tired of living in a city and that I'd like to move to a smaller town. I couldn't tell her what had really happened. She would never hire me then!

Discussing Ideas. Which of the following questions seems more polite? Why?

A. Why are you quitting your job in Toronto?

B. I'd like to know why you are quitting your job in Toronto.

Why do you think that Ellen is quitting her job? Give at least three possibilities.

A. Clauses with Embedded Questions

Information questions may be changed to noun clauses. Question words such as *when, why, what,* and *who(m)* are used to introduce these embedded questions. When the question is changed to a noun clause, the subject must come *before* the verb, as it does in statements.

Information Questions	Noun Clauses with Question Words
When will you start your new job?	I wanted to know **when** I would start my new job.
How much will you make?	I'm not sure **how much** I'll make.
Who is going to be your supervisor?	Could you tell me **who** is going to be my supervisor?
Why did you leave your last job?	She asked me **why** I had left my last job.

1 The following are typical questions asked on a job application or in a job interview. Change them from direct questions to noun clauses with question words. Use the examples as models.

Examples: application / What is your name?

On an application, you will be asked what your name is.

interview / Why will you be an asset to the company?

During an interview, you may (might, could) be asked why you will be an asset to the company.

1. application / Where did you go to school?
2. application / Where do you live?

3. application / What work experience do you have?
4. application / Why do you want to work here?
5. interview / What are your strengths and weaknesses?
6. interview / Why should we hire you?
7. interview / How would you describe yourself? What kind of a person are you?
8. interview / How much money do you hope to earn?

B. Clauses with If *and* Whether

Yes/no questions may be changed to noun clauses by using *if* or *whether (or not)* to introduce them. *Whether* is preferred in formal English. It also implies choice among alternatives rather than a strict yes/no decision. Remember that the subject must come *before* the verb in the noun clause.

Yes/No Questions	Noun Clauses with *If, Whether*
Do you have any job openings?	I asked **if** they had any job openings.
Should I talk to the manager?	I would like to know **whether (or not)** I should talk to the manager.
Is the manager here now?	Do you know **if** the manager is here now?

2 Jobs are not the only situations that require interviews. Colleges and universities often use interviews to help in admissions and placement, especially with non-native English speakers. The following list includes some typical questions used in academic interviews. Change them from direct questions to noun clauses with *if* or *whether*. Use the example as a model.

Example: Are you applying to several schools?
I will (may, might) be asked if (whether) I am applying to several schools.

1. Do you have your high school (or college) transcripts?
2. Do you have letters of recommendation?
3. Is your family supporting you? Do you have a scholarship? Will you need financial aid?
4. Have you taken the TOEFL test? Did you find certain sections more difficult than others?
5. Did you take the admissions test (SAT, ACT, GRE, etc.)? Have you received your scores?
6. Are you planning to live with your parents? Have you ever lived on your own before?

3 The following are typical questions asked during job interviews in specific careers. Imagine that you had interviewed for one of these jobs. Tell about the questions you were asked. Change the direct questions to indirect questions. Use the question words to begin your clauses or add *if* or *whether* when necessary. Pay close attention to shifts in verb tenses in the noun clauses.

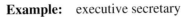

Example: executive secretary
How fast do you type?
The interviewer asked (wanted to know, inquired about) how fast I typed and whether I could. . . . Then she wanted to know. . . .

1. executive secretary
   a. Can you use a fax machine?
   b. What other office machines do you know how to use?
   c. Which office software are you familiar with?
   d. Are you comfortable with the Internet?

2. truck driver
   a. Do you have a license for driving trucks?
   b. Have you ever hauled a load of over ten tons?
   c. Do you have a good driving record?
   d. Where did you last work?

3. graphic artist
   a. Who have you worked for?
   b. Which design software programs have you used?
   c. Have you had any experience with digital imaging?
   d. Do you have a portfolio?

4. restaurant manager
   a. How many people have you supervised?
   b. What kinds of restaurants have you worked in?
   c. How many meals did the restaurant serve per day?
   d. What hours was the restaurant open?

4 After you return to your office from lunch, your assistant hands you a message from Janet. You know several women named Janet. In pairs, use the following cues to ask and answer questions about this message.

Examples: what / last name
A. Did she tell you what her last name was?
B. Sorry, she didn't tell me.

where / call her

A. Did she say where I could call her?

B. No, she didn't leave her number.

1. what / want
2. if (whether) / call back
3. when / call back
4. how long / be in town
5. where / call from
6. if (whether) / be important
7. how / get my number
8. if (whether) / be free tomorrow

DATE 9/27 HOUR 1:00

TO MARY

WHILE YOU WERE OUT

M JANET

OF

PHONE AREA CODE PHONE NUMBER

TELEPHONED		RETURNED CALL		LEFT PACKAGE	
PLEASE CALL		WAS IN		PLEASE SEE ME	
WILL CALL AGAIN	✓	WILL RETURN		IMPORTANT	

MESSAGE WANTS TO SEE YOU

SIGNED

Form 529 • ASSOCIATED LOOSE LEAF CO. • 873-8700

5 A coworker has just told you that your boss is angry and wants to see you immediately. With a partner, complete the following list of questions to ask the coworker. Then find a different partner. Your second partner will play the part of coworker.

Example: *Did she say who she was angry with?*
Did she mention whether I was involved?

1. Did she tell you why ____________________
2. Do you know whether ____________________
3. I need to know when ____________________
4. Did she mention where ____________________
5. ____________________
6. ____________________

6 Do you plan to work after you have finished your studies? Will you be looking for a job in the near future? What are some of your concerns? Complete the following sentences in your own words, telling about your hopes, fears, and goals. Use a question word (*how much, how often, where, when, why, if, whether,* etc.) to begin each clause that you add.

Example: Everything depends on *when I finish school.*

1. I'm concerned about. . . .
2. I'm interested in. . . .
3. I don't really care about. . . .
4. I'm (not) worried about. . . .
5. I've been thinking about. . . .
6. So far, I haven't paid attention to. . . .
7. Sometimes I'm nervous about. . . .
8. Right now I'm tired of. . . .

Using What You've Learned

7 Whether you have worked or not, most of you have probably been interviewed at one time or another. Sharpen your skills by role-playing interviews for various jobs. No doubt few of you will have tried these jobs, so be sure to use your imagination as you ask and answer job-related questions. Interview for some of these jobs or add your own.

Jobs

lead singer in a rock group	brain surgeon	ESL teacher
jet pilot	beautician	smuggler
florist	genetic engineer	bartender
auto mechanic	ballet dancer	computer hacker

Be sure to ask for the following information.

Interviewers

1. personal data: name, address, and so forth
2. previous work experience in general and previous experience in this area
3. reasons for leaving last job
4. hopes, plans, career goals

Interviewees

1. hours and salary
2. vacation time
3. benefits
4. working conditions
5. job security

Useful Expressions

I would like to know (if, whether, when, how much, etc.). . . .
Could (Would) you explain (describe, tell me, etc.) . . . ?
Would you mind explaining (telling me, etc.) . . . ?
It's important for me to know when (how, how often, etc.). . . .

When you are finished, report to the class about which job your partner was seeking, whether you hired him or her, and why or why not.

PART 3 Statements and Requests of Urgency

Setting the Context

Prereading Questions. When the economy is growing, does everyone benefit?

Equality for All?

In many ways, the U.S. economy is the envy of the world. Now, after entering the new millennium, the economy is riding the wave of a ten-year expansion with the average income for workers at a record high and unemployment at a 30-year low. However, all the news is not good. One very troubling aspect of the "miracle economy" is the difference in income between rich and poor. In the last 20 years, the money made by wealthier Americans has increased dramatically. At the same time, when adjusted for inflation, the income of the poorest 20 percent has actually dropped by almost 10 percent.

Some economists say that differences in income levels are an essential part of the capitalist economic system. They believe that higher incomes are the reward of harder work and more important contributions to the economy. Other experts argue that such a huge disparity in wealth is harmful to society. They say that it undermines the ideas of opportunity and equality that the nation was built upon and thus it leads to increases in violence and crime. In their opinion, it is essential that the government close the income gap between rich and poor. For example, they insist that the minimum wage* be increased significantly and that new educational opportunities be given to those in greatest need.

Discussing Ideas. What reasons can you give for the gap in income in a wealthy nation such as the United States? What do you think should be done to close this gap between the rich and the poor?

A. Statements of Urgency with That

In formal English, the subjunctive mood is used in clauses with *that* following adjectives of urgency.

Adjectives	Examples	Notes
advisable best crucial desirable essential imperative important necessary urgent vital	It is **essential** that he **be** on time. It is **important** that you not **arrive** late. It was **urgent** that they **discuss** the matter. It is **vital** that she **make** a decision soon.	This subjunctive form is the same as the simple form of the verb (*be, go, have,* etc.). *Not* comes before the verb in the negative. These statements are similar to commands but less direct and thus "softer." Compare: *Be on time! It's crucial that you be on time.*

Note: Modal verbs are not used in the noun clause with this type of construction.
Correct: It was desirable that they *talk*.
Incorrect: *It was desirable that they *should talk*.

**minimum wage* the legal minimum amount of money a person can be paid per hour

1 Rephrase these sentences to begin with *It is important* (*essential, urgent,* etc.). Make any other necessary changes.

In a recent speech, an activist for economic change demanded the following:

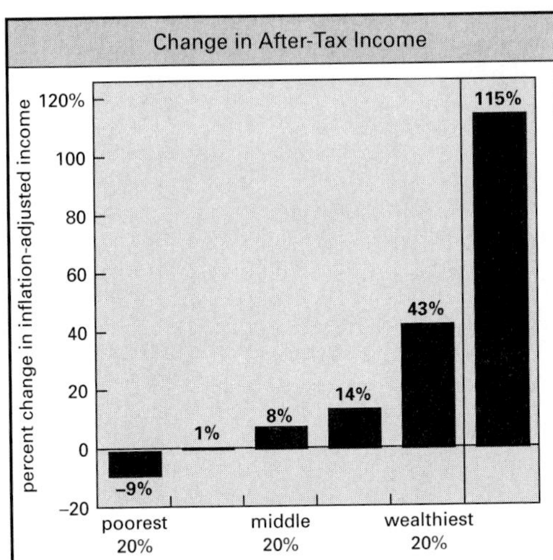

An analysis by the Center on Budget and Policy Priorities (CBPP), a research group that studies government policies affecting the poor, found that in the past two decades, the wealthiest Americans' incomes have skyrocketed, while the poorest have seen a decline in inflation-adjusted income.

Example: People must be made aware of employment issues.

It is essential that people be made aware of employment issues.

1. The gap between rich and poor must be closed.
2. Sex or race must not be used to judge workers.
3. Employers must not discriminate against women or minorities.
4. Every qualified person must have equal opportunity for employment.
5. Every person in the country must have access to a quality education.
6. The company should try to hire people from all parts of the population.
7. There should be more minorities in management positions.
8. There must be more economic development in poorer areas.

Culture Note

Some economists say that when the rich are getting richer, this is an indication of a good economy and that it is good for everyone. They say that a rising tide lifts all boats. While there may be some truth to this argument, the tide obviously lifts some boats much higher than others. In 1999, the wealthiest 20 percent in the United States received over 50 percent of the income. The poorest 20 percent received only 4.2 percent of the income.

B. Urgent Requests with That

The subjunctive mood is also used in noun clauses with *that,* which follow certain verbs of request. This form of request is formal and polite yet fairly strong.

Verbs	Examples	Notes
advise ask command require urge demand insist desire propose recommend request suggest	We **asked** that the manager **attend** the meeting. We were going to **request** that the vice president also **participate.** We **demand** that something **be** done about these problems. We **desire** that everyone **be** aware of the problems.	The verb in the main clause may be in any tense. The simple form is used for the verb in the noun clause. In conversational English, infinitives are normally used after the verbs *advise . . . urge,* rather than clauses with *that.* With the verbs *demand . . . suggest,* infinitives are not normally substituted.

Note: As with statements of urgency, modal verbs are not used in noun clauses with this type of construction.

2 Every workplace has rules that employees are required to follow. "Soften" the following commands by changing them to strong requests. Begin each request with *My boss asks that . . . , requests that . . . , insists that . . . , requires that . . .*, and so forth. Make any other necessary changes.

Example: be on time

My boss requires that I be on time.

1. Don't make personal calls.
2. Keep your breaks to 15 minutes.
3. Don't leave before five o'clock.
4. Plan your vacations in advance.
5. Work fast but try not to make mistakes.
6. Be friendly but efficient.
7. Stay off the Internet.
8. Come to me if you have any problems.

3 Unions traditionally have tried to bring better salaries and working conditions to workers at lower income levels. The following is a list of issues that a union has brought to a software corporation named Macrohard. Change the list so that each item includes a noun clause with *that.*

Example: The union asked Macrohard to improve the salaries of the lowest-paid workers.

The union asked that Macrohard improve the salaries of the lowest-paid workers.

1. The union asked Macrohard to provide health insurance to all employees.
2. The union asked the company to provide child care.
3. The workers demanded to be given equal pay for equal work.
4. The union requested the company to publicize all job openings.
5. The workers demanded to be given equal consideration for promotions.
6. The union urged the company to forbid all forms of sexual harassment.
7. The workers asked the company to allow job sharing.
8. The union advised Macrohard to allow flexible schedules.
9. The union urged the company to give one-month vacations.

4 Imagine that you are a union representative for one of the groups listed in the following. You are concerned with the health, safety, pay, and benefits of your union members. What are some of the "demands" that you will make to the workers' employers? Use your own ideas to complete each sentence. (A *local* is a union branch, or group.)

Unions

Truck Drivers' Local 441

Farm Workers' Local 70

Nuclear Power Plant Workers' Local 10

Textile Workers' Local 55
Restaurant Workers' Local 12
Brain Surgeons' Local 617
Secret Agents' Local 007

1. I (will) ask that. . . .
2. I (will) demand that. . . .
3. In my opinion, it's necessary that. . . .
4. In fact, it's vital that. . . .
5. Because of . . . , it's urgent that. . . .
6. In conclusion, I request that. . .

5 Mrs. Jones is the manager of a large insurance office. Her assistant, Bill Thomas, has just arrived late. It is 9:45. As you read the following conversation, imagine that you are Bill Thomas. Using reported speech, pretend that you are retelling this conversation to a friend later in the day. Make all necessary changes in verbs, pronouns, and adverbs.

Mrs. Jones: You're late! You were late yesterday, too. I hope that you won't continue this.

Bill: I'm sorry, Mrs. Jones. The bus broke down today.

Mrs. Jones: What happened yesterday?

Bill: I'm really sorry. I forgot to tell you that I had a doctor's appointment. The appointment was for 7:45, but the doctor ran late with the patient before me. I wasn't able to get in to see him until 8:15.

Mrs. Jones: That's understandable. However, I ask that you tell me these things. I also ask that you come on time. It is essential that we run on schedule here.

Bill: Sorry again, Mrs. Jones. I hope that you'll forgive me.

Mrs. Jones: All right, but don't let it happen again. Now, where is that report that you promised me? When will you be finished with the Weir account? Have you found all the information that you need?

Using What You've Learned

6 In pairs, role-play some of the following situations involving problems between an employer and employee or add a few original situations. Take turns role-playing the boss and the employee. Try to use these expressions in your role plays:

It's vital that. . . .
I (We) demand that. . . .
It's urgent that. . . .
We insist that. . . .

It is essential that. . . .
I (We) request that. . . .
I (We) ask that. . . .
I wonder why (how, etc.). . . .
I would like to know if (why, when, etc.). . . .
Could you tell me why (how, who, etc.) . . . ?

Problems

1. X works full time but doesn't make enough money to support his/her family. X wants a significant raise.
2. W is late to work more often than he/she is on time.
3. J's boss often requires that J stay after 5:00 P.M. to do extra work. J feels he is being taken advantage of.
4. Y's knowledge of computers is very important to the business, but he/she spends a lot of time surfing the Internet while at work. Other employees believe he/she doesn't work as hard as they do.
5. Z gossips about fellow employees and has created some serious problems. Many of the other employees are upset and are threatening to quit.
6. X's wife is about to give birth. X wants to take six months off work because he is about to be a father.

PART 4 Clauses as Subjects of Sentences

Setting the Context

Prereading Questions. In your opinion, do most people like their jobs? Why or why not?

Job Satisfaction

While Studs Terkel was writing his book *Working,* he asked 135 people, from elevator operators to company presidents, "How do you like your job?" The overwhelming majority answered, "I don't!"

Why people dislike their jobs is often obvious. In today's world of mass production and division of labor, few people are doing a job that is unique. Most workers perform tasks just like thousands or millions of other workers. As a result, few workers feel truly necessary or important. They seldom get the feeling of satisfaction that comes from accomplishing something.

That job satisfaction is related to productivity is also obvious. Although workers today have better pay and benefits, safer working conditions, and more job security, their productivity level has fallen throughout the world. Dissatisfied workers do not perform as well as those who are satisfied. What seems to give most people satisfaction is to complete an entire project. Yet the organization of business today rarely allows workers that opportunity.

Discussing Ideas. What are some of the most boring jobs you can think of? What are the most interesting? Can you do a good job if you hate what you are doing?

A. Clauses as Subjects of Sentences

A noun clause may be used as the subject of a sentence. In this case, the noun clause *must* begin with a connecting word and takes a singular verb.

Words or Phrases as Subjects	Noun Clauses as Subjects
Their job is difficult.	**What they do** is difficult.
His mistakes are numerous.	**What he is known for** is his mistakes.
Something is certain.	**That he is a troublemaker** is certain.

B. Anticipatory It *Clauses with* That

In conversational English, *it* is often used to begin sentences rather than placing the noun clause in subject position. Of course, sentences with *it* and adjectives of urgency (*vital, urgent, necessary,* etc.) are followed by verbs in the subjunctive mood.

Noun Clauses as Subjects	Anticipatory *It*
That he is a corporate spy is now certain.	**It** is certain **that he is a corporate spy.**
That we arrest him is necessary.	**It** is necessary **that we arrest him.**

1 Change the following sentences to begin with *it* instead of noun clauses.

Example: That Harry dislikes his job so much is a shame.
It's a shame that Harry dislikes his job so much.

1. That Harry is unhappy in his job is obvious.
2. That he hasn't already quit is surprising.

3. That he has stayed at this job so long amazes me.
4. That he will quit soon is almost certain.
5. That he find a better-paying job is essential.
6. That he might not make enough to support his family worries us.

2 Do you intend to work? What are your job prospects? Will you be able to find a job that you like and that pays well? Form at least six sentences on this topic. Begin them with *It's (un)likely (fairly certain, doubtful, too bad, lucky,* etc.) *that. . . .*

3 English speakers will often answer a question by beginning with a noun clause formed from the question. This is particularly common when the person is trying to avoid answering the question. Change the following questions to noun clauses and use the clauses as subjects to complete the phrases. *Note:* With yes/no questions, only *whether* is used.

1. Where is Harry today?	. . . is a mystery to me.
2. Why isn't he at work?	. . . is not important.
3. Is he sick again?	. . . is none of our business.
4. Why does he have so many days off?	. . . doesn't concern us.
5. How does he get any work done?	. . . doesn't really matter.
6. Has the boss decided to fire him?	. . . is irrelevant.
7. How much does he make?	. . . is his business.
8. Does he have a company car?	. . . is confidential.

4 English speakers will also begin sentences with noun clauses formed from questions in order to stall. Rephrasing the original question into a clause allows the person a little time to think over the answer. In pairs, take turns asking and answering the questions that follow. You may want to talk about work and experiences with jobs, or you may answer more generally about your schoolwork, hobbies, and so forth. Begin your responses with noun clauses.

Example: What do you like to do the most?
What I like to do most is to talk with people.
or
What I like to do most is to spend time outdoors.

1. What do you like to do the most?
2. Why do you like to do this?
3. What do you least like to do?
4. How do you work best (slowly, under pressure, etc.)?
5. Where do you work best (at home, in an office, etc.)? Why?
6. When do you work best (in the morning, on rainy days, etc.)? Why?
7. What do you like to wear to work (casual clothes, a suit and tie, etc.)?
8. When do you take breaks (when you finish a project, when you feel like it, etc.)?

5 Many factors are involved in job satisfaction, but not everyone places the same value on each factor. Whether you have worked, are working now, or may work in the future, consider the following list of concerns. In your opinion, what is or is not important in thinking about working and the job market? Form noun clauses from the information and use them to complete the following sentences.

place of employment	amount of money
type of work	hours of work per day
amount of job security	type of benefits
amount of responsibility	amount of vacation time
type of working conditions	number of sick days

1. . . . concerns me because. . . .	**5.** . . . doesn't concern me. . . .
2. . . . worries me. . . .	**6.** . . . doesn't worry me. . . .
3. . . . matters to me. . . .	**7.** . . . doesn't matter to me. . . .
4. . . . is important to me. . . .	**8.** . . . isn't important to me. . . .

Example: place of employment

Where I work isn't really important to me because I can live almost anywhere.

or

Where I work concerns me because I don't want to live in a large city.

6 **Error Analysis.** Exploitco, Inc., has decided to cut its costs. It plans to lay off workers, and the workers, obviously, are not happy about this. The following sentences have errors in their use of noun clauses. Find and correct the errors.

Example: Exploitco ~~announces~~ *announced* that it was going to lay off 50 workers.

1. The workers asked why was the company going to do this.
2. The management said them that the company was losing money.
3. The workers asked to the management if the company had considered alternatives.
4. According to the management, it was necessary that workers were laid off.
5. The workers told to the management that they would like to discuss the situation.
6. The workers suggested that everyone took pay cuts.
7. What would that do was to save all the jobs.
8. Working together, the workers and management decided how would they solve the problem.

Using What You've Learned

7 Do you have some complaints about your home, school, or job? Choose one of the following combinations and in pairs or small groups role-play your complaints!

two roommates
a teacher and a student
a student and a person in the school administration
a parent and a child
a boss and an employee

Useful Expressions

What bothers (irks, irritates) me is. . . .
What drives me crazy is. . . .
What I can't stand is. . . .
What I don't like is. . . .
Why I get angry (upset, etc.) is. . . .

8 Imagine that you are a gossip columnist and your job is to get as much information as possible during an interview. Your interviewees are often upset by your questions and do their best to avoid answering. Work in pairs and role-play your interviews.

Interviewees

Bill Gates	a rock star	the president
your teacher	a sports figure	a movie star

Useful Expressions

. . . is none of your business.
. . . is private.
. . . doesn't (shouldn't) concern you.
. . . is irrelevant.
. . . is top secret.
. . . is not something I can reveal.
. . . must be kept confidential.

PART 5 Reduction of Noun Clauses to Infinitive Phrases

Setting the Context

Prereading Questions. How would you define stress? When do you feel stress? What jobs do you consider the most stressful?

Job Stress

All jobs create some type of stress. Perhaps your boss asks you to work overtime to complete a report by a certain deadline. Perhaps it is necessary for you to stand in the same spot at an assembly line eight hours a day, five days a week. Perhaps there are days when you are forced to sit at your desk with nothing to do, watching the clock, but you must not leave because you are at work. Each of these situations creates stress.

Web Note

Stress affects every part of our lives, and it can cause serious health problems. If you feel under a great deal of stress and feel that you may need help in coping, consult Stress Management and Emotional Wellness Links at *http://imt.net/~randolfi/StressLinks.html. This site will link you to places near you that can be of help. Another good site is* The International Stress Management Association *out of the United Kingdom. This registered nonprofit organization provides help and worldwide links at www.isma.org.uk/.*

Through many years of evolution, your body has learned how to respond to stress based on its instinct for survival. Just as if you were in the wilderness facing a wild animal, your body reacts to stress by preparing for fight or flight. Your muscles tense. Your blood vessels constrict. Your pulse rate shoots up, and your blood pressure soars.

Learning how to cope with stress is of primary importance in today's work world. Stress affects job performance, relationships, and the personal well-being of millions of people. The U.S. Clearinghouse for Mental Health Information claims that American businesses lose $17 billion annually because of employees' stress-related disabilities. Health authorities estimate that as many as 60 percent of all doctor visits in the United States are due to psychological stress rather than specific illnesses.

Discussing Ideas. Do you believe that 60 percent of all doctor visits in the United States are due to stress? What are some physical and emotional reactions that you have when you are under stress? Some people perform better under moderate stress. Are you one of these?

A. Reduction of That *Clauses in the Subjunctive Mood*

Noun clauses in the subjunctive mood are commonly reduced to infinitive phrases. All adjectives of urgency preceded by *it* (it is important, vital, etc.) can be reduced as in the following chart. Only the following verbs of request are normally reduced to infinitives: *advise, ask, command, require, urge.*

Noun Clauses	Infinitive Phrases
It's **important** that you **call.** It's **essential** that he **have** the money.	It's **important for you to call.** It's **essential for him to have** the money.
I **advised** that he **call** right away. He **urged** that I **see** a lawyer.	I **advised him to call** right away. He **urged me to see** a lawyer.

1 Working conditions are often a source of stress on the job. As Japanese manufacturers have shown, improvements in working conditions can often make a tremendous difference in employee productivity. The recommendations that follow are based on Japanese methods. Change the noun clauses to infinitive phrases.

Example: To reduce stress, it is important that a person take periodic breaks to relax.
To reduce stress, it is important (for a person) to take periodic breaks to relax.

1. It is best that workers have a pleasant place to relax.
2. It is advisable that workers get regular exercise time on the job.
3. It is crucial that people work in a healthy environment.
4. It is essential that a worker have proper lighting.
5. It is vital that workers breathe clean air.
6. It is imperative that workers feel safe.
7. It is necessary that management provide training on new equipment.
8. It is important that management and workers have regular safety reviews.

2 Decision making is another area where many Japanese companies have used effective strategies. Through participating in decision making, workers feel more responsibility for their work. This, in turn, reduces the stress that comes from feeling insecure in a position. In the following sentences, change the noun clauses to infinitive phrases. Include an indirect object when necessary.

Example: Workers around the world are asking that their employers give them more power.

Workers around the world are asking their employers to give them more power.

1. Workers have asked that management allow them to participate in major decisions.
2. Negotiators have advised that management give workers more responsibility.
3. Workers have urged that companies reward employees for suggesting improvements.
4. Workers have asked that management allow them to do more of their work at home.
5. Workers have urged that management meet regularly with employees.
6. Negotiators have advised that management treat employees with respect.
7. Workers have asked that management consider dramatic changes.
8. Management has asked that workers be patient.

3 Imagine that you are in the following situations. What can you do to promote the health, well-being, and productivity of everyone on the job? Express your ideas by completing the following sentences in your own words. Use infinitive phrases.

1. You are a manager in a large insurance office. Most of your workers spend eight hours a day at a desk, working on computers, meeting customers, or answering phones. What do you feel is important for maximum efficiency in the office?
   a. In my opinion, it's important. . . .
   b. It's also necessary. . . .
   c. In fact, it's essential. . . .
   d. It's best. . . .

2. You are an assembly-line worker in an automobile manufacturing plant. Each person on the line adds, checks, or paints one part of the automobile. You work with heavy machines that can be dangerous. What would you request of the management to make your work safer, more productive, or more pleasant?
   a. I would ask. . . .
   b. In fact, I have advised. . . .
   c. The government should require. . . .
   d. I strongly urge. . . .

B. Reduction of Indirect Commands, Requests, and Embedded Questions

Reduction of Commands

Commands can be reduced to infinitive phrases in reported speech. The infinitive phrase expresses the same meaning as *should* + verb. The verbs *advise, beg, command, direct, encourage, order, urge,* and *warn* follow the same pattern as *tell* in the infinitive phrases. The indirect object must be included.

Commands	Reported Speech	Infinitive Phrase
Stop it!	She said that we should stop it.	She said to stop it.
Finish the job.	She told us that we should finish the job.	She told us to finish the job.

Reduction of Requests for Action and for Permission

Requests with *Will you . . . , Would you . . . ,* and *Could you . . .* can be reduced to infinitive phrases. The indirect object *must* be used with the infinitive phrase. Requests with *May I . . . , Could I . . . ,* and *Can I . . . ,* can also be reduced to infinitive phrases, but *no* indirect object is used.

Requests for Action	Reported Speech	Infinitive Phrase
Will you help me?	She asked (me) if I could help her.	She asked me to help her.
Could you lend me $5?	She asked (me) whether I could lend her $5.	She asked me to lend her $5.

Requests for Permission	Reported Speech	Infinitive Phrase
Could I leave early?	John asked (me) if he could leave early.	John asked to leave early.

Reduction of Embedded Questions

Yes/no and information questions with modal auxiliaries may be reduced to infinitive phrases. In reduced yes/no questions, *whether (or not)* is always used in an infinitive phrase. With both types of questions, the speaker and the subject of the question *must* be the same person(s).

Yes/No Question	Embedded Question	Infinitive Phrase
Should I come early?	Jay asked if he should come early.	Jay asked whether to come early.

Wh Question	Embedded Question	Infinitive Phrase
Which pages should I read?	I asked (her) which pages I should read.	I asked (her) which pages to read.

4 Losing a job is difficult, psychologically as well as financially. Imagine that you have been laid off from your job. The following are things you would like to know. Rephrase the questions to use infinitive phrases.

Example: How can I find a new job?
I would like to know how to find a new job.

1. How long should I wait before applying for another job?
2. What kind of job should I look for?
3. How much money can I expect?
4. Where should I look?
5. What should I write on my resume?
6. What can I do with so much free time?
7. How can I avoid becoming depressed?
8. How can I qualify for unemployment benefits?

5 Losing a job and being unemployed presents a number of dilemmas. Rephrase the following questions to use infinitive phrases.

Example: Should I borrow money to pay my bills?
I don't know whether to borrow money to pay my bills.

1. Should I go back to school?
2. Should I wait for a good job?
3. Should I take a low-paying job?
4. Should I ask my family for help?
5. Should I give up my apartment?
6. Should I move in with my parents?
7. Should I get a roommate?
8. Should I go to an employment agency?

6 Finding a job can be difficult, and sometimes you have to be very resourceful to come up with good possibilities. Imagine that a friend of yours is looking for a job. Give him or her some advice. Change the following commands to statements with infinitive phrases. Use the example as a model.

Example: Go to the city employment office.
I would tell (urge, advise) my friend to go to the city employment office.

1. Read the want ads.
2. Ask everyone you know about possible jobs.
3. Don't wait for people to call you.
4. Visit all the major businesses in the area.
5. Talk to the counselors at your school.
6. Put an ad in the paper under "Situations Wanted."
7. Don't give up.
8. Try every possible method.

7 Do you have any other suggestions for someone who is job hunting? Make a list of at least five sentences with infinitive phrases.

Using What You've Learned

8 You and your classmates are employed in an automobile assembly plant. Several years ago, your company borrowed heavily from a bank, and the loan has come due. Unfortunately, your company has been losing money and cannot repay the loan. The bank has agreed not to demand its money immediately if your company reduces its budget by 25 percent.

Divide into two groups: one, the management, and the other, the employees. In your groups, decide what areas you would like to see the 25 percent reduction come from. Be sure to adopt a hard-line bargaining position as well as a more moderate position. For example, even though you are willing to accept a 5 percent salary decrease, you might begin by demanding that your salary stay the same.

Finally, meet with members of the other group and try to negotiate a new contract. If you don't reach a compromise by the end of the class, the bank will foreclose and all of you will lose your jobs. Use the following data as you plan your strategy and negotiate.

EXPLOITCO, INC.
Management: 10 people
Workers: 200

PERCENTAGE OF BUDGET	
Production costs	20%
Research and development	15%
Company psychiatrist	3%
Recreational facilities	3%
Campaign contributions	5%

	MANAGEMENT	EMPLOYEES
Salaries	15%	15%
Pensions	5%	5%
Health insurance	4%	4%
Paid vacation	1%	1%
Free lunches	2%	2%

As you negotiate, you might want to use the following expressions:

I (We) would like to know. . . .
Could you explain (tell us, etc.). . . .
I (We) don't understand. . . .
What we want is. . . .
What we are trying to do is. . . .
Why we are . . . is. . . .
How we. . . .
We demand (insist, ask, etc.). . . .
It is necessary (essential, crucial, advisable, etc.). . . .

Video Activities: Telecommuting

Before You Watch. Sometimes people work from home. What are some advantages and disadvantages of telecommuting? List them below. In small groups, discuss your answers.

Advantages to Workers	Advantages to Employers
1. ______	1. ______
2. ______	2. ______
3. ______	3. ______
Disadvantages to Workers	**Disadvantages to Employers**
1. ______	1. ______
2. ______	2. ______
3. ______	3. ______

Watch. Take notes on the benefits of telecommuting from different perspectives.

1. As you listen, note the benefits of telecommuting from a worker's perspective.

   ____

   ____

2. As you listen, note the benefits of telecommuting from an employer's perspective.

   ____

   ____

Watch Again. Answer these questions in small groups.

1. Listen for these numbers and write what each one represents.
   a. 20,000,000 ______________
   b. 12,000–13,000 ______________
   c. 10,000 ______________
   d. 3,000–4,000 ______________
2. The phrases *gridlock* and *bumper-to-bumper* refer to ______________.
   a. traffic accidents b. slow traffic c. very heavy traffic
3. When someone is *goofing off,* they are ______________.
   a. sleeping b. working c. playing
4. The expression *saving a bundle* means ______________.
   a. saving a lot of money
   b. working harder
   c. getting work done faster
5. Another word for *telecommuter* is ______________.
   a. telephoner b. telenetter c. teleworker

After You Watch. Change the following quotations to reported speech.

1. One worker said, "Telecommuting has changed my life."
2. The reporter asked, "How do companies benefit from allowing employees to work at home?"
3. The narrator said, "Telecommuting is now so popular that AOL is adding 40,000 modems a month."
4. One employer said, "If I give them a quota of x and they produce 2x, I don't care if they're watching 'Oprah' and eating bonbons."

Focus on Testing

Noun Clauses and Noun Clause Reductions

Problem areas with noun clauses often appear on standardized English proficiency exams. Check your understanding of these structures by completing the sample items that follow.

Remember that . . .

- With reported speech, you must be consistent in changes in verb tenses, modal auxiliaries, pronouns, and adverbials.
- The word order of a question changes when it is placed within a noun clause.
- The simple form of the verb is used in noun clauses following statements of urgency or urgent requests.
- Many noun clauses can be reduced to infinitive phrases.

Part 1. Circle the best completion for the following.

Example: Susan said ________ would like me to help.

a. that
b. then
(c.) she
d. if

1. David promised that he ________ arrive yesterday.
   a. will
   b. can
   c. would
   d. had
2. Annette wanted to reach a consensus about ________ the work.
   a. if to finish
   b. when she should finished
   c. whether to finish
   d. finished
3. She was interested in how ________ process the new information.
   a. rapid I could
   b. rapidly could I
   c. could I
   d. rapidly I could
4. He asked ________ fulfillment from a hard day's work.
   a. do you gain
   b. did I gain
   c. whether I gained or not
   d. whether or not I gained

Part 2. Each sentence has one error. Circle the letter below the word(s) containing the error.

Example: We were going to (A) request (B) that (C) the president also participates (D).

1. It (A) is essential that everyone is (B) on time to the meeting and that everyone be (C) well prepared (D).
2. Debra demanded (A) that we terminated (B) our involvement in the project before she returned (C) from her furlough (D) in South America.
3. Exactly where is (A) Roberto today is (B) something that the boss insists (C) that she ascertain (D) immediately.
4. What did I advise (A) Brad and Margie was to confer (B) with a trained and licensed marriage counselor before they (C) even contemplated getting a divorce (D).

Chapter 8

Breakthroughs

IN THIS CHAPTER

Part 1 The Simple Tenses

Part 2 The Perfect Tenses

Part 3 The Continuous Tenses

Part 4 The Modal Auxiliaries

Part 5 Review of Chapters 5 to 8

Introduction

In this chapter, you will study the forms and uses of verbs in the passive voice. You will notice that the time frame of a passive verb may be the same as that of an active verb, but the focus of the passive sentence is quite different. As you study the chapter, pay careful attention to the focus of the passive constructions.

The following passage introduces the chapter theme "Breakthroughs" and raises some of the topics and issues you will cover in the chapter.

The Gifts of History

If the last 100 years is associated with anything, it is technological change. In transportation, for example, we have gone from the horse and buggy to the space shuttle. In medicine, diseases that could not even have been recognized a few years ago are now being diagnosed with sophisticated equipment and treated with genetic therapy, laser surgery, or newly synthesized drugs. How has so much been done in such a short time? The answer is that it hasn't. In such a short time, that is.

Of course, it is true that countless great advances have been made in our lifetimes. Yet, it is just as true that today's technological "miracles" are based on concepts of engineering, biology, physics, and chemistry that were discovered hundreds, if not thousands, of years ago. Thus, today's "unprecedented" achievements should not be viewed in isolation. They are the fruit of our technological inheritance that has been accumulated over centuries.

As Albert Einstein wrote when reflecting on his lifetime of work, "My inner and outer life is built upon the labors of my fellow men, both living and dead."

Discussing Ideas. What does the expression *the fruit of our technological inheritance* mean? Can you think of examples where current advances are directly based on years of inherited knowledge?

PART 1 The Simple Tenses

Setting the Context

Prereading Questions. How important is technology to our lives? Have we become accustomed to too many machines?

No Escape!

How important is technology? Take a moment and look around. It hardly matters what time it is or where you are. Almost everything that you own, use, or even touch in the course of a normal day was created through technology.

In the morning, your toast is made and the coffee is brewed by electronic machines. You are transported to school or work by bus, train, car, or bike. During the day, you receive messages that are transmitted via phone, fax, or the Internet.

Back home, dinner is prepared in a microwave, and programs are delivered to your television via antenna, cable, or satellite dish. And these are only a few examples.

You may like technology or hate it, but one thing is certain. In today's world, technology is almost impossible to escape.

Discussing Ideas. Which machines are most important to you? Could you live without machines? Why or why not?

A. Introduction to the Passive Voice

Transitive verbs (verbs that take an object) can appear in either the active or the passive voice. The voice does not normally affect meaning but it *does* change focus. In the active voice, the focus is on the agent or doer of the action. To shift the focus to the receiver of the action, use the passive voice. Compare:

	Examples
Active	Subject Verb Object My dog bit the mailman.
Passive	The mailman was bitten by my dog. Subject Verb Agent

1 In each of the following sets of sentences, underline the verb(s) and indicate which verbs are passive and which are active. Then, circle the noun that has the main focus in each sentence.

Example: passive (The telephone) was invented by Alexander Graham Bell in 1876. active (Alexander Graham Bell) invented the telephone in 1876.

1. __________ Since 1876, many advances have been made in the field of communications.

   __________ Since 1876, we have made many advances in the field of communications.

2. __________ Several companies began to produce personal computers in the 1970s.

   __________ Personal computers began to be produced by several companies in the 1970s.

3. __________ Today computers make some sales calls.

   __________ Today some sales calls are made by computers.

4. __________ By the early 1990s, the Internet was being used to communicate all over the world.

   __________ By the early 1990s, people were using the Internet to communicate all over the world.

5. __________ By last year, technicians should have connected most colleges in the United States to the Internet.

   __________ By last year, most colleges in the United States should have been connected to the Internet.

6. __________ Now, hundreds of thousands of students are doing research electronically.

   __________ Now, research is being done electronically by hundreds of thousands of students.

7. __________ How will our lives be changed by this technology in the future?

   __________ How will this technology change our lives in the future?

B. The Simple Tenses

The passive voice of verbs in simple tenses is formed in this way: *will be, am, is, are, was, were* + past participle (+ *by* + agent). Adverbs of frequency usually come after the first auxiliary verb. The passive forms have the same general meanings and time frames as verbs in the active voice.

	Active	Passive
Past	Samuel Morse **invented** the Morse Code.	The Morse Code **was invented** by Samuel Morse.
Focus	Samuel Morse	The Morse Code
Present	Inventors **make** new discoveries every day.	New discoveries **are made** by inventors every day.
Focus	Inventors	New discoveries
Future	Technology **will control** our lives.	Our lives **will be controlled** by technology.
Focus	Technology	Our lives

2 Underline all uses of the passive voice in the passage "No Escape!" on pages 242 to 243. Give the tense and time frame of each.

3 Which of the following sentences can be changed to the passive voice? First, underline the subjects(s) and double underline the verb(s) in each and circle any direct objects. Then change the sentences to the passive voice if possible.

Example: Scientists discover (new technological advances) everyday.
New technological advances are discovered by scientists everyday.

1. New technological advances usually arrive in major cities first.
2. Satellites transmit overseas telephone calls.
3. Computers design cars.
4. Athletes use computers to monitor their workouts.
5. Laser scanners read food prices in supermarkets.
6. Scientists compete to be the first to develop new products.
7. Hundreds of new products flood the market each year.
8. Some technologies spread very quickly.

C. By + *Agent*

By + noun (or pronoun) can be used in passive sentences to tell who or what performed the action of the verb. However, most passive sentences in English do not contain these phrases. Use *by* + agent only if the phrase gives the following information:

	Examples
Information that is necessary to the meaning of the sentence	Houses **will be run** by computers.
A particular name or idea that is important in the context	Nine magnificent symphonies **were composed** by Beethoven.
New or unusual information	The telephone **was invented** by Alexander Graham Bell. It **was invented** in the 1870s.

4 Read the following sentences and omit *by* + agent where it is not necessary.

Example: Today, television is transmitted ~~by people and machines~~ to and from almost every part of the globe.

1. Television was originally created by people purely for entertainment.
2. Today, television is used by people for all types of purposes.
3. Television was made possible by researchers through a variety of technological breakthroughs.
4. In 1884, a scanner disk was developed by a German, Paul Nipkow.
5. Using this disk, an image was broken down into thousands of dots by Nipkow.
6. Later, a device was created by V. K. Zworykin that was used by him to scan and duplicate images using electron beams.
7. The cathode-ray picture tube was perfected and the first TV sets were produced by Allen B. DuMont in 1939.
8. On February 1, 1940, the first official program was broadcast in the United States by the National Broadcasting Company (NBC).
9. Soon, a variety of programs were being broadcast by companies around the United States.
10. These early programs were all transmitted by the companies in black and white.
11. Later, color transmissions were achieved by researchers.
12. Today, very clear color transmissions are sent by companies across the globe in a matter of seconds.

5 Change the sentences to the passive. Omit *by* + agent when appropriate.

Example: From about 1850 to 1910, many technological advances altered day-to-day life.

From about 1850 to 1910, day-to-day life was altered by many technological advances.

Edison's first electric lamp

1. Elisha Otis exhibited the first modern elevator at the New York World's Fair in 1853.
2. From the 1850s to the 1880s, many inventors improved the steel-making process.
3. Cheap production of steel made stronger and taller buildings possible.
4. Using steel construction and elevators, builders soon built structures with more than five or six stories.
5. Thomas Edison of the United States and Joseph Swan of Great Britain simultaneously produced the first electric lamps in the late 1870s.
6. Willis Carrier invented air conditioning in 1911.
7. Air conditioning opened up entire new parts of the United States and the world for habitation.
8. People built hundreds of new houses in hot places like Houston, Texas, and Phoenix, Arizona.

D. Common Expressions in the Passive Voice

Notice the variety of prepositions that follow these expressions; *by* is also used, depending on the context.

be accustomed to	be formed of (from, by)	be made up of
be based on	be known for (as)	be noted for
be connected to	be known to + *verb*	be related to
be covered with	be involved in (with)	be shown in (at, on)
be derived from	be linked to	be suited for
be equipped with	be located in (at, on)	be used for (as, with)
be filled with (by)	be made of (from)	be used to + *verb*

Note: Verbs of emotion such as *amaze, bore, interest* are often used in passive constructions. (*He's interested in sports. I'm amazed at her progress.*)

6 Use appropriate expressions from the preceding list to complete the following sentences. Use present or future tenses.

Example: In the future, even powerful computers _will be made_ of portable components.

1. Today, most people ____________ (still) to using paper, pencil, and their hands to do many chores.
2. Much of our day-to-day work ____________ up of manual tasks, such as opening and closing things, lifting and carrying things, writing and typing things.
3. In the future, our houses and apartments ____________ with amazing devices to help us communicate, do our work and shopping, and manage our homes.
4. Many of the devices ____________ to a central house computer.
5. Some of these futuristic devices ____________ to control the lighting and temperature in the house.
6. Other robotlike devices ____________ for cleaning the house, doing laundry, and cooking.
7. Computer monitors ____________ in the kitchen, the home office, and other important areas.
8. Your desk ____________ (not) with papers; instead, it will have only a computer.

E. Get + *Adjective or Past Participle*

	Examples	Notes
get + adjective	I **got angry** about the situation.	*Get* (meaning *become*) + adjective or past participle is frequently used in conversation. This form of the passive is seldom used in writing.
get + past participle	I **got upset** about the situation. I **got worried** about the situation.	

7 Use *get* + adjective or past participle to complete the following to make true statements.

1. I get frustrated when . . . .
2. I always get sick when . . . .
3. When I'm late for class, I get . . . .
4. Before difficult exams, I get . . . .
5. If I don't sleep well, I get . . . .
6. I get bored when . . . .
7. I get really excited (about) . . . .
8. I get confused . . . .

F. *Anticipatory* It

The passive voice is often used with *it* to avoid mentioning the agent or source. *By* + agent is rarely used with these constructions.

	Examples	Notes
Active **Passive**	**People said,** "The earth is flat." **It was said,** "The earth is flat." **It was said** that the earth was flat.*	*It* is often used with the passive form of verbs such as *believe, confirm, deny, estimate, fear, hope, mention, report, say,* and *think.* Past expressions like *it was believed* indicate that these ideas have changed.

* *That* is added when a direct quote is changed to reported speech. In reported speech, verbs often shift to past tenses. See Chapter 7.

8 As we learn more about our world, many beliefs change. Expressions such as *it was believed, felt,* or *said* are followed by noun clauses to indicate past beliefs that have changed. In these cases, the verbs in the noun clauses normally take past forms. Rephrase the quotations by using *It was believed, said, felt, thought,* or *feared.*

Example: Telephones will ruin the postal service.

It was believed that telephones would ruin the postal service.

1. "A telephone will always be too expensive for most people to have."
2. "Television will eliminate the movie industry."
3. "Faxs are useful only in large businesses."
4. "Computers are too complicated for ordinary people to use."
5. "All employees need to work in the office every day."
6. "It is too dangerous to have automatic tellers."
7. "Most people don't want to have a lot of electronic gadgets in their homes."
8. "Videotape is useful only for advertising firms."

9 Complete the following passage with active or passive forms of the verbs in parentheses. Use simple verb tenses and add negatives and adverbs when indicated.

Electronic Mail Networks

E-mail *is commonly used* (use / commonly) on many university campuses by faculty and students who wish to communicate more easily and frequently among

themselves. In an English as a second language course last semester, for example, class discussions _______________ (take) place by e-mail. During that course, homework assignments _______________ (give/sometimes) out over the network, and "chat lines" _______________ (organize) so that the students could practice their language skills by e-mail.
(blanks numbered 1, 2, 3)

Some students _______________ (overwhelm) by today's communication technology. However, most universities _______________ (offer) workshops for those who want to learn about e-mail. Once e-mail learners _______________ (equip) with the basic knowledge of how to use the network, they _______________ (link) into not only a local but also a global network.
(blanks numbered 4, 5, 6, 7)

Web Note

Are you interested in an e-mail pen pal, or would you like to find more ways of practicing English on the Web? Try Dave's ESL Cafe *at www.pacificnet.net/~sperling/eslcafe.html.*

10 One of the great technological innovations in the last 200 years was the process of refining oil into gasoline. Without this, the internal combustion engine would not have been practical, and cars might not have been developed.

The refining process is explained in the following passage, which is written entirely in the active voice. First, read the passage for meaning. Then improve it stylistically by changing some of the sentences to the passive voice. Remember to omit the agent when appropriate. Finally, in small groups, compare the changes you made and explain why you made them.

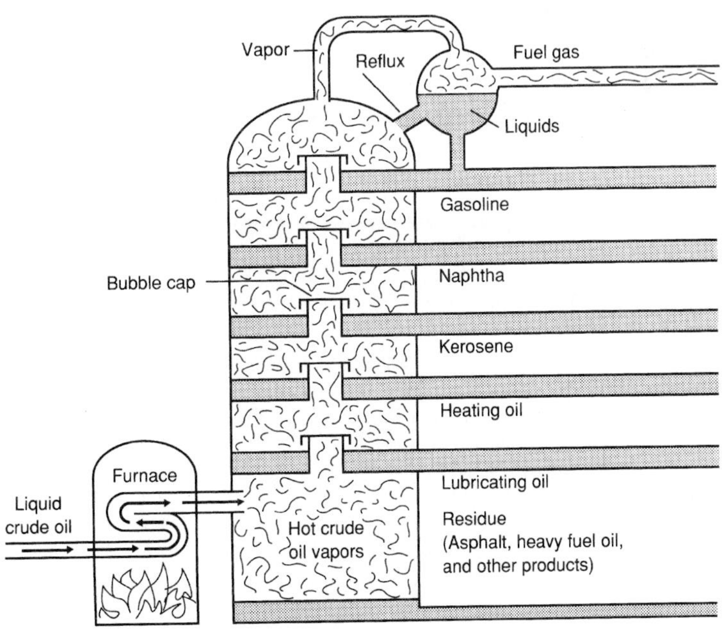

Refineries

People use a variety of techniques to refine oil, but the most common is separation. The separation process has several steps. First, technicians heat the oil in a large furnace, and from there they send it into a fractionating tower. This tower is a steel cylinder about 130 feet (40 meters) high. When the hot oil enters the tower, it turns into vapor. This vapor rises naturally. As it rises, its temperature begins to fall, and the components of the oil separate according to their weight. At this time, workers take the heavy oil from the bottom of the tower. During the process, workers also remove lubricating oil, kerosene, and gasoline from higher points. Uncondensed gas rises to the top of the tower, where a mechanism releases it through a pipe. Another mechanism recycles this gas into the tower for further separation.

Using What You've Learned

11 Many of you have developed hobbies or have worked in a particular field or career. Consider some of the processes involved in your hobby or your work and how you can explain one or two of them step by step. Then, in pairs or small groups, give a clear, but fairly detailed, explanation of the process to your classmates.

For example, if you are a civil engineer, you may want to describe how a road is built, how land is surveyed, or how a bridge is constructed. If you have a hobby such as photography, perhaps you could talk about how film is developed or how pictures are enlarged.

Other possibilities include how photosynthesis takes place, how water is purified, how a familiar item is made, or how illegal items are smuggled in and out of countries.

PART 2 The Perfect Tenses

Setting the Context

Prereading Questions. What changes have occurred in medicine in the last 150 years? What breakthroughs have taken place in our knowledge of medical care and treatments?

Miracles in Medicine

Just imagine that you were alive 150 years ago and that you were in a serious accident or had a serious illness. What were your chances of survival?

At that time, only a few truly effective medicinal remedies had been developed. For example, cinchona bark (quinine) was used to fight malaria, and digitalis was used to treat heart failure. Other infections or diseases simply had to run their course, and the patient either died or recovered, with little medical help.

Since those days, medicine has been completely transformed by a large number of discoveries. Antibiotics, for example, have made it possible to treat bacterial infections; the development of antimalarial drugs has been a very important factor in allowing people to live productively in the tropics; and vaccines have been effective in preventing many diseases. In fact, small pox has been virtually eliminated from the face of the earth.

Your chances of surviving both a very bad accident and a serious illness have increased markedly.

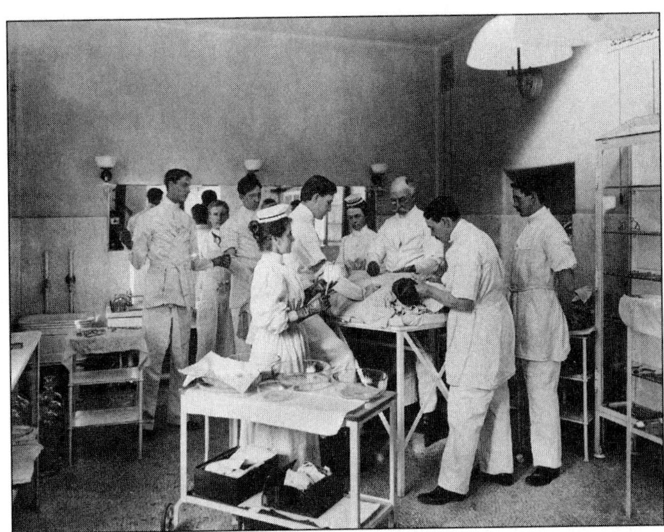

A Victorian-era operating room

Discussing Ideas. What serious infectious diseases, which were formerly common, have now become rare? Can you name other important therapeutic drug discoveries?

A. The Perfect Tenses

The passive voice of verbs in the perfect tenses is formed in this way: *have (will have, have, has, had)* + *been* + past participle (+ *by* + agent). Adverbs of frequency generally come after the first auxiliary verb.

	Examples	Notes
Future Perfect	Within the next few years, companies **will have developed** several new drugs.	Within the next few years, several new drugs **will have been developed.**
Focus	Companies	Several new drugs
Present Perfect	Drug companies **have developed** many new antibiotics since the 1950s.	Many new antibiotics **have been developed** since the 1950s.
Focus	Drug companies	Many new antibiotics
Past Perfect	Until the 1950s, scientists **had developed** few antibiotics.	Until the 1950s, few antibiotics **had been developed.**
Focus	Scientists	Few antibiotics

Note: The perfect continuous tenses (*will have, have, has,* or *had been* + verb + *ing*) are not used in the passive voice.

1 Quickly reread the passage "Miracles in Medicine." Find all sentences in the passive voice and tell the subject and verb in each. Do any of the passive sentences include an agent?

2 Which of the following sentences are in the active voice, and which are in the passive voice? Label each. Then label the subject (S), verb (V), object (O), and/or agent (A) in the sentence.

Example: active Throughout most of history, humans (S) had known (V) little (O) about the causes of and cures for disease.

passive Throughout most of history, little (S) had been known (V) about the causes of and cures for disease. no agent

1. ________ Until the end of the 19th century, the idea of microbes had been regarded as "nonsense."
2. ________ Given the lack of understanding of infection, most doctors had believed diseases to be "imbalances" in a person's body fluids.
3. ________ Sick patients had been viewed as "overexcited" or "exhausted."
4. ________ Bloodletting had been seen as the best way to purge a patient.
5. ________ Until 1844 and Horace Wells' discovery of "laughing gas" (nitrous oxide), tooth extractions and surgeries had been performed without anesthesia.
6. ________ After Pasteur had proposed his theory of germs as the source of infections, Joseph Lister developed antiseptics to clean instruments and treat wounds.
7. ________ Since Alexander Fleming's discovery of the healing properties of penicillin in 1928, antibiotics have become second only to aspirin as the most commonly used drugs in the world.
8. ________ Many diseases have been eradicated through immunizations, better hygiene, and better nutrition.
9. ________ Postsurgical infections have declined ever since doctors began washing their hands between patients.
10. ________ Pure drinking water and pasteurized milk have helped to eliminate cholera, typhoid, and typhus in many parts of the world.
11. ________ In recent years, a great deal of research has been devoted to controlling or curing diseases such as cancer and AIDS.
12. ________ Within the upcoming decades, more breakthroughs will have been made in laser surgery, electronic imaging, and organ transplants.

3 Using the example as a model, form complete sentences from the following cues. Use the past perfect passive in your sentences. Begin each sentence with *Before antibiotics . . . .*

Example: cinchona bark / use / malaria

Before antibiotics, cinchona bark had been used to treat malaria.

1. sulfa drugs / prescribe / for infections
2. brandy, cold water, and castor oil / use to treat pneumonia
3. bloodletting / recommend for almost any disease
4. whisky / give for exhaustion
5. opium / use for many ailments
6. small doses of mercury / prescribe to treat syphilis

Bloodletting was a common practice.

4 Older remedies are not necessarily bad remedies. In fact, many excellent remedies have been passed down through the centuries. Chinese remedies are some of the most interesting and best tested. Tell about some of them by forming complete sentences from the ten cues that follow. Use the present perfect tense, passive voice.

Gingko

Example: some of these remedies / test in laboratories, but others have not

Some of these remedies have been tested in laboratories, but others have not.

1. all of these remedies / test "clinically" in China over centuries
2. the gingko tree / use in Chinese medicine for almost 4,000 years

Culture Note

Alternative medicine is becoming more and more important in the United States. A recent survey showed that over one in three Americans (almost 35 percent) use alternative forms of medicine: chiropracty, acupuncture and acupressure, and herbal remedies, among others.

3. asthma, bronchitis, and tuberculosis / treat with ginkgo seeds and fruit for hundreds of years
4. gingko leaves / prescribe in Europe for strokes and blocked arteries
5. dried sea horse / use to treat swollen thyroid glands for thousands of years
6. ulcers / treat with licorice root
7. licorice root / find to have steroidlike characteristics
8. dried mandarin orange rind / burn to keep mosquitoes away for over a thousand years
9. orange rind / use as a cure for digestive ailments for many centuries
10. sweet wormwood / successfully prescribe for malaria for over 1,500 years

5 Imagine that you work in a hospital emergency room, and a patient who had been in a car accident has just been admitted. In pairs, go over the following checklist. Ask questions using the present perfect tense of the passive voice. Give short answers using the past participle.

Example: notify the patient's family
A. Has the patient's family been notified?
B. Notified.

1. take the patient's temperature
2. check his blood pressure
3. take the patient's pulse
4. treat the patient for shock
5. draw blood samples
6. order X rays
7. bandage his wounds
8. give the patient plasma

6 What medical breakthroughs will occur during the next 50 years? The following are a few that doctors expect. Complete each of the eight sentences with the future perfect passive form of the verbs in parentheses.

Example: Within the upcoming years, several important medical research projects will have been completed (complete).

1. By the year 2050, medicine as we know it today ______________ (transform / completely).
2. Within the upcoming years, much more ______________ (learn) about human genetics.
3. Within the next 50 years, many new drugs ______________ (develop) to fight bacteria that have become resistant to antibiotics.
4. New types of sutures* ______________ (create) for closing wounds.
5. By the year 2050, hundreds of thousands of organ transplants ______________ (perform).

**suture* fiber used to sew parts of the living body

6. New drugs __________ (develop) to counteract the body's rejection of transplanted organs.
7. Within the next 50 years, numerous forms of laser surgery __________ (perfect).
8. By the time we reach old age, incredible advances __________ (make/certainly) in medicine.

7 Use present forms—simple or perfect—of the verbs in parentheses to complete the following passage. Choose between active and passive forms. Note any cases where more than one tense may be appropriate.

The Healing Power of Plants

We _often think_ (think/often) of medicine as human-made capsules or tablets. Yet, the truth ____1____ (be) that over 25 percent of the drugs that ____2____ (sell) yearly in the United States ____3____ (derive) from plants. Birth control pills, aspirin, digitoxin, and morphine ____4____ (develop) from plants. When we ____5____ (buy) these substances, however, their original appearance ____6____ (alter) completely. The active chemicals ____7____ (extract/already) from the plants, and they ____8____ (press) into pills or ____9____ (scoop) into capsules along with inactive substances. Thus, despite the "antiseptic" appearance of these drugs, they ____10____ (have) very "earthy" origins. They ____11____ (derive) from bark, dried leaves, flowers, or roots.

8 Use simple or perfect forms of the verbs in parentheses to complete the following passage. Choose between active and passive forms. Note any case where more than one tense may be appropriate.

Aspirin

For centuries, many cultures _have recognized_ (recognize) the healing power of the willow tree. Long before the beginnings of modern medicine, willow bark ____1____ (use) to treat fever and inflammation. The ancient Greeks ____2____ (have) a very creative explanation for its success. They ____3____ (notice) that even though this tree ______ (4) (grow) along river banks and its "feet" ______ (5) (be) damp, it ______ (6) (remain) healthy. The Greeks ______ (7) (reason) that the tree ______ (8) (protect) by its bark.

The active ingredient in willow bark, *salicin,* ______ (9) (be) extremely bitter and ______ (10) (irritate) many patients. As a result, until this century, the bark ______ (11) (prescribe/often) by doctors but ______ (12) (nottake/always) by their patients, who ______ (13) (feel) that the cure ______ (14) (be) worse than the disease.

Then, in 1897, ______ (15) (come) a major breakthrough. Felix Hoffman, who ______ (16) (work) for Bayer of Germany, ______ (17) (discover) a derivative of salicin, acetylsalicylic acid.

Of all the wonder drugs, aspirin ______ (18) (be/perhaps) the most remarkable. In history, no other drug ______ (19) (use) so widely and for so many purposes. Since its discovery, aspirin ______ (20) (ease) the pain of millions of people, especially those who ______ (21) (suffer) from arthritis.

Before aspirin, bark from willow trees was used to treat illness.

Using What You've Learned

9 What do you know about home remedies? Work together in small groups, and share your knowledge of these cures. What have they been used for? Which have medical bases, and which do not?

castor oil	garlic and garlic juice
celery juice	ginseng
copper bracelets	moldy bread

10 In the past 150 years, a complete transformation has occurred in medicine and health care. Prepare a brief report for your class on a breakthrough in medicine of particular interest to you. Use one of these topics, or choose one of your own. Be sure to include the following: What is it? When was it developed? By whom? How is it used? What had been used before its development?

antibiotics	MRI
burn treatment	organ transplants
cancer treatment	pasteurization
contact lenses	PET
diagnostic X ray	radiation therapy
insulin	ultrasound
kidney dialysis	vaccines
laser surgery	vitamins

PART 3

The Continuous Tenses

Setting the Context

Prereading Questions. How has farming changed during the last 200 to 300 years? Can you give any specific examples?

Food for Thought

In the history of the Earth, settled agriculture has a relatively short chapter. It was only about 10,000 years ago that animals were first being domesticated and crops were being cultivated and harvested. Before that time, humans had fed themselves through fishing, hunting birds and animals, and gathering wild food.

During most of the past 10,000 years, agricultural development progressed slowly. Cultivation began with crops such as rice, corn, and gourds. By the time of the ancient Greeks, some products were actually being imported and exported, especially grains from Egypt. By the fall of the Roman Empire, new farming methods were being introduced all over Western Europe.

It wasn't until the 19th century, however, that major changes in agriculture took place. Migration to the American plains led to the development of both tools and techniques for higher production. At the present time, the United States has achieved such efficiency that a large surplus of food products is being produced.

Discussing Ideas. What do you think are the most important crops for a society to grow? What climate is required for these crops?

A. The Continuous Tenses

The passive voice of verbs in the present and past continuous tenses is formed in this way: *be (am, is, are, was, were)* + *being* + past participle (+ *by* + agent). Adverbs of frequency generally come after the first auxiliary verb.

	Active	**Passive**
Present Continuous	Today farmers **are using** sophisticated machinery to plant and cultivate their farms.	Today, sophisticated machinery **is being used** to plant and cultivate farms.
Focus	Farmers	Sophisticated machinery
Past Continuous	A century ago, farmers **were using** oxen to pull cultivators.	A century ago, oxen **were being used** to pull cultivators.
Focus	Farmers	Oxen

Note: The future continuous tense (*will be* + verb + *ing*) and the present and past perfect continuous tense (*have, has,* or *had been* + verb + *ing*) are not used in the passive voice.

1 Quickly reread the passage "Food for Thought" and underline all passive voice verbs. What is the tense and time frame of each? Do any of the passive sentences have agents?

2 Complete the following eight sentences using the past continuous tense, passive voice of the verbs in parentheses.

Example: Through history, agricultural development took place relatively slowly, but by the Middle Ages, oxen were being bred (breed) for farm work, crops were being rotated (rotate), and some irrigation was being used (use).

1. By the Middle Ages, a wide variety of crops ______________ (produce) throughout Europe.
2. In Spain, sugarcane ______________ (grow) and merino sheep ______________ (raise) for their wool.
3. In Italy, silk from silkworms ______________ (harvest) and rice ______________ (cultivate).
4. By the 1800s, many new farming techniques ______________ (use), but most work ______________ (do / still) by hand or by animals.
5. By 1850, horse-drawn reaping machines ______________ (use).
6. Soon after, steam engines ______________ (attach) to a variety of farm equipment.
7. A hundred years later, however, most farming worldwide ______________ (do / still) using human and animal power.
8. Between 1950 and 1970, major changes occurred in mechanization, and by 1970, tractors ______________ (use) in most parts of the world.

3 Throughout history, humans have tried to breed better plants and animals. Today, with our increasing knowledge of plant genetics, amazing changes are taking place. Form complete sentences from the following cues. Use the present continuous tense, passive voice.

Example: Many new techniques / currently develop in agriculture and plant genetics.
Many new techniques are currently being developed in agriculture and plant genetics.

1. New techniques / develop to allow for direct planting of rice.
2. Soybeans / use to make a variety of new high-protein food products.
3. Shorter wheat stalks / develop to withstand damage from storms.
4. Strawberries / breed to resist damage from frost.
5. Beans / engineer to create their own fertilizer.
6. Gene banks / establish in many countries to preserve important seed material.
7. Freeze-drying / perfect to allow for rapid, economical preservation of many vegetables.
8. Potatoes / breed to grow in a much wider variety of climates.

4 **Review.** Complete the following with active or passive forms of the verbs in parentheses. Use appropriate verb tenses and add negatives and adverbs when indicated.

The Webs That Scientists Want to Weave

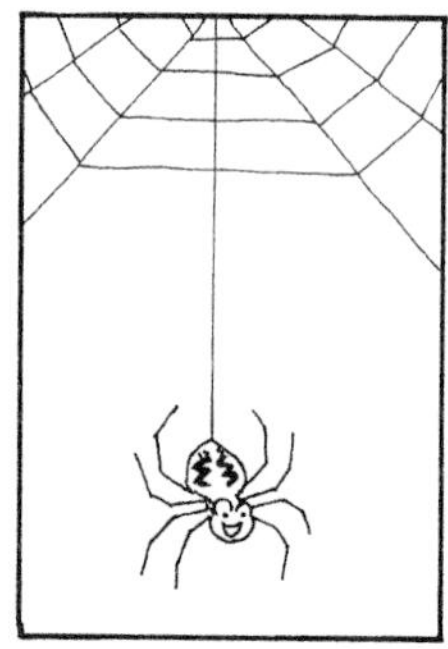

During the 18th century, French scientists *filled* (fill) barns with spiders in hopes of harvesting their webs to spin into thread. Millions of spiders ______ (1) (need) because it ______ (2) (take) several thousand just to make enough thread for a single dress! Unfortunately, though, the spiders ______ (3) (not cooperate) with the French scientists, and the experiment ______ (4) (consider) a disaster.

The scientists ______ (5) (try) to colonize spiders in the same way as silkworms, which ______ (6) (colonize / successfully) for centuries. Why ______ (7) this experiment ______ (8) (fail)? When the spiders ______ (9) (group) together in large numbers, they ______ (10) (fight) fiercely or ______ (11) (eat) each other.

The French experiment ______ (12) (fail), but over the years, interest in spider silk ______ (13) (persist) because of its unique properties. It ______ (14) (be) the strongest material that ______ (15) (find) on earth—five times stronger than steel. At the same time, it ______ (16) (be) 30 percent more flexible than nylon and ______ (17) (be) able to absorb three times the impact force of materials that ______ (18) (use / currently) to make bulletproof vests.

Today, many researchers ____________ (continue) to search for the keys to
19
spider silk, and one group ____________ (begin) to study the gene that
20
____________ (determine) spider silk formation.
21

In the future, it is possible that spider silk ____________ (use) for a multitude
22
of purposes, such as sutures, suspension bridges, and "improved" bulletproof vests!

Using What You've Learned

5 Use the resources in your library (encyclopedias, newspaper articles, journals, etc.) or from the Internet to gather information on recent research in your field. Try to choose an area of your field that particularly interests you and that will interest your classmates. For example, it may be your own research or the research of a colleague. After you have gathered your information, write a brief composition explaining the work. Later, in pairs or small groups, take turns telling (not reading) about this research. Do your best to explain in language that everyone will understand.

PART 4 The Modal Auxiliaries

Setting the Context

Prereading Questions. How long do you think the world's oil supplies will last? What would happen if we ran out tomorrow?

Low on Energy

It is difficult to overstate the importance of coal, oil, and natural gas—the so-called fossil fuels. Without them, most industries could never have mechanized, and industrialization might not have occurred. Without them, virtually every engine would die, and the vast majority of lights would suddenly be extinguished.

Nowadays the question is no longer if we will ever run out of these precious resources; the question is when. It took perhaps 500 million years for fossil fuels to develop. In another 50 years, supplies may well be exhausted. At that point, we might plunge into a preindustrial world in which millions would die of hunger and the rule of law would collapse.

As we begin the new millennium, it is clear that much time has been lost. Policies encouraging conservation and alternative energy sources should have been started decades ago. Still, the situation is far from hopeless. With the world's best minds working on the problem, a practical alternative to fossil fuels could certainly be found. But do we have the resolve necessary to search for the solution, and is there enough time?

Discussing Ideas. What alternatives to fossil fuels do you know of? Which do you think is the most important? What steps do you think should be taken concerning our energy needs?

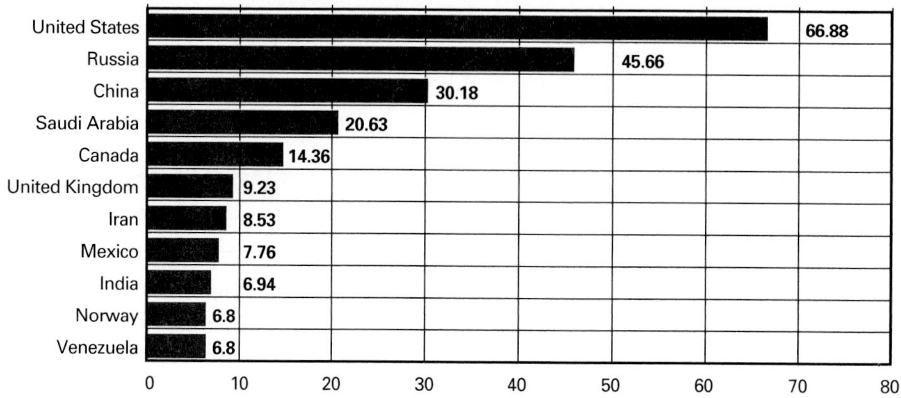

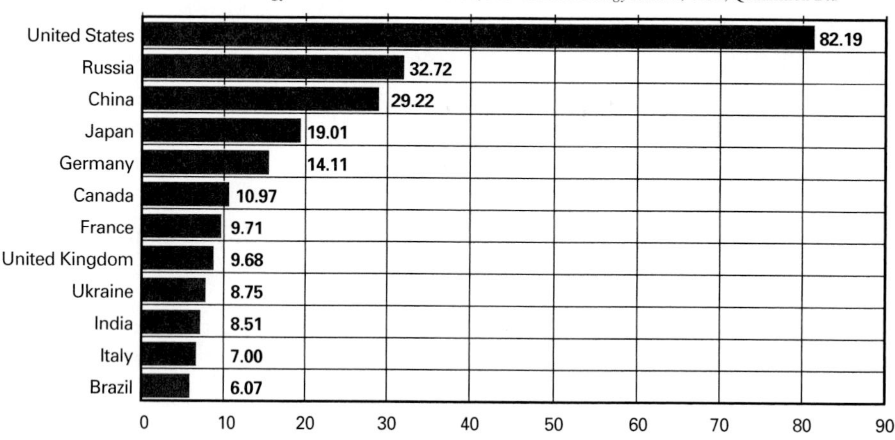

A. The Modal Auxiliaries

The simple passive voice of modal auxiliaries is formed in this way: modal (*can, could, may, might, must, ought to, shall, should, will, would*) + *be* + past participle (+ *by* + agent). The perfect passive form follows this pattern: modal + *have been* + past participle.

Simple Modals	Active	Passive
can, could, may, might, must, ought to, shall, should, will, would	We **could conserve** more oil today.	More oil **could be conserved** today.
Focus	We	More oil

Perfect Modals	Active	Passive
can, could, may, might, must,* ought to, shall, should, will, would	We **could have conserved** more oil in the past.	More oil **could have been conserved** in the past.
Focus	We	More oil

**Note:* The perfect form of *must* gives the meaning of probability only; it does not express need. Compare: *The work must be finished* (probability or need, depending on the context). *The work must have been finished* (probability only).

1 In the following sentences, change the verbs from the active voice to the passive voice whenever possible. Omit the agent unless it is important to the meaning of the sentence.

Example: We should recycle bottles and cans.
Bottles and cans should be recycled.

1. We should have developed solar power sooner.
2. We might use methane now instead of other fuels.
3. We ought to develop new biodegradable plastics.
4. We should car pool as much as possible.
5. We must educate people about energy.
6. We ought to have researched alternative energy sources a long time ago.

2 Complete these sentences with the active or passive forms of the modals and verbs in parentheses.

1. Most experts agree that solar power ____________ (will / become) an important energy source, but there is little agreement on when this ____________ (can / accomplish).
2. Today, the world is almost completely dependent on oil, so a long transition period ____________ (will / need) before solar power ____________ (can / replace) oil.
3. Which fuel ____________ (should / use) until solar energy ____________ (can / produce) in sufficient quantities? Clearly, the choice ____________ (must / come) from fossil fuels. Our entire industrial capacity depends on fossil fuels.
4. Thus, fossil fuels ____________ (cannot / abandon). But which of the fossil fuels ____________ (should / use) during the transition to solar power?
5. Coal and oil are such heavy polluters that they ____________ (should / avoid). Natural gas is clean burning, but it ____________ (cannot / find) in necessary quantities.

6. What we need is an energy source that is nonpolluting and one that we __________ (can / find) in unlimited quantities.
7. The incredible truth is that such a fuel has existed for millions of years. This fuel __________ (can / recover) easily, and no new technology __________ (will / require) to use it.
8. This seemingly magical substance is methane. We __________ (can / find) this highly efficient fuel almost anywhere. Methane is a natural by-product of decomposing organic matter.
9. Whenever leaves, bits of food, or dead animals decay and return to the soil, methane __________ (produce). This process __________ (can / control), and the gas __________ (can / collect).
10. It __________ (can / put) to many uses. For example, it __________ (might / replace) natural gas for cooking.

3 The following passage is written entirely in the active voice. It contains sentences that could be improved by using the passive voice. Rewrite the selection using sentences in the passive voice when appropriate. Omit the agent if it is not necessary to the meaning of the sentence.

Energy Planning

Since the 1800s, when oil first became an important resource, we have known that the supply could not last forever. Today, it is obvious that we should not use these supplies freely. In fact, many people believe that governments ought to regulate them.

We should have created a general energy plan decades ago. Just when the government could have enacted such a plan is debatable. However, surely after World War II, the direction of our industrial development was clear, and people could have done something.

Today, with the size and complexity of our industrial system, it would be extremely difficult to begin a strict energy plan. However, if people had developed a plan in the 1940s, we probably could have enforced it. In this way, we might manage our resources in a more efficient way.

---

4 **Error Analysis.** Many of the following sentences have errors in their use of the active or passive voice. Find and correct all errors. Note that there may be more than one way of correcting each error.

Example: In the 1890s, several industries were developed pedal-powered machines.

Correction: In the 1890s, several industries developed pedal-powered machines.

or

Pedal-powered machines were developed by several industries in the 1890s.

1. Three times as much power can delivered by the legs as by the arms.
2. By the late 1890s, tools such as saws and grinding wheels was being powered by bicycle-like machines.
3. Unfortunately, pedal power was abandoned soon after the development of gasoline engines.
4. However, it has "rediscovered" recently.
5. Today "people-powered" tools are making several different manufacturers.
6. These tools are been used by some craftspeople and farmers.
7. A number of tasks may be performed by "people-powered" tools.
8. For example, grain can ground, water can pumped, and land can cleared, plowed, and cultivated.

5 **Review.** Complete the following with the active or passive voice of the verbs in parentheses. Use any of the verb tenses and/or modals covered in this chapter.

Geothermal Power

One energy source that *has been used* (use) for hundreds of years is geothermal power. Geothermal power is simply the heat that ______(1) (produce) by volcanic activity below the earth's surface. This natural energy source ______(2) (put) to use in many ways. In Iceland, for example, geothermally heated water ______(3) (use) since 1930. Today, a large majority of homes there ______(4) (heat) geothermally. Electricity ______(5) (generate/also) by turbines that ______(6) (power) by naturally heated water. In fact, geothermal power ______(7) (develop) to such an extent in Iceland that dependence on fossil fuels ______(8) (reduce). Plus, this use of geothermal power ______(9) (bring) a tremendous side benefit; air pollution ______(10) (cut/drastically).

Unfortunately, up until now, few countries ______(11) (follow) Iceland's example. Nations such as the United States and Canada ______(12) (bless) with numerous geothermal areas that ______(13) (exploit) safely and easily. Both hot water and electricity ______(14) (provide) at low prices. Yet, neither country ______(15) (take) advantage of its geothermal resources. Currently,

only a small number of hot springs ______ (use) to provide hot water, and
16
many fewer ______ (produce) electricity.
17

6 **Review.** Complete the following with the active or passive voice of the verbs in the parentheses. Use any of the verb tenses or modals covered in this chapter.

Hydroelectric Energy

The world relies heavily on fossil fuels, yet other excellent sources of energy *have already been developed* (already/develop). Hydroelectricity, for example, is a very attractive form of energy. Its power source ______ (renew/regularly) by rain and snow. And, obviously, hydroelectricity ______ (not pollute) the atmosphere. Because of these advantages, hydroelectric sites ______ (exploit) in many parts of the world. In Sweden, for example, over 75 percent of their energy needs ______ (provide) by hydroelectricity.
1 2 3 4

Unfortunately, however, most of the untapped hydroelectric sites ______ (find) in parts of the world where people ______ (not need) a large amount of energy. Sites with great promise ______ (exist) in Canada, Latin America, India, and Russia, yet they ______ (not exploit). Sadly, despite its great potential as a source of clean, renewable energy, only a few countries are making hydroelectricity a top priority.
5 6 7 8

Itaipu dam on the borders of Brazil and Argentina.

7 **Review.** Complete the following passage by using either the active or passive forms of the verbs and modals in parentheses. Use any of the tenses and modals covered in this chapter.

Chasing Windmills

During the 1970s, a wind-power industry began to emerge in the United States. It *grew* (grow) out of the search for alternatives to oil as energy sources. A major project ______ (1) (fund) by the U.S. government to construct a wide variety of large wind turbines. At the time, it ______ (2) (believe) that wind power ______ (3) (become) a globally used, pollution-free, renewable source of energy. But, by the 1980s, United States interest in wind power ______ (4) (disappear/almost), except in California.

In California, wind-power projects ______ (5) (not abandon). Both individuals and power companies ______ (6) (pursue) the idea. Today, wind power ______ (7) (use) to produce almost 2 percent of the entire state's electricity. The same amount of energy ______ (8) (produce) by wind as ______ (9) (produce) by one nuclear reactor.

In Europe, wind power never lost favor as it did in the United States. Several countries ______ (10) (persist) in conducting research and developing projects.

In order for wind power to become truly workable, many improvements ___11___ (made). Better turbines ___12___ (build), and affordable ways of harnessing the wind ___13___ (design). Today, numerous wind-power projects ___14___ (plan), and it ___15___ (expect) that wind-power production will increase 400 percent by 2000.

Using What You've Learned

8 In pairs or small groups, talk about a practice in a field with which you are familiar—for example, engineering, construction, cooking, teaching chemistry (English, etc.). First, give a careful description of how the practice is currently done. Then give your opinion on ways this practice could be improved. State your recommendations on what *must, has to, should,* or *ought to be done.*

9 In pairs or small groups, examine a problem your country or the world is facing today. Examples include inflation, unemployment, foreign debt, pollution, crime, and drug use. After you have described the problem, examine its roots and discuss what exactly caused this problem. Finally, offer your opinions on what *could, should,* or *ought to have been done* five, ten, or twenty years ago to avoid the current situation.

Focus on Testing

Use of the Passive Voice

Verbs in the passive voice are frequently tested on standardized English proficiency exams. Review these commonly tested structures and check your understanding by completing the sample items that follow.

Remember that . . .

- The passive is formed in this way: (modal auxiliary) + *be* + past participle.
- The verb *be* is singular or plural depending on the subject of the passive sentence.
- The verb *be* gives the appropriate tense and time frame for the sentence.

Part 1. Circle the best completion for the following.

Example: Morse Code ______________ by Samuel Morse.

a. invented
b. was invent
(c.) was invented
d. did invent

1. Do you know if Mary ____________ the Smiths?
   a. be related to
   b. be related with
   c. is related with
   d. is related to

2. Robotlike machines ____________ to do a variety of household tasks.
   a. can now be used
   b. can be now used
   c. can now use
   d. can now be using

3. Aspirin ____________ the bark of the willow tree.
   a. is derived to
   b. are derived to
   c. is derived from
   d. are deriving from

4. Potatoes, now a major source of food worldwide, ____________ brought to Europe by Spaniards in the 16th century.
   a. was
   b. were
   c. had been
   d. was being

Part 2. Each sentence has one error. Circle the letter below the word(s) containing the error.

Example: E-mail commonly is used (Ⓐ) on many university campuses by faculty (B) and students who wish (C) to communicate (D) more easily and frequently.

1. In humankind's (A) thousands of years on earth, many resources (B) including wood, wind, water, and coal have been using (C) to produce (D) energy.

2. Measures should be taken (A) decades ago to decrease (B) the world's (C) dependence on oil; amazingly, such measures are still being debated (D).

3. It was assumed (A) that fossil fuels will last (B) forever and that as technology developed (C), it would simply become (D) easier to extract these precious resources.

4. Natural gas is (A) a much (B) cleaner source of energy than coal or oil but unfortunately are not found (C) in sufficient quantities to be used (D) extensively worldwide.

PART 5

Review of Chapters 5 to 8

1 **Review.** Complete the following with active or passive forms of the verbs in parentheses. Use appropriate verb tenses and forms of modal auxiliaries. Add negatives or adverbs when indicated.

The Silver Screen

Our world _changed_ (change) dramatically one cold winter night in Paris just minutes from the fabulous Paris Opera. On December 29, 1895, cinema ___1___ (bear).

That night, Auguste Lumiere and his two sons Auguste and Louis ___2___ (reveal/first) their now immortal film to the public. This first movie film ___3___ (project) onto a screen that ___4___ (locate) in the middle of the dark basement of the Grand Cafe. The audience ___5___ (seat) on both sides of the screen because the film ___6___ (can/view) from either direction. The apparatus that ___7___ (use) to show the film ___8___ (be) the same one that ___9___ (use) to take the film: the Lumieres ___10___ (invent) a reversible filming machine. Though remarkable, the film itself ___11___ (not be) fascinating. It ___12___ (show) a train that ___13___ (enter) a station and workers who ___14___ (leave) a factory in Lyons.

In the days after this first movie ___15___ (show), only two small Parisian newspapers ___16___ (report) the event. The Lumieres ___17___ (believe) that their machine ___18___ (will/have) no future and even ___19___ (refuse) to sell it to another Frenchman, Georges Melies. Melies ___20___ (obtain/finally) the device, however, and between 1896 and 1908, he ___21___ (produce) over 400 movies, some very short and others lengthy.

Culture Note

The film industry does almost $7 billion in business in the United States each year. For example, $6,949,000,000 was spent in theaters in 1998. The film industry also licenses movies for home viewing. In 1998, more than 700 million videotapes were available for rental. Watching movies at home in DVD format is the newest trend. Almost 100 percent of American households have a color TV, over 90 percent have a VCR, and home viewing is becoming increasingly popular.

While the Frenchmen ______ (22) (develop) their machines, Thomas Edison, the famous American inventor, ______ (23) (work) hard at perfecting his. Edison ______ (24) (create) his kinetiscope, and in 1903, he ______ (25) (make) the first American movie. Of course, it ______ (26) (be) a western, *The Great Train Robbery,* and ______ (27) (include) a moustached bandit.

Since these first magic moments of the silver screen, the popularity of movies ______ (28) (explode). During the last 100 years, audiences worldwide ______ (29) (delight), ______ (30) (frighten), ______ (31) (bore), and ______ (32) (astound) by images on the screen. Movies ______ (33) (reach) almost every part of every continent. Their content ______ (34) (evolve) from simple scenes and landscapes to the complex screenplays and computer graphics possible today. Numerous genres ______ (35) (develop), from documentaries to horror shows, science fiction, drama, fantasy, escapism, and even cartoons.

2 **Review.** First skim the following passage for meaning. Then complete it by adding appropriate connecting words. Note that the passage contains adjective, adverb, and noun clauses.

Fads and Fashions

Imagine *that* it is the end of the 1800s and ______ (1) you are a female. What will you wear ______ (2) you go out today? Your attire will depend in large part on ______ (3) you are and ______ (4) you live.

For those of you in the middle class ______ (5) live in the Americas or Europe, you will probably wear your corset. This is a construction ______ (6) will cover over one-quarter of your body and ______ (7) is made of cloth with steel ribs. The back has eyelets and several yards of laces ______ (8) are used to fasten the corset. You will wear your corset ______ (9) your waist will appear to be extremely small. And ______(10)______ it may be summertime, you will wear two or three layers of clothing over your corset. On your feet, you will wear boots ______(11)______ go up to your knees and ______(12)______ also have long laces as fasteners. ______(13)______ you are finally finished dressing and go outside, you will notice ______(14)______ every other female is wearing similar attire.

Now return to the present! ______(15)______ women worldwide have much more freedom today ______(16)______ they did in the past, you can probably put on almost anything you want. Of course, your age, your religion, and your personality will probably affect ______(17)______ you choose a dress, a suit, or pants, for example. Your economic status will affect ______(18)______ expensive that outfit is. And your size, your physical condition, your eyes and hair will probably affect ______(19)______ color you choose. But the reality is ______(20)______ today you probably have a choice, ______(21)______ your counterparts ______(22)______ were living only a few decades ago did not.

Web Note

If you are interested in fashion, consult the Web! For Armani, try www.modaonline.it/armani_e_ps/default.asp.

For Donna Karan, see www.donnakaran.com/.

For more general information, try First View *at www.firstview.com/.*

3 Rephrase the following story about four friends whose car broke down when they were driving in the desert. Use reported speech and make all necessary changes in verbs, adverbs, and pronouns.

Example: "What are we going to do?" asked Steve.
Steve asked what they were going to do.

Improvisational Technology

"Don't worry, Steve," Tina reassured him. "Let's get out and start walking. I'm sure help is not too far away." As Tina said this, she dismantled the rearview mirror from the car.

"What are you doing?" asked Gail.

"I'm taking the mirror so that we have it with us. We might need to signal someone for help."

"What a good idea!" Gail nodded, and then she began to take a hubcap off the car.

"What are you doing?" asked Frank. He was the last one to get out of the car.

"I'm taking this hubcap. We can use it to shade us from the sun if it gets really hot," Gail replied.

"That's smart," Frank said as he looked around him. "I think I'll take the radiator. That way if we get thirsty, we'll have water to drink."

"Good idea," said both Gail and Tina.

Then, when they were ready to begin walking, Gail, Tina, and Frank noticed that Steve had taken off one of the car doors and was trying to carry it.

"What are you doing with that door?" the three friends shouted.

"Well," said Steve as he dragged the door over to where they stood, "I thought that if it gets hot, we could roll down the window!"

4 **Review.** Combine the following seven sets of sentences and then rewrite them in paragraph form. Use commas when necessary, and add other information if you wish.

Example: 1989 was a year.
This year brought innumerable changes to our globe.
1989 was the year that brought innumerable changes to our globe.

1. In the fall of 1989, the Berlin Wall was torn down.
   It had stood as a physical and psychological barrier between East and West for almost 30 years.
2. A new government was elected in Poland in September 1989.
   It was the first noncommunist government since World War II.
3. The Polish people elected a new type of leader.
   Their leader had been a dedicated communist.
4. It was also in 1989.
   Hungary, the former Czechoslovakia, East Germany, and the former Soviet Union all opened their borders to the West then.
5. Many of the changes had been put in motion decades earlier.
   These changes occurred in 1989.
6. One can see the influence of history on the present.
   The events of 1989 are compared to the events of the 1870s, the 1920s, and the 1940s.
7. Many of the countries had been parts of larger empires years earlier.
   These countries gained freedom in the 1980s.
8. The new borders may remain. These borders were created in recent years. The new borders may change again someday soon.

Video Activities: Advances in Medicine

Before You Watch. Discuss these questions in small groups.

1. What do you think happens if the nerves that control your muscles die? Do you know the name of the disease that kills these nerves?
2. Have you ever known anyone who had a disease that affected his or her movement? How did this disease affect his or her life?

Watch. Circle the correct answers.

1. The main idea of this video segment is that ________________.
   a. ALS is a very difficult disease to have
   b. a cure will soon be found for ALS
   c. there is hope for people with ALS
2. Jerry Lineberger controls his wheelchair and his computer by moving his ________________.
   a. legs and arms
   b. hands and feet
   c. head and eyes

3. Dr. Jeffrey Rosenfeld's treatment ______________.
   a. has cured some people
   b. may help some people live longer
   c. is dangerous and difficult

Watch Again. Write answers to these questions.

1. How long has Jerry Lineberger had ALS? __________
2. What are the initials of the protein that Dr. Rosenfeld uses in his treatment?

   ____

3. Use the words below to complete the description of Dr. Rosenfeld's treatment.

abdomen	catheter	implanted	inserted
pump	release	spinal fluid	vertebra

A __________ the size of a hockey puck is __________ in the __________. A __________ is __________ between two __________. Tiny holes continuously __________ the drug into the __________.

4. *Diagnosed* is a verb. The noun is __________.
5. *Optimistically* is an adverb. The adjective is __________.
6. Listen and write words that have these meanings.
   a. incredible __________
   b. a doctor who specializes in the nervous system __________
   c. to increase the amount of time __________
   d. unproved theory __________

After You Watch. Complete the following sentences with the active or passive form of the verb in parentheses.

1. Until recently, patients with ALS __________ (give) any hope.
2. Dr. Rosenfeld's procedure __________ (not / perform) in many hospitals.
3. Dr. Rosenfeld hopes that many more patients __________ (help) in the future.
4. After Dr. Rosenfeld __________ (implant) the pump, he __________ (insert) a small catheter.
5. Thousands of people across the country __________ (suffer) from ALS.

Focus on Testing

Review of Problem Areas from Chapters 5 to 8

A variety of problem areas are included in this test. Check your understanding by completing the sample items that follow.

Part 1. Circle the best completion for the following.

Example: By 9:00 Ned ____________ his breakfast.

a. has finished
b. finishing
(c.) had finished
d. had been finishing

1. Mary said it was very important to her that she ____________ her work.
   a. is liking
   b. like
   c. likes
   d. liked
2. Around the world, copper cables ____________ glass fibers used to transmit electronic messages.
   a. are been replaced by
   b. are being replaced
   c. are replacing by
   d. are being replaced by
3. It is imperative ____________ to the meeting.
   a. that he comes
   b. that he come
   c. he comes
   d. he must come
4. Fossil fuels, such as oil and natural gas, ____________ plant and animal material deposited on the sea floor millions of years ago.
   a. are formed to
   b. is formed from
   c. are formed from
   d. is formed to
5. A child's brain is one mass, ____________ an adult's brain is separated into two hemispheres.
   a. when
   b. while
   c. why
   d. how
6. ____________ the nonviolent means that Mohandas K. Gandhi advocated, his followers often resorted to violence.
   a. Despite of
   b. In spite
   c. In spite of
   d. Despite the fact that
7. ____________ he decides to tell the truth, we will never know who killed that poor woman.
   a. Unless
   b. When
   c. Although
   d. Consequently
8. She exclaimed ____________ to play tennis.
   a. what it was a beautiful day
   b. was it a beautiful day
   c. what a beautiful day was it
   d. what a beautiful day it was

Part 2. Each sentence has one error. Circle the letter below the word(s) containing the error.

Example: Within the upcoming years, several important medical research projects will have be (A) completed (B) and breakthroughs will have been (C) made. (D)

1. With over 400,000 words, English is said (A) to be (B) one of the most richest (C) languages in the world in terms of (D) vocabulary.
2. Because (A) her tireless work with the wretched (B) and the sick, Mother Teresa was awarded (C) the (D) Nobel Peace Prize in 1979.
3. The (A) first major (B) oil fields in Saudi Arabia was discovered (C) in 1923 by Socal, a (D) United States oil company.
4. That elderly, gray-haired (A) man must have been (B) confuse (C) about the time of his appointment because he arrived two hours ahead of schedule (D).
5. The (A) Russian physiologist I. P. Pavlov conducted experiments with dogs in order to (B) he could learn (C) more about responses to a variety of stimuli (D).
6. When questioned (A) by the police, the young woman said that (B) she has left (C) the store before the robbery took (D) place.
7. Galileo put (A) in prison because (B) of his public statements regarding (C) the rotation (D) of the earth around the sun.
8. While (A) Sputnik was launched (B) by the Soviets (C) in 1957, the race to space began in earnest (D).

Chapter 9

Art and Entertainment

IN THIS CHAPTER

Part 1 Gerunds

Part 2 Infinitives

Part 3 Verbs Followed by Either Infinitives or Gerunds

Part 4 Infinitives and Gerunds As Subjects and Complements; Parallelism

Introduction

In this chapter, you will study some of the forms and uses of infinitives and gerunds. As you study, pay close attention to which verbs are followed by infinitives and which are followed by gerunds. Also, note any difference in meaning when both an infinitive and a gerund may be used. In Chapter 12, you will study additional forms and uses of infinitives and gerunds.

The following passage introduces the chapter theme "Art and Entertainment" and raises some issues that you will cover in the chapter.

What Is Art?

Trying to define art is almost impossible because each individual has an opinion on what *is* or *is not* art. For some, art is only certain types of music or painting or sculpture, while for others, art includes any creative act. The best way, then, to define art may be to consider what it does rather than what it is.

For most people, the function of art is to be pleasing to the eye or ear. In fact, art has served as decoration since prehistoric times. Yet, does something have to be beautiful to be art? Can a disturbing or distasteful piece be considered art? Does the definition of art as beauty exclude works like Picasso's *Guernica,* shown on page 279, which portrays the destruction of an entire town?

According to some critics, art goes beyond beauty. It involves making the world understandable by bringing order to the chaos of human experience. But can this definition be appropriate when one considers the chaos in works such as Michelangelo's *Last Judgment* or Erik Satie's *Through the Looking Glass?*

Perhaps we can define art only by giving a more general explanation of its function. Art historian John Canaday expresses this idea by saying that art is meant to clarify, intensify, or otherwise enlarge our experience of life.

Discussing Ideas. How many types of art can you name? Do you believe all creative work qualifies as art?

PART 1 Gerunds

Setting the Context

Prereading Questions. Many people say that jazz is the only truly American art form. What do you know about jazz? Do you like jazz music?

Jazz

Jazz musicians are unique as creative artists. Many poets, painters, and novelists are accustomed to working alone, but this is often impossible for jazz musicians. Because of the nature of jazz, most of their playing and practicing must be with other musicians. They need each other's sounds and impulses to become inspired.

To develop their own styles, jazz musicians must be ingenious and versatile. Playing jazz involves remembering hundreds of musical phrases and improvising on them during a solo. Each musician's personal style develops through various ways of improvising.

Some jazz musicians are so skillful at improvising that they can even improvise on their mistakes. The late trumpeter Dizzy Gillespie was famous for using any mistake to begin a new improvisation. By using a mistake to begin a new melody, he created a whole new piece of music.

Jazz legend Dizzy Gillespie

Discussing Ideas. What does it mean to improvise? There is so much improvisation in jazz that every time musicians play a particular song, they change it. Do you know of any type of music other than jazz in which improvisation is so important?

A. Functions of Gerunds

Gerunds may be used in place of nouns as the subject or the complement of a sentence. They may also be used as the object of a verb or preposition. *Not* is used before the gerund to form the negative. A possessive noun or adjective can precede it as the subject of the gerund. In conversational English, however, object forms (rather than possessive forms) are also used as subjects of the gerund.

Function	Examples
Subject	**Singing** is a lot of fun.
Complement	My favorite pastime is **listening** to music.
Object of a Verb	I enjoy **dancing.**
Object of a Preposition	I often relax by **playing** the guitar.
Negative Gerund	**Not owning** a guitar makes it difficult for me to practice.
Subjects of Gerunds	I always enjoy **Michael's (his) guitar playing.**
	He's used to **my sitting and listening** for hours.
	He's used to **me sitting and listening** for hours.*

*This form is incorrect but is frequently used in conversational English.

B. Gerunds As Objects of Prepositions

If a verb form is used after a preposition, it must be the gerund form. Gerunds commonly follow these expressions.

List of Words		Examples
be afraid of	insist on	We're excited **about going** to the concert.
be excited about	plan on	Let's plan **on leaving** early.
be interested in	succeed at (in)	I'm thinking **about getting** season tickets.
be good at (in)	think of (about)	Good musicians improve **by practicing** everyday.
be (get) tired of		He was tired **after practicing** for five hours.

C. To + *Gerund*

To is used as a preposition in the following expressions. These expressions *must* be followed by a gerund if a verb form is used.

List of Verbs	Examples
be accustomed to	I **am accustomed to spending** a lot of time outdoors.
be given to	I **am used to spending** a lot of time outdoors.*
be used to	I'**m looking forward to going** to the beach.
look forward to	
object to	
plead innocent (guilty) to	

*Do not confuse *used to* (habitual past) with *be used to (be accustomed to).*

1 What kinds of music do you like? Do you play any instruments? Would you like to learn any? Using your own ideas, complete the following sentences with appropriate prepositions and gerunds or gerund phrases.

Example: I am (I wish I were) good _at playing_ the flute.

1. I'm interested ________ ________ more (about) music.
2. I'd like to be better ________ ________ different kinds of music.
3. I'm planning ________ ________ some new records this week.
4. I get tired ________ ________ the same kinds of music.
5. Instead ________ ________ to a ball game, I'd much rather go to a concert.
6. I'm looking forward ________ ________ to a concert soon.
7. I'm also thinking ________ ________ . . . .

2 Add some of your own comments on different instruments, music, or musicians. Use gerunds or gerund phrases with the following cues to form at least six sentences.

(not) be interested in	object to
(not) be used to	plan on
(not) care about	take advantage of
(not) be successful at	in spite of
look forward to	instead of

Culture Note

Drug use was common among jazz musicians in the 1950s. Jazz greats such as Charlie Parker, Billie Holiday, Miles Davis, and Stan Getz all had problems with addiction. Getz and Davis gave up drugs and had very long and successful careers. Parker and Holiday remained addicted. As their health declined, so did their ability to create music. Holiday died at age 43, Parker at only 35.

3 The following sentences use infinitives of purpose to explain how someone did something. Rephrase each sentence to use *by* + a gerund. Use the example as a model.

Miles Davis, a brilliant trumpeter, was a high-school student in St. Louis in the early 1950s when he met jazz greats Charlie Parker and Dizzy Gillespie. He moved to New York City at age 18, began playing with Parker and Gillespie, and became a star.

Example: Miles Davis came to New York to learn more about jazz music.
Miles Davis learned more about jazz music by coming to New York.

The jazz great, Miles Davis

1. At first in New York, he worked several odd jobs to make money.
2. Miles played with jazz greats Dizzy Gillespie and Charlie Parker to learn more about a new movement in jazz called "bebop."
3. Eventually, he started his own band to give himself more musical freedom.
4. In the following years, Miles blended many types of jazz to create his own special sound.
5. While playing, he often turned his back to the audience to keep his concentration.
6. In the 1950s, he began using illegal drugs to try to escape loneliness.
7. He gave up drugs in the 1960s to improve his health.
8. Throughout most of his career, Miles traveled around the world to give his music a wider audience.

Web Note

Today, many organizations exist to help musicians who want to conquer addictions and stay drug free. One is the Musicians Assistance Program. You can learn about it at www.map2000.org/.

D. Gerunds as Objects of Verbs

If a verb form is used after the following verbs, it must be the gerund form.

admit	can't help	enjoy	involve	recommend
appreciate	consider	finish	mention	spend time
avoid	discuss	forgive	mind (dislike)	suggest
be worth	dread	imagine	miss	understand

4 Imagine that you have gone to a concert. Tell about it by completing the following sentences with gerunds or gerund phrases formed from the cues in parentheses.

Example: We all enjoyed (go / to the concert).
We all enjoyed going to the concert.

1. It certainly was worth (see).
2. I wouldn't mind (see that group again).
3. I admit (not like all the music).
4. We certainly appreciated (you / give us the tickets).
5. We are considering (go to another concert).
6. It will involve (make plans well in advance).
7. I'd recommend (you / buy tickets soon).
8. I suggest (call the box office today).

5 Using your own words, form complete sentences from the following cues.

1. appreciate / take
2. consider / return
3. discuss / return
4. imagine / see
5. involve / plan
6. don't mind / drive
7. recommend / see
8. spend time / visit
9. suggest / go
10. can't help / wonder

6 In pairs, take turns asking and answering the following questions.

1. Do you spend a lot of time listening to music?
2. What types of music do you enjoy? Are there any types you dislike?
3. Do you enjoy going to concerts? What types of concerts do you enjoy most?
4. Whom would you recommend seeing in concert?
5. Name some musicians that you think are worth paying a lot of money to see.
6. Would it be worth driving an hour to see these musicians?

7 Do you plan on going to a concert soon? In pairs, role-play a phone call or a visit to a theater box office to get information about tickets. Use as many of the following as possible in your role play.

I'm interested in. . . .	I suggest. . . .
Would you mind . . . ?	I'd recommend. . . .
I (would) appreciate. . . .	I hope that you'll enjoy. . . .
Is it worth . . . ?	If you don't mind. . . .

E. Subjects of Gerunds

A possessive noun or adjective is often used as the subject of a gerund. However, if the subject is a long noun phrase or if it is not a person, *the* + [gerund] + *of* + [subject] can be used.

	Example
Gerund Without a Subject	Beautiful **singing** is something I always enjoy.
Possessive As Subject	**Her singing** was truly magnificent. **Ella's singing** has thrilled countless audiences. I will never forget **Ella Fitzgerald's singing.**
The* + Gerund + *of	I will never forget **the singing of the jazz great, Ella Fitzgerald.** I will never forget the sound of **the shattering of glass** as her voice reached a high note.

8 Rephrase the following sentences to include gerund forms of the verbs in parentheses. Include the subject of the gerund with each sentence. In cases where possessives and phrases with *of* are possible, show both.

Louis Armstrong

Wynton Marsalis

1. There is only one "Mr. Jazz." Louis Armstrong's playing (Louis Armstrong / play) has influenced jazz ever since the 1920s. Through ____________ (he / improvise), "Satchmo" actually changed the art of trumpet playing. He made the trumpet do things that were supposed to be impossible. ____________ (he / "bend") of trumpet sounds astonished musicians everywhere.
2. ____________ (represent) the legacy of Louis Armstrong, Dizzy Gillespie, and Miles Davis among modern jazz trumpet players is Wynton Marsalis. His

__________ (understand) of the major trends in the history of jazz are evident in his distinctive performances. __________ (complement) this is his technical brilliance. __________ (train) for years as a classical musician has given his __________ (play) a distinctive refined sound. For years, Marsalis considered __________ (dedicate) himself to classic music. Today, he is primarily involved in __________ (perform) jazz. However, he still enjoys __________ (appear) in some classical concerts.

3. It is not difficult to name great jazz vocalists of the past. __________ (Billie Holiday/sing) was the personification of swing. __________ (Joe Williams/sing) the personification of blues, and __________ (Ella Fitzgerald/sing) the personification of modern jazz.

F. Direct Objects of Gerunds

Like verbs, gerunds may have direct objects. Gerunds that have direct objects may be phrased in two ways.

	Examples	Notes
Gerund + Object ***The* + Gerund + *of* + Object**	**Arranging music** can be difficult. **The arranging of music** is a major focus of the graduate program.	Using *the* with the gerund and *of* with the object places stronger emphasis on the gerund in its use as a noun.

9 Complete the following sentences by forming gerund phrases that use *the* and *of.*

Example: Jazz developed through *the combining of many styles* (combine/many styles) of music.

1. Jazz was born through __________ (mix/different races, cultures, and music).
2. The earliest forms of jazz began in New Orleans with __________ (blend/work songs, spirituals, blues, folk, and traditional music).
3. New Orleans provided the right atmosphere for __________ (interweave/black and white music).
4. Jazz always involves much more than __________ (play/musical notes).
5. It is __________ (express/one's individuality) through music.
6. For the musician, the heart of jazz is __________ (release/tension and emotion) through music.

Using What You've Learned

10 Longfellow said, "Music is the universal language of mankind." In small groups, discuss whether all music is, in fact, a language that everyone can understand. As you talk, share your own ideas on music. What is music? Is everything that we hear today really music? What kinds of music do you prefer? What kinds of music are popular today?

11 How can you become a good musician? How do you learn to play a guitar, a piano, a flute, a harp, a violin, or a saxophone? If you know about an instrument, give a brief description of the basic steps in learning to play it. For example, "You can become a good musician by practicing every day. . . ." Or, "If you're interested in playing the piano, you start by learning the scales. . . ." If you don't play an instrument, tell about another art form such as dance or acting, or a hobby or sport that you enjoy.

PART 2

Infinitives

Setting the Context

Prereading Questions Today, artists use everything from blowtorches to computers in their work. Yet some of the most beautiful work is still done by hand. Which tools did (do) traditional artists from your culture use?

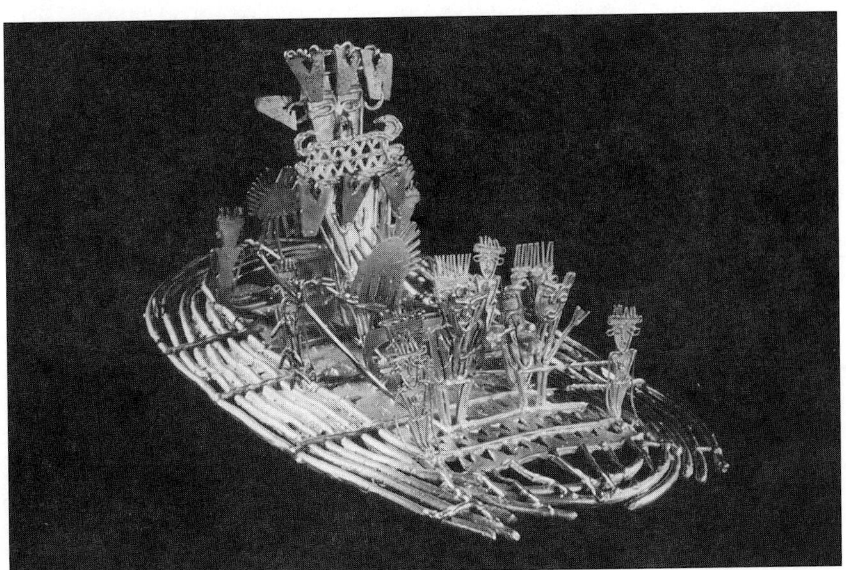

"El Dorado" gold work was from Colombia, created before the arrival of the Europeans.

Pre-Colombian Gold Work

Using gold for trade was rare among the Indians in ancient America because gold was sacred. Symbolic of great power, gold was believed to have a direct link to the gods, especially the sun god. Thus, it was too precious to use as money.

Instead, gold was an offering. It was a special tribute for an individual to give to the gods or to a patron. Above all, gold was important in funeral practices. Exquisite ornaments were used to decorate important graves, and most of the pre-Colombian gold work still in existence comes from such burial sites.

Unfortunately, much of the gold work that European explorers acquired was melted down to send to Europe. As a result, the gold work that remains has been found, for the most part, in more recently discovered graves.

Discussing Ideas. What happened to the gold work that the European explorers found? Can you think of other examples of art that has been taken or destroyed by outsiders?

A. Functions of Infinitives

An infinitive may be used in the following ways: in place of a noun as the subject or complement of a sentence, as the subject after "anticipatory" *it,* or as the object of a verb. Infinitives of purpose may also be used at various points within a sentence. *In order* can be used before an infinitive of purpose, but it is not necessary and is often omitted. *Not* is used before the infinitive to form the negative. *For* + a noun or object pronoun can precede an infinitive as its subject.

Function	Examples
Subject	**To visit** South America is one of my goals.
Complement	One of my goals is **to visit** South America.
With Anticipatory *It*	It's one of my goals **to visit** South America.
Object of a Verb	I would like **to visit** South America.
Negative Infinitive	It would be a shame **not to go.**
Subjects of Infinitives	It would be a shame **for him not to go.**
Infinitives of Purpose	**In order to see** everything, you should plan to spend several months there.
	To see everything, you should spend several months there.

B. Infinitives As Objects of Verbs

Infinitives may be used as objects of the following verbs.

List of Verbs				Examples
agree	decide	mean	seem	They **agreed to help.**
appear	forget	offer	serve	We **decided to leave** early.
be	happen	plan	tend	He **forgot to call.**
be about	hope	prepare	wait	She **refused to help.**
be supposed	learn	proceed		You **seem to be** upset.
come	manage	refuse		We **waited to say** "good-bye."

1 Imagine that you went to the Gold Museum in Bogotá, Colombia. Tell about your visit by completing the following sentences, using appropriate infinitive forms. Be sure to include negatives or subjects when indicated.

Example: We planned / go / to the Gold Museum.
We planned to go to the Gold Museum.

1. Everyone agree / meet / at the museum.
2. There appeared / be / hundreds of people at the museum.
3. We happened / choose / a busy day.
4. We had hoped / go / when it wasn't crowded.
5. We waited / the crowds / leave.
6. We decided / not / stay.
7. We agreed / come back / later.
8. We plan / never / go / there on a holiday again.

2 Working with a partner, create a story of approximately 20 sentences. Form sentences from each of the following cues and include these sentences in your story. When you are finished, present your story to the class.

1. agree / wait
2. decide / not go
3. hope / return
4. learn / ask
5. offer / help
6. prepare / leave
7. seem / not want
8. manage / understand

C. Verbs That May Be Followed by (Pro)nouns and Infinitives

The following list of verbs may use an infinitive object or a (pro)noun object and an infinitive.

Form	Examples	List of Verbs	
Verb + Infinitive	I asked **to go.**	ask	need**
Verb + Pro(noun) + Infinitive	I asked **her to go.**	beg	prefer†
		choose	promise
		dare	want
		expect	wish
		help*	would like†
		intend	

**Help* may be followed by an infinitive or by the simple form of a verb. Compare: *I helped her to do it. I helped her do it.*

**In certain cases, *need* may be followed by a gerund. Compare: *I need to wash my car. My car needs washing.*

†See Part 3 for more information on these verbs.

D. Verbs That Must Be Followed by a (Pro)noun Object Before an Infinitive

In the active voice, the following verbs *must* have a (pro)noun object *before* an infinitive. In the passive voice, the infinitive may follow the verb directly.

Form	Examples	List of Verbs	
Verb + (Pro)noun + Infinitive **Passive Verb + Infinitive**	We hired **him to do** the research. (active voice) He **was hired to do** the research. (passive voice)	believe cause convince enable encourage forbid force get* hire	instruct motivate order permit remind show . . . how teach tell use

**Get* is not used in the passive voice. In the active voice, it normally uses a (pro)noun object. In some idiomatic expressions, however, it is directly followed by an infinitive: *I get to go.* (I am allowed or permitted to go.) *I've got to go.* (I must go.)

3 Complete the following by using appropriate infinitive forms. Add a noun or pronoun object when necessary and include negatives when indicated.

Example: We asked / stay.

We asked to stay. No (pro)noun object is necessary.

We convinced / not / stay.

We convinced her not to stay. A (pro)noun object is necessary.

1. He chose / not / stay.
2. The extra money helped / pay for the trip.
3. The extra money enabled / stay longer.
4. They told / stay.
5. We were told / stay.

4 South America has a wealth of material for anyone interested in arts or crafts: music, dance, poetry, novels, painting, sculpture, architecture, and beautiful and varied craft work.

Imagine that you have the opportunity to go anywhere in South America. In pairs, take turns completing, asking, and answering these questions about your travels.

1. Where would you choose to . . . ?
2. Why would you like to . . . ?
3. How would you plan to . . . ?
4. Would you decide to . . . ?
5. What do you hope to . . . ?
6. Do you intend to . . . ?
7. Whom would you ask to . . . ?
8. Would you prefer to . . . ?
9. Who(m) would you want to . . . ?
10. What would you expect to . . . ?

E. Adverbs, Adjectives, and Nouns Followed by Infinitives

Adverbs + Infinitives	Notes
Pure gold is **too** soft **to use** in jewelry. Pure gold is not hard **enough to use** in jewelry. Can you tell me **where to buy** nice jewelry? (Can you tell me where I can buy some?)	*Too* and *enough* are often used with infinitives. *When, where,* and *how* can also be followed by infinitives. These phrases are reduced forms of noun clauses.

Adjectives + Infinitives	Notes
It was **wonderful to visit** the Gold Museum. I was **happy to go** there. It was **great to be able to go** there. It was **fascinating to see** the exhibit. It was **fascinating (to me) to learn** about gold. I was **the last (person) to leave.** It was **nice of you to join me.**	Adjectives such as *excited, happy, pleased, sad* are frequently followed by infinitives. Present participles such as *boring* and *interesting* are also followed by infinitives. *To* or *for* are often used to include a subject with the participle. Infinitives can also follow ordinals or superlatives *(first, last)* and *it* + adjective. *Of* (not *for*) is used with these.

Nouns + Infinitives	Notes
There are so many **things to see.** (There are so many things that we can see.)	Infinitives may be used after nouns as reduced forms of adjective clauses.

5 Consider these examples of pre-Colombian workmanship. Imagine the tools and the working conditions involved in making them. What are your reactions to them? Complete the following sentences, using appropriate infinitives as you express your opinions.

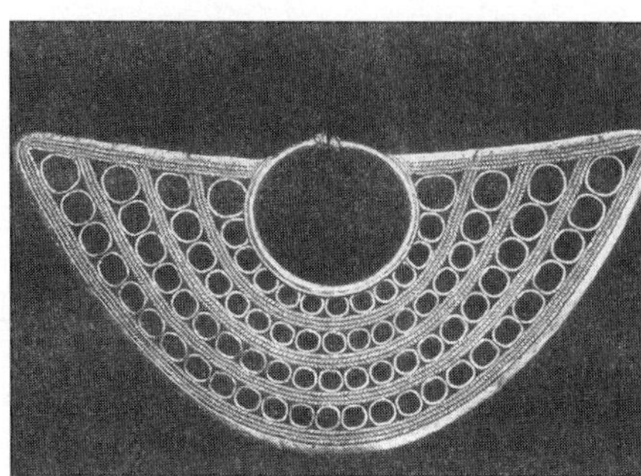

Example: It is amazing *to see the quality of workmanship in these pieces.*

Web Note

You can learn more about Colombia's Gold Museum and see examples of incredible metal crafting at www.banrep.gov.co.

1. I wonder if it was difficult. . . .
2. How did the artists get enough . . . ?
3. How were they able . . . ?
4. These pieces seem too. . . .
5. The artists must have worked hard. . . .
6. I wonder who was the first. . . .
7. I wonder if it was easy. . . .
8. I would enjoy learning how. . . .
9. It would be nice. . . .
10. I would like to know where. . . .

6 Complete the passage by using appropriate infinitive or gerund forms of the verbs in parentheses.

Example: Craftsmen in Colombia and Peru had known how ___*to work*___ (work) with gold well before 400 B.C.

1. Despite the primitive quality of their tools, they were able ________ (master) almost every technique for ________ (work) with gold known today.
2. These craftsmen learned how ________ (heat) gold until it was soft.
3. This allowed artists ________ (stretch) and ________ (hammer) the gold without ________ (break) it.
4. Normally, gold tends ________ (break) easily.

5. Later, these craftsmen developed the lost wax technique, which involved ________ (melt) gold and ________ (pour) it into molds.
6. In order ________ (use) this technique, the artist had ________ (be) skillful at ________ (work) with gold.
7. Some artists were so highly regarded that they were not permitted ________ (do) any other form of work.
8. These ancient smiths were so advanced that only a few of today's methods of ________ (work) gold were unknown to them.

7 Complete the following by using appropriate infinitive or gerund forms of the verbs in parentheses.

White Gold

It is soft, yet tough enough *to pull* (pull) and ________ (1) (pound) into almost any shape. It can be melted down ________ (2) (use) again. It gleams in the sun and is better at ________ (3) (reflect) light than anything else.

It is silver—a metal people have treasured for at least 5,000 years. During that time, they have managed ________ (4) (dig) up nearly a million tons of it, almost enough ________ (5) (make) three solid columns each the size of the Washington Monument, which is 555 feet high.

Much of the world's silver has been used ________ (6) (make) coins. The first silver coins are believed ________ (7) (date) from around 600 B.C. People had used chunks of silver for ________ (8) (trade) long before that time, but ________ (9) (trade) became easier with the use of coins.

Like gold, pure silver is malleable; a good silversmith knows how ________ (10) (pound) or ________ (11) (beat) it into shape without ________ (12) (break) it. Objects made of pure silver are normally too soft ________ (13) (use), though. A silversmith needs ________ (14) (add) other metals ________ (15) (strengthen) the silver. Sterling silver, for example, consists of 925 parts silver mixed with 75 parts copper.

8 Complete the following passage by using appropriate infinitive or gerund forms of the verbs in parentheses.

Precious Metals in the Americas

Silver played almost as big a part as gold in *bringing* (bring) many Europeans to the Americas. The Incas and the Aztecs had mined both of these precious metals, and word of their riches was enough ________ (1) (bring) thousands of Europeans who hoped ________ (2) (become) rich in the Americas. For 200 years after ________ (3) (discover) the Americas, Spain was the wealthiest nation in the world, and merchants in many places refused ________ (4) (accept) any form of money other than the Spanish silver dollar.

Since the early days of the Americas, silver has brought a different sort of wealth as people have learned ________ (5) (employ) it in a variety of important ways. ________ (6) (coat) mirrors, X rays, and photographic film and ________ (7) (conduct) electricity are only a few of its uses. In fact, silver is even used for ________ (8) (make) rain; pilots seed clouds with crystals of silver salts, which causes rain ________ (9) (form).

9 **Error Analysis.** All of the following sentences contain errors in the use of infinitives or gerunds. Find the errors and make the necessary corrections.

Example: Pure gold is ^*too* soft to use in jewelry.

1. I would enjoy to learn how to make jewelry.
2. She asked me going with her to South America.
3. Everyone agreed meeting me at the steps in front of the concert hall.
4. Marguerite refused helping me with the painting.
5. Miles Davis playing is beautiful.
6. The playing jazz is a difficult art form.
7. I can't help to go to at least once a week.
8. The students are very excited about to visit the Louvre Museum.
9. Marina isn't used to practice the piano yet.
10. I like to relax by paint with oil.

Using What You've Learned

10 What artistic activities do you participate in during your free time? Are you interested in painting or drawing? Taking photographs? Playing music? Do you like to go to concerts and museums? What kinds of art or artistic activities do you dislike? Which do you avoid? Discuss your interests with a partner, using as many of the words and expressions from the following list as possible. Remember which are followed by gerunds and which are followed by infinitives.

It's fun. . . .	be accustomed to	enjoy
It's boring. . . .	be interested in	expect
It's enjoyable. . . .	avoid	plan
It's interesting. . . .	encourage	plan on
It's relaxing. . . .	(someone)	

11 Think of all the tools or materials that you work with on a daily basis: pencils, erasers, notebooks, rulers, dictionaries, bicycles, cars, spoons, knives, faucets, chairs, and so forth. Choose one item, exotic or ordinary, and write at least a six-sentence description of how and why it is used. Later, read your description to the class, *but* do not tell your classmates what the item is. Let them guess, based on your description of it.

12 Cultures around the world have special crafts. The Chinese are famous for their porcelain, their brush paintings, and their carpets. Middle Easterners are famous for their rugs, as well as their ceramics and ironwork. Central and South American groups are noted for weaving, pottery, and basketry. Africans are renowned for wood carving.

Is there a highly developed craft that is typical in your culture? Or perhaps there is another art form such as music or dance that is a cultural specialty. Individually or in small groups, prepare a brief presentation (five to ten minutes) on an art or craft in your culture. Try to bring examples to help illustrate your presentation. As you prepare, use as many infinitives and gerunds as possible.

PART 3 Verbs Followed by Either Infinitives or Gerunds

Setting the Context

Prereading Questions. Are you familiar with impressionist art? Who are some of the more famous impressionist painters?

The Impressionists

On April 15, 1874, a small group of artists including Pissarro, Degas, Cézanne, Sisley, Monet, Morisot, and Renoir held their first exhibition in Paris. The paintings that they displayed are recognized today as masterpieces. However, at that time, this artwork caused the public to react with disappointment and disgust.

Impression, Sunrise by Claude Monet

It seemed for a moment as though all of Paris had stopped to criticize the radical style of these artists.

Art critics were virtually unanimous in their panning* of the exhibition. Some even advised burning all of the paintings. One critic sarcastically labeled the group's technique impressionist, after seeing *Impression, Sunrise,*** a painting by Claude Monet. The critic had meant to ridicule† the techniques of the group, yet it was this name that the group adopted. The group had already been trying to define their technique for some time. After hearing these remarks, the painters stopped looking for definitions and began to call themselves impressionists.

Discussing Ideas. Though impressionist art was ridiculed in the beginning, today it is appreciated around the world. Are people always resistant to new trends or revolutionary ideas? What are some current trends in art, music, or fashion that some people cannot accept? Do you think any of these trends will one day become as popular as the impressionist paintings?

A. Verbs Followed by Either Infinitives or Gerunds

Verbs with Little or No Difference in Meaning When Followed Either by a Gerund or an Infinitive		
Verbs	**Examples**	**Notes**
begin can(not) bear can(not) stand continue start	I **began studying** art several years ago. I **began to study** art several years ago.	These verbs are commonly followed by either infinitives or gerunds with little difference in meaning.
attempt intend neglect	I've **attempted to do** an oil painting several times. I've **attempted doing** an oil painting several times.	Both forms are correct, but infinitives are used more often after these verbs.
hate (dis)like love prefer	I **like to go** to museums. I **like going** to museums. I **would like to go** to the Museum of Fine Arts in Boston.	Both forms are often used, but only infinitives are used when the verbs are in the conditional.

**pan* strongly criticize
***impression* in this sense, an idea or memory that is not distinct, precise, or well defined
†*ridicule* make fun of

Verbs That Have Different Meanings When Followed Either by a Gerund or an Infinitive

	Examples	Notes
Infinitives with *Forget, Regret,* and *Remember*	I **forgot to tell** you what happened. I **regret to give** you this news. Did you **remember to tell** him the story?	Infinitives follow *forget, regret,* and *remember* when these verbs express a first (or earlier) action. The infinitive expresses the second (or later) action. *To inform, to say,* or *to tell* are the most common infinitives used after *regret.* Other verbs normally use the gerund form after *regret.*
Gerunds with *Forget, Regret,* and *Remember*	Have you **forgotten** (about) **telling** him that? I **regret not giving** him more advice. Do you **remember promising** me that you would tell him?	Gerunds follow these verbs when the verb expresses the second action. The gerund expresses the first action.
Infinitives with *Try*	I **tried to talk** to him, but he was too busy. (I didn't talk to him.)	When *try* means *attempt,* it is followed by an infinitive.
Gerunds with *Try*	I **tried talking to him,** but he wouldn't change his mind. (I talked to him.)	*Try* can also mean *experiment* (with different alternatives). In this case, it is followed by a gerund.

Verbs That Have Different Meanings When Followed Either by a Gerund or an Infinitive (*Continued*)

	Examples	Notes
Infinitives with *Stop* and *Quit*	We **stopped to take** a break. (We stopped our work in order to take a break.)	When an infinitive follows *stop* or *quit,* it tells the reason or purpose for stopping.
Gerunds with *Stop* and *Quit*	We **stopped taking** long breaks. (We used to take long breaks, but we don't anymore.)	When a gerund follows these verbs, it tells *who* or *what* was stopped.
Infinitives with *Mean*	Did you **mean to spend** so much?	*Mean* followed by an infinitive means *intend* or *plan.*
Gerunds with *Mean*	It **means not having** enough money for the rest of the month.	*Mean* followed by a gerund means *involve* or *signify.* An impersonal subject (*this, that, it,* etc.) is normally used with *mean* + a gerund.
Infinitives with *Propose*	I **propose to nominate** John at the next meeting.	*Propose* followed by an infinitive means *intend.*
Gerunds with *Propose*	I **propose asking** him first before you nominate him.	*Propose* followed by a gerund means *suggest.*

Verbs That Are Followed by Gerunds or Infinitives, Depending on the Use of a (Pro)noun Object		
	Examples	**Notes**
Verb + Gerund	I advise **taking** your camera.	These verbs may be followed by gerunds if no (pro)noun object is used.
Verb + (Pro)noun + Infinitive	They **advised** me **to take** my camera.	If a (pro)noun object is used, it is followed by an infinitive. Infinitives are also used when these verbs are in the passive voice.
advise	encourage	permit
allow	forbid	teach

Note: In certain cases a gerund is used after *teach* + object. This most often occurs with common school subjects such as reading, painting, and singing. (*I teach [children] reading and writing.*)

1 Many of the sentences in the following conversation may be completed by using either infinitives or gerunds. In cases where only one form is possible, explain why.

Anne: I can't believe this: I'm leaving for Europe tomorrow, and I haven't even started <u>packing (to pack)</u> (pack) yet! Talk about disorganized. I'm sure I'll forget ________ (1) (take) my passport, or my tickets, or something.

Joan: I'd love ________ (2) (go) with you, especially to Paris. How long will you be there?

Anne: I'll be there for five or six days. I'd prefer ________ (3) (spend) a year or two in Paris, but even a few days is fine with me. I'm going to try ________ (4) (visit) as many museums as I can—the Louvre, the Musée Rodin. . . .

Joan: Remember ________ (5) (visit) the Musée Marmottan. It has some of Claude Monet's most beautiful paintings, including many of the *Water Lilies* series. Try ________ (6) (spend) at least an afternoon there. I meant ________ (7) (spend) a day there myself, but I wasn't able to. It would have meant ________ (8) (change) our plans.

Anne: I remember ________ (you / tell) me about that. Didn't you try ________ (go) several times, but the museum was closed?
9 10

Joan: I'd tell you the story again, but you should stop ________ (talk) and start ________ (pack).
11 12

2 Form complete sentences from the following.

1. That museum does not permit you / take pictures.
2. At least, they do not permit / use a flash.
3. You are forbidden / use a flash.
4. My friend teaches people / take pictures without a flash.
5. She could teach you / take good pictures without your flash.
6. Flash cameras can cause the colors / fade.
7. The museum encourages people / buy prints there instead.
8. The prints are very good. I advise / buy several.

3 Complete the following passage by using infinitive or gerund forms of the verbs in parentheses.

Impressionism

Before Monet painted *Impression, Sunrise,* art critics had used the word *Impressionism* to suggest (suggest) incompleteness or a superficial vision of the subject. The impressionists decided ________ (adopt) the name and wished ________ (find) a suitable definition for it. One suggestion was ________ (paint) in terms of light rather than in terms of physical shape.
1 2 3

In order ________ (define) impressionism, one must remember ________ (consider) the impressionists' concern for light rather than form. Instead of ________ (analyze) the form of an object, the impressionists allowed themselves ________ (see) only the light reflected from the object. This is because they were interested in ________ (reproduce) the effect of the light alone. Thus, flowers in the distance that appeared ________ (be) blurs of color were painted as blurs, even if the artist hap-
4 5 6 7 8 9

pened _____10_____ (know) the flowers well enough _____11_____ (reproduce) them exactly from memory.

4 Complete the following passage by using infinitive or gerund forms of the verbs in parentheses.

The Bar at the Folies Bergere, 1882 by Édouard Manet

Culture Note

Great artists have often been ignored. Vincent van Gogh, one of the most brilliant and most troubled of the impressionist painters, provides a tragic example. The son of a minister, van Gogh was multilingual and widely traveled. He had enormous talent and many connections in the art world. Still, he doubted his own ability and suffered from severe depression. Vincent van Gogh committed suicide in 1890 at the age of 37. Though hundreds of his works are considered priceless today, he sold only one painting during his lifetime.

Édouard Manet

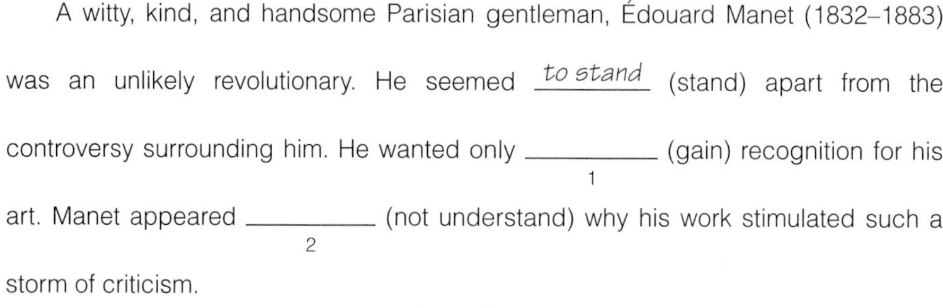

A witty, kind, and handsome Parisian gentleman, Édouard Manet (1832–1883) was an unlikely revolutionary. He seemed __to stand__ (stand) apart from the controversy surrounding him. He wanted only _____1_____ (gain) recognition for his art. Manet appeared _____2_____ (not understand) why his work stimulated such a storm of criticism.

Yet Manet was a revolutionary. His paintings *Déjeuner sur l'herbe* and *Olympia* caused the entire Parisian art world _____3_____ (shake) with amazement. Manet was the first _____4_____ (begin) the new trends of modernism. A great innovator, he disliked _____5_____ (follow) old styles. _____6_____ (he/handle) of form, color, and light shows a completely modern way of _____7_____ (think). He was the first in the Parisian art world _____8_____ (ask), Is art simply a recording of reality? Does it have _____9_____ (imitate) the past? Are artists forbidden _____10_____ (create) their own interpretations?

The importance of Manet's work goes beyond the quality of his painting. It anticipated many trends ________ (come). He borrowed from the old masters but
11
avoided ________ (imitate) them. In essence, Manet was successful at ________
12 13
(take) ideas from old art and ________ (redefine) these ideas in terms of the new.
14
His struggle ________ (define) his vision encouraged a generation of young artists
15
________ (explore) their own vision of art.
16

Using What You've Learned

5 The pieces of art that follow were considered revolutionary and in some cases "crude," "simplistic," "distasteful," or "disgusting" when they were first shown. The appearance of each, however, prompted irreversible changes in the art world of the time. In small groups, discuss your own opinions of these particular works of art. Which do you like or dislike? Can you imagine why they were considered outrageous? In your discussion, try to use as many of these words or phrases as possible.

avoid	understand	know (how)	be successful at
can't help	be accustomed to	(would) like	be / get tired of
can't stand	be used to	(not) mind	(not) care for
enjoy	be fascinated with	prefer	(not) approve of
imagine	be interested in	tend	object to

The Little White Girl: Symphony in White, No. 2 by James Whistler

Burning of the Houses of Parliament by J.M.W. Turner

Mont Sainte-Victoire by Paul Cézanne

The Invalid by Henri Matisse

The Starry Night (1889) by Vincent van Gogh

The Scream by Edvard Munch

PART 4

Infinitives and Gerunds as Subjects and Complements; Parallelism

Setting the Context

Prereading Questions. Are you familiar with traditional African art? What materials have Africans traditionally used to create art forms?

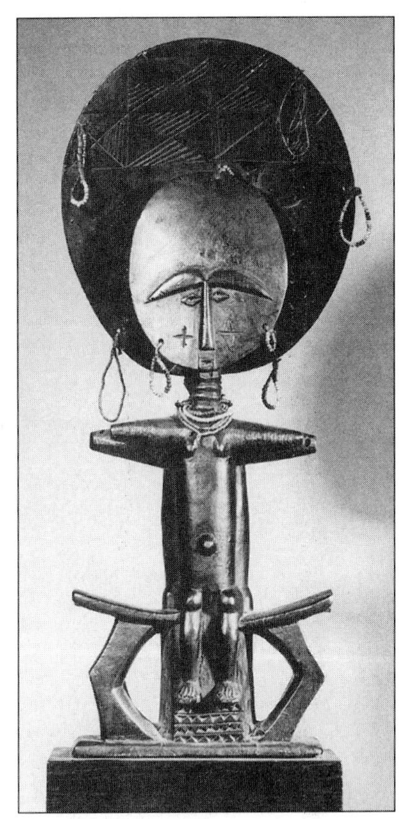

African Art

For many people, to create art is to express the moral and religious beliefs that form the basis of their lives. This has been particularly true in the case of African art. African sculpting, dancing, storytelling, and music all developed from religion. Because of this religious influence, African art had two chief characteristics: variety in form and similarity in style. Different areas of Africa specialized in different forms—statues, drums, dances, masks—because the beliefs and rituals of African religion were varied. Yet the basic art styles throughout Africa were remarkably similar because everything was a variation on traditional religious themes. Most of African art has had this consciously religious function. The sculpting, dancing, singing, and drum music have all been designed to reinforce the creative energy of life. Far from being primitive, African art is a highly stylized expression of spirituality.

Discussing Ideas. In the early 1900s, many revolutionary artists such as Picasso, Braque, and Matisse looked to African art as a source of inspiration. Much of today's popular music has its roots in African music. In which kinds of music can you see the strongest evidence of African influence?

A. Infinitives and Gerunds As Subjects and Complements

Both infinitives and gerunds may be used as subjects and complements of sentences. Gerunds are more commonly used as subjects; however, infinitives often follow *it* as the subject of a sentence. Both appear as complements, although infinitives are more common.

	Examples	Notes
Gerund Subject	**Sculpting** is one of the important types of art from Africa. **Sculpting** in Africa has been dated to ancient times. **Working** with bronze was a specialty of artists from Benin.	Gerunds are often used as subjects to express a process or an action in progress.
Gerund Complement	A specialty in Benin was **working** with bronze.	Gerunds may be used as complements after *be*, but infinitives are used as complements after other linking verbs.
Infinitive Subject	**To produce** (or **producing**) a detailed figure may take anywhere from a few hours to several weeks.	Infinitives are occasionally used as subjects to refer to a goal, purpose, or intention.
Infinitive with Anticipatory *It*	**It** can take several weeks **to produce** a detailed figure.	An infinitive often follows the verb when the "anticipatory" *it* is the subject of the sentence.
Infinitive Complement	A difficult part of the task is **to select** the best type of wood for a particular carving.	Infinitives are often used as complements with the linking verbs *be*, *seem*, and *appear*.

1 Today, machines do much of our work for us. As a result, some of the qualities associated with handmade items have been lost. Our clothing may be cheaper, but it is no longer unique. Most of the fabrics are synthetic. Our food is processed from start to finish. Even much of our music is electronic.

Do you think we have sacrificed quality by relying so heavily on machines? Have we already lost the skills to make things carefully by hand? Do you believe that it is important to protect folk or traditional arts and crafts? Give your own opinions on this subject by completing the following with infinitive phrases.

Example: It's (not) important *to preserve traditional arts and crafts.*

1. It would be a shame. . . .
2. It's difficult. . . .
3. It's much more interesting. . . .
4. It's better. . . .
5. It would also be fascinating. . . .
6. It's hard. . . .
7. It's necessary. . . .
8. It's (im)possible. . . .

Now rephrase your sentences to begin with gerunds.

Example: *Preserving traditional arts and crafts is (not) important.*

B. Parallelism

Sentences with more than one infinitive or gerund should use the same form (infinitive *or* gerund, *not both*) whenever possible. This is especially true when coordinating conjunctions are used or when a series of items is listed.

Parallel Structures	Traditional art in Africa includes **sculpting, dancing,** and **storytelling.**
Lack of Parallel Structures (poor style)	Traditional art in Africa includes **sculpting, dancing,** and **to tell** stories.

2 Complete the following eight sentences with appropriate infinitive or gerund forms of the verbs in parentheses. In some cases, either form will be appropriate, so be sure to use parallel structures in your sentences.

Example: Non-Africans often consider *sculpting* (sculpt) as the greatest traditional African art, but to Africans, *dancing* (dance) is perhaps their most important art form.

African Dance

1. __________ (dance) is a way of __________ (unite) two important parts of African life: religion and community life.
2. African dance can be a part of a ceremony for __________ (mark) the start of a hunt or __________ (give) thanks for a successful harvest.
3. It is often used __________ (commemorate) a birth or death or __________ (celebrate) a marriage.
4. Often dance is festive, a time __________ (honor) special spirits, or it is purely recreational, a time __________ (people enjoy) themselves.
5. For Africans, __________ (dance) is __________ (move) spontaneously to the rhythm of the drums.
6. African __________ (drum) involves __________ (create) an individual rhythm, __________ (follow) the other drummers, and __________ (respond) to their rhythms.

7. African drums are constructed __________ (produce) dozens of sounds, and every drummer attempts __________ (make) new combinations of sounds.
8. Frequently it is impossible __________ (Westerners / duplicate) or even __________ (follow) complex African rhythms.

3 Complete the following sentences by using infinitive or gerund forms of the verbs in parentheses. If you believe that either may be appropriate, explain why.

1. An African woodcarver's main function was _to create (creating)_ (create) sculpture for religious purposes.
2. ______________ (attract) and ______________ (keep) specific spirits inside a carving was a way to protect the village from harm.
3. ______________ (express) energy or life force in physical form is still the goal of African woodcarvers.
4. It must have been important ______________ (combine) art and practicality because household items such as cups, spoons, and stools have shown amazing workmanship.
5. ______________ (wear) carved wooden masks was a part of many religious dances, and the mask itself was believed to have special powers.

6. __________ (collect) African sculpture became a favorite pastime of Europeans and Americans; as a result, few original pieces remain in Africa today.
7. Today, __________ (carve) religious or household items has been replaced by __________ (produce) souvenirs for tourists.
8. Now it is almost impossible __________ (find) carvings of the same quality as in the past.

4 **Error Analysis.** Many of these sentences contain errors in the use of infinitives and gerunds. Find any errors and make the necessary corrections.

1. Long before Europeans came ~~for~~ to explore tropical Africa, the powerful nation of Benin had been flourishing in what is now southern Nigeria.
2. Benin society was dignified, law abiding, and well ordered; it was headed by a king, or *Oba,* who was all powerful yet tolerant enough to allow a good deal of personal freedom in his kingdom.
3. In spite of not to have a written language, the Beninese left beautiful bronze plaques and figures as records of their civilization.
4. The *Oba* hired artists to design the plaques in order to decorate his palace.
5. These plaques recorded numerous scenes of life in Benin, and many showed two important aspects of the culture: hunting and to trade.
6. Only the strongest Beninese men could become hunters and then only after to complete rigorous training.
7. Young hunters had to learn how to track animals, moving quickly and quietly and surviving in the forest for days without food.
8. When European explorers arrived, they couldn't help to be amazed at the amount of commerce in Benin.
9. Benin was the commercial center of western Africa, and Beninese merchants were clever enough outthinking the Europeans, who had expected dealing with simple natives.
10. Beninese merchants had an elaborate money system, and they dealt in the buying and to sell of ironwork, weapons, farm tools, wood carvings, and food.

Using What You've Learned

5 Oral tradition and the art of storytelling are important aspects of African life. A storyteller may be able to recount the 500-year history of his or her family or village.

In small groups, take turns telling stories about your family, town, or region. Your story may be a favorite from childhood: When my great-grandfather was a young boy, Indians in northern Wisconsin took care of him and helped raise him. . . . Or it may be a story from your town: In San Joaquin, they tell the story of *la llorona. La llorona* is a ghost who is often heard crying for her lost baby. . . .

As you tell your story, try to talk continuously for at least four minutes. Do your best to include as many infinitives and gerunds as you can.

Video Activities: Women in Jazz

Before You Watch. Discuss these questions in small groups.

1. Which of these musicians played jazz?

   a. Billie Holiday b. the Beatles c. Luciano Pavarotti

2. Do you ever listen to jazz? Do you know any other famous jazz musicians?

Watch. Circle the correct answers.

1. What kind of music does Rosetta Records publish?
   a. songs by modern female jazz musicians
   b. songs from early jazz musicians
   c. early songs by female jazz musicians
2. According to Rosetta Weitz most people today do not realize that women ______________.
   a. sang with jazz bands
   b. had a powerful influence on jazz
   c. were better jazz musicians than men
3. Successful female jazz musicians had ______________.
   a. wealth and power
   b. everything but power
   c. to depend on men
4. What did early female jazz singers sing about?

   a. love b. war c. pride d. abandonment e. poverty

Watch Again. Answer these questions in small groups.

1. Complete the names of these jazz musicians. Put a check mark (✓) next to the women.

Jazz Musicians	Women?
a. ______________ Cox	______
b. ______________ McKinney	______
c. Maxine ______________	______
d. Lester ______________	______
e. ______________ Calloway	______
f. ______________ Ellington	______
g. ______________ Basie	______
h. ______________ Humes	______

2. *Impact* means the same as ______________.
   a. destruction b. influence c. connection
3. Something that is *quintessential* is ______________.
   a. a perfect example b. necessary c. successful
4. *Alongside* means the same as ______________.
   a. near b. with c. instead of

After You Watch. Complete the following sentences with a gerund or an infinitive.

1. I don't really enjoy __________ (listen) to jazz.
2. Marcus is thinking of __________ (become) a musician.
3. Rosetta Weitz hopes __________ (preserve) the works of early female jazz musicians.
4. Instead of __________ (play) rock and roll, you should be playing jazz.
5. Cab Calloway's sister taught him __________ (play) jazz.

Focus on Testing

Use of Infinitives and Gerunds

Problem areas with infinitives and gerunds often appear on standardized English proficiency exams. Check your understanding of these structures by completing the sample items that follow.

Remember that . . .

- Certain verbs can be followed by gerunds, others by infinitives, and some verbs by either.
- Gerunds (not infinitives) are used after prepositions.
- A possessive noun or adjective is often used as the subject of a gerund.
- Some verbs must be followed by a (pro)noun object before an infinitive.

Part 1. Circle the best completion for the following.

Example: We convinced her not __________.
a. she stay
b. stayed
(c.) to stay
d. stay

1. Mike is interested __________ to the store.
   a. in go
   b. at going
   c. in going
   d. with going
2. I recommend __________ the assignment.
   a. to finish
   b. that you finishing
   c. finishing
   d. finished
3. She took that class __________ her English.
   a. in order improve
   b. to improve
   c. in order improving
   d. improve
4. We agreed __________ at the theater.
   a. to meet
   b. meeting
   c. in order to meeting
   d. for meeting

Part 2. Each sentence has one error. Circle the letter below the word(s) containing the error.

Example: Dance can be (A) a festive time for honor (Ⓑ) special spirits or it can be (C) a purely recreational time for people to enjoy (D) themselves.

1. Jack and Mary were forced to (A) selling (B) their home because (C) they couldn't make (D) the house payments.
2. They expected (A) for her (B) to go (C) to that restaurant because she always liked trying (D) different kinds of food.
3. The job was tiring, (A) so the workers stopped taking (B) a break and relaxed (C) on a (D) bench in the sun.
4. I advised Frank and Julie (A) seeing (B) a marriage counselor before (C) their relationship really started to deteriorate (D).

Chapter 10

Conflict and Reconciliation

IN THIS CHAPTER

Part 1 *Hope* Versus *Wish*

Part 2 Imaginary Conditions: Present and Unspecified Time

Part 3 Perfect Modal Auxiliaries

Part 4 Imaginary Conditions: Past and Present Time

Part 5 Factual Conditions: Present, Future, and Unspecified Time

Introduction

In this chapter, you will look at ways to express hopes and wishes, and you will study conditional sentences. With these, you will study more about the subjunctive mood and about modal auxiliaries.

The following passage introduces the chapter theme "Conflict and Reconciliation" and raises some topics and issues you will cover in the chapter.

Humans and the Environment: Conflict or Coexistence?

"We have forgotten the earth, forgotten it in the sense that we fail to regard it as the source of our life."

FAIRFIELD OSBORN

Humans have a history of trying to control the environment. We have learned to produce a constant food supply through farming, to regulate our temperature through use of clothing and heating and cooling systems, and to build shelters that can withstand even the greatest extremes in weather.

Our history has been a constant struggle to survive the rigors of our environment. Because of this struggle, we often look at the world as an opponent to be conquered, dominated, and exploited. But as we change the environment to fit our needs and desires, we damage the fragile balance of nature, sometimes irreparably. Unfortunately, there are too many people for us to continue this battle with our earth. If the population were small, our impact would not be significant. But the impact of over 5 billion people is tremendous.

Today the world is at a crossroads. Many plants and animals are near extinction, and the all-important food chain is in jeopardy. If we had tried to live with our environment instead of fighting against it, we would not have caused such widespread damage, and the environment would not be in danger today. If we continue to abuse our world, we will almost certainly destroy it.

Discussing Ideas. In what ways does the environment of an area change when a large population moves into it? From your experience, are people generally careful to respect their environment? How can humans reconcile their conflicts with the environment?

PART 1 *Hope* Versus *Wish*

Setting the Context

Prereading Questions. Think again about the major problems we face today. Can one person do anything to help solve these problems?

Taking Responsibility

What kind of country do you want? What kind of world? What can you, the average person, do to help achieve this kind of world?

There are many who believe that it is impossible for an individual to have an effect on the world situation. These people often wish that the situation were different and that our problems had never developed. Still, they do nothing. They may hope that solutions are possible or that the problems will disappear, but they think that the solutions are completely out of their control.

Others feel that giving up and withdrawing from the world is the worst possible decision. They believe in activism and personal involvement. They hope that through their activities they will be able to effect changes and thus to influence leaders and policies.

Discussing Ideas. Where do you stand? Are you someone who tries hard to make changes and to find solutions, even for major problems? Can you think of individuals who have had a profound effect on major world problems?

A. Hope *Versus* Wish

The verb *hope* is generally used to express optimism, that something is possible. The verb *wish* is often used to express impossibility or improbability, that the speaker wants reality to be other than it is. Both verbs are often followed by noun clauses. Compare the following:

	Examples	Implied Meaning
hope wish	I **hope** that our team **will win** tonight. I **wish** that our team **could win** tonight. I **wish** that our team **were going** to win tonight.	I think that they have a chance to win. I doubt that they can win.
hope wish	I **hope** the team **won** last night. I **wish** the team **had won** last night.	I don't know if they won, but it's possible. I know the team lost last night.

Note: Wish also has an optimistic meaning in certain expressions: *We wish you a happy birthday! I wish you a merry Christmas.*

1 What can you do to help make changes? One possibility is writing petitions to local, regional, or even world leaders. The following petition was written to the United Nations by middle-school students in Northville, Michigan. Underline the verbs in the noun clauses. Indicate whether the verbs express past, present, or future time frames.

Example: We hope that you will read our proposals carefully. future

1. We hope that you, as world leaders, are concerned about the survival of all humans. ______________
2. We hope that you recognize the seriousness of today's problems. ______________
3. We wish that we were in the position to do something about the serious problems of today: war, disease, environmental damage and catastrophe, and more. ______________
4. We wish that all countries had begun long ago to work on the problems of the world. ______________

Culture Note

People in the United States often use petitions as a way of focusing on a problem or of getting support for or against possible solutions. A petition is a request, usually to a governmental body or authority. A petition can be signed by only one person, but it will generally carry more weight with more signatures. Specific interest groups may gather thousands of signatures in support of or against an issue.

5. We wish that people everywhere had more concern for the world around them. ______________
6. We wish that governments had faced the problems of drugs and arms trafficking long ago. ______________
7. We wish that people had cared more about the environment many decades ago. ______________
8. We wish there were a way to end all civil wars. ______________
9. We wish that all countries were working together to create a better world. ______________
10. We wish that all nations could live in peace. ______________
11. We hope that future generations will have a peaceful, healthy environment. ______________
12. We hope that the leaders of the world will face these problems so that today's young people will have a world in the future. ______________

B. Subjunctive Forms with Wish

In general, the verb *wish* is followed by a verb in the subjunctive mood. Modal auxiliaries are sometimes used with present and future forms. *That* is optional in sentences with *wish* and *hope*.

	Examples	Notes
Wishes About the Future	I **wish** that the situation **were going** to change. I **wish** the situation **would (could)** change.	Present and future wishes are expressed by using *would, could,* or a subjunctive verb form. In most cases, this form is the same as the simple past tense. In formal English, *were* is used for all forms of the verb *be*. In informal English, *was* is often used with *I, he, she,* and *it.*
Wishes About the Present	Tony **wishes** he **were** still young. I **wish** I **could leave** right now. I **wish** that we **saw** them more often.	
Wishes About the Past	I **wish** they **had arrived** earlier. I **wish** that they **hadn't stayed** so late. She **wishes** she **could have gone.**	Past wishes use the past subjunctive. The past form is the same as the past perfect (*had* + past participle). In conversation, perfect modals are sometimes used.

2 Quickly reread the passage "Taking Responsibility." Then do the following:

1. Find the two clauses that follow *wish* in the second paragraph. Underline the verb(s) in each of these clauses. What is the time frame in the first clause? What about the second?

2. Find the two clauses that follow *hope* in the second paragraph. Underline the verbs and identify the time frame in each.

3 Friends of the Earth is an international environmental group working to improve the quality of life all over the world, primarily through education and political action. Read the quotations from Friends of the Earth. Then add correct verb forms to the personal statements that follow.

- *Overpopulation:* "Projections of current growth rates suggest that the earth's population will increase to 8 billion by the year 2012."

Debbie L., Westwood, California: "I wish that more people realized/would realize (1) (realize) the dangers of the population explosion. I wish we ________ (2) (begin) to control our growth long ago. I hope that we ________ (3) (be) able to do something before it's too late."

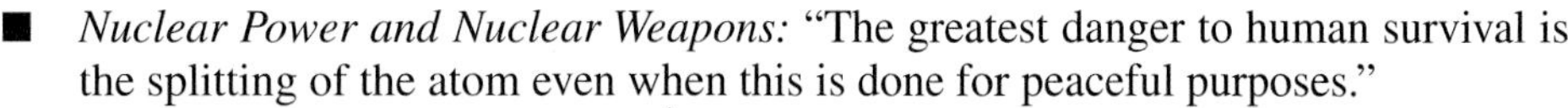

- *Nuclear Power and Nuclear Weapons:* "The greatest danger to human survival is the splitting of the atom even when this is done for peaceful purposes."

Culture Note

The United States has dozens of organizations devoted to enjoying and helping protect the environment. Some of these organizations are at the local level only, but many are national and even international. The major organizations are also heavily involved in political action and, as a group, form the second most powerful lobby in the United States. Most use peaceful means, such as education, land preservation, establishment and maintenance of parks and trails, pollution monitoring, and cleanup, to achieve goals. A few environmental organizations are much more militant, however, and are sometimes labeled "ecoterrorists" for the lengths members will go to in order to achieve their goals.

Gunter N., Heidelberg, Germany: "I hope that people ________ (4) (begin) to realize how dangerous our situation is. I hope they ________ (5) (understand) our present capability to destroy ourselves. I wish everyone ________ (6) (know) how much radiation escapes from nuclear power plants every day. We must stop nuclear development now! I wish that we ________ (7) (learn / never) how to split the atom."

Luis G., Caracas, Venezuela: "I'm an engineer, and I believe that use of nuclear power is necessary. I wish that people ________ (8) (understand) more about our energy situation worldwide. I wish they ________ (9) (realize) how soon we'll run out of oil. We need other sources of energy. I hope that attitudes about nuclear power ________ (10) (change)."

- *Pollution of the Oceans:* "The oceans could be dead within a decade or two unless our neglect and abuse of them is swiftly reversed. . . . Pollution is not the only immediate threat to the seas. . . . Overfishing has depleted many fish species to the point where their recovery is in doubt."

Rodney U., Gloucester, Massachusetts: "I'm a deep-sea fisherman. . . . I wish our world leaders ________ (11) (join) me on a fishing trip. I wish they ________ (12) (see) the damage we've already done to our oceans. Pollution spreads far out to sea now. So

many areas are overfished. I hope that countries around the world ______ (start) to
13
cooperate before it's too late. We've got to work together to save our oceans."

Web Note

Following is a list of some of the largest environmental groups in the United States. Today, these and most others have offices, programs, and activities around the world, and some have Websites in multiple languages:
Friends of the Earth, *www.foe.org/;*
Greenpeace *www.greenpeace.org;*
The National Audubon Society, *www.audubon.org;*
The Nature Conservancy, *www.tnc.org/home1.html;*
The Sierra Club, *www.sierraclub.org/.*

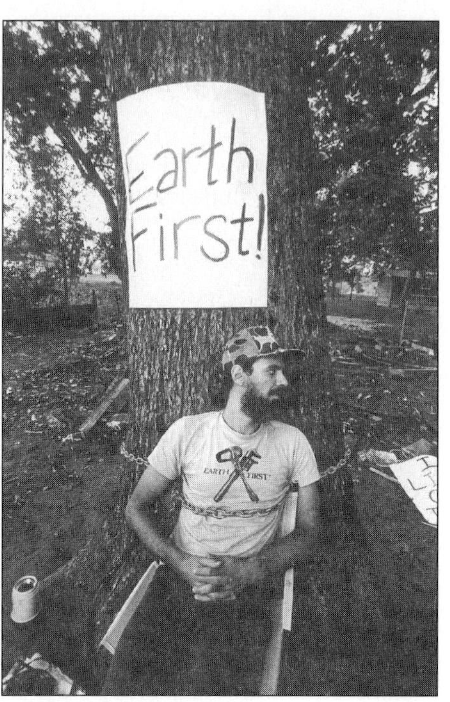

Some environmental groups are highly militant and will use unusual means to fight what they view as injustice. Other groups use more peaceful and conventional means.

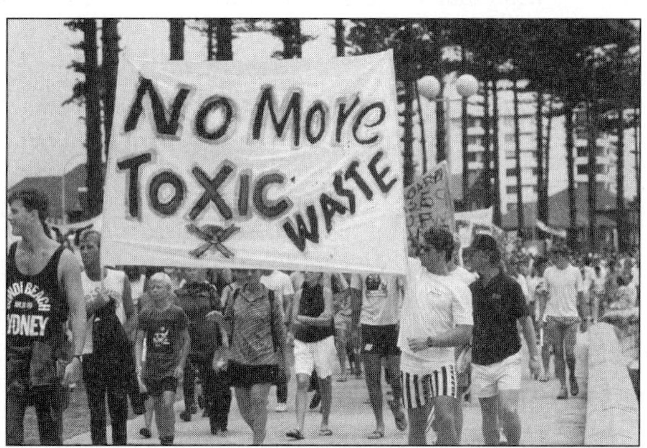

4 For the last four decades, Colombia has been torn by armed conflicts. This ongoing conflict has affected all aspects of Colombian life, and it has also severely affected the Colombian environment.

Following are pictures and a news report about the conflicts in Colombia and a Colombian's commentary on the situation. First, read the captions and the commentary for meaning. Then, complete the passage, using appropriate past, present, or future forms of the verbs in parentheses. Add negatives, adverbs, and modal auxiliaries as indicated or as necessary.

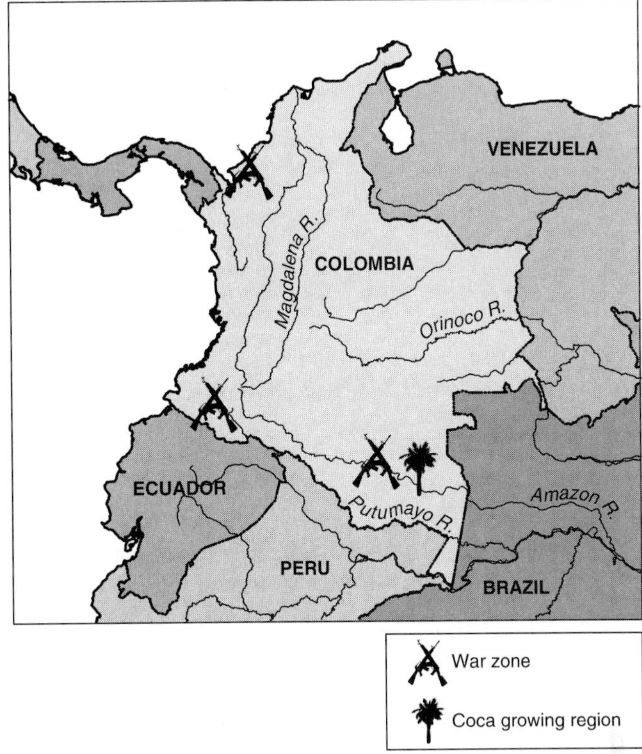

Guerrillas have targeted oil, Colombia's main export, as a tactic in their war against the state, staging some 1,000 assaults on oil pipelines since 1986.

War, Drug Trade Cause Colombia Ecological Disaster

BOGOTÁ, COLOMBIA, Dec. 28, 2000—Warring leftist guerrillas and far-right paramilitaries, and the illegal drug trade in the world's top cocaine producer are causing an ecological disaster of "unsuspected proportions" in Colombia, according to an army report published in December 2000. The report, titled "The scars on 'Mother Earth,'" said the rebel groups' tactic of blowing up oil pipelines has polluted the Andean nation's ecosystem with more than two million tons of crude oil in the last decade. The drug trade has been contaminating the soil with 200,000 tons of chemicals a year and causing deforestation at a pace that is rapidly destroying the country's jungles. "Guerrillas and paramilitaries have caused this ecological catastrophe which, . . . if the current rate of deforestation continues, will turn half the country's jungles into pasture in 17 years."

Colombia is one of the world's five top countries in terms of water resources and biodiversity, the Environment Ministry says. . . . The army calculates that about 3,600 square miles (9,300 square kilometers) of jungle and agricultural land has been lost in the past decade. At the same time, the war has claimed 35,000 lives in the past decade alone.

The Colombian government report calls the drug trade "one of the direct causes of the destruction of biodiversity," saying coca leaf, poppies, and marijuana cultivation has caused serious deforestation. Thirty-three hundred square miles (8,500 square kilometers) of jungle have been destroyed in the last 30 years. Furthermore, some 200,000 tons a year of 28 types of chemicals used in the processing of coca leaf and poppies for cocaine and heroin have been seeping* into the water and soil.

(REUTERS NEWS SERVICE, www.reuters.com)

Commentary by Alfonso G., born and raised in Colombia, now a U.S. citizen

My Country

It *breaks* (break) my heart to see the damage that *has been done* (do) until now and ________ (1) (do/still) to my native country. So much land ________ (2) (ruin/already). So many lives ________ (3) (affect). So many people ________ (4) (injure), ________ (5) (die), or ________ (6) (assassinate). It is a horrific tragedy for me and my country.

I ________ (7) (wish) that none of this ________ (8) (happen/ever). I ________ (9) (wish) that, in the past, the Colombian people ________ (10) (have) good earnings, decent government, and peaceful surroundings. I ________ (11) (wish) the fighting ________ (12) (start / never). Today I wish that people ________ (13) (not die) because of the conflict. I wish that children and

---

**seep* enter slowly, as in a liquid slowly entering a solid

teenagers ____________ (not draft / now) to work for the guerrilla or the
14
paramilitaries. I wish that people in the United States and other countries ____________ (stop) consuming drugs. I wish that all sides ____________ (come)
15 16
together to resolve these terrible conflicts.

What ____________ I ____________ (hope) for? Today, I ____________
17 18 19
(hope for / only) for an end to the conflicts and for some resolution. Tomorrow, I ____________ (hope) that someday I ____________ (be) able to return to my
20 21
country and ____________ (help) it recover. I ____________ (hope) that I
22 23
____________ (help) rebuild my grandparents' village, and that I ____________
24 25
(share) my knowledge and experience by teaching at my former university. I ____________ (hope) that I ____________ (see / once again) a beautiful, peaceful
26 27
Colombia with people working together to improve all our lives.

5 Life is a constant series of choices. Unfortunately, many decisions are based on temporary needs or desires rather than on long-term goals. Can you think of any examples of this from your society? Choose two of the following five points that are relevant to your region or country. Then give a detailed description based on these questions.

a. What exactly happened?
b. What do you wish had happened instead?
c. What is happening now, as a result?
d. What do you wish were happening?

1. a period of social change (changes in family structure, roles, education, mobility, etc.)
2. economic changes
3. a period of political change (a revolution, elections, a political scandal)
4. an environmental crisis (pollution, overcrowding, destruction of a particular area, the loss of human, animal, or plant life)
5. a natural disaster and the preparation for it (an earthquake, a tidal wave, a volcanic eruption)

Example: economic changes

a. Venezuela is an oil-producing country. In the early 1970s, the rise in oil prices caused drastic changes in our society. We began to import most of our food, clothing, medicine, and machinery. We relied on oil money.

b. I wish we had realized the effect of this. I wish we had planned for the future instead of spending all our income so quickly.
c. Today, Venezuela has serious economic and political problems. These have also caused many social problems.
d. I wish we produced more of our own products. I wish we were saving our oil for the future. I wish we could solve our social problems, too.

Using What You've Learned

6 What are your opinions on the problems raised in the preceding exercises? Do you view them as solvable? Or do you believe that the opportunity for solutions has passed? Give your reactions by making at least two statements about each question. Use *hope* or *wish* in your statements.

7 In small groups, write a petition to the United Nations or to world leaders. It may be about one particular issue, such as population or environmental concerns, or it may be a more general statement of your hopes and wishes. Include at least six statements using *wish* and *hope*.

8 Do some research on the Web. Visit the Websites of several environmental organizations, and then choose one that particularly interests you. Find out what the primary focus of the organization is—that is, activities such as camping and canoeing, land preservation, or political action, for example. Then find out what the organization is doing in your area or country. Finally, give a brief report to the class on what you've learned.

PART 2

Imaginary Conditions: Present and Unspecified Time

Setting the Context

Prereading Questions. Are there any societies in existence today that are virtually free of conflict? Could such a society ever exist?

Model Societies

The 20th century has witnessed some of the most amazing and most rapid changes in history. Many of these changes have helped humans immensely, but others have created a number of complex problems that threaten our very existence.

Yet these problems are not unsolvable. Both individuals and groups are actively searching for solutions. Some people are even designing model societies that would not suffer from many of today's ills.

As we are beginning the 21st century, think about the type of society you would like to live in. Then, imagine that you had the opportunity to create it. If you actually had the opportunity, could you plan a new society? Should you have this chance, you would first have to recognize the shortcomings of societies today. Next, you would be faced with the monumental task of designing a society that would not develop similar or worse problems. How would you accomplish this?

Discussing Ideas. What are *shortcomings?* In your opinion, what are some of the major shortcomings in modern societies?

A. Otherwise: *Present Time*

Otherwise is a transition that is used to contrast reality with wishes and dreams. It means "if not" or "if the situation were different." Like other transitions, *otherwise* is often used after a semicolon. The auxiliaries *would, could,* and *might* are frequently used after *otherwise.*

Examples	
That city has terrible smog;	**otherwise,** the summers **would be** beautiful.
	otherwise, I **could enjoy** living there.
	otherwise, we **might move** there.

1 Sahelia is an imaginary Third World country. Read each of Sahelia's problems. Then use *otherwise* to complete the sentences that follow.

Example: *Problem:* few schools. The minister of education steals 50 percent of the education budget; otherwise, *Sahelia might have more schools.*

1. *Problem:* few qualified teachers. Sahelia pays its teachers $1 a week; otherwise, ...
2. *Problem:* underdeveloped economy. Sahelia exports 90 percent of its natural resources; otherwise, ...
3. *Problem:* few industries. The military budget consumes 75 percent of the country's G.N.P. (gross national product); otherwise, ...
4. *Problem:* shortage of skilled workers. Most of the skilled workers are in the military; otherwise, ...
5. *Problem:* hunger. Sahelia exports most of its food; otherwise, ...
6. *Problem:* disease. There are few doctors in Sahelia; otherwise, ...

B. Imaginary Conditions: Present and Unspecified Time

Imaginative conditional sentences express conditions that are hypothetical or that the speaker thinks of as untrue, contrary to fact. They may be wishes and dreams, or they may express advice.

In these conditional sentences, a subjunctive form of the verb is used in the *if* clause. It is the same as the simple past except that *were,* not *was,* is used for the verb *be.*

Examples	Implied Meanings
If Sahelia **had** more doctors, there **would be** less disease.	Sahelia has few doctors. Because of this, disease is a serious problem.
If the educational system **were** better, they **could train** more doctors.	The educational system is not adequate, and, as a result, Sahelia cannot train many doctors.
If developed countries **gave** more aid, Sahelia might **develop** more industries.	Developed countries do not give Sahelia much aid, so Sahelia hasn't been able to develop many industries.

2 Imagine that you are a citizen of Technologica, an imaginary country with a set of problems quite different from Sahelia's. Study Technologica's list of problems. Then form sentences with *if* that explain what would, could, or might happen if the wishes that follow came true.

Problems

pollution (air, water, land are unsafe)
lack of energy (all oil is imported)
lack of food (almost all food is imported)
high unemployment and inflation rates
high crime rate
negative trade balance
lack of open space

Example: I wish fewer people drove cars. If *fewer people drove, the air would be cleaner.*

1. I wish the industries were more concerned about pollution. If . . . .
2. I wish Technologica had its own source of energy. If . . . .
3. I wish the government managed the economy better. If . . . .
4. I wish the wealth of the country were distributed more equally. If . . . .
5. I wish Technologica produced more of its own food. If . . . .
6. I wish we had more natural resources. If . . . .

3 Consider the following situation. The United Nations has chosen you to develop the plans for a model society. Choose one of the statements in each of the following sets. Then make one or more sentences using *if* to explain the reasons for your choice.

Example: There would be free medical care.
Everyone would pay for medical care.
In my model society, there would be free medical care. If there were free medical care, we could eliminate many common diseases. If we were able to eliminate most diseases . . . .

In my model society, ...

1. There would be only one ethnic group.
All ethnic groups would be welcome.
2. There would be complete freedom of religion.
Only one religion would be allowed.

3. The government would control the press.
   There would be no control of the press.
4. The military would be small.
   The military would be large.
5. All people could own and carry guns.
   There would be strict gun-control laws.
6. There would be free housing.
   Housing would not be free.

4 In Activity 3, you discussed some ideas about a model society. Now consider some more fundamental issues. In small groups, discuss the following questions. Then write notes on the advantages and disadvantages of each option. Finally, use these notes to create sentences with *if*.

1. What type of economy would you set up?

	Advantages	Disadvantages
capitalist	*economy develops quickly*	*a large class of poor people*
	______	______
	______	______
socialist	*some people very rich*	*inflation, unemployment*
	______	______
	______	______
	______	______

Example: *If we had a capitalist economy, the economy would develop quickly and some people would become very rich. However, a large class of poor people might form, and inflation and unemployment would be constant problems.*
If we had a socialist system, there might be. . . . However, ...

2. What would the most important economic activity be?

	Advantages	Disadvantages
heavy industry	______	______
	______	______
	______	______
high tech	______	______
	______	______
	______	______
agriculture	______	______
	______	______
	______	______

services	______________________	______________________
	______________________	______________________
	______________________	______________________
	______________________	______________________
	______________________	______________________

3. What type of government would you establish?

	Advantages	**Disadvantages**
religious	______________________	______________________
	______________________	______________________
	______________________	______________________
	______________________	______________________
secular	______________________	______________________
	______________________	______________________
	______________________	______________________
	______________________	______________________
	______________________	______________________

4. Who would make important decisions?

	Advantages	**Disadvantages**
supreme leader	______________________	______________________
	______________________	______________________
	______________________	______________________
	______________________	______________________
	______________________	______________________
	______________________	______________________
parliament	______________________	______________________
	______________________	______________________
	______________________	______________________
	______________________	______________________
	______________________	______________________
	______________________	______________________
computer	______________________	______________________
	______________________	______________________
	______________________	______________________
	______________________	______________________
	______________________	______________________
	______________________	______________________

5 Answer one of the questions from Activity 4 in writing. Begin your composition with a statement about which option you would select. (*In my model society, there would be a capitalist economy. . . .*) Then support this opinion by listing the advantages of this option over the other(s). Use *if* clauses whenever possible.

C. *Imaginary Conditions with* Should *or* Were + *Infinitive*

Should or *were* + infinitive is sometimes used instead of *if.* In this case, *should* or *were* comes before the subject. With *should,* delete *if* and use the simple form of the main verb. With *were,* delete *if* and use the infinitive form of the main verb.

	Examples	
With *if*	**If** our military **became** weak,	our country **might be invaded.**
Without *if*	**Should** our military **become** weak,	
	Were our military **to become** weak,	
With *if*	**If** a world war **started,**	it **would be** terrible.
Without *if*	**Should** a world war **start,**	
	Were a world war **to start,**	

Note: Should and *were* + infinitive are occasionally used without deleting *if.* Compare:

If I { came / were to come / should come } to the meeting later, there would be trouble.

6 One of the most important problems any society must face is crime. In your model society, what would happen to people who broke the law? Use *should* and *were . . . to* and suggest penalties for the following crimes.

Example: robbing a bank
Should you rob a bank, you would go to prison for two years.
Were you to rob a bank, you could spend two years in jail.

1. stealing a car
2. rioting
3. trying to overthrow the government
4. throwing a tomato at the supreme leader
5. spying for a hostile country
6. buying goods on the black market

7 Complete the following by adding the correct forms of the verbs in parentheses.

Arcosanti

Architect and visionary Paolo Soleri *believes* (believe) that it ______ (be, still) possible to create model communities. According to Soleri, if all buildings in a

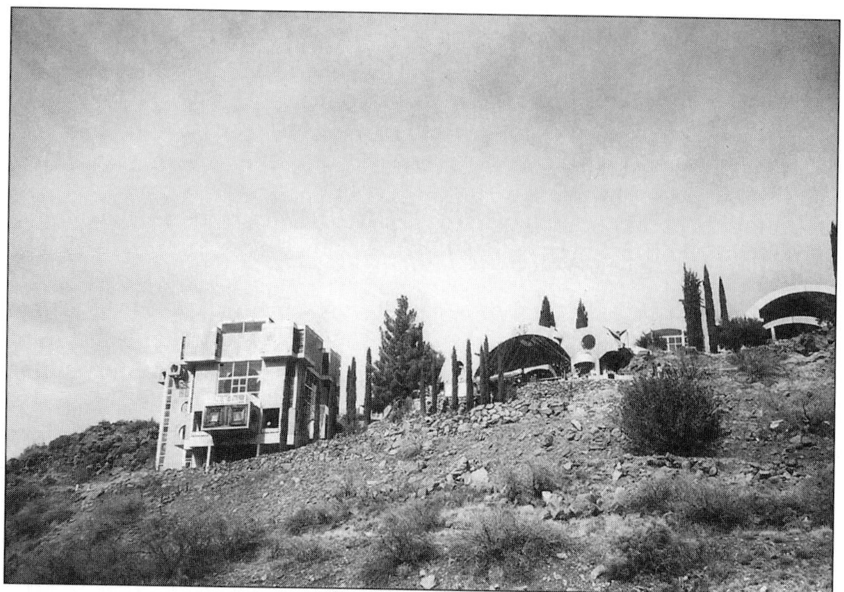

Arcosanti, Pablo Soleri's model community in Arizona

community ______2______ (be) constructed in a small area, large tracts of open space ______3______ (surround) the community. If all the buildings ______4______ (be) close together, people ______5______ (have) little need for cars. They ______6______ (walk) to their destinations. In this way, people ______7______ (get) daily exercise, which ______8______ (help) them stay in better health. They ______9______ (know/also) their neighbors much better. Should this ______10______ (be) true, it ______11______ (cut) down on crime.

To prove his point, in 1970, Soleri ______12______ (begin) to build a town called Arcosanti in the desert near Phoenix, Arizona, in the southwest region of the United States. He ______13______ (design) Arcosanti using his ideas for a model community. Now, over 30 years later, thousands of city planners and other visitors ______14______ (flock) to Arcosanti each year to experience its unique environment.

Many of us wish the world ______15______ (be) a more livable place. Soleri and other planners ______16______ (do) something about it!

Using What You've Learned

8 An old saying is that if you wish upon the first star of the night, your wish will come true. Practice five wishes now, and then later, look for the first star of the evening to wish *for real!*

Your five wishes may be for anything or anyone—for yourself, your family, a friend, your country. Write your wishes and follow each with an explanation using *if.* Then, share your wishes with your classmates.

Example: *I wish the TOEFL test didn't exist. If the TOEFL test didn't exist, I could go out tonight instead of studying for it.*

9 What are some of the penalties for crimes in your hometown or country? For example, what is the penalty for speeding? For running a red light? For using a weapon? Share your information in pairs or small groups. Take turns telling about crimes and justice in different places. In your examples, try to use clauses with *if, should,* or *were* + infinitive.

Example: *In my country, should you run a red light, probably nothing would happen because nobody pays attention to the traffic signals.*

10 Is the situation in your community similar in some ways to that in Sahelia or Technologica? Does it have a different set of problems? In pairs, pretend that you are the newly appointed chief adviser to the leader of your country. It is your job to suggest solutions to the country's problems. After your partner (the leader) explains a problem, suggest a possible solution, using *If I were you.* Then explain what *would, could,* or *might* happen if the leader followed your advice.

Example: *Leader:* We have a terrible problem with air pollution.

Adviser: If I were you, I'd outlaw all private cars, and the air pollution problem would be solved. On the other hand, were you to outlaw cars, there might be a revolution!

11 Imagine that volcanoes have just formed a new island in the Pacific Ocean. It is over a thousand miles from the nearest land, so it does not belong to any country. Although there is no vegetation at present, the island has rich soil, beautiful white sand beaches, and an ample supply of natural resources.

In pairs or in small groups, design the ideal society for this island. You might begin by naming the island and drawing a map to show its size, shape, and position in the world. Next, consider the questions mentioned earlier concerning the economy, political system, judicial system, and the ethnic background of the people. Give as much specific information as possible. For example, if the society were industrial, which industries would you establish and how would the island feed itself? If it were agricultural, which crops would it grow, and how would it get industrial goods?

Would the island export any of its products? If so, to where? Would the island form any alliances with other nations? If so, which nations? How large would the population be?

When you are finished, have one member of your group give a brief presentation summarizing the most important characteristics of your ideal society.

PART 3 Perfect Modal Auxiliaries

Setting the Context

Prereading Questions. What is the largest city that you know of? What is its population? What are conditions like in this city? Is the situation improving or getting worse?

Too Late?

Many of the world's large urban areas are suffering from multiple problems that have resulted from massive growth without careful planning. Shortages of safe drinking water, severe air pollution, poorly developed public transportation systems, and high crime rates are common features of population centers around the globe.

With proper planning, we could have avoided many of these problems. For example, governments might have managed growth. They could have provided systems of transportation and sanitation so important to quality of life. They should have limited the use of automobiles and developed clean energy sources.

They might have, they could have, they should have done all these things. The unfortunate truth is that they didn't. That is *we* didn't. Now it's too late.

Or is it?

Discussing Ideas. Does your city have the problems mentioned in the passage? Do you think the problems could have been avoided? How? The writer seems to think it is really too late to make basic improvements in our environment. Do you agree?

A. Perfect Modal Auxiliaries

Perfect modal auxiliaries can be used to express activities or situations in the past that were not real or that did *not* occur. Often they express our wishes in hindsight. Perfect modal auxiliaries follow this pattern: modal + *(not) have* + past participle.

	Examples	Notes
Unfulfilled Intentions and Preferences would (not) have would rather (not) have	We **would have moved,** but we couldn't find another place. We **would rather have moved** to the country than have stayed in the city.	*Would have* refers to past intentions that were not fulfilled. *Would rather have* refers to past preferences that were not fulfilled. *Than* + simple form is often added for comparisons of wishes with reality.
Unfulfilled Advice should (not) have ought (not) to have	We **should have sold** our house before the company built the factory across the road.	*Should have* and *ought to have* refer to actions that were advisable but that did *not* take place. *Ought to have* is less common than *should have.*
Past Possibilities could (not) have might (not) have may (not) have	We **could have protested** the building of the factory. He **might have listened** to our complaints. Some of the neighbors **may have spoken** to the owners.	*Could have, might have,* and *may have* refer to past possibilities. In some cases, these express alternatives that were not taken. In others, the speaker or writer is uncertain whether the action took place. In some contexts, *could have* also refers to past abilities.
Past Probabilities must (not) have	The company **must not have been concerned** about our health and well-being. They **must have cared** more about making money.	*Must have* refers to past probabilities. The speaker or writer is fairly certain of the accuracy of the statement.

Note: In rapid speech, perfect modals are seldom pronounced clearly. *Have* is often pronounced as *a* or *of,* as in *shudda* or *shudduv.*

1 Quickly reread the passage "Too Late?" Then do the following:

1. Underline the modal auxiliaries in the second and third paragraphs. Do these modal auxiliaries refer to real events or situations? If not, what do they refer to?
2. What form of the main verb is used after these auxiliaries?

2 **Rapid Oral Practice.** Go around the class in a chain, changing the following to include perfect modal auxiliaries.

Example: A: I wouldn't do that.
B: I wouldn't have done that.

A. She could help us.

B. She could have helped us.

1. We should leave.
2. They couldn't help us.
3. It must be right.
4. He may have a problem.
5. I ought to go.
6. It might not work.
7. She may call.
8. I wouldn't try that.
9. He'd rather stay home.
10. We might go there.
11. It couldn't be true.
12. We'd like to discuss it.
13. I'd rather not tell you.
14. She could do it.
15. We ought to tell him.
16. They might stop him.

3 Use your imagination to give at least two answers to the following questions. Use *would have* or *would not have* + *but* or *except that.*

Example: Why didn't you move to Rio last year?

I would have moved there, but (except that) I didn't have the money.

Why did you stay here all summer?

I would not have stayed, but I couldn't get any time off work.

1. Santiago has a terrible air pollution problem. Why haven't city officials done something to clean the air?
2. Your parents moved to Santiago 20 years ago. Why did they originally move there?
3. They left Santiago and bought a small farm in the country. Why didn't you go with them?
4. You have had a terrible cough for over a week. Why haven't you been to a doctor?
5. You are a month overdue in paying your rent. Why haven't you paid it?
6. You haven't handed in your last homework assignment. Why not?

4 Complete the thought in the following statements by using *would rather have* or *would rather not have.*

Example: Today, Sam went to work early.

He would rather have stayed home.

He would rather not have gone to work.

1. Yesterday afternoon at 5:00, Sam was in downtown Dreckville.
2. There was a terrible traffic jam, so he decided to park his car and wait.
3. He got out of his car and began to walk.
4. After a while, he found a fast-food restaurant.
5. He ate a hamburger.
6. The traffic jam never cleared up, so he slept in his car.

5 Dreckville, an imaginary city in the center of the United States, has many problems. Make suggestions on what Dreckville *could have, might have,* or *should have done* to avoid the following problems. Give at least four suggestions for each problem.

Example: Dreckville has little greenery. There is one major park area, but it is in a financial and industrial district. Most residential areas have no green space. Two-thirds of Dreckville's population live in dense apartment complexes. Children play in the street for lack of other areas to play in.

Dreckville could have planned a park system. Dreckville should have designed small squares or plazas in the center of each neighborhood.

1. Dreckville has no real city center. Its businesses and industries are spread out over a large area. They are connected by a complicated network of freeways. The average commute to work by car takes 35 minutes; some commuters travel over an hour and a half each way.
2. Dreckville has a limited bus service but no subway system. Most of the suburbs are not on bus lines. The average fare is $4.45. Most of the bus lines do not have frequent service. The average time between buses is 30 minutes. Only 10 percent of the population uses the system.
3. A river runs through Dreckville. Its water is highly polluted. Most of the industry around Dreckville is located just outside the city limits, along the river. Several factories dump their wastes into the river.
4. Dreckville has an average of 150 smog-alert days per year (days when children and older people should stay indoors because the air quality is so poor).

Culture Note

The Environmental Protection Agency of the U.S. government monitors air quality around the United States. It uses the Pollutant Standard Index, measuring levels of carbon monoxide, ozone, and other chemicals. A level of 0 to 50 reflects good air quality, while 200 to 299 shows very unhealthy air, and 300 to 500 is hazardous. From 1995 to 1997, the Riverside/San Bernadino area of California had almost 350 days over 100 on the index. Bakersfield and Los Angeles, California, were second and third, respectively, on the list of days over 100.

6 Read the statements that follow and then use *must have, could have, may have,* and *might have* to suggest answers to the questions. Give at least two answers for each.

Example: There are no birds left in Dreckville. What happened to them?

The pollution must have killed them. The birds could have died from a disease. They might have moved south and never come back!

1. Yesterday at 7:30 A.M., an empty bus was parked in the middle of Dreckville's largest street. What was wrong with the bus? Where was the bus driver?
2. Francesca waited for 30 minutes for the bus to come. Finally, she gave up. How did she get to work?
3. She went by the river on the way to work and noticed that several dead fish were floating on top of the water. What killed the fish?
4. She arrived at work 45 minutes later. Her boss was angry. What did he say to her?
5. When she returned home, she found a window broken and all of her clothes thrown on the floor. What had happened while she was at work?
6. Francesca looked at the mess in her house. What did she do?

Using What You've Learned

7 Are you good at making up excuses for things you haven't done? Who in your class is the best at making up excuses? First, make a list of five things that you haven't done but that you should have done. Then, think up your excuses and take turns telling them to the class. If you wish, take a vote on whose excuses are the best, worst, or most creative.

Example: *I haven't written to my parents. Well, I would have written them last week, but I lost all of my pens and my dog ate all my stationery.*

8 The mayor of Dreckville disappeared mysteriously two months ago. At first, most people thought that he had been kidnapped. However, in the last few days, the following information has been leaked to the press.

- The mayor is living in a mansion in Rio de Janeiro.
- More than $5 million is missing from the city treasury.
- The mayor has a Swiss bank account containing $20 million.
- He accepted bribes from chemical companies that were polluting the river and from an oil company.
- He used his money and influence to block the development of mass transportation.
- Just before the last three elections, he tampered with the computers that count votes.
- The police have been investigating the mayor for over a year, and they were about to arrest him.

Separate into groups of three or four. Pretend that you are members of a special task force to fight corruption in government and that you must give a report to the city council of Dreckville. First, use modals of probability / possibility to speculate on what exactly the mayor did and why he did these things. Then draw up a list of actions that the police and the city council *should have, could have,* or *might have taken* to prevent this scandal. Finally, make a set of recommendations for the future. Be sure to address how the mayor can be brought to justice and how the government could or should prevent this type of corruption in the future. Remember, the mayor may not be the only corrupt official in the government. When you are finished, have one member of your task force report your findings and recommendations to the class.

PART 4

Imaginary Conditions: Past and Present Time

Setting the Context

Prereading Questions. What are some of the technological changes of the last century? Has this advancement of technology always had a beneficial effect?

Albert Einstein

Progress?

The tremendous impact of change in our lives constantly presents us with new issues, new challenges, new questions to resolve. As our technological awareness grows, we develop new and "better" systems for controlling our world. Yet, are these systems really better? Is technology really a key to solving our problems?

As we look at past accomplishments, we can say that much of our technological progress is associated with a few great people. If minds like Galileo's, Watt's, Edison's, and Einstein's hadn't existed, our technology would not have advanced as quickly, and the world would be a much different place. But would it be a worse place to live in, or might it in some ways be better?

Discussing Ideas. Think about the final question in the passage and imagine our world without the technological progress of the past 200 years. Without such progress, how would our world be worse? How might it be better?

A. Otherwise: *Past Time*

In past time, *otherwise* means "if not" or "if the situation had been different." *Would have, could have,* and *might have* + past participle are commonly used with *otherwise.*

Examples
James Watt invented the steam engine in the 1700s; **otherwise,** the Industrial Revolution **might not have begun** then. The Wright brothers invented the first airplane. **Otherwise,** they **wouldn't have become** famous.

1 The advent of agriculture led to radical changes in human society. In the following sentences, substitute *otherwise* for the connecting word and make all necessary changes.

Example: Humans began cultivating food about 10,000 years ago; in this way, they developed a stable food source.

Humans began cultivating food about 10,000 years ago; otherwise, they wouldn't (couldn't) have developed a stable food source.

1. Tribes no longer had to follow herds of animals, so they settled in permanent villages.
2. People had more than enough food; therefore, they had time to develop new technologies.
3. People had more free time, so they devoted themselves to music, art, and other creative efforts.
4. Some areas were naturally suited for agriculture; thus, tribes fought over these areas.
5. War became a common occurrence, so people developed new and more sophisticated weapons.
6. Humans learned how to use metal; hence, they were able to fabricate spears, knives, and later, guns.

B. Imaginary Conditions: Past Time

Conditional sentences with *if* can be used to speculate about past situations or events that did *not* take place. In these conditional sentences, the verb in the *if* clause is *had* + the past participle. Sometimes *if* is deleted and the auxiliary *had* is placed before the subject. In negative sentences where *if* is deleted, *not* follows the subject. The verb in the main clause is usually *would have, could have,* or *might have* + past participle.

Examples	Implied Meanings
If humans **had not learned** to use metal, they **would** never **have invented** guns. **Had** humans **not learned** to use metal, they **would** never **have invented** guns.	Humans learned to use metal, and one result was the invention of guns.
People **could not have grown** crops in many areas if they **hadn't learned** how to irrigate. People **could not have grown** crops in many areas **had** they **not learned** how to irrigate.	People were able to grow crops in many areas because they learned how to irrigate.

2 The following is a list of some of the early historical events that led to improved weaponry. Use *if* to connect each event with its results. Create at least eight new sentences.

Example: The Greeks learned to bend and laminate wood. They created new farming tools. They invented the bow and arrow.

If the Greeks hadn't learned to bend and laminate wood, they wouldn't have created new farming tools or invented the bow and arrow.

1. The Chinese invented gunpowder. They invented fireworks.
2. Ancient Egyptians needed a sharp, durable tool for harvesting wheat. They made the first metal sword.
3. Ancient East Africans developed an iron industry. They made new and more effective spears and knives. They were able to defeat invaders. They became successful traders.

4. Europeans traveled to China in the 13th century. They started to import spices. They found new ways to preserve meat. They learned about gunpowder. They developed firearms.

3 Complete the following sentences by adding the correct forms of the verbs in parentheses. Use the modal auxiliaries *would, could,* and *might.*

Example: If Otto Lilienthal hadn't died (not die) in a gliding accident, he might have invented (invent) the first "powered" aircraft.

1. The Wright brothers built and flew the first airplane. If the Wright brothers _______________ (not be) wealthy, they _______________ (not afford) to work on this project.
2. Had they _______________ (not study) the design of earlier German gliders, it _______________ (take) them years to design their own.
3. Consistent strong winds were necessary for the first flights. The Wrights _______________ (not move) to Kitty Hawk, North Carolina if it _______________ (not have) the best wind conditions for test flights.
4. On December 17, 1903, they made the world's first powered flight. Flier 1 _______________ (not fly) if the Wrights _______________ (not develop) a lightweight gasoline engine.
5. A number of French and German inventors were working on planes at the same time. Someone else _______________ (develop) the first plane in a few months if the Wrights _______________ (not succeed).
6. Aircraft didn't become important until World War I. Had the war _______________ (not break out), the development of the airplane _______________ (take) much longer.

The Wright brothers with one of their early airplanes.

4 Read the following historical events. List some of the things that happened at that time because of the event. Then form sentences with *if* that show how the results were connected. Use the example as a model.

Example: People learned to farm.
They didn't have to hunt for all of their food. They built cities. . . .
If people hadn't learned to farm, they would have had to hunt for all of their food. If they had had to hunt for all of their food, they wouldn't have built cities.

1. People learned to use metal.
2. People developed ocean-going boats.
3. Columbus discovered the "New World."
4. James Watt invented an efficient and inexpensive engine.
5. Gregor Mendel did landmark work in understanding genetics.
6. Alexander Fleming discovered penicillin.
7. Marie Curie learned the properties of radium.
8. Einstein developed theories about the atom.

C. Imaginary Conditions: Past and Present Time

Conditional sentences with *if* can be used to describe past actions or situations that have affected the present. The verb in the *if* clause is *had* + a past participle. The verb in the main clause is usually *would, could,* or *might* + a simple or continuous verb. *If* can be deleted and the subject and verb (auxiliary) inverted.

Examples	Implied Meanings
If Columbus **hadn't claimed** the "New World" for Spain, most South Americans **might speak** Portuguese today.	Columbus claimed the "New World" for Spain, and therefore, most of South America is Spanish-speaking.
Had Einstein **not lived,** we **would have** a much different world.	Einstein and his work played a major role in developments that affect our lives today.

5 Complete the following sentences, giving at least two imaginary present results for each *if* clause.

Example: If the car hadn't been invented, *we might still be using horses as a major means of transportation.*
. . . we might not have so much air pollution.

1. If humans hadn't developed systems for writing . . . .
2. Had the gun been banned 50 years ago . . . .
3. If aircraft had never been developed . . . .
4. If penicillin hadn't been discovered . . . .
5. If satellites had never been launched . . . .
6. If a nuclear war had started five years ago . . . .

6 Technological advances have led to both great achievements and disasters. Read the following four summaries and react to each by writing at least three sentences using *if* clauses. Include both past and present conditional clauses in your sentences.

Example: Because of political problems in the mid-1970s, Portugal postponed planting new cork oaks. People cut the existing forests for cork or for firewood, and no new plantings were started. The result was a worldwide shortage of cork for use in wine bottles. Today, manufacturers use half-plastic, half-cork stoppers even for vintage wines.

If Portugal hadn't been having political problems, this situation might not have occurred.

If Portugal had replanted the trees, there wouldn't have been a cork shortage.

If there hadn't been a cork shortage, manufacturers wouldn't be using plastic corks.

1. The extensive nuclear testing in Nevada in the 1950s spread deadly radiation throughout the area. After one explosion in 1953, 4,300 sheep died. Today, hundreds of residents living near the testing area have developed cancer. They sued the government and won millions of dollars.
2. A farmer near Newburgh, New York, fertilized his field too early in the spring of 1979; as a result, he killed thousands of birds. Approximately 10,000 birds of varying species were found dead. They died because they ate the powerful fertilizer pellets. Because the ground was still hard, the pellets did not sink in, and the birds mistook the pellets for food.
3. In the Philippines in 1979, river water polluted by upstream copper mining was used to irrigate rice fields, and approximately 2,500 acres (1,000 hectares) of young rice plants died. Over 2,000 farmers lost their crops.
4. Off the coast of India in the Maldive Islands, cutting of hardwood trees (a secondary export) has removed the primary food of rats, which lived on the fruit of the trees. The rats, therefore, started to eat coconuts. They destroyed about half the islands' coconut crop, which is the main export.

Web Note

Exxon has a Website devoted to the Valdez *oil spill. You can learn more about this tragic spill and its effects at www.oilspill.state.ak.us.*

The 1989 oil spill from Exxon's tanker *Valdez* was one of the worst human-created ecological disasters of all time. Here volunteers try to clean off the oil which covered the shores, killing thousands of plants and animals along the coast.

7 Imagine that it is now the year 2099. Your home is earth, and it is a very pleasant place. As the 22nd century approaches, you are looking back and imagining what might have or might not have happened during the 21st century. Use past subjunctive forms of the verbs in parentheses or add perfect modal auxiliaries to complete the following passage.

Looking Back at the Years 2000–2098

Life in the 21st century has been very pleasant, thanks to a memorable event in the year 2010. In that year, the entire world decided to work together. The 21st century *would (might) have been* (be) very different if that event ______ (1) (happen/never).

If we ______ (2) (not decide) to work together, there ______ (3) (be) a total disaster. Our environment ______ (4) (damage) beyond repair if we ______ (5) (not control) pollution, use of resources, and farming and fishing methods. The population of the world ______ (6) (continue) to grow, and more and more people ______ (7) (move) to the cities.

If the earth's population ______ (8) (continue) to grow, we ______ (9) (not provide) free medical care and education for everyone. There ______ (10) (be) problems with jobs. And of course, there ______ (11) (not be) enough food to go around.

Fortunately, though, at the beginning of the 21st century, our governments were very wise. As a result, we have a healthy environment, sufficient food and medical care, free education, and safe, interesting jobs for everyone. By working together, we have created a very nice place for all the citizens of the earth.

Using What You've Learned

8 Choose one political, social, economic, or technical development that has significantly affected our lives. Research your topic and prepare a brief presentation. Include a "capsule" history of the development and a short list of its positive and negative effects. Finally, speculate on what would (not) have happened and how our lives would be different had this development not taken place.

9 Think about some turning points in your own life. Think about some of the choices that you have made and the events or changes that have occurred because of them. Then write a short composition about one of these. Describe how your life changed because of the decision, and then describe how it might have been or might be if you had done things differently. You can choose from the following ideas or create some of your own. Finally, share your thoughts in a small group discussion with your classmates.

- If you had chosen a different language to study, what might it have been? How would this have affected your current work or studies?
- If you had chosen a different career, what might you have studied? Why?

- If you had grown up in a different place, where might it have been? How would your life be different today because of it?
- What if you had gotten married at age 16? How would your life have been different? What would you be doing today?

Focus on Testing

Use of Subjunctive and Conditional Forms

Subjunctive and conditional forms are frequently tested on standardized English proficiency exams. Check your understanding of these structures by completing the sample items that follow.

Remember that . . .

- In formal English, a subjunctive form is used after the verb *wish.*
- A modal auxiliary is generally not used in clauses with *if;* the subjunctive is usually used.
- Modal auxiliaries are followed by the simple form of the main verb; perfect modal auxiliaries are formed with *have* + past participle or *have* + *been* + past participle.

Part 1. Circle the best completion for the following.

Example: I hope the team ______________ last night.

a. win (c.) won
b. had won d. will win

1. If Mary ______________ her work, she would probably change jobs.
   a. doesn't like c. hasn't liked
   b. didn't like d. hadn't liked
2. Were she ______________ there, she could pick up the package for us.
   a. to going c. going
   b. to go d. go
3. If I ______________ more money, I could have taken a trip with them.
   a. had c. would have had
   b. would have d. had had
4. He has often wished ______________ able to change careers.
   a. that he were c. he could be
   b. he was d. that he is

Part 2. Each sentence has one error. Circle the letter below the word(s) containing the error.

Example: The 20th century might have been (A) different then (B) it was (C) if that event has never happened (D, circled).

1. If English didn't have (A) so many (B) vocabulary words, it might (C) have seemed (D) easier to learn.

2. If (A) they had had (B) more time, they could had (C) visited the Statue of Liberty, along with (D) the United Nations.

3. If Orville and Wilbur Wright hadn't (A) went (B) to Kitty Hawk, North Carolina, to test their flying machines, they might not have encountered (C) the right winds to make the launch possible (D).

4. Should the Prime Minister to receive (A) another vote (B) of no confidence, she would (C) be forced to dissolve (D) her government.

PART 5

Factual Conditions: Present, Future, and Unspecified Time

Setting the Context

Prereading Questions. Did Native Americans of the past regard the earth in the same way as most Americans do today? If not, what are some of the differences between the two points of view?

Plundered Earth

He treats his mother, the earth, and his brother, the sky, as things to be bought, plundered, sold like sheep or bright beads. If man does not learn, he will destroy the earth and leave behind only a desert.

You must teach your children that the ground beneath your feet is the ashes of our grandfathers. If you tell your children that the earth is rich with the lives of our kin, they will respect the land. Teach your children that the earth is our mother. Whatever befalls the earth, befalls the sons of the earth. If men spit upon the ground, they spit upon themselves.

CHIEF SEATTLE, 1854

Discussing Ideas. Who was Chief Seattle describing in the first paragraph? What did he want people to learn? What are some of the things that have happened to our earth since Chief Seattle's time?

1 Review. Complete the paragraph with the appropriate forms of the verbs in parentheses.

Acid Rain

Since the 1930s, industrial plants and automobiles around the world *have released/have been releasing* (release) larger and larger quantities of chemicals into the air. Whenever certain chemicals ________ (1) (combine) in the atmosphere, they ________ (2) (produce) acids. When certain wind patterns exist, these acids ________ (3) (stay) in the upper atmosphere. The acid mixture ________ (4) (travel) thousands of miles before it ________ (5) (return) to the earth as rain, snow, or fog. This phenomenon ________ (6) (cause) ecological damage worldwide for several decades. Although the phenomenon ________ (7) (have) many scientific terms, it ________ (8) (be) generally known as *acid rain.*

The effects of acid rain on a statue in *Boston.*

A. Factual Conditions: Present or Unspecified Time

Factual conditional sentences may refer to habitual activities or to situations that are true in general.

Examples	Notes
If nitrogen and sulfur dioxide **mix,** they **form** an acid solution. You **shouldn't mix** chemicals unless you **know** what you are doing.	Conditional sentences with *if* and *unless* generally use either the simple present or modal auxiliaries such as *should* or *can. Unless* is similar in meaning to *if not* in many sentences.

2 Form complete sentences with *if* or *when* by combining each cause with its result. Make all necessary changes and add articles where they are needed.

Example: smokestacks release sulfur into the air → sulfur reaches high altitudes
If (When) smokestacks release sulfur into the air, the sulfur reaches high altitudes.

(a)

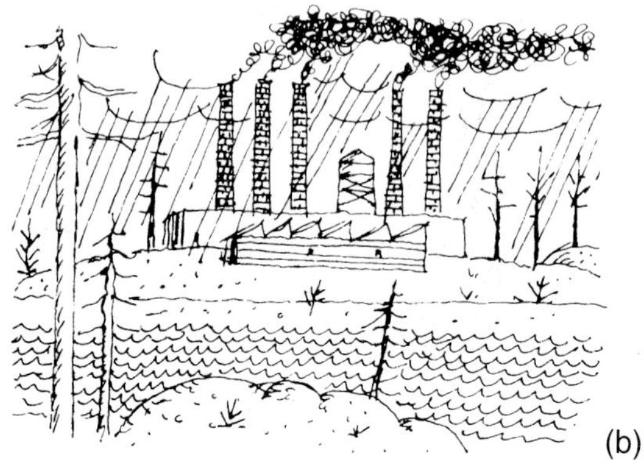
(b)

Web Note

Acid rain is a global threat that demonstrates very clearly how interconnected we are on earth. Pollutants from one region can affect rainfall hundreds, even thousands of miles away. For more information and some interesting experiments, check the Environmental Protection Agency's *Website at www.epa.gov/airmarkets/acidrain/index.html.*

	Causes		Effects
1.	sulfur dioxide mixes with clouds	→	drops of acid rain form
2.	acid rain falls to the ground	→	soil becomes acidic
3.	forests become acidic	→	young trees die
4.	acid contents of rivers rise	→	fish stop reproducing
5.	drinking water becomes more acidic	→	water pipes dissolve

B. Factual Conditions: Future Time

Factual conditional sentences that refer to the future normally express intentions or causes and effects. The intention or effect in the main clause will or will not occur depending on the cause or condition expressed in the *if* clause.

Examples	Notes
If we **continue** to abuse the earth, we **will destroy** it. **Unless** we **learn** from our mistakes, we **may repeat** them.	These conditional sentences with *if* and *unless* generally use the simple present in the *if* clause and a modal in the main clause (*will, may, might, can, should*).

3 Read the information on pesticides and use it to complete the exercise that follows.

Pests and diseases destroy approximately one-third of the world's agricultural harvests each year. In agriculture, any organism that damages or destroys valuable plants is a pest: microorganisms, insects, birds, animals, and other plants. To control these pests, farmers worldwide use pesticides (chemical poisons). There are advantages and disadvantages to pesticide use.

Advantages

Harvests increase dramatically.
Losses during storage are lower.
Crops are easier to export.

Disadvantages

Pests develop a resistance to the chemicals.
Pesticides often kill the natural enemies of the pest.
Pesticides accumulate in nature and can reach lethal amounts.
Pesticides concentrate in animal and human fat.

Form at least six sentences with *if* to show the good and bad effects of pesticides. Use the future tense.

Example: *If farmers use pesticides, they will lose fewer crops.*
If farmers don't use pesticides, their losses will increase.

4 Restate your sentences from Activity 3 to use *unless* instead of *if.*

Example: *Unless farmers use pesticides, they will lose many of their crops.*

5 Use *if, when,* and *whenever* with present and future verbs to rephrase the following sentences.

Example: We use pesticides. We affect more than just the pest.
When we use pesticides, we affect more than just the pest.

1. We use pesticides. We also affect birds and animals that feed on the pest.
2. For example, aphids eat crops that have been sprayed. The poison enters the aphids' systems.
3. A ladybug eats poisoned aphids. The poison accumulates in the ladybug.
4. A sparrow eats the ladybug. The sparrow absorbs the poison.
5. A larger bird such as a hawk eats the sparrow. The bird also eats the accumulated poison from thousands of insects.
6. A hawk consumes large amounts of the poison. The hawk is not able to reproduce.

6 Acid rain, pesticide poisoning, and other forms of pollution are tremendous threats to the environment. However, these pollutants seem almost insignificant when compared to the ultimate man-made ecological disaster—a nuclear war or a nuclear accident. Examine the chart and then answer the questions, using complete sentences.

1. If there were a nuclear explosion in your city,
   a. how high would the temperature climb?
   b. how many people living within 20 miles would survive?
   c. approximately how many people would die instantly?
2. If you are 50 miles from a nuclear explosion,
   a. will you die instantly?
   b. will you get sick?
   c. where will you find food that is safe to eat and water that is safe to drink?
3. If you lived 1,000 miles from the nearest explosion,
   a. would you be safe?
   b. what problems would you probably have?
   c. what might be the effect on your future children?
4. If you think a nuclear war is about to start,
   a. whom will you contact?
   b. what plans will you make?

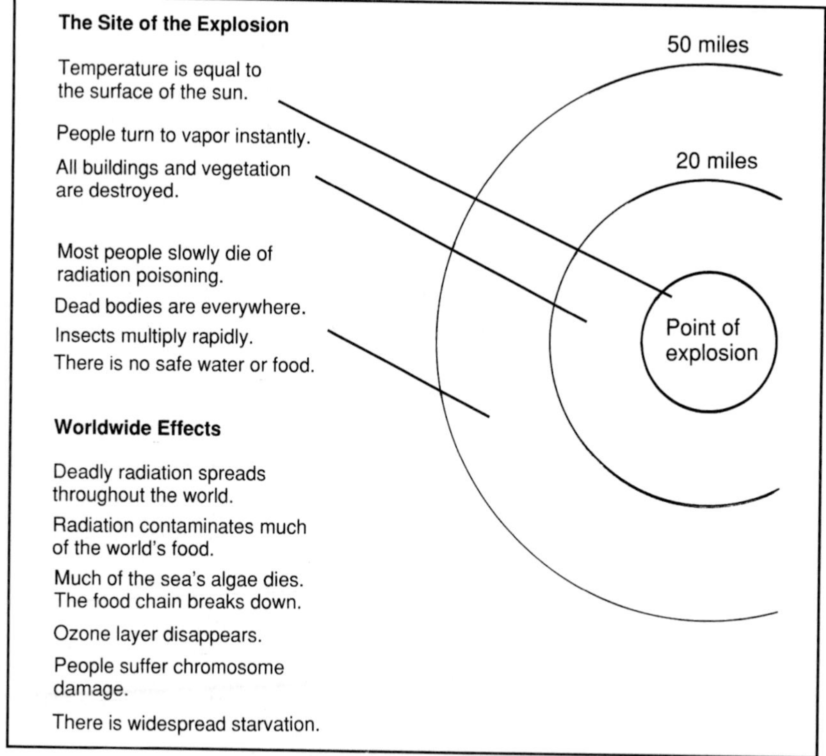

The Site of the Explosion
Temperature is equal to the surface of the sun.
People turn to vapor instantly.
All buildings and vegetation are destroyed.
Most people slowly die of radiation poisoning.
Dead bodies are everywhere.
Insects multiply rapidly.
There is no safe water or food.
Worldwide Effects
Deadly radiation spreads throughout the world.
Radiation contaminates much of the world's food.
Much of the sea's algae dies. The food chain breaks down.
Ozone layer disappears.
People suffer chromosome damage.
There is widespread starvation.
50 miles
20 miles
Point of explosion

Using What You've Learned

7 Reread the opening passage "Humans and the Environment: Conflict or Coexistence?" on page 312. Then consider all of the problems raised in this chapter, along with other issues not raised here. Additional possibilities are listed on the next page.

In small groups, discuss the various issues that seem most critical to you. Talk about what the current situation is, how it developed, how it might have developed differently, and what its impact on the future might or will be. As you discuss, make some notes and begin to organize your ideas.

After your discussion, choose the one issue that you believe needs the most urgent attention. Use your notes and any additional ideas as the basis for a composition. In your composition, look at both reality and unreality. First, describe the current situation. Then, hypothesize about the past, present, and future—if things had been done differently. Finally, work again in the same groups and share your compositions.

- Abortion
- AIDS
- Air and water pollution
- Cancer
- Disposal of nuclear waste
- Extinction of species
- Global weather changes
- Hazardous waste disposal
- Population growth and control
- Storage or elimination of nuclear weapons
- Urban migration

Video Activities: A Strike

Before You Watch. Discuss these questions in small groups.

1. Why do workers go on strike?
2. Are government workers allowed to go on strike?

Watch. Circle the correct answers.

1. What have the unionized workers of the county of Los Angeles decided to do?
   a. go back to work b. go on strike c. go to court
2. How much of a pay increase is the union asking for?
   a. 15.5% over three years b. 15% over two years c. 5% in one year
3. How much of a pay increase is the county offering the union?
   a. 19% over five years b. 9% over three years c. 11% over two years

Watch Again. Answer these questions in small groups.

1. Check the employees that are mentioned in the video segment.
   _______ a. librarians _______ d. teachers _______ f. typists
   _______ b. nurses _______ e. cooks _______ g. cashiers
   _______ c. building maintenance workers
2. Which of the employees above are going back to work tomorrow? _______
   ____

3. According to the woman in the video, which two of these problems do the nurses have?
   a. too little pay b. too much work c. poor working conditions
4. *Principal* means ______________________.
   a. the most important b. the smallest c. the leader
5. When something is *booming,* it is ______________________.
   a. just starting b. growing rapidly c. declining
6. If something is *critical,* it is ______________________.
   a. dangerous b. expensive c. necessary

After You Watch. Complete the following sentences.

1. The nurses wish that the judge ______________________________.
2. If the county had more money, ______________________________.
3. ______________________________, the workers wouldn't be on strike.
4. If the strikers win, ______________________________.
5. ______________________________, the workers will lose money.

Focus on Testing

Use of Conditional Sentences

Conditional sentences are frequently tested on standardized English proficiency exams. Check your understanding of these structures by completing the sample items that follow.

Remember that . . .

- In formal English, a subjunctive form is used after the verb *wish.*
- A modal auxiliary is generally not used in clauses with *if;* the subjunctive is usually used.

Part 1. Circle the best completion for the following.

Example: We ______________________, but we couldn't find another place.
   a. moved (c.) would have moved
   b. will move d. had moved

1. If it ______________________, they won't go to the beach.
   a. be raining c. is rain
   b. will be raining d. is raining

2. If humans ________________ metal, we would still be living in the Stone Age.
   a. didn't learn to use
   b. hadn't learned to use
   c. hadn't learned using
   d. didn't learn using

3. Were there to be a problem, the manager ________________ notify all workers immediately.
   a. should
   b. should to
   c. has to
   d. had to

4. Unless Billie ________________ on the test, she won't be able to continue her work.
   a. doesn't do well
   b. won't do well
   c. does good
   d. does well

Part 2. Each sentence has one error. Circle the letter below the word(s) containing the error.

Example: He might have listened to our complaints if we have been more
A B C
organized when we presented our case.
D

1. Despite her feeling that she should had been able to help, there was nothing
A B C
that she could have done.
D

2. Although economists use many different economic indicators to judge the
A B C
value of a country's currency, the prices at McDonald's may have been the
D
clearest indicators of all.

3. Unless all countries will begin to reduce emissions from fossil fuels, acid
A B
rain will become an even more serious problem.
C D

4. It was sold out; otherwise, we would had gone to see the movie.
A B C D

Chapter 11

Medicine and Science

IN THIS CHAPTER

Part 1 Adjective Clause to Phrase Reduction

Part 2 Verbs Followed by Participial Constructions; The Verbs *Lay/Lie, Raise/Rise*

Part 3 Adverb Clause to Phrase Reduction

Part 4 Causative and Structurally Related Verbs

Introduction

In this chapter, you will learn how to reduce clauses into phrases. You will also study certain verbs that are generally followed by phrases.

The following passage introduces the chapter theme "Medicine and Science" and raises some issues that you will cover in the chapter.

Aging

Aging is one of the few things assured in this changeable world. It is our grandparents, our parents, and perhaps even you and I graying, balding, and sagging . . . suffering a progression of indignities associated with our years.

Biologically speaking, aging is characterized by the physiological weakening of cells and organs leading to a point where disease becomes inevitable. "Old age," said one old-timer, "is like living on an island steadily shrinking in size."

But no matter how dreaded, old age is not without desirable aspects. Senior citizens, having been observers of life for several decades, carry with them a special wisdom tied to their years of experience. They are often the heads of large families, enjoying the love and respect of the younger members of their clans. As grandparents, they can love the new children in the family while avoiding the burdens of parenthood. And, finally, as actor Maurice Chevalier noted when asked whether he minded growing old, "Not if I consider the alternative."

Discussing Ideas. What comes to mind when you think of the word *old?* At what age does middle age begin? What about old age? In your culture, are people treated with more respect as they get older? What is the alternative to old age that Maurice Chevalier alludes to?

PART 1 Adjective Clause to Phrase Reduction

Setting the Context

Prereading Questions. What are some major medical advances that have taken place in the last century? How have these advances affected the length of people's lives?

Life Span

Having benefited from the medical and nutritional advances of the past 80 years, people are on the average living much longer lives than their ancestors. With diseases like polio, malaria, and tuberculosis eliminated or controlled, life into old age is now the norm, particularly in developed countries. The average American's life span, believed to have been 45 years in 1900, today stands at 74.

This change is quite impressive, but there is still a great deal of progress to be made. Fewer people are dying of childhood diseases, and as a result, many more people live into their 60s and 70s. Still, the life expectancy after 65 has increased little in the 20th century. A man 65 or over can expect to live one and a half years longer than the same man (65 or over) in the 19th century would have, and a woman three and a half years longer. There has been no significant increase in the life expectancy of white males over 65 in the United States since 1789.

That's the bad news. The good news is that the research currently being done by thousands of scientists may soon change all that, bringing with it dramatically longer life and, perhaps more important, a longer youth.

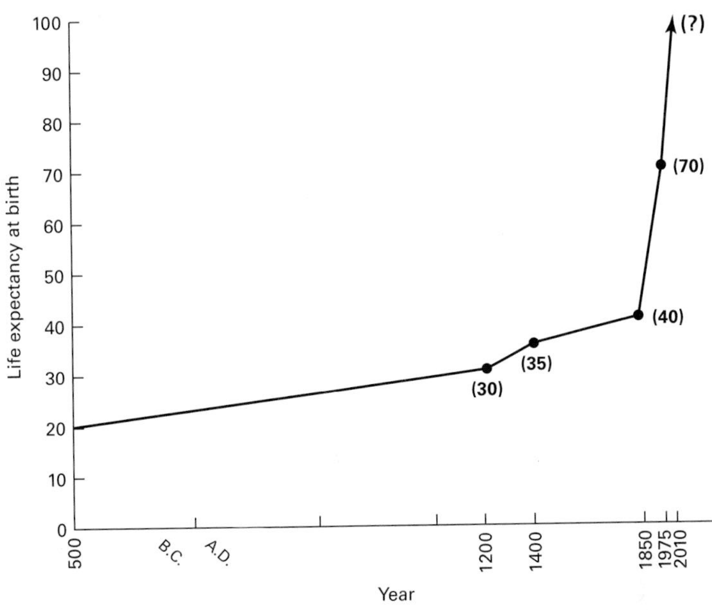

Culture Note

"Baby boomers" is a name for people born between 1946 and 1964. This generation, some 75 million strong in the United States, has had a major social, political, and economic effect on the nation. Now this generation is aging, and some of its members are beginning to retire. By the time they have all retired, this group will form the largest group of "senior citizens" in U.S. history.

Discussing Ideas. How much longer is the life span of an average American today than it was in 1900? How much longer is the life expectancy of a person of 65 than it was 100 years ago? According to the passage, what is the good news?

A. Introduction to Participial Phrases

A participial phrase is a phrase that includes a present or past participle. Participial phrases can be formed from adjective clauses if the relative pronoun is the subject of the adjective clause. The time frame of these phrases is determined by the verb in the independent clause or by the general context.

B. Reduction of Adjective Clauses with Verbs in the Active Voice

	Examples	Notes
Clause	There are several researchers **who are studying aging in rats.**	In adjective clauses with verbs in the active voice, eliminate the connecting word and use the present participle of the main verb. The present participle is used to replace verbs in a variety of tenses. If the adjective clause has commas, the phrase has commas; otherwise, it does not.
Phrase	There are several researchers **studying aging in rats.**	
Clause	The rats **that eat the least** live the longest.	
Phrase	The rats **eating the least** live the longest.	
Clause	Rats **that did not follow this diet** had normal life spans.	
Phrase	Rats **not following this diet** had normal life spans.	To form the negative, use *not* at the beginning of the participial phrase.

1 Underline the adjective clauses in the following sentences and then change them to participial phrases.

Example: Humans enjoy the longest life span of any mammal that inhabits the earth.
Humans enjoy the longest life span of any mammal inhabiting the earth.

1. Still, after age 60, people begin to suffer from a number of complications that eventually lead to disability and death.
2. Most people who are still living at the age of 70 die within ten years.
3. The number of Americans who live past 90 represents less than .5 percent of the population.
4. Only around 13,000 people who reside in the United States are currently over 100.
5. There are only a few verified cases of Americans who survived past 110.

C. Reduction of Adjective Clauses with Simple-Tense Verbs in the Passive Voice

	Examples	Notes
Clause	This tree, **which was discovered in 1965,** is over 4,000 years old.	In adjective clauses with verbs in the passive voice, eliminate the connecting word and *be*. If the adjective clause has commas, the phrase also has commas; otherwise, it does not.
Phrase	This tree, **discovered in 1965,** is over 4,000 years old.	
Clause	Newer research **that is not yet completed** suggests that there are even older living things.	
Phrase	Newer research **not yet completed** suggests that there are even older living things.	To form the negative, use *not* at the beginning of the participial phrase.

2 Underline the adjective clauses in the following sentences and then change them to participial phrases. Include any necessary punctuation.

Example: According to most scientists, the oldest organisms that are known are trees.
According to most scientists, the oldest organisms known are trees.

Bristlecone pine

Sea anemone

1. Sequoias and redwoods, which are found in the Pacific Northwest, have maximum life spans that are estimated at 3,000 years.
2. There are bristlecone pines that are thought to be at least 4,500 years old.
3. Perhaps even older than these pines are sea anemones, which are believed to have the potential for immortality.
4. This plantlike animal, which is intensively studied all over the world, stays "young" by constantly replacing parts of its simple anatomy.
5. One group of sea anemones, which was transported to England in 1804 and placed in an aquarium, lived over 90 years without showing any sign of aging. (They died of unknown causes, which apparently had nothing to do with aging.)

D. Reduction of Adjective Clauses with Continuous-Tense Verbs in the Passive Voice

	Examples	**Notes**
Clause	Cancer, **which is being studied around the world,** may be cured some day.	In adjective clauses with verbs in the continuous tense and passive voice, eliminate the connecting word and *is, are, was,* or *were. Being* + the past participle remain.
Phrase	Cancer, **being studied around the world,** may be cured some day.	

3 Underline the adjective clauses in the following sentences and then change them to participial phrases.

Example: For some gerontologists,* old age is a disease <u>that is being studied</u> so that it can be cured.

For some gerontologists, old age is a disease being studied so that it can be cured.

1. Life extension experiments that are being performed on animals have shown promising results.
2. A number of tests that are being carried out concern the lowering of body temperature.
3. The cold-blooded animals that are being subjected to lower temperatures live up to ten times longer.
4. The mammals that are being given similar tests also show a significant increase in longevity.
5. Some monkeys and rats that are being fed temperature-lowering drugs have added years to their lives.

**gerontologist* scientist who studies aging

E. Reduction of Adjective Clauses with Verbs in Perfect Tenses

Adjective clauses with verbs in the perfect tenses may be reduced in two ways. Either (1) *have* is changed to *having* or (2) *have* is eliminated and the main verb of the clause is changed to a present participle.

	Examples	Notes
Clause	The rats **that have followed the special diet** have little heart disease.	
Phrase	The rats **following (having followed) the special diet** have little heart disease.	*Having* + the past participle is used to emphasize the completion of the activity.
Clause	The other rats, **which had been fed more,** led shorter lives.	
Phrase	The other rats, **having been fed more,** led shorter lives.	With clauses in the passive, *having* + *been* + the past participle is normally used.

4 Underline the adjective clauses in the following sentences and then change them to participial phrases. Add all necessary punctuation.

Example: In the 1920s, Clive McCay, who had already worked with temperature control, decided to vary the diet of rats.

In the 1920s, Clive McCay, having already worked with temperature control, decided to vary the diet of rats.

1. He found that rats that had been fed only two-thirds of the normal number of calories lived twice as long as those that had followed a normal diet.
2. Other scientists who have studied McCay's findings are conducting similar experiments.
3. Roy Walford of the University of California at Los Angeles is running tests on rats that have fasted every other day for their entire lives.
4. Walford, who has extended the lives of these rats, is convinced that his findings apply to humans.
5. Walford and others who have seen the results of fasting in rats hope to find similar results in humans.

5 Read the following passage and underline all adjective clauses. Then change these clauses to participial phrases. Pay close attention to the punctuation.

Roy Walford

Roy Walford is a pathologist who does research and teaches at U.C.L.A. Walford, who is considered an expert on aging, believes that the key to the fountain of youth is a lower body temperature. There are two ways to achieve lower temperatures. One is to slow one's heartbeat through the yoga techniques that are currently being practiced in India. Unfortunately, this method takes years of training. The other way is through what Walford calls "undernutrition."

Walford bases his conclusions on his research that is being done with rats that have been systematically underfed. These rats, which are thought to be the oldest in history, weigh 25 percent less than "normal" rats but live twice as long. Like other scientists, Walford believes these findings apply to humans. Unlike his colleagues, Walford is doing research not only on the animals who inhabit his lab but also on himself.

Walford, who plans to live to be 130 to 140, has adopted a diet in some ways similar to the diet of his rats. At five feet, eight inches and 140 pounds, he fasts two days a week and eats carefully designed meals the other five. Walford predicts that this diet, which consists mostly of vegetables, fruit, grains, and vitamin supplements, will help him lose an additional 30 pounds (he has already lost 10) and lengthen his middle age considerably. Scientists have known of evidence that supports the value of undernutrition for over 70 years. However, Walford is the first scientist who has applied the principles to himself.

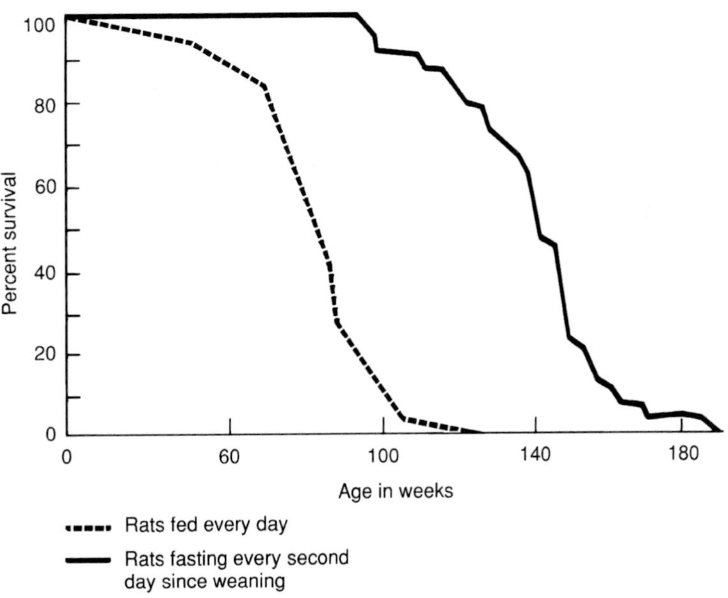

F. Review of Restrictive and Nonrestrictive Adjective Clauses

Restrictive clauses identify the noun(s) they describe. They give information that is necessary to the meaning of the sentence. Nonrestrictive clauses give extra information about the noun(s) they describe. For more information on restrictive and nonrestrictive clauses, see Chapter 4, Part 1.

Examples	Notes
Dr. Jeffery, **who runs the experiments,** lives near Los Angeles.	Nonrestrictive clauses are set off by commas. *That* cannot be used as a relative pronoun.
The man **who (that) works with him** lives in San Diego.	Restrictive clauses are not set off by commas. *That* can, in most cases, be used as a relative pronoun.

G. Placement of Nonrestrictive Participial Phrases

Nonrestrictive participial phrases are reduced from nonrestrictive adjective clauses. When a nonrestrictive phrase modifies the subject of the main clause, it can be placed at different points within a sentence.

	Examples	Notes
Clause	Walford, **who has worked in this field for over 20 years,** is considered an expert.	A nonrestrictive participial phrase may be placed either immediately before or after the subject of a main clause. It is also occasionally placed at the end of the sentence if there is no confusion about which noun it modifies.
Phrase	Walford, **having worked in this field for over 20 years,** is considered an expert. **Having worked in this field for over 20 years,** Walford is considered an expert. Walford is considered an expert, **having worked in this field for over 20 years.**	

6 Change the following adjective clauses into participial phrases, using present or past participles. Put the phrase in three different positions. Then discuss which position sounds the best and why.

Example: Walford, who believes that humans could profit from undernutrition, began to fast and diet several years ago.

Walford, believing that humans could profit from undernutrition, began to fast and diet several years ago.

Believing that humans could profit from undernutrition, Walford began to fast and diet several years ago.

Walford began to fast and diet several years ago, believing that humans could profit from undernutrition.

1. Walford, who has decided not to wait for long-term studies, is, in essence, acting as his own guinea pig.*
2. Most people, who think that undereating would be too difficult, will probably never try undernutrition.
3. Walford, who finds this type of diet enjoyable, plans to continue indefinitely.
4. Eating, which is often done out of habit rather than need, may be our biggest health problem.

Web Note

To learn more about Walford and his work, visit Walford's Website at www.walford.com/. You can also look at a Public Broadcasting program on aging, which included information on Walford's work, at www.pbs.org/stealingtime/living/history.htm.

Using What You've Learned

7 Someone once said that age is a state of mind. When and how do we age? Is aging a slow, steady process that is inevitable for all of us? Or is aging a series of abrupt stages that each of us goes through? Do physical, emotional, and intellectual maturing and aging occur at the same time and at the same rate?

---

*_guinea pig_ small mammal frequently used for laboratory experiments; also, a term often applied to the subject of any experiment

Separate into small groups and spend ten to fifteen minutes discussing your ideas. Share stories from your life and the lives of your friends and family as well as your thoughts on the general topic of aging. Take notes as you talk. Then use your notes as the basis for a short composition on one aspect of the aging process.

PART 2

Verbs Followed by Participial Constructions; The Verbs *Lay/Lie, Raise/Rise*

Setting the Context

Prereading Questions. Who is the oldest person that you know? Are there certain areas of the world where people tend to live a long time?

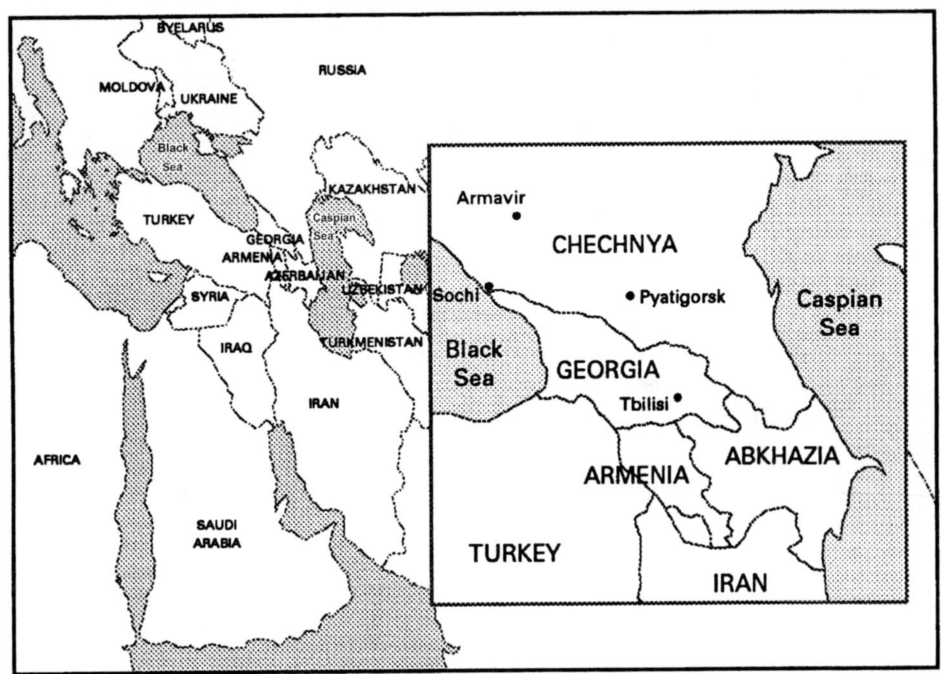

Khfaf

It may be difficult to believe, but while traveling in Abkhazia, I discovered a woman living an active life at the age of 139. Her name was Khfaf Lazuria. When I met her in 1974, she was perhaps the oldest woman alive.

I was taken to visit Khfaf by her grandnephew, an eminent Abkhazian poet. As we drove up to the house, we saw her in the courtyard sitting comfortably in the shade of a large tree. Although she had not been told of our coming, Khfaf was clearly delighted to have visitors. After being introduced and receiving her warm greetings, I began to question her. She seemed to enjoy the interview and sat answering me for well over an hour. I was fascinated by her face, smooth with very few wrinkles. At times she noticed me staring at her, but she responded warmly, kissing my cheeks as an expression of her approval.

Sula Benet

Discussing Ideas. How old was Khfaf when the author met her? Did she seem her age? In what ways did she seem younger?

A. Verbs with Two-Part Objects

Catch, find, keep, leave, and *send* can be followed by a (pro)noun and a second verb.

	Examples	Notes
Present Participle	They **caught him cheating** on his taxes. We **left** her **working** in the field.	The present participle is used for the second verb to describe an activity in progress.
Past Participle	He **kept** the horse **tied** to a tree. We **found** the key **hidden** in a chest.	The past participle describes a completed activity. The past participle rarely follows *catch* or *send.*

1 For decades, there have been rumors of extraordinarily old people living in Abkhazia, a republic that was once in the Soviet Union, as well as in Vilcabamba, Ecuador. Following are some sentences about these people. Form participial phrases from the words in parentheses.

Web Note

For more information on the peoples of Abkhazia, you can check this Website: http://hypatia.ss.uci.edu/gpacs/abkhazia/.

Example: These rumors sent (officials / search / for verification).
These rumors sent officials searching for verification.

1. The verification process kept (researchers / work / for years).
2. In the end, the researchers caught (some older people / lie / about their age).
3. Still, for every 100,000 people, they found (71 / live / past the age of 100).*
4. The researchers left (these elderly people / work / their fields) and (live / their poor but healthy lives).
5. These findings about the elderly have sent (many) researchers / look into / the keys to longevity.

*The rate in the United States is about 6 per 100,000

B. Verbs of Perception

The verbs *feel, hear, listen to, look at, notice, observe, perceive, see, smell, taste,* and *witness* can be followed by a noun or object pronoun + a second verb. The second verb can be a present participle *or* a simple form, usually with little difference in meaning. However, with certain verbs that express "finality," there is a difference. Compare:

	Examples	Notes
Simple Form	We **watched** the sun **go** down. We **saw** the man **die.**	The simple form implies the completion of an action.
Present Participle	I **watched** the sun **going** down. I **saw** the man **dying.** I **noticed** him **being helped** into the car. We **saw** him **being rushed** to the hospital.	The present participle refers to an action in progress. Only the present participle can be used with passive constructions. These constructions can imply either completed actions or actions in progress.

2 Many visitors have gone to Vilcabamba and Abkhazia to study these amazing people. Complete the following sentences about the visitors' findings, using the words in parentheses. Discuss the differences in meaning (if any) when both the simple and *-ing* form of the second verb are possible.

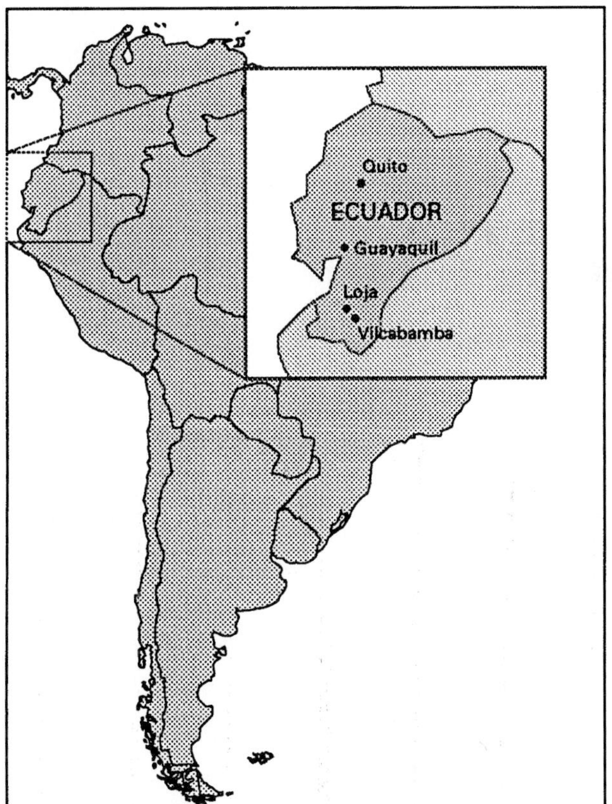

Example: The visitors have watched (100-year-olds / ride / horses).
The visitors have watched 100-year-olds ride (riding) horses.
(Ride and riding give similar meanings, but riding emphasizes that the action was in progress.)

1. The visitors have seen (they / swim / vigorously).
2. They have observed (they / work / fields).
3. The visitors have noticed (they / participate / in all family and community activities).
4. They have witnessed (the elders / be / honor / at feasts).
5. They have listened to (these senior citizens / talk / to their great-great-great-grandchildren).
6. They have heard (the old ones' advice / be / seek / by young people).
7. They have witnessed (true respect / be / give / to them / by younger people).
8. In Abkhazia, they've heard (a few / discuss / their part / in the Crimean War, fought in the 1850s).

3 Every culture is unique. Mention some of the differences between two cultures you know well, using *watch, see, observe, notice, listen to, witness,* and *hear.* Try to give at least five original sentences.

Example: *I've noticed more assertiveness here. People in Japan aren't as assertive.*

C. By *with Phrases of Means or Manner*

Participial phrases placed after the verb often explain "how" or "in which way" an action is carried out. *By* can come before these phrases in some cases.

Examples	Notes
How does Don make a living? He makes a living **(by) farming** a small plot of land.	*By* can be added if the participle phrase answers a "how" question.
What does he do in the evenings? In the winter, he sits next to the fire **reading.**	*By* is not possible in this sentence.

4 In the late 1970s, Gabriel Erazo of Vilcabamba was 132. The following is from one researcher's account of an interview with him. Form participial phrases from the words in parentheses. Add *by* when it is possible to do so. Add all other necessary prepositions.

Gabriel Erazo

[. . .] Soon the son disappeared (leave/us/alone).[1] At first sight, Gabriel Erazo looked rather comical. The old man was sitting on his porch (wear/two hats).[2] He amused himself greatly (explain/the reason)[3]. This way he only had to remove one hat when going to bed, Erazo told me playfully. At 132, Erazo wore no glasses, had perfect hearing, and moved with the agility of a young man.

We passed the afternoon (talk/his long life)[4]. He had married as a young man, but after over 50 years with him, his wife had died. Since then, he had spent his time (bring up/his youngest child)[5] and (farm/his small piece of land)[6]. At times he would stand (point/the green field)[7] in which he worked and the path which led to it. Erazo told me that he got plenty of exercise (walk/this step path)[8] some 15 times a day. After a while, he led me to this field (take/my hand in his)[9]. He demonstrated how he farmed (work/the ground/with his primitive hoe)[10]. Later, as we walked up the path, we stopped several times, for I was winded and in need of rest. We ended the day (stand/his veranda)[11] (watch/the glorious sunset)[12].

D. Lay/Lie, Raise/Rise

Both native and second-language speakers tend to confuse the verbs *lay/lie* and *raise/rise*. To understand the distinction, note which verb in each set is transitive and which is intransitive.

Lay *Versus* Lie

Lay means "to place someone or something on a surface." It is transitive and therefore is followed by an object.

	Examples
Present	Gabriel **lays** the baby in the crib when she needs a nap.
Past	Boris **laid** the book on the table.
Past Participle	He has **laid** it there many times.
Present Participle	Ana is **laying** the tiles for the floor.

Lie means "to be in a place or position."* It is intransitive and therefore is not followed by an object.

**Lie* can also mean "not to tell the truth." This verb is intransitive and its forms are regular: *He lied to me yesterday.*

	Examples
Present	Abkhazia **lies** 500 miles east of here.
Past	Mary **lay** down on the beach and rested.
Past Participle	She has **lain** there for 30 minutes.
Present Participle	She will be **lying** there for the rest of the day.

Raise *Versus* Rise

Raise means "to lift, to make bigger," "to bring up" (children), or "to cultivate" (plants). *Raise* is transitive.

	Examples
Present	Ben **raises** his hand in class every day.
Past	After the game, Mary **raised** the trophy over her head in victory.
Past Participle	Maria has **raised** her children alone since her husband died.
Present Participle	The men are **raising** their voices in protest.

Rise means "to move up without assistance" or "to increase." *Rise* is intransitive.

	Examples
Present	In summer the sun **rises** about 6:00 A.M.
Past	Ernesto **rose** slowly from his chair.
Past Participle	The price of oil has **risen** in the last two weeks.
Present Participle	The moon is **rising.**

5 Circle the correct verb form in the following sentences.

1. I met an old couple (laying / lying) in a pasture under a tree.
2. They (laid / lay) a blanket down next to them and invited me to join them.
3. They lived alone; they had already (raised / risen) their five children.
4. For food, they (raise / rise) corn and have chickens, which (lain / lay) eggs.
5. After an hour, the wind began to (raise / rise) and the sky became clouded.
6. I suddenly realized the time and (raised / rose) to leave.

6 Choose the correct verb: *lay, lie, raise,* or *rise.* Then fill in the correct form in the following eight sentences.

Example: During the summer, the sun <u>always rises</u> (always) before 6:00 A.M.

1. I normally arise before daybreak. The alarm goes off at 5:00 A.M., and I __________ in bed for about half an hour before getting up.

2. However, one particular morning last summer, the sun __________ (already) by the time I got up.
3. Light was streaming in the window when I __________ (finally) my head from the pillow to see what kind of day it was going to be.
4. It was my day off so, after I __________ in bed for an extra hour, I got up and called some friends to invite them for a hike.
5. The weather was perfect. We spent the morning hiking and the afternoon __________ on a beach near a lake.
6. Around 4:00, everyone started feeling hungry. After we __________ our food on a blanket, we sat eating and talking for what seemed like hours.
7. With the sun low in the sky, I __________ down in the tall grass and closed my eyes.
8. When I awoke, it was pitch black. While I was __________ under a canopy of stars, a harvest moon began __________.

Using What You've Learned

7 Imagine that you have the opportunity to travel to Vilcabamba, Abkhazia, or another unique area. Use your imagination to envision your trip. Then, in small groups, give a description of your experiences, using as much detail as possible. Finally, write a short composition describing what you saw, heard, felt, witnessed, or noticed.

PART 3

Adverb Clause to Phrase Reduction

Setting the Context

Prereading Questions. In your opinion, what are the most important elements in good health and a long life?

An Abkarian shepherd with his great grandson

The Good Life

Wanting to discover the secret to longevity, gerontologists, biologists, medical doctors, and sociologists have flocked to Abkhazia and Vilcabamba. They have put the older citizens through exhaustive medical examinations and have conducted numerous studies concerning their lifestyles and social roles. But after working within these communities for years, scientists still have few concrete answers as to why so many people there live so long. Many researchers believe that the diet of these people is the most important reason. Others cite factors such as clean air and water, genetics, and exercise. Perhaps the best answer comes from the elderly people themselves. When asked why they were young so long, several old people of Abkhazia and Vilcabamba shrugged their shoulders and answered that they led the "good life." What do you think they meant by the good life? In your opinion, what steps should a person take to live a long healthy life?

A. Adverb Clause to Phrase Reduction

When an adverb clause has the same subject as the main clause of the sentence, the adverb clause can often be reduced to a phrase. In these phrases, the subjects are omitted and the verbs are changed to present participles. This type of phrase is generally placed before the independent clause.

Clause	Phrase	Notes
Before the doctors left, they had examined several people.	**Before leaving,** the doctors had examined several people.	Adverb clauses with *before, after, since, as, while, when, because,* and *despite (in spite of) the fact that* are often reduced to phrases.
After the doctors had left, they published their findings.	**(After) having left,** the doctors published their findings.	*After* is often omitted when the phrase has a reduced perfect verb.
When they were leaving the village, the doctors gave the children candy.	**(When) leaving the village,** the doctors gave the children candy.	*When* and *while* are sometimes omitted from these phrases.
Because they needed money, the villagers were happy to help.	**Needing money,** the villagers were happy to help.	*Because* and *as* are always omitted from these phrases.
Despite the fact that they were tired, they kept working.	**Despite being tired,** they kept working.	With *despite (in spite of) the fact that,* delete *the fact that.*
Since he was examined, the man has recovered from the disease.	**Since being examined,** the man has recovered from the disease.	With passives, the first auxiliary verb *(be* or *have)* becomes the present participle.

B. Elliptical Phrases

When the subjects in the main and adverb clauses are the same, adverb clauses with the verb *be* can often be reduced. To do this, omit both the subject and the verb *be.*

Clause	Phrase	Notes
When they were finished with the research, they left the village.	**(When) finished with the research,** they left the village.	*When* and *while* can be omitted in elliptical phrases.
Although she was tired and hungry, she kept traveling.	**Although tired and hungry,** she kept traveling.	*Although* and *if* are never omitted in these phrases.
Because Grace was tired and hungry, she stopped to rest.	**Tired and hungry,** Grace stopped to rest.	*Because* is always omitted in these phrases.

1 Change the dependent clauses into phrases in the following sentences. Where appropriate, omit the connecting word and make changes in nouns and pronouns.

Example: While scientists were studying the centurions (people 100 or over), they tried to isolate the elements of the "good life."

While studying the centurions, scientists tried to isolate the elements of the "good life."

1. The researchers assumed that diet was important even before they arrived in the villages.
2. After doctors had examined hundreds of elderly people, they realized that the number-one killer in the West, heart disease, was virtually absent there.
3. Because the villagers eat little meat and few dairy products, they have no problem with cholesterol.
4. The villagers remain thin but amazingly healthy because they consume about 60 percent of the calories and 40 to 50 percent of the protein common in the Western diet.
5. Despite the fact that they eat little protein, they have enormous amounts of energy.
6. If they were bored by their simple diet, they certainly disguised it well.
7. When they were offered Western food by visitors, the elderly were interested at first but preferred their own diet.
8. Illness is rare, but if they are sick, the villagers eat less, rest, and take herbal remedies.

2 Expand the phrases in the following sentences into dependent clauses.

Example: Having small farms, most of the elderly people lead demanding lives.

Because they have small farms, most of the elderly people lead demanding lives.

1. Not having modern tools, they must devote much of their time to strenuous physical labor.
2. If tired of working to support themselves, few of the older people complain about this.
3. When questioned about their lifestyle, the older people saw nothing unusual about the way they lived.
4. After having moved from their mountain villages to large cities, the children of the elderly rarely live past 80.
5. Studying the people who had moved away from Abkhazia, scientists found a high incidence of heart disease.
6. Living the "good life," the people of Abkhazia almost never suffer from heart disease.

3 Imagine that you are a researcher who has just arrived in a village that has no heat, running water, or electricity. You plan to study the elderly there. Tell about your "work" by completing the following sentences with phrases. Delete the words in parentheses.

Example: Before . . . , I had to find a place to stay.

Before beginning my research, I had to find a place to stay.

1. After . . . , I found a small room to rent.
2. I talked to hundreds of people while. . . .
3. (Because) . . . , I tried to be very polite.
4. Despite . . . , I was accepted into the community almost immediately.
5. (When) . . . , I became sad.
6. Before . . . , I packed my film and notes and said good-bye to the many friends I had made.

C. Dangling Phrases

Phrases that have been reduced from adverb clauses must have the same logical subject as the independent clause. Phrases that do not are ungrammatical "dangling" phrases. To correct a dangling phrase, either expand the phrase into a full clause or change the independent clause so that it has the same logical subject as the phrase.

Dangling Phrase	Implied Meaning	Corrected Sentence
Having lived for 100 years, the doctors were amazed at my grandfather.	The dangling phrase implies that the doctors had lived for 100 years.	Because he had lived for 100 years, the doctors were amazed at my grandfather.
After finishing the operation, the patient was given a sedative.	The dangling phrase would imply that the patient finished the operation!	After finishing the operation, the doctor gave the patient a sedative.
If sick, his family cares for him.	The dangling phrase implies that the family is sick.	If sick, he is cared for by his family.

4 A researcher rode a horse through miles of rough terrain to interview 124-year-old José Molina. The following is from the researcher's account of the visit. Some of the sentences have "dangling phrases." Find these dangling phrases and correct the sentences by expanding the phrases into adverb clauses. If a sentence is correct, don't change it.

Example: While traveling in the country, the weather was hot.
While I was traveling in the country, the weather was hot.

1. Having worked since early in the morning, José Molina welcomed the chance for a rest.
2. After shaking my hand, we walked to a large tree and sat down.
3. While talking about his life and family, my horse stood nearby nibbling on the grass.
4. José had made his living as a farmer since coming to Vilcabamba some 90 years before.
5. Living a simple life and having few possessions, money was not important to José.
6. If ill, his wife made him a special type of herbal medicine.
7. José had to get back to work after talking to me for over an hour.
8. Although tired and hungry, there was plenty of work left to do.
9. Riding back to town, the view of the mountains was spectacular.

5 Go back to the sentences with dangling phrases in the previous activity and rewrite them by changing the subject of the independent clause. You may have to change the meaning of the independent clause.

Example: While traveling in the country, the weather was hot.
While traveling in the country, I became hot.

6 Underline the dependent clauses in the following passage. When it is possible, change these clauses into phrases. Make changes from pronoun to noun where appropriate and make any other changes in sentence structure.

Status of the Elderly

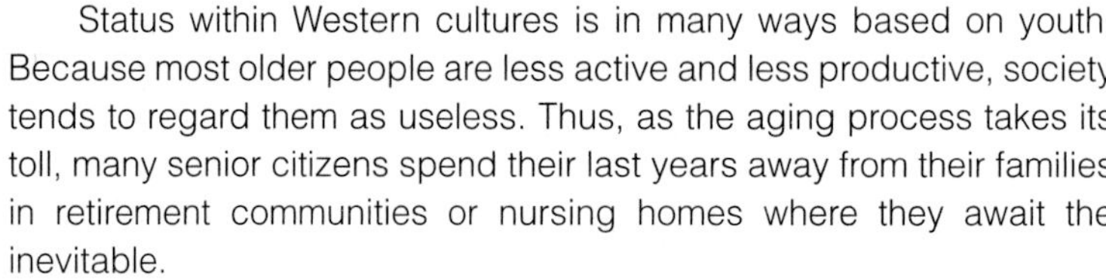

Status within Western cultures is in many ways based on youth. Because most older people are less active and less productive, society tends to regard them as useless. Thus, as the aging process takes its toll, many senior citizens spend their last years away from their families in retirement communities or nursing homes where they await the inevitable.

This situation is reversed in Vilcabamba and Abkhazia. While the elderly are growing older in these cultures, they gain social prestige and importance rather than lose it. Because they live in close-knit families, the older citizens are never separated from their loved ones. Even when they are very old, they continue to help with the household responsibilities. And if they are sick, several generations of family are nearby to care for them.

The elderly never lose sight of their roles within the family and community. While they are surrounded by sons, daughters, grandchildren, and great-grandchildren, the old ones are constantly told, "You are the reason we are here; you are first in the family; we need your superior wisdom; we need your wise judgments." Because many older people in the West believe they are useless, they age quickly and die young. Because the old of Vilcabamba and Abkhazia know that they are not useless, they continue to lead productive lives well into their hundreds.

Using What You've Learned

7 "A bullet cannot kill you; it is only destiny that determines when you die."

MIGUEL CARPIO, 127 YEARS OLD, VILCABAMBA

Some people believe that everything about our lives is predetermined. Others feel that chance plays a major role in determining the future. Still others think that what happens to us is neither predetermined nor accidental—that we control our own destiny. What do you believe?

In small groups, discuss your ideas on human destiny. Give as many examples as you can to support your point of view. As you talk, make notes. Then use these notes as the basis for a short composition on how one's life is determined. In your composition, use as many adverb phrases as possible.

PART 4

Causative and Structurally Related Verbs

Setting the Context

Prereading Questions. What are some things that are supposed to slow or prevent aging? Do you believe these things work?

Forever Young

People have dreamed of eternal youth for thousands of years. Since ancient times, unusual beliefs have surrounded this dream. In China, for example, the Taoists thought that proper breathing could make people live forever. Masters in this discipline helped converts limit the number of breaths they took. When a Taoist could go 1,000 normal respirations without breathing, he or she supposedly became immortal. In Europe and the Middle East, the breath of virgins was believed to cure the problems of old age. As a result, King Solomon had unmarried women surround him during the later years of his life. During the Roman Empire, it was thought that human blood would make old age disappear. Thus, officials had the bodies of dying gladiators saved. Then they let aged men and women drink the blood of these slain warriors.

Discussing Ideas. The passage gives three examples of methods that were used to prevent aging. In your own words, describe each of these methods and tell where each originated.

A. Causative and Structurally Related Verbs

Several verbs in English use special constructions with the simple form, the infinitive, or the past participle of the second verb.

	Examples	Notes
help	We **helped** him **(to) enter** the pool.	*Help* takes a (pro)noun + the simple form or infinitive of a second verb.
let allow	She **let** him **swim** in the stream. She **allowed** him **to swim** in the stream.	*Let* has the same meaning as *allow*, but they are followed by different constructions. *Let* is followed by (pro)noun + simple form. *Allow* is followed by (pro)noun + infinitive.
make force	She **made** him **leave** after ten minutes. She **forced** him **to leave** after ten minutes.	*Make* and *force* have similar meanings, although *force* is stronger. *Make* is followed by (pro)noun + simple verb. *Force* is followed by (pro)noun + infinitive.
have	He **had** a lab **test** the water. He **had** the water **tested** (by a lab). She **had** the servant **bring** a drink to her. She **had** the drink **brought** to her (by a servant).	*Have* is similar in meaning to *arrange for. Have* may be followed by (pro)noun + simple verb. Also, *have* may be followed by a passive construction: (pro)noun + past participle. (You *have* someone *do* something, or you *have* something *done.*)

1 For thousands of years, people have believed that certain waters could revitalize older people. Complete the following sentences about such treatments by forming a phrase from the words in parentheses.

Example: Can some substances make (age / disappear)?
Can some substances make age disappear?

1. In Greek mythology, Zeus's wife Hera visited a spring that made (the signs of age / vanish).
2. Hera forced (other beautiful women / stay / away from this spring).
3. The Roman god Jupiter let (certain people / enter the special waters of Juventas).
4. Jupiter allowed (these lucky bathers / regain / their youth).
5. Of course, these waters helped (the bathers / feel / young again).
6. The Bible mentions the "fountain of life" from which the Lord let (Adam and Eve / drink).
7. In search of the "fountain of youth," Ponce de León had (native guides / take / him to present-day Florida) in 1512. Unfortunately, he found an Indian arrow instead and died at age 61.

2 Change the following sentences from the active to the passive voice. Delete the nouns in italics.

Example: The emperors of China had *officials* hire alchemists to prescribe cures for aging.
The emperors of China had alchemists hired to prescribe cures for aging.

1. The alchemists had *people* bring gold and mercury to them because they believed these elements stopped aging.
2. Unfortunately, dissatisfied emperors had *guards* execute their alchemists.
3. Isabella and Ferdinand of Spain had *explorers* investigate stories about a fountain of youth.
4. Several monarchs had *magicians* create potions to make them young again.
5. Alfonso of Colombia had *craftsmen* design special jewelry to prolong his life.

3 Many anti-aging treatments of questionable value have been developed in the 20th century. In 1931, a Swiss doctor named Paul Niehans was called to the hospital to treat a woman suffering from convulsions because her thyroid gland had been removed by mistake during an operation. Complete these sentences about Dr. Niehans and his treatments by using either the past participle or simple form of the verbs in parentheses.

1. Dr. Niehans went to a nearby slaughterhouse and had the thyroid gland of a steer _removed_ (remove) and _packed_ (pack) in ice.
2. Niehans then had technicians ________ (mince) this gland, ________ (put) it into a neutral solution, and ________ (inject) the woman with the mixture.
3. When this treatment was successful, Niehans became convinced this type of "cell therapy" was the key to organ regeneration. In 1933, he had the first buildings ________ (erect) for his now famous Clinique La Prairie.
4. When a patient entered the clinic, the doctor would have assistants ________ (run) tests to isolate the patient's weak organs.
5. Then Niehans had the patient ________ (inject) with cells taken from the corresponding organ of newly slaughtered lambs. Thus, if the patient suffered from heart disease, the cells would come from the lamb's heart.
6. Little proof has ever been given to support the effectiveness of "cell therapy." Still, thousands had Niehans ________ (give) them his mysterious and expensive treatment.
7. Somerset Maugham, Pope Pius XII, Winston Churchill, Charles de Gaulle, and Niehans himself had this treatment ________ (perform) on them, though none of these men is alive to describe its effects.

Web Note

For more information about Clinique La Prairie, including a video, go to www2.laprairie.ch/eng/.

4 If you were the owner of a true fountain of youth, what would you do? Complete the following sentences with your own opinions.

Example: I would let my mother *use it for free.*
I would allow my grandmother *to pay a reduced price.*

1. I would (not) let my friends . . . .
2. I would (not) allow my family . . . .
3. I would make other people . . . .
4. I would force my grammar teacher . . . .

5. I would have the police . . . .
6. I would have trespassers (passive) . . . .
7. I would (not) help scientists . . . .

5 Fill in each blank with the present or past participle, gerund, infinitive, or simple forms of the verbs in parentheses.

Frozen in Time

On January 12, 1967, a 73-year-old man *named* (name) James H. Bedford lay ____________ (1) (die) of lung cancer in a small convalescent home near Los Angeles. In the early evening, his condition was grave, and he began ____________ (2) (gasp) for breath. A short time later, after ____________ (3) (find) no vital life signs, Bedford's physician, Dr. Renault Able, pronounced him dead.

So began the world's first human experiment in cryonics. Dr. Able had assistants quickly ____________ (4) (connect) Bedford's body to a heart-lung machine ____________ (5) (flood) it with nutrients and oxygen. At the same time, he prevented Bedford's blood from clotting by ____________ (6) (inject) it with the chemical heparin. Then, Dr. Dante Brunol, from the Los Angeles Cryonic Society, helped Able ____________ (7) (freeze) Bedford's body as quickly as possible. First, they had dry ice ____________ (8) (pack) around the body. Then, into Bedford's bloodstream, they added DSFO, a chemical "antifreeze" that prevents ice crystals from ____________ (9) (form) in living tissue when the tissue freezes. When the body temperature reached freezing, they let assistants ____________ (10) (disconnect) the heart-lung machine. By 2:00 A.M., Bedford's body temperature was 100 degrees below zero. Next, a seven-foot-long "cryogenic storage capsule," ____________ (11) (design) by a California engineer, was brought into the room. The doctors watched Bedford's frozen body ____________ (12) (be) wrapped in aluminum foil and placed inside the capsule. After ____________ (13) (be) sealed, the capsule was flooded with liquid nitrogen, a gas with a temperature of 320 degrees below zero. The temperature of this

gas made Bedford's body ______________ (become) as brittle as glass. The
14
following day, the capsule was flown to Arizona for storage.

If in the future a cure for lung cancer is found, doctors may be able to awaken James Bedford and allow him ______________ (start) his life where he left it.
15

6 **Review.** The following passage is fiction; however, it is based on a true story. Combine each set of sentences into one sentence. Use adverb, adjective, and noun clauses and participial phrases. Also use verbs of perception, causative verbs, and so forth to join sentences. Omit unnecessary words and add all needed punctuation.

Example: I had been driving for 14 hours. I stopped the car and rested. There was still a long drive ahead.

After driving for 14 hours, I stopped the car and rested even though there was still a long drive ahead.

1. My wife and I were sitting in a roadside restaurant. People were talking about a "rejuvenation machine." This machine was located in the middle of a California desert. I heard this.
2. We had been in California for a few days. We drove out toward Twenty-Nine Palms. We wanted to find this rejuvenation machine and its inventor, George Van Tassel.
3. I first saw George W. Van Tassel. He was sitting by an impressive dome. The dome was surrounded by desert.
4. I greeted him and explained my purpose. He let us examine his machine, the "Integratron." Extraterrestrials had supposedly helped him design the Integratron.
5. The Integratron was a dome. The dome was 38 feet high and 53 feet in diameter. The dome resembled an old-fashioned observatory.
6. The machine could produce up to 100,000,000 volts of electricity. The machine was inside the dome. Van Tassel explained this to us.
7. A person needed only to walk under the arc of the electricity. The person wanted to become young again. Van Tassel told us this.

8. The Integratron was financed by contributions. The contributions came from the Ministry of Universal Wisdom, Inc. This ministry is a nonprofit organization. This organization is owned by his family. Van Tassel revealed this to me.
9. Van Tassel wanted to get in touch with us in the future. He copied our address and phone number. We let him. We returned to our car.
10. We were leaving. I heard him. He was talking to an older couple. The couple had just driven up.

7 Why do you think that Van Tassel asked for the author's address? Do you think Van Tassel contacted the author? Imagine that you are the author. Complete the story with at least five original sentences. Use as many different types of clauses and phrases as you can.

Using What You've Learned

8 In small groups, review the information in Activity 3 (on Paul Niehans), Activity 5 (on Renault Able and James Bedford), or Activity 6 (on George Van Tassel and the Integratron). Then create a humorous skit loosely based on this information.

Use your imagination to develop the characters of your skit fully. You may even want to "invent" one or more new characters. Add an inventive ending to the skit. When you are finished, perform your skit for the class.

Video Activities: Stealth Surgery

Before You Watch. Answer these questions in small groups.

1. What kinds of pictures does an X ray machine take? Have you ever had an X ray?
2. Do you know the name of any other machines that can take pictures of the inside of a body? What are they? How are they different from X rays?

Watch. Answer these questions in small groups.

1. What is Leonard Novak's favorite free time activity? Why is it unusual?

   ____

2. What health problem did Leonard Novak have recently?

   a. eye problems b. bad headaches c. a cancerous tumor

3. What is the name of the new treatment that Novak received? ____________
4. Why is this treatment better than traditional surgery? ____________

Watch Again. Answer these questions in small groups.

1. Use the words below to complete the description of the new treatment.

anatomical	converted	creates	CT
images	MRI	placed	scans

Two hundred or more ________ and ________ ________ of the patient's head are fed into the computer and ________ into 3D ________. Then a band ________ on the patient's head ________ an ________ map.

2. *He was benched* means that he ________.
   a. couldn't play b. was hit with a bench c. got sick
3. *She threw him a curve ball* means that she ________.
   a. hit him b. pitched the ball to him c. surprised him
4. The word *invasive* is an adjective related to ________.
   a. invalid b. invasion c. invent
5. The *skull* is the ________.
   a. bone of the head b. the nose c. the neck bone
6. *Stealth* refers to the action of moving ________.
   a. quickly b. secretly c. carefully

After You Watch. Complete the following sentences.

1. After ________, Leonard was told not to play baseball for a month.
2. The doctor watched a video monitor while ________________.
3. Because ____________________, it leaves a very small scar.
4. Despite ________________________, the tumor returned.
5. When ____________________________, he is unhappy.

Focus on Testing

Use of Participial Phrases and Related Structures

Problems with participial phrases and related structures always appear on standardized tests of English proficiency. Check your understanding of these structures by completing the sample items that follow.

Remember that . . .

- The present participle is used to replace verbs in a variety of tenses.
- *Having* + past participle is used to emphasize the completion of the activity.
- An adverb clause having the same subject as the main clause of the sentence can often be reduced to a phrase.

Part 1. Circle the best completion for the following.

Example: Cancer, ______________ around the world, may be cured some day.

a. to be studied
(c.) which is being studied
b. being studied
d. that is being studied

1. The rats ______________ the least live the longest.
   a. which eats
   c. had eaten
   b. that eating
   d. eating

2. That tree, ______________ in 1965, is over 4,000 years old.
   a. discover
   c. which was discovering
   b. discovered
   d. that was discovered

3. The patients ______________ a special diet had little heart disease.
   a. followed
   c. having followed
   b. who had followed
   d. having been followed

4. We found the notebook ______________ in an old dusty drawer.
   a. hidden
   c. having hidden
   b. hiding
   d. it was hidden

Part 2. Each sentence has one error. Circle the letter below the word(s) containing the error.

Example: When (A) they was leaving (B, circled) the village, the doctors gave (C) the children candy and waved (D) good-bye to them.

1. After considering (A) the matter carefully, mother had (B) me gave (C) the toy back to my brother and apologize (D) to him.

2. Harriet, having left (A) the children working (B) in the field, she (C) hurried back to prepare dinner (D).

3. Every afternoon after an arduous (A) day of seemingly endless work, Harold lied (B) down on the sofa and raised (C) his (D) feet for an hour or more.

4. While hiking (A) along the Inca Trail as the weather cleared (B) after a rain shower, the beauty (C) of the mountains was overwhelming (D).

Chapter 12

The Future

IN THIS CHAPTER

Part 1 Passive, Continuous, and Perfect Infinitives

Part 2 Passive and Perfect Gerunds

Part 3 Review

Introduction

In this chapter, you will review infinitives and gerunds and learn about their perfect and passive forms. At the conclusion of the chapter, you will find a general review of the grammar presented in this book.

The following passage introduces the chapter theme "The Future" and introduces some topics that you will cover in this chapter.

A Glimpse of the Future

What will life on earth be like 50 years from now? What changes can we expect to have taken place? Here are a few glimpses of what the future may hold:

- The life expectancy, at least in developed countries, will be 100 years or more because cures for many diseases, including AIDS and some forms of cancer, will have been found.
- Scientists' having figured out the human genetic code will allow many genetic defects to be repaired before a baby is born.
- Computerization will enable more and more people to "telecommute," that is, work at home while being connected to the office via computer.
- Developments in engineering will make it possible for icebergs to be towed to dry areas and for a bridge to be built across the Strait of Gibraltar.
- Nations will be able to reduce their dependence on petroleum because alternative sources of energy will have been developed. Ultralight "hypercars" will be able to travel across the United States on one tank of gas.
- Overpopulation will have become a tremendous problem. By the year 2050, demographers expect the world's population to have doubled.
- Many people will be living and traveling in space. Within 50 years, thousands of people are expected to be living and working on space colonies.

Web Note

Learn about the Human Genome Project and the decoding of our genetic heritage at www.ornl.gov/hgmis/.

Discussing Ideas. Do you believe that the developments described in the preceding list will really happen? In what ways do you think they will affect you and your family personally? What other changes—both positive and negative—do you expect in the next 50 years?

PART 1

Passive, Continuous, and Perfect Infinitives

Setting the Context

Prereading Questions. Would you like to travel or live in space? Do you think this will be possible in your lifetime?

Space Colonies

The idea of space colonies may appear to be farfetched at present, but as the earth's population grows and as its resources diminish, the idea will need to be considered seriously. Princeton physicist Gerard O'Neill, a leading proponent of space colonization, expects such colonies to have become a reality by the middle of the 21st century. He thinks that competition among nations will help accelerate such development. O'Neill, along with other scientists, is advising government officials to begin planning space colonies soon. If this is done, O'Neill predicts that within 100 years, 200 million people can expect to be making routine trips into space each year.

O'Neill explains that it will be cheaper to build a number of small colonies than one extremely large one. To facilitate communication, the colonies will be clustered together. They will be small in scale and simple in government. Being decentralized, they will manage to avoid many of the problems that currently face our large urban areas.

Discussing Ideas. Why do you think it will be cheaper to build several small colonies rather than one big one? Which nations do you think will be willing to pay for these colonies to be developed?

A. Review of Active and Passive Forms of Simple Infinitives

	Affirmative	Negative
Active **(*not*) *to*** + **verb**	Many people would be afraid **to live** in a space colony.	We were warned **not to walk** on the surface of the planet.
Passive **(*not*) *to be*** + **Past Participle**	The space shuttle is scheduled **to be launched** tomorrow.	We expect **not to be delayed.**

Note: See Chapter 9 for lists of verbs followed by infinitives.

1 Review. Fill in the blanks with the active or passive form of the infinitive phrase.

Space Colonies of the Future

What can we expect the space colonies of the late 21st century *to be* (be) like? According to Gerard O'Neill, it will be cheaper ______ [1] (build) several small colonies than one large one. Thus the colonies will tend ______ [2] (spread out) and small. Perhaps in this way they can manage ______ [3] (not become) overcrowded.

The colonies can be located almost anywhere in the solar system; however, they will need ______ [4] (build) outside the shadow of any planet ______ [5] (enable) them ______ [6] (take) advantage of solar energy. Huge mirrors will be used ______ [7] (gather) sunlight, which scientists will try ______ [8] (adjust) to the same intensity that exists on earth. In addition, it will be necessary for the earth's gravity and atmosphere ______ [9] (duplicate) so that flowers, trees, and crops will be able ______ [10] (grow). Because of the earthlike conditions, it will be possible for people ______ [11] (participate) in outdoor activities, just as they do now on earth.

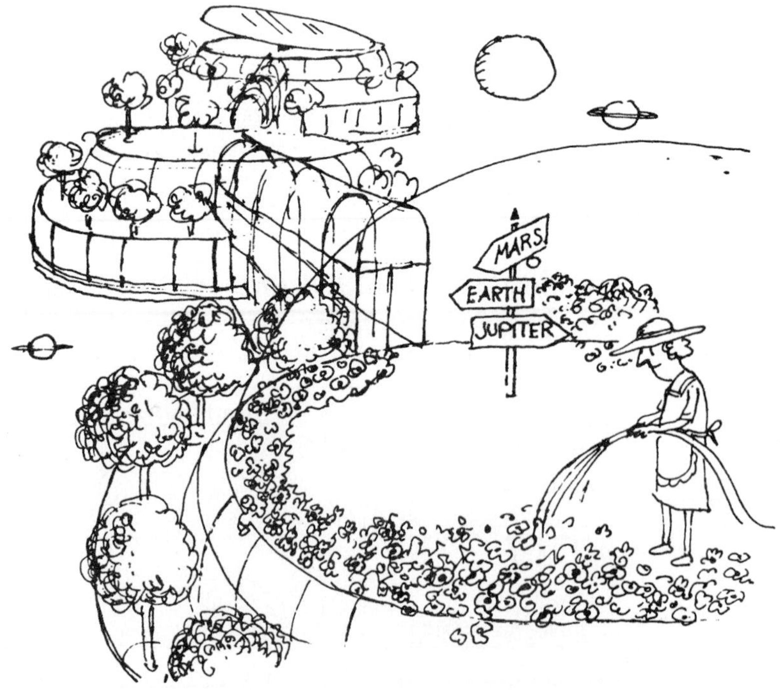

Web Note

Learn more about current space projects by visiting NASA's *Website at www.nasa.gov/today/index.html.*

The idea of a clean, peaceful, and uncrowded place to live is exciting to many people. Unfortunately, though, we must expect the first space colony ________ (not complete) before the end of the 21st century.
12

B. Perfect and Continuous Forms of Active Infinitives

Form	Examples	Notes
Continuous ***(not) to be* + verb + *-ing***	Many people can expect **to be living** in space within 100 years.	Continuous infinitives emphasize that the action of the infinitive is in progress at the time of the main verb. They often occur after the verbs *agree, appear, arrange, happen, hope, expect, plan, pretend, promise, seem.*
Perfect Active ***(not) to have* + past participle**	The UFO appears **to have landed.**	The action of the perfect infinitive happened before the time of the main verb.
Perfect Passive ***(not) to have been* + past participle**	People appear **not to have been warned** concerning the arrival of the UFO.	Perfect infinitives often occur after the verbs *appear, claim, expect, happen, hope, pretend, seem.*

Note: The perfect continuous form exists but is almost never used: *By the year 2100, people can expect* ***to have been traveling*** *in space for many years.*

2 Quickly reread the passage "Space Colonies of the Future" on page 380. Underline all the infinitives and label their forms as active or passive and simple, continuous, or perfect.

3 The year is 2081, and a number of space colonies have been established. Space shuttles deliver needed supplies from earth. Following are excerpts from a conversation between the captain and the navigator of one of the shuttles. Complete the conversation with the simple, perfect, or continuous infinitive forms of the words in parentheses.

Navigator: I'm glad you've returned from your nap, sir! There's a large object behind us. It appears *to have changed* (change) direction within the last few minutes. In fact, it now seems ________ (head) directly toward us.
1

Captain: Relax. That's nothing but a meteor.

Navigator: Captain, that "meteor" happens ________ (gain) on us. At current speed, it will reach us in three minutes.
2

Captain: What? That's impossible! No meteor could move that fast.

Navigator: Sir, maybe you should put on your glasses. That "meteor" appears ________ (be) an alien spaceship.
3

Captain: Why didn't you notice this sooner?

Navigator: I tried to tell you, but . . .

Captain: Never mind! Take evasive action! With our speed, these aliens cannot hope ________ (keep up) with us.
4

Navigator: Sorry, sir, but our engines seem ________ (stop) working.
5

Captain: Then prepare to fire weapons.

Navigator: More bad news, captain. All of our weapon systems appear ________
6
(malfunction) at the moment.

Captain: I should never have gotten up from my nap.

Navigator: Sir, we've just received a message from the alien vessel. They claim ________ (come) from a distant galaxy. They expect ________ (board) our ship
7 8
within a few minutes.

4 You are inside your house when you hear a tremendous crash. You rush out to investigate and find something very unexpected. Use the following cues to complete the phrases containing the active or passive perfect form of the infinitive.

Example: An alien spacecraft appear / crash-land on the street in front of your house.
An alien spacecraft appears to have crash-landed on the street in front of your house.

1. None of your neighbors appear / hurt. ______________________________

2. However, the two aliens on board the spacecraft seem / injure. ______________________________

3. They can speak. They claim / send / on a peace mission. ______________________________

4. They expected / complete their mission by now. ______________________________

5. Unfortunately, their spacecraft seem / develop mechanical problems. ______________________________

6. It seem / damage. ______________________________

C. More Verbs Followed by Infinitive Objects

Form	Examples	List of Verbs		
verb + *to* + verb	We can't afford **to move** to a space colony now. The alien pretended **to be dying.** I deserve **to have been selected** to go on a space mission.	arrange (can't) afford care claim consent	demand deserve endeavor fail hesitate pretend	prove struggle swear threaten volunteer
verb + (pro)noun + *to* + verb	The captain commanded the officers **to abandon** ship. He urged us **to take** extra supplies on our trip.	appoint caution challenge command	compel direct implore oblige	persuade require urge warn

5 The spaceship in which you are traveling has been hijacked by hostile aliens. The following is a list of the aliens' demands. Complete the sentences, using active or passive infinitive phrases. Add nouns or pronouns as needed.

Example: We urge ___you to obey___ (obey).

1. We demand ____________ (take) to your leader.
2. We caution ____________ (not resist).
3. We command ____________ (give) us your flight log.
4. We have arranged for your captain ____________ (transfer) to our planet.
5. If you do not obey, we will not hesitate ____________ (kill) you.
6. Do not pretend ____________ (understand / not) our orders.
7. You must not fail ____________ (do) as we instruct you.
8. It is useless to implore ____________ (change) our minds.

6 You are the leader of one of the first space colonies. There is much work to do, and there are many problems to solve. Use the following cues to give your workers instructions containing infinitive phrases. There are many possible answers for each item.

Example: arrange / receive

I will arrange for you to receive all the necessary tools.

Sachiko, please arrange to receive the necessary equipment.

1. endeavor / solve
2. warn / be careful
3. direct / build
4. volunteer / repair
5. consent / live
6. caution / not stand
7. require / follow instructions
8. don't hesitate / ask

7 A common use of infinitives is in sentences expressing commonly held beliefs or ideas. In these sentences, the main verb is normally passive. Verbs used this way include *assume, believe, expect, know, suppose,* and *think.* Following are some commonly held beliefs concerning space and the universe. Convert them to passive-voice sentences containing infinitives.

Web Note

Visit Mars (and other planets) via the National Air and Space Museum! *At the museum's Website, you can learn a great deal about the "red planet":* www.nasm.edu/ceps/etp/mars/.

Example: We consider life on Mars to be impossible.

Life on Mars is considered to be impossible.

1. We know that the universe is expanding.
2. We think that the earth was formed billions of years ago.
3. We assume that aliens are trying to communicate with us.
4. We know that sunspots are thousands of miles in height.
5. We expect space travel to be commonplace within 100 years.
6. We know that the former Soviets sent the first woman into space.
7. We suppose that the next satellite to Mars will be launched soon.
8. We believe that the Russians are training people to live in space permanently.

8 **Review.** The following sentences contain examples of changes that can be expected in the future. Use the cues to complete the sentences with infinitive phrases. In some cases, there is more than one correct answer.

Example: Here are a few changes that we can expect *to have taken place* (take place) by the year 2030.

1. Advances in technology promise ____________ (provide) millions of people with a higher standard of living and more leisure time than ever before.
2. Genetic engineering techniques will enable food supplies ____________ (expand) greatly.
3. By the end of the 21st century, millions of people can expect ____________ (telecommute) to their jobs from home.

4. The use of computers in schools will make it possible __________ (education / be) much more individualized.
5. Lengthened life spans will probably cause people __________ (get married) several times.
6. Advances in aeronautics will enable the trip from New York to Tokyo __________ (make) in three hours.
7. We all would like nuclear weapons __________ (eliminate) once and for all.
8. Cures are expected __________ (find) for many forms of cancer.
9. Scientists also hope __________ (develop) a cure for AIDS.
10. Unfortunately, conditions in many developing countries will tend __________ (not improve) greatly by the year 2030.
11. In many places, conditions __________ (get) worse by then.
12. These problems challenge __________ (governments / work) together to find solutions.

9 **Review.** In the following sentences, some students are talking about their future hopes and plans. Use the cues to complete the sentences with infinitive phrases. Use perfect forms whenever possible.

1. *Sachiko:* By the year 2006, I hope <u>to have completed</u> (complete) my Ph.D. in electronic engineering.
2. *Martin:* I plan __________ (work) for myself within ten years.
3. *Alex:* If I get a chance, I will volunteer __________ (send) on a mission to outer space.
4. *Leda:* As soon as I finish my education, I intend __________ (go back) to my country and __________ (work) as an architect.
5. *Pablo:* My greatest wish is __________ (people / find) a way to live together peacefully.
6. *Camila:* There are so many fascinating places __________ (visit) that I hope __________ (have) a job that includes lots of traveling.
7. *Galia:* As a musician, I want __________ (accept) to a great conservatory and afterwards __________ (become) a concert pianist.
8. *Joseph:* In the near future, I just hope __________ (not draft) into the army when I return to my country.

9. *Kim:* I would like for North and South Korea ________________ (reunite) so that I can visit my relatives in the north.
10. *Dmitri:* Within ten years I hope ________________ (earn) enough money ________________ (buy) a house and ________________ (start) a family.
11. *Jan:* I am expected ________________ (take over) my family's business some day, but to tell you the truth, I would prefer ________________ (not work) with my relatives.
12. *Betty:* In about two months, my family's new house is supposed ________________ (finish). I plan ________________ (spend) a few weeks decorating and arranging it before I start looking for a job.

Using What You've Learned

10 Share your knowledge about the universe by making as many comments as you can on the following subjects. Use the verbs *know, believe, consider, think, assume, feel, suppose, expect,* or *hope* in the passive voice. When you are finished with the six subjects, add at least six more of your own and continue the discussion.

Example: Jupiter

Jupiter is thought to have small amounts of water. It is known to be the largest planet in our solar system.

1. Earth	3. Mars	5. the Milky Way
2. the moon	4. Saturn	6. space stations

11 Working in small groups, take turns telling your classmates about your hopes and plans . . .

- five years from now.
- ten years from now.
- 20 years from now.
- 50 years from now.

Refer to the list of verbs followed by infinitives on page 383, and try to use as many of them as possible in your discussion.

PART 2 Passive and Perfect Gerunds

Setting the Context

Prereading Questions. How are robots portrayed in movies? Have you ever seen a real robot? What did it look like? What did it do?

Web Note

You can see a wide variety of amazing robots on the Web. Try these sites:
Carnegie Mellon Robotics Institute: *www.ri.cmu.edu/projects/project_153.html;*
Honda: *http://world.honda.com/robot/;*
Integrated Surgical Systems: *http://www.robodoc.com/;*
MIT *(Massachusetts Institute of Technology: www.ai.mit.edu/projects/humanoid-robotics-group/kismet/kismet.html;*
NASA: *http://learn.arc.nasa.gov/education/topics/robotics.shtml.*

Robots and Robotics

Robot is the Czech word for forced or compulsory labor. Despite having been coined by playwright Karel Capek in 1921, the term did not become popular until the appearance in 1950 of Isaac Asimov's classic book *I, Robot*. Already at that time, a few companies had begun producing robots for use in heavy industry. Then, as today, robots were used mostly for hazardous and boring jobs such as welding, spray painting, and handling dangerous materials.

In the last 20 years, the combining of robots with computers has led to advances in the science of robotics. New computer software has made robots more flexible and adaptable and has given them the senses of vision and touch. As a result, sales by U.S. robotics companies have increased greatly. At the same time, however, large numbers of blue-collar workers have become worried about being replaced by robots. Industry's not having taken worker concerns into account has already led to occasional unrest and even sabotage of the robots in some factories.

Discussing Ideas. Which jobs can robots do better than humans? Which jobs can probably never be done by robots?

A. Review of Active and Passive Forms of Simple Gerunds

Form	Examples	Notes
Active ***(not)* verb + *-ing***	In industry, robots are used mostly for **performing** boring, difficult tasks.	Gerunds commonly function as subjects, subject complements, objects, and objects of prepositions.
Passive ***(not) being* + past participle**	Some workers worry about **being replaced** by machines.	**Reminder:** In formal English, a possessive pronoun (e.g., *your*) is used to modify a gerund: *The teacher complained about* ***our*** *coming late to class.*

Note: See Chapter 9 for practice with the various functions of gerunds in a sentence.

B. Perfect Forms of Gerunds

Form	Examples	Notes
Active ***(not) having*** **+ past participle**	After **having installed** robots, the company retrained its workers.	In many cases, the simple gerund and the perfect gerund may be used. Thus, in the example, *installing* is also correct. The perfect form may be selected when the speaker wants to emphasize the sequence of events in the sentence. The action in the gerund phrase occurred earlier than the action of the main verb.
Passive ***(not) having been*** **+ past participle**	After **having been coined** in 1921, the term *robot* was not widely used until the 1950s.	*Being coined* is also possible. The perfect passive form is rarely used.

1 Reread "Robots and Robotics." Underline all the *-ing* forms. Analyze which ones are verbs, which ones are adjectives (participles), and which ones are gerunds. Label the gerunds as simple or perfect, active or passive.

2 In the following sentences, change the form of the gerund from simple to perfect. Your teacher may direct you to do this exercise orally.

Example: After working on the computer for nine hours, I had a backache.
After having worked on the computer for nine hours, I had a backache.

1. The teacher was upset about the student's lying to her.
2. I appreciate your helping me with my math homework.
3. I regret not going to college when I had the chance.
4. Ana was pleased about being chosen for the scholarship.
5. My husband was angry at me for not giving him an important message.
6. I don't remember hearing that man's name before.
7. I can't forgive your taking my car without permission.
8. John's failing the entrance exam makes him ineligible to attend the college.
9. She felt hurt about not being invited to the party.
10. Not finishing college did not stop Arthur from becoming a millionaire.

3 Complete the following sentences using the active or passive gerund forms of the words in parentheses. Note the cases where the simple or the perfect form could be used.

Robots in Science Fiction

Robots have been central characters in many science fiction stories. In some early stories, after *having been viewed (being viewed)* (view) initially as loyal servants,

The robots C3PO and R2D2 from the movie *Star Wars*

the robots turn out to be evil and threatening. The robots are portrayed as ______ (1) (have) the potential to isolate us, restrict our privacy, and even destroy us. In one eerie story by Ray Bradbury, the robots, after ______ (2) (destroy) humankind, continue ______ (3) (function) as before, ______ (4) (dust) the furniture and ______ (5) (water) the lawns of their former "masters."

In contrast, other stories present robots in a positive light. The original *I, Robot,* published in 1938 by Eando Binder, is about a gentle and all-too-trusting robot who becomes tired of ______ (6) (use) by misguided humans and decides to "commit suicide" by ______ (7) (disconnect) his own battery. Isaac Asimov provides another example. In his 1950 version of *I, Robot,* there is a nursemaid robot who "simply can't help ______ (8) (be) loving and helpful and kind."

In recent years robots—some evil, some good—have become popular characters in many television shows and movies. For example, millions of people all over the world remember ______ (9) (see) *Star Wars* with its lovable robots R2D2 and C3PO, who couldn't seem to avoid ______ (10) (get) into trouble and ______ (11) (need) to be rescued by their human companions.

4 The following sentences concern the entry of Japan into the robotics industry. Complete the sentences using the simple active or passive gerund forms of the words in parentheses. Afterwards, read the passage again. Whenever possible, change the gerunds to the perfect form.

1. After *leading / having led* (lead) the world in the development of robot technology for many years, the United States is worried about ______ (surpass) by Japan.

Web Note

Learn more about Japanese robotics. Try these Websites: Honda: *http://world.honda.com/robot/;* Koganei System: *www.koganei.co.jp/;* The University of Tsukuba: *www. roboken.esys.tsukuba.ac.jp/;* Toray Engineering: *www.toray-eng.com/.;* *And don't forget to check* Tomoe Co., *creators of sushi-making robots!: www.sushi-master.com/.*

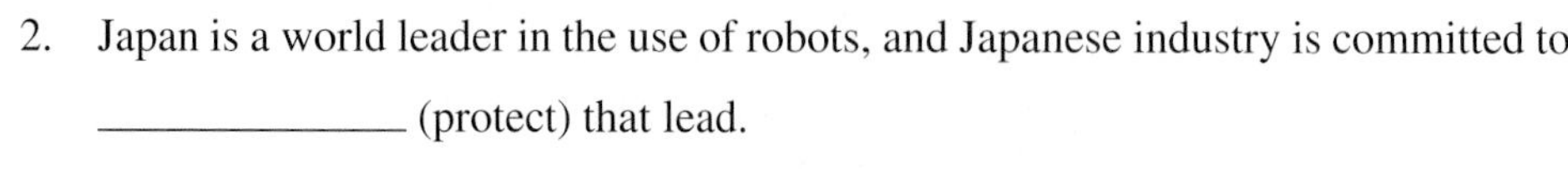

2. Japan is a world leader in the use of robots, and Japanese industry is committed to ____________ (protect) that lead.
3. As a result of ____________ (use) robots in the semiconductor industry, Japanese companies have been able to acquire a significant share of the world semiconductor market.
4. Although Japanese industry is committed to ____________ (use) robots, Japanese workers are not overly concerned about ____________ (replace) by machines. This is because human and robot workers typically perform different tasks. For example, a French reporter recently told of ____________ (visit) a Japanese engine factory that operated with a small crew of human workers during the day and continued ____________ (produce) engines at night by ____________ (use) robots. In an automated equipment factory, parts are assembled into finished products during the day after ____________ (make) by robots during the night.

5. Currently, the Japanese are working on ____________ (develop) a new generation of robots that will be able to handle objects with great precision. ____________ (accomplish) this goal will lead to the robots' ____________ (use) in many new industries.

5 Working in pairs, interview one another about the following topics. Write your partner's answers in complete sentences.

Example: something you enjoy doing early in the morning

A. Tell me something you enjoy doing early in the morning.

B. Early in the morning, I enjoy sleeping!

Ask about something your partner . . .

1. hates doing alone
2. likes having done for him or her
3. regrets not doing (not having done) when he or she had the chance
4. enjoys doing on a rainy day
5. resents being asked to do
6. feels guilty about not doing more often

C. More Verbs Followed by Gerund Objects

List of Verbs			Examples
anticipate	detest	recall	She **anticipates getting** a good raise this year.
complete	escape	resent	We shouldn't **delay buying** the new equipment.
defer	excuse	resist	Do you **recall meeting** him?
delay	postpone	risk	She **resented having** to work every weekend.
deny	prevent	tolerate	

6 Complete the following sentences with active or passive gerund phrases. Add subjects and negatives when indicated.

Example: Some workers risk losing (lose) their jobs if the company installs robots.

1. Management anticipates ____________ (profits/go up) 25 percent next year if robots are installed in the factory.
2. The workers resented ____________ (not consult) about the use of robots in the assembly plant.
3. Management risks ____________ (anger) the labor unions by using robots.
4. The angry workers did not deny ____________ (attempt) to damage the robots.
5. Management deferred ____________ (make) a decision about the installation of robots in the assembly plant.
6. The workers say they will not tolerate ____________ (replace) by machines.
7. We have postponed ____________ (explain) to the workers about the new robots.

7 Today, most robots are used in heavy industries. However, before long, robots will be doing common household chores for their owners. In the following exercise, imagine that a woman is giving instructions to the family robot concerning a dinner party she is preparing to give. Complete each sentence with a gerund or gerund phrase. Add subjects and negatives where possible and try to use the perfect and passive gerund forms.

Example: The guests will be arriving in less than an hour and this place is a mess! You mustn't delay . . . *cleaning up the living room!*

1. This is the second time this year you have been late preparing for a party. I won't tolerate . . . .
2. Over 100 guests phoned to say they were coming, but I'm sure I didn't invite that many. In fact, I can only recall . . . .
3. The pot roast won't be ready for at least three hours. We may have to postpone . . . .
4. Oh my! Something in the oven is burning. You must try to prevent . . . . We mustn't risk . . . .
5. The pot roast is burned to a crisp! I hope my guests will forgive . . . .
6. I ordered you to prepare for this party last week. Don't deny . . . . I resent . . . .

8 **Review.** Complete the following passage by using the gerund or infinitive forms of the verbs in parentheses. Use either the active or the passive voice.

Humans Versus Machines

As the Industrial Revolution began *to unfold (unfolding)* (unfold) in the 19th century, English workmen attempted ______ (1) (destroy) new textile machines because the machines seemed ______ (2) (take away) the workers' jobs. Two centuries later, workers around the world have been trying ______ (3) (use) similar tactics against the new robots that have begun ______ (4) (appear) in more and more industrial plants. Anxious ______ (5) (protect) their jobs, workers are willing ______ (6) (do) whatever is necessary, even if it means ______ (7) (damage) or ______ (8) (destroy) expensive machines.

Gerrit Nijland, a professor of industrial robotics at Berenschot Management Training Center in the Netherlands, studies the acceptance of automatons in his country, where around 70 firms currently use robots. He finds that the most common form of sabotage is ______ (9) (slow down) the machines: Workers feed parts to the machines in the wrong order ______ (10) (confuse) the machines, or they repair the machines improperly ______ (11) (cause) them ______ (12) (break down) quickly. Workers have even mixed sand with the engine oil ___13___ (destroy) the gears and bearings of these robots. Whatever the form of sabotage, Nijland says that workers want management ___14___ (disappoint) with robot performance. This would, in theory, make the workers' jobs more secure. In one metal-construction plant, workers' resistance to robots forced production ___15___ (reduce) for more than six months. Other companies are certain ___16___ (face) with similar troubles, says Nijland, unless management decides ___17___ (hold) and encourages workers ___18___ (attend) joint management/worker discussions about the effect robots will have on jobs.

Using What You've Learned

9 The robots have taken over! Imagine a factory in which robots are the bosses and humans are the workers. The humans are lazy and inefficient. They make many mistakes, some of them dangerous. The robot bosses are angry and frustrated. Write a story or dialogue about this situation that includes at least six verb + gerund combinations. Here are a few possibilities, but try to create your own as well.

deny / steal	delay / finish
admit / break	recall / tell
tolerate / replace	risk / injure
resent / tell lies	recommend / fire
excuse / not tell	spent time / train

10 Divide the class into two teams to play a game that will help you review gerunds and infinitives as objects of verbs. The members of each team should form a line. Flip a coin to decide which team will go first.

Your teacher or a classmate will pick a verb from the list on page 391. Your team has one minute to work together to make a sentence using that verb and an infinitive or gerund. The first student in line should then say the sentence out loud. After speaking, this person should go to the end of the line. Then it will be the other team's turn.

Example: *Teacher:* forbid
Student: *The teacher forbids us to talk during exams.*

Your team will get one point for each correct sentence. If the speaker makes a mistake, the class will work together to fix it.

Focus on Testing

Use of Gerunds and Infinitives

Infinitives and gerunds are frequently tested on standardized English proficiency exams. Review these commonly tested structures and check your understanding by completing the sample items that follow.

Remember that . . .

- Certain verbs are followed by infinitives and certain verbs are followed by gerunds.
- Only gerunds may follow prepositions.
- In formal English, a possessive (not object) form is used before a gerund.

Part 1. Circle the best completion for the following.

Example: Many people can expect __________ in space within 100 years.

a. live
b. living
(c.) to be living
d. to lived

1. Before __________ out with friends, I cleaned up my room.
   a. went
   b. to go
   c. going
   d. to have gone
2. I recommend __________ an umbrella, as it's sure to rain.
   a. you to take
   b. you taking
   c. taking
   d. to take
3. I look forward __________ my grandparents during winter vacation.
   a. to visiting
   b. to visit
   c. your visiting
   d. visit
4. This suit needs __________ before the dinner party next week.
   a. clean
   b. cleaned
   c. to be cleaned
   d. to have cleaned

Part 2. Each sentence has one error. Circle the letter below the word(s) containing the error.

Example: An alien spacecraft <u>appears</u> (A) <u>to has</u> (Ⓑ) crash-landed <u>on the street</u> (C) <u>in front of</u> (D) your house.

1. <u>Having grown</u> (A) <u>up</u> (B) in a large house with many sisters and brothers, Emily is unaccustomed <u>to</u> (C) <u>live</u> (D) by herself.
2. <u>As</u> (A) roadways <u>leading</u> (B) out of the city become more and more congested, the idea <u>of building</u> (C) a new freeway will need <u>being</u> (D) considered seriously.

3. Within 50 years, lightweight cars made (A) of plastic instead of (B) steel will enable drivers traveling (C) from Los Angeles to New York on (D) one tank of gas.

4. Fred's (A) having lied (B) on his job application made (C) him ineligible to working (D) at the company.

PART 3

Review

1 **Review.** In the following exercise, choose the correct verb form from the two that are given in parentheses.

Future Family

It is a spring afternoon in the year 2030; the Jones family has gathered to celebrate Junior's 13th birthday. There's Dad and his third wife, Mom and her second husband, Junior's two stepbrothers from his mother's husband's previous marriages, 100-year-old Great-Grandpa, assorted aunts, uncles, and stepcousins.

As Junior blows out the candles on his cake, he makes a wish—that he didn't have so many relatives.

Culture Note

Divorce is still very common in the United States, but the rate of divorce is falling somewhat. For example, the 1998 statistics of 4.2 divorces per thousand was the lowest in more than 20 years. Divorces peaked in 1979 at 5.3 per thousand. Today, there are almost 20 million divorced people in the United States, almost 10 percent of the adult population.

Web Note

You can learn more about possibilities for the future by visiting the Website of the World Future Society, *a nonprofit organization researching new technologies, emerging issues, and social change: www.wfs.org.*

As the preceding passage demonstrates, the 21st century family will certainly be more ((complicated)/complicating) than today's family as a result of people's (live/living)[1] longer and (marry/marrying)[2] more than once. In fact, we can expect the "divorce-extended" family (being/to be)[3] the normal family unit of the future. Like Junior, most children will have several sets of stepparents and grandparents, aunts, uncles, and cousins, as well as former spouses and in-laws. As a result of (belong/belonging)[4] to several different family groups at the same time, children are likely (to be/being)[5] more independent. Children as young as 12 may be allowed (to choose/choosing)[6] the parent they will live with after a divorce.

Although extended families will be larger in the future, "natural families" will be smaller in many developed countries as couples decide (to have/having)[7] fewer and fewer children. With (fallen/falling)[8] birthrates, the government may have to find ways to (get/let)[9] people (to have/have)[10] more children. Some futurologists foresee governments' (offer/offering)[11] money to couples (to have/having)[12] more children.

Sociologists predict that the reorganization of the family unit will be largely beneficial. For one thing, the complexity of the divorce-extended family will require that family members (be/are)[13] more communal and cooperative. Regardless of the changes that lie ahead, the human need for love makes it essential that, in one form or another, the family (survive/survives)[14].

2 Review. In the following passage, choose the correct word from the two that are given in parentheses. Where there is an X, the word in parentheses may not be needed.

Housing in the Future

((The)/A) houses of (the/X)[1] future will give families far more (the/X)[2] comfort and convenience (than/as)[3] ever before. (Although/In spite of)[4] (the/a)[5] house in the year 2050 (may/can)[6] resemble many of today's homes in outward appearance, technology will cause some (surprised/surprising)[7] differences on the inside, (where/which)[8] a computer may turn lights on and off, regulate the temperature, (but/and)[9] even call the police (whether/if)[10] it detects strange movements, smoke, (and/or)[11] fire. In (the/X)[12] kitchen, the computer will be able to defrost and cook a dinner so (that/which)[13] it is hot (when/while)[14] people come home from (work/to work)[15]. (The/One)[16] decade from now, (the/X)[17] robots (may/had better)[18] be able to take care (of/from)[19] dusting, vacuuming, and other (cleaned/cleaning)[20] chores.

(The/X)[21] smaller families and (the/X)[22] growth of single-person households mean that homes will be smaller. (Over/While)[23] the next 20 years, (a/one)[24] single-family home will decline (from/to)[25] an average size of 1,500 square feet (from/to)[26] perhaps 1,000 square feet. (In addition/However)[27], (with/inside)[28] the home, more creative uses of windows, glass doors, skylights, and two-story ceilings will make less space (feel/to feel)[29] like more. The living room and dining room (should/may)[30] be replaced (by/from)[31] (a/the)[32] large, multiuse living area. Houses will have more built-in furniture (to/for)[33] conserve space. (As a result/For example)[34], tabletops will slide (in/into)[35] walls (when/until)[36] not in use, and the type of bed (that/X)[37] folds into a wall or closet will be commonplace. All in all, families will have more flexibility in changing floor plans through (the/X)[38] use of movable walls, (and/X)[39] modular furniture, and built-in features.

3 **Review.** What do you imagine a business trip will be like in the 21st century? To get an idea, read the following list of sentences. Then recombine the sentences into a well-written paragraph. Use compound and complex sentences, pronouns, and transitions to give your paragraph coherence. Pay close attention to punctuation.

An executive leaves home in a single-seat car.
The car gets 100 miles per gallon.
The executive steers the car into an automated traffic lane.
The driver reads the news on a dashboard video monitor.
Electronic sensors guide the vehicle to a "railport."
At the railport, the executive boards a train.
The executive straps himself or herself into a soft, pneumatic seat.

The train levitates above the ground.
The train travels at 300 miles an hour.
The train reaches the airport within minutes.
The executive boards a giant aircraft.
One thousand other passengers board the aircraft.
The aircraft is made of plastic.
The overseas flight is smooth.
The overseas flight is at supersonic speed.
The plane is entirely controlled by computers.
The trip is from the executive's front door in San Francisco, California, to Paris, France.
The trip has taken just three hours.

4 Error Analysis. Each of the following sentences contains one or more errors. The errors may be in sentence structure, verb form, pronoun reference, agreement, parallelism, transition choice, word order, or punctuation. Find the errors and correct them.

1. Education in the next 50 years, it will be revolutionized by the use of computers.
2. Computers will bring knowledge to people wherever they are—at home, on the job, by a hospital bed, in the car, as well as a traditional classroom.
3. Education will be individualized on the basis of tests that they will reveal how each person can learn most easily.
4. Students whom learn best through hearing information would receive much of his education orally.
5. If a learner would have a visual orientation, he would spend more time reading and writing on computer screens.
6. By 2020, less people will study engineering and other applied skills due to computers will do most of the works in these fields.
7. In spite of to use personal computers to read and write, books will not completely disappear for many years.
8. Education expert David Brostrom reports that by 2033, more than 60 percent of American adults would attend college, compared with 30 percent today.

9. The revolution in genetics promises transforming the treatment of disease.
10. By the years 2010, researchers will not only have a complete map of all human genes, but also they will be able to make changes in some of these genes.
11. They will know how to regulating normal growth of cells.
12. Medical advances will enable people for to live longer, healthier lives.
13. Scientists will discover treatments for major diseases and allowing people live 100 years or more.
14. New techniques with lasers and advances in radiation will make many of today's medical operations to become obsolete.
15. Tremendous advances will be made in the treatment of disease; though, the cost of medical care will probably increase.

5 **Review.** Fill in each blank with the active or passive form of the verbs in parentheses. In some cases, more than one answer may be possible.

The "Third Wave"

Futurist Alvin Toffler views history as a succession of rolling, overlapping waves of change. The "first wave," as he *calls* (call) it, ________ (1) (begin) around 8000 B.C. and ________ (2) (last) until the Industrial Revolution. At the beginning of the first wave, most humans ________ (3) (live) in small, often migratory groups and ________ (4) (feed) themselves by fishing or hunting. Then agriculture ________ (5) (invent), and it was no longer necessary for people to wander in search of food. Instead, they could settle in one place. This first wave of change ________ (6) (not end/yet) when the Industrial Revolution ________ (7) (break out) at the end of the 17th century. This ________ (8) (be) the beginning of the second wave. Industrialization ________ (9) (begin) moving across Europe and competing with the agricultural societies that ________ (10) (be) predominant up to that point. Thus, two separate and distinct processes of change ________ (11) (roll) across the earth simultaneously.

Today very few first-wave societies ________ (12) (remain). Only a few primitive tribes in Africa or New Guinea, for example, ________ (13) (not/industrialize). Meanwhile, the second wave ________ (14) (spread/still). Many countries, which before now _____15_____ (be) basically agricultural, _____16_____ (devote) their resources and manpower to the construction of automobile plants, textile factories, railroads, and so forth. The momentum of industrialization _____17_____ (feel/still) all over the world.

Since the end of World War II, however, a new force _____18_____ (move) over the earth, and it _____19_____ (transform) everything it _____20_____ (touch). This force _____21_____ (call) the third wave. It _____22_____ (initiate) in the 1950s by the introduction of the computer, commercial jet travel, the birth-control pill, and many other high-impact innovations. Since then, it _____23_____ (reach) Britain, Japan, the Soviet Union, the United States, and most of the other industrialized nations. Today all the high-technology nations _____24_____ (shake) by the collision between the third wave and what Toffler calls "the obsolete, encrusted economies and institutions of the second."

According to Toffler, third-wave civilizations _____25_____ (develop) a variety of energy sources, all of them renewable. Within a few years, for example, a fusion reactor _____26_____ (test/successfully). Third-wave civilization _____27_____ (base) on a far more diversified technological foundation springing from biology, genetics, electronics, outer space, and undersea operations. Within ten years, these types of industries _____28_____ (surpass/already) steel, autos, and chemicals, the current world leaders. Furthermore, much third-wave technology _____29_____ (design) to use less, not more, energy. As it _____30_____ (be) in first-wave societies, the home _____31_____ (be) the central unit of the society of tomorrow. Once again, large numbers of people _____32_____ (live and work) in their homes. In this sense, our civilization _____33_____ (come) full circle from where it began.*

---

*Adapted from Alvin Toffler, *The Third Wave* (New York: Bantam, 1981), pp. 14–15.

Using What You've Learned

6 Have you ever written a poem in your native language? Have you ever written poetry in English? You may be surprised to discover that writing poetry in a second language can be an enjoyable and liberating experience. Since poetry is based on images and not grammar, it offers writers an unparalleled opportunity to be creative. Because poetry is an art form, poets don't have to follow every grammatical rule. They only need to be sure that their messages can be understood.

As a final activity, write an eight- to ten-line poem about your vision of the future. You can do this individually, in small groups, or as a class. You may also like to write a poem about a notable family member, classmate, or place. Use the following instructions to guide you, or feel free to change them.

Line 1: Give a four- to five-word sentence with a subject and a verb.
Line 2: Add three modifiers to describe a noun in Line 1.
Line 3: Compare the noun to something. Use the word *like.*
Line 4: Add a participial phrase that gives motion to the noun(s) in Line 3.
Line 5: Add two or three adverbs or adjectives to describe the motion in Line 4.
Line 6: Use a metaphor to make this action either very great or very small.
Line 7: Give nouns and adjectives that refer to your idea in Line 1.
Lines 8 (9, 10): Give your opinion or final comment on the idea from Line 1.

Here is a sample poem.

Space
Will there be a time when there won't be space anymore—
Open space, free space, space to move around?
Space is like a huge ocean wave.
Moving outward, upward, roaring toward the edge,
Completely free,
More freedom than cars on a freeway or apartments in a city.
So little space that everything seems airtight, can't breathe, no light,
Too many things crowded together,
Not enough space for clear skies, sunlight, or me.

Video Activities: Concept Cars

Before You Watch. Answer these questions in small groups.

1. What does the word *concept* mean?
   a. beginning b. idea c. imagination
2. Describe the kind of car that you would like to own. You can describe one that exists, or use your imagination.

Watch. Answer these questions in small groups.

1. Which of these statements is true?
   a. All concept cars become production cars.
   b. Car manufacturers use concept cars to "try out" new ideas.
   c. Concept cars are too expensive to build.
2. Which of these concept cars did not become production cars?
   a. the Avalanche
   b. the Lacrosse
   c. the PT Cruiser
   d. the Prowler
3. Write the name of the concept car next to the correct description.
   __________ a. video monitors and voice-activated lights and turn signals
   __________ b. a popular design
   __________ c. a combination of a truck and an SUV

Watch Again. Circle the correct answers.

1. Which of these car companies are mentioned in the video segment?
   a. Ford
   b. Mercedes
   c. Chrysler-Daimler
   d. Chevrolet (Chevy)
   e. Toyota
   f. Buick
2. It's a real *eye-popper* means it looks __________.
   a. great b. dangerous c. terrible
3. *I'm a Ford man* means __________.
   a. he works for Ford b. he buys Ford cars c. his name is Ford
4. "The club *just got its motor running* last December" means that it just __________.
   a. bought a car b. fixed an engine c. started

After You Watch. Complete the sentences with the correct form of the verb in parentheses.

Example: Here are a few changes that we can expect <u>to have taken place</u> (take place) by the year 2030.

1. By 2050, experts expect that many changes in transportation __________ (take place).
2. New breakthroughs in engine design will enable manufacturers __________ (increase) fuel efficiency.
3. In the United States, most people expect __________ (own) several cars in their lifetimes.
4. The use of computers will make it possible for __________ (cars / be) much safer.

Focus on Testing

Review of Problem Areas from Chapters 9 to 12

A variety of problem areas are included in this test. Check your understanding by completing the sample items that follow.

Part 1. Circle the best completion for the following.

Example: He urged us ______________ our things.

a. that we take
b. take
(c.) to take
d. took

1. John is known for ______________ about his work.
   a. complaining never
   b. never complaining
   c. never to complain
   d. never to be complaining

2. Since the 1930s, industry and automobiles ______________ large amounts of pollution into the air.
   a. had been releasing
   b. had been released
   c. are releasing
   d. have been releasing

3. The universe is known ______________.
   a. to have expand
   b. to be expanding
   c. expanding
   d. having expanded

4. When ______________, he was cared for by both family and friends.
   a. sick
   b. he is sick
   c. to be sick
   d. he sick

5. Much of the world's silver has been used ______________ coins.
   a. to making
   b. made
   c. make
   d. to make

6. She wishes ______________ there now.
   a. that she was
   b. she was
   c. she were
   d. that she is

7. We couldn't afford ______________ out for dinner.
   a. go
   b. going
   c. to go
   d. gone

8. If the majority of eligible voters had actually voted, he ______________ the election.
   a. might win
   b. could have won
   c. could had won
   d. might had won

Part 2. Each sentence has one error. Circle the letter below the word(s) containing the error.

Example: He might have listened (A) to our complaints if (B) we have been more (Ⓒ) organized when we presented (D) our case.

1. Much (A) research that (B) showing the (C) value of undernutrition has been conducted (D) in recent years.
2. If humans did not learn (A) how to work (B) with metal, it would (C) never have been possible to create the assorted (D) weaponry we have today.
3. Benin, which (A) a powerful country in tropical Africa, was headed (B) by an *Oba* or king, who was all-powerful yet (C) tolerant enough to grant (D) a great deal of freedom.
4. The look of contempt (A) on the pianist's (B) face made the audience feeling (C) extremely uncomfortable (D).
5. Were they place (A) another order shortly (B), we would have great difficulties in meeting (C) the production (D) deadline.
6. A reporter's job consists (A) of gathering (B) information and to write (C) news (D) stories.
7. Chris had gone (A) to check on (B) the status of the final reports (C) before he saw Alex submitted (D) the project.
8. Mary would liking (A) to hear (B) from you if you have (C) the (D) time to write her.

Appendices

Appendix 1

Irregular Verbs

Simple Form	Past	Past Participle
arise	arose	arisen
awake	awoke/ awaked	awaked/ awoken
be	was/were	been
bear	bore	borne/born
beat	beat	beat
become	became	become
begin	began	begun
bend	bent	bent
bet	bet	bet
bite	bit	bitten
bleed	bled	bled
blow	blew	blown
break	broke	broken
breed	bred	bred
bring	brought	brought
broadcast	broadcast	broadcast
build	built	built
burst	burst	burst
buy	bought	bought
cast	cast	cast
catch	caught	caught
choose	chose	chosen
cling	clung	clung
come	came	come
cost	cost	cost
creep	crept	crept
cut	cut	cut
deal	dealt	dealt
dig	dug	dug
do	did	done
draw	drew	drawn
drink	drank	drunk
drive	drove	driven
eat	ate	eaten
fall	fell	fallen
feed	fed	fed
feel	felt	felt
fight	fought	fought
find	found	found
flee	fled	fled
fly	flew	flown
forbid	forbade	forbidden
forget	forgot	forgotten
forsake	forsook	forsaken
freeze	froze	frozen
get	got	got/gotten
give	gave	given
go	went	gone
grind	ground	ground
grow	grew	grown
hang	hung/hanged	hung/hanged
have	had	had
hear	heard	heard
hide	hid	hidden
hit	hit	hit
hold	held	held
hurt	hurt	hurt
keep	kept	kept
know	knew	known
lay	laid	laid
lead	led	led
leap	leapt	leapt
leave	left	left
lend	lent	lent
let	let	let
lie	lay	lain
light	lit/lighted	lit/lighted
lose	lost	lost
make	made	made
mean	meant	meant
meet	met	met
overcome	overcame	overcome
pay	paid	paid
prove	proved	proved/proven*
put	put	put
quit	quit	quit
read	read	read
ride	rode	ridden
ring	rang	rung
rise	rose	risen
run	ran	run
say	said	said
see	saw	seen

Simple Form	Past	Past Participle	Simple Form	Past	Past Participle
seek	sought	sought	sting	stung	stung
sell	sold	sold	strike	struck	struck/stricken*
send	sent	sent	strive	strove	striven
set	set	set	swear	swore	sworn
shake	shook	shaken	sweep	swept	swept
shoot	shot	shot	swim	swam	swum
show	showed	showed/shown*	swing	swung	swung
shut	shut	shut	take	took	taken
sing	sang	sung	teach	taught	taught
sink	sank	sunk	tear	tore	torn
sit	sat	sat	tell	told	told
sleep	slept	slept	think	thought	thought
slide	slid	slid	throw	threw	thrown
slit	slit	slit	thrust	thrust	thrust
speak	spoke	spoken	understand	understood	understood
spend	spent	spent	upset	upset	upset
spin	spun	spun	wake	woke/waked	woken/waked
split	split	split	wear	wore	worn
spread	spread	spread	weave	wove	woven
spring	sprang	sprung	wind	wound	wound
stand	stood	stood	withdraw	withdrew	withdrawn
steal	stole	stolen	write	wrote	written
stick	stuck	stuck			

*These participles are most often used with the passive voice.

Appendix 2

Spelling Rules and Irregular Noun Plurals

Spelling Rules for -s, -ed, -er, -est, *and* -ing *Endings*

This chart summarizes the basic spelling rules for endings with verbs, nouns, adjectives, and adverbs.

Rule	Word	-S	-Ed	-Er	-Est	-Ing
For most words, simply add *-s, -ed, -er, -est,* or *-ing* without making any other changes.	clean	cleans	cleaned	cleaner	cleanest	cleaning
	cool	cools	cooled	cooler	coolest	cooling

Spelling changes occur with the following.

Rule	Word	-S	-Ed	-Er	-Est	-Ing
For words ending in a consonant +*y*, change the *y* to *i* before adding *-s, -ed, -er,* or *-est.*	carry	carries	carried	carrier		
	happy			happier	happiest	
	lonely			lonelier	loneliest	
	study	studies	studied			
	worry	worries	worried	worrier		
Do *not* change or drop the *y* before adding *-ing.*						carrying
						studying
						worrying
For most words ending in *e*, drop the *e* before adding *-ed, -er, -est,* or *-ing.*	dance		danced	dancer		dancing
	late			later	latest	
	nice			nicer	nicest	
	save		saved	saver		saving
	write			writer		writing
Exceptions:	agree					agreeing
	canoe					canoeing
For many words ending in one vowel and one consonant, double the final consonant before adding *-ed, -er, -est,* or *-ing.* These include one syllable words and words with stress on the final syllable.	begin			beginner		beginning
	hot			hotter	hottest	
	mad			madder	maddest	
	plan		planned	planner		planning
	occur		occurred			occurring
	refer		referred			referring
	run			runner		running
	shop		shopped	shopper		shopping
	win			winner		winning

Rule	Word	-S	-Ed	-Er	-Est	-Ing
In words ending in one vowel and one consonant, do *not* double the final consonant if the last syllable is not stressed.	enter happen open travel visit		entered happened opened traveled visited	 opener traveler		entering happening opening traveling visiting
Exceptions: including words ending in *w*, *x*, or *y*	bus fix play sew	buses	bused fixed played sewed	 fixer player sewer		busing fixing playing sewing
For most words ending in *f* or *lf*, change the *f* to *v* and add *-es*.	half loaf shelf	halves loaves shelves	halved shelved	 shelver		halving shelving
Exceptions:	belief chief proof roof safe	beliefs chiefs proofs roofs safes				
For words ending in *ch*, *sh*, *s*, *x*, *z*, and sometimes *o*, add *-es*.	church wash class fix quiz tomato zero	churches washes classes fixes quizzes tomatoes zeroes				
Exceptions:	dynamo ghetto monarch piano portfolio radio studio	dynamos ghettos monarchs pianos portfolios radios studios				

Irregular Noun Plurals

person	people	foot	feet	deer	deer	ox	oxen
child	children	tooth	teeth	fish	fish	series	series
man	men	goose	geese	sheep	sheep	species	species
woman	women	mouse	mice				

Irregular Noun Plurals with Foreign Origins

alumnus	alumni	analysis	analyses	basis	bases	crisis	crises
criterion	criteria	curriculum	curricula	hypothesis	hypotheses	oasis	oases
memorandum	memoranda	synthesis	syntheses	thesis	theses	radius	radii
phenomenon	phenomena	nucleus	nuclei	stimulus	stimuli		
syllabus	syllabi or syllabuses						
index	indices or indexes						

Appendix 3

The with Proper Nouns

With *the*		**Without *the***	
The is used when the class of noun (continent, country, etc.) comes before the name: *the* + class + *of* + name. *The* is used with most names of regions. *Exceptions:*	the continent of Asia the United States of America the U.S.A. the West the Midwest the equator New England southern (northern, etc.)	*The* is not used with names of planets, continents, countries, states, provinces, cities, and streets. *Exceptions:*	Mars Africa Antarctica Russia Ohio Quebec Austin State Street (the) earth the world the Netherlands
The is used with plural islands, lakes, and mountains. *The* is used with oceans, seas, rivers, canals, deserts, jungles, forests, and bridges.*	the Hawaiian Islands the Great Lakes the Alps the Pacific Ocean the Persian Gulf the Mississippi River the Suez Canal the Sahara Desert the Black Forest the Golden Gate Bridge	*The* is not used with singular islands, lakes, and mountains. *Exceptions:*	Oahu Fiji Lake Superior Mt. Whitney the Isle of Wight the Matterhorn (and other mountains with German names that are used in English)
The is generally used when the word *college, university,* or *school* comes before the name: *the* + ... + *of* + name.	the University of California the Rhode Island School of Design	*The* is not used when the name of a college or university comes before the word *college* or *university.* *Exception:*	Boston University Amherst College the Sorbonne
The is used with adjectives of nationality and other adjectives that function as nouns.	the Germans the Japanese the rich the poor the strong	*The* is not used with names of languages. *Note: The* is used with the word *language: the German language.*	German Japanese
The is used in dates when the number comes before the month.	the twenty-eighth of March	*The* is not used in dates when the month begins the phrase.	March 28
The is used with decades, centuries, and eras.	the 1990s the 1800s the Dark Ages	*The* is not used with specific years.	1951 1890
The is used with names of museums and libraries.	the Museum of Modern Art the Chicago Public Library		

*The class name is often omitted with well-known oceans, deserts, and rivers: *the Atlantic, the Nile.*

Appendix 4

Verbs Not Normally Used in the Continuous Tenses

The following verbs are seldom used in the continuous tenses. In some cases, the continuous form is used in certain idiomatic expressions or in descriptions of the definite action.

Thoughts or Feelings		Examples	Notes
appear appreciate be believe consider* desire dislike doubt feel* hate know like love	mean* mind miss need prefer realize recognize remember seem think* understand want*	We **need** to discuss the situation. We **think** that this is a serious issue. We **consider** it to be a problem. We **want** to make several improvements. *Compare:* Bob **is thinking** about his problems. He **has been considering** a variety of solutions. He **has been meaning** to talk to you about it.	These verbs are rarely used in a continuous tense; the verbs with an asterisk (*), however, sometimes appear in a continuous tense (especially the present perfect continuous). The verbs *think* and *consider* occasionally appear in the present continuous tense, also.

Perceptions		Examples	Notes
feel* hear* look see	smell sound taste	The ocean **looks** cold today. The wind **feels** very cold and damp. *Compare:* I **am looking** at the ocean now. I **am feeling** a little seasick.	These verbs sometimes appear in a continuous tense in the description of a specific action or in certain idioms.

Possession		Examples	Notes
belong to cost have*	own possess	We **own** a house. It **belongs** to my sister and me. The house **has** four bedrooms. *Compare:* We**'ve been having** fun lately. We**'re having** a party next weekend.	These verbs almost never appear in continuous tenses, except for the verb *have*. In idiomatic use, *be having* has several meanings, including "be experiencing" or "be eating, drinking."

Appendix 5

Modal Auxiliaries and Related Structures

Modal Auxiliaries

Auxiliary	Function and Time Frame	Examples
can	present ability	I **can swim** very well.
	present impossibility	I **cannot finish** this exercise.
	informal present request	**Can** you **help** me?
could	past ability	I **could speak** French when I was younger.
could have	past ability (unfulfilled)	With some help, I **could have finished** earlier.
may	present request or permission	**May** I **help** you?
	present possibility	He **may be sleeping** now.
may have	past possibility	He **may have gone** out somewhere.
might	present possibility	I **might go** to the movies or I **might stay** home.
	present advice or suggestion	You **might see** a doctor if your cold doesn't improve.
might have	past possibility	She **might have gone** to the library.
must	present need	Everyone **must pay** his taxes.
	present probability	He's not eating. He **must not be** hungry.
must not	present prohibition	Students **must not cheat** on tests.
must have	past probability	You **must have been** tired after the game.
ought to	present advice	You **ought to work** faster.
	present expectation	The check **ought to come** tomorrow.
ought to have	past advice (not taken)	We **ought to have finished** this long ago.
	past expectation	She **ought to have gotten** the check yesterday.
should	present advice	You **should be** very careful if you go there.
	present expectation	The mail **should arrive** soon.
should have	past advice (not taken)	We **should have started** this weeks ago.
	past expectation	He **should have arrived** an hour ago.
will	present requests	**Will** you please **help** us?
	future intentions	He**'ll help** us if he can.
would	present request	**Would** you please **help**?
		Would you **mind helping** me?
	past habits	As a child, I **would play** outside everyday after school

Related Structures

Related Structures	Function and Time Frame	Examples
be able to	present ability	We **aren't able to** leave now.
	past ability	We **weren't able to** see the play.
had better	present advice	You **had better not** eat that.
have got to	present need	She **has got to** leave now.
have to	present need	She **has to** leave now.
not have to	present lack of need	It's early. We **don't have to** leave yet.
had to	past need	I **had to** work last Saturday.
didn't have to	past lack of need	I **didn't have** to work last Sunday.
used to	past habits	We **used to** relax on the weekend, but now we work.

Appendix 6

Summary of Gerunds and Infinitives

Verbs Often Followed by Gerunds

admit	complete	discuss	forgive	postpone	resist
anticipate	consider	dread	imagine	practice	risk
appreciate	defer	enjoy	involve	prevent	spend time
avoid	delay	escape	mention	recall	suggest
be worth	deny	excuse	mind	recommend	tolerate
can't help	detest	finish	miss	resent	understand

Verbs Often Followed by Infinitives

afford	claim	fail	mean	refuse	volunteer
agree	come	forget	offer	seem	wait
appear	consent	happen	plan	serve	
arrange	decide	hesitate	prepare	struggle	
be	demand	hope	pretend	swear	
be supposed	deserve	learn	proceed	tend	
care	endeavor	manage	prove	threaten	

Verb + (noun or pronoun) + infinitive

ask	choose	expect	intend	prefer	want	would like
beg	dare	help	need	promise	wish	

Verb + noun or pronoun + infinitive

appoint	command	encourage	implore	permit	show ... how	warn
believe	compel	forbid	instruct	persuade	teach	
cause	convince	force	motivate	remind	tell	
caution	direct	get	oblige	request	urge	
challenge	enable	hire	order	require	use	

Verbs followed by Either Infinitives or Gerunds with No Change in Meaning

attempt	cannot bear	continue	intend	love	prefer
begin	cannot stand	hate	like	neglect	start

Verbs followed by Either Infinitives or Gerunds with Changes in Meaning

forget	mean	propose	quit	regret	remember	stop	try

Verbs followed by Either Infinitives or Gerunds, Depending on the Use of a Noun or Pronoun Object

advise	allow	cause	encourage	forbid	permit	teach

Phrases with Prepositions That Are Often Followed by Gerunds

approve of (disapprove of)
be accustomed to
be afraid of
be capable of
be excited about
be given to
be good at
be famous for
be interested in
be proud of
be sorry about
be successful at
be (get) tired of
be (get) used to

Also: instead of, in spite of

care about
depend on
forget about
insist on
look forward to
plan on
plead innocent (guilty) to
rely on
speak about
succeed at
take advantage of
think of (about)
worry about

Index

A

A/an, 55, 63
Abstract nouns, 47
Active voice. *See also* Passive voice
  gerunds and, 387–388
  get and, 289n
  infinitives and, 379–381
  introduction to, 243
  modal auxiliaries and, 262–263
  reduction of clauses to phrases in, 351
  in simple tenses, 245
  verbs and, 289
Adjective(s). *See also* Clause(s), adjective
  comparative forms of, 195–196
  conjunctions and, 91, 93
  count nouns and, 47
  expressions of quantity and, 59
  gerunds and, 284
  get and, 247
  infinitives and, 291
  irregular, 196
  noncount nouns and, 49
  of parts of speech, 3
  possessive, 52
  probability and, 34
  quantifiers and, 64, 65
  reported speech and changes in, 214
  with *so . . . that,* 202
  superlative forms of, 195–196
  testing on, 53–54
  of urgency, 222, 227
Adverb(s). *See also* Clause(s), adverb
  comparative forms of, 195–196
  complements and, 5
  coordinating conjunctions and, 91
  of frequency, 9, 149, 244, 251, 258
  infinitives and, 291
  irregular, 196
  negative, 79
  of parts of speech, 3
  phrases, 149–150, 191
  probability and, 34
  with *so . . . that,* 202
  superlative forms of, 195–196
Adverbials, 214
Advice, 37, 329
After, 149, 154, 165, 365
Agreement, subject/verb, 65, 67, 68
All (of), 64–65, 65n, 134
Allow, 370
Along with, 68
Although, 178, 365
Always, 9
And, 89, 91
Appear, 5
Articles, 3, 47, 55, 62–63, 83–84
As, 149, 154, 166, 365
As a consequence, 159
As a result (of), 96, 159
As soon as, 149, 154, 166
As well as, 68, 197
As . . . as, (not), 195, 197

B

Be, 5, 9, 79
Be going to, 10
Because (of), 159, 365
Become, 5
Before, 149, 154, 165, 365
Both . . . and, 68, 92–93, 197
But, 89, 91
But also, 68
By, 165, 247, 360
By + agent, 245, 248
By the time (that), 165

C

Catch, 358
Causative verbs, 369–370
Cause, showing, 159
Clause(s). *See also* Clause(s), adjective; Clause(s), adverb; Complex sentences
  of cause, 159
  of comparison, 196–197
  conjunctions and, 89, 91, 92–93
  defined, 4
  dependent, 101
  with embedded questions, 217
  with *if,* 218

Clause(s)—*Cont.*
join, ways to, 107
nonrestrictive, 355
noun, 102, 211, 214, 218, 223, 227
parallel forms and, 80
reduction to phrases, 232, 351–352, 353–354, 356, 364–365
restrictive, 355
of result, 159
sentence fragments and, 108
as subjects of sentences, 227
testing on, 239–240
time, 148–149, 154, 165, 166
with *whether,* 218
Clause(s), adjective
anticipatory *it* with, 125
complex sentences and, 101
expressions of quantity and, 134
nonrestrictive, 115–116, 134, 355–356
reduced to phrases, 253, 351, 352, 354
restrictive, 115–116, 355–356
subject/verb agreement and, 135
testing on, 138–139
with *that,* 121, 127–128, 129
with *when,* 132–133
with *where,* 132–133
with *which,* 121, 127–128, 129
with *who,* 121
with *whom,* 127–128, 129
with *whose,* 123, 130
Clause(s), adverb
cause and result and, 159
complex sentences and, 101–102
of contrast, 178, 183–184
placement and punctuation of, 149–150
of purpose, 191
reduced to phrases, 364–365
of result, 202
testing on, 207–208
Collective nouns, 77–78
Comma splices, 107
Command sentences, 4, 83–84, 87, 214, 234
Comparisons, 195–197
Complements, 5, 303
Complex sentences
main clause as focus of, 104–105
overview of, 101–102
with *so, such, so many/much,* 202n
testing on, 111–112
with *that,* 121, 128, 129, 133
Complex sentences—*Cont.*
with *when,* 133
with *where,* 133
with *which,* 121, 128, 129, 133, 134
with *who,* 121, 128, 129
with *whom,* 128, 129, 134
with *whose,* 123, 130
Compound sentences, 89, 96, 105, 111–112
Concrete nouns, 47
Conditional sentences
factual, 341, 342
imaginative, 321–322, 325, 334, 336
testing on, 339–340, 346–347
Conjunctions
adverb clauses of result and, 202n
coordinating, 89, 91, 107, 304
correlative, 92–93
of parts of speech, 3
subordinating, 102, 107
Connecting words, 101–102, 173–174
Consequently, 159
Contrast, 178, 183–184
Correlatives, 92–93
Count nouns. *See also* Noncount nouns
adjectives and, 59
articles and, 55
defined, 47
definite article and, 62–63
expressions of quantity and, 59
nouns that are both noncount and, 50
plural, 47
pronouns and, 59
quantifiers and, 65
singular, 47
with *so many . . . that,* 202
units of measurement with, 58

D

Dangling phrases, 367
Definite articles, 62–63
Despite (in spite of) the fact that, 178, 365
Due to/due to the fact (that), 159, 159n
During, 166

E

Either of, 134
Either . . . or, 68, 92–93
Elliptical phrases, 365

Enough, 64, 65, 291
Even though, 178
Exclamation, as sentence type, 4

F

Factual conditional sentences, 341, 342
Feel, 5
Find, 358
For, 89, 91, 291
Force, 370
Forget, 296
Fractions, 65
Fragments, sentence, 108
Future continuous tense, 15, 20
Future perfect continuous tense, 24, 28, 149
Future perfect tense, 28, 149, 251

G

Gerunds
  active forms of, 387–388
  direct objects of, 286
  functions of, 281
  noncount nouns and, 49
  as objects of prepositions, 282
  as objects of verbs, 283
  parallel structures and, 304
  passive forms of, 387–388
  perfect forms of, 388
  subjects and, 284, 303
  testing on, 308–309, 394–395
  to +, 282
  verbs and, 296–297, 391
Get, 5, 247, 289n

H

Habitual past tense, 12
Have, 370
Help, 370
Hence, 159
Hope vs. *wish,* 313
How, 291
However, 96

I

If
  clauses with, 218
  elliptical phrases and, 365
If—Cont.
  factual conditions and, 341, 342
  imaginary conditions and, 321–322, 325, 334, 336
Imaginary conditions, 321–322, 325, 334, 336.
    See also Conditional sentences
In addition to, 68
In order that, 191
In order to, 191
In spite of the fact (that), 178
Indefinite articles, 55
Infinitives
  active forms of, 379, 381
  adjectives and, 291
  adverbs and, 291
  commands and, 234–235
  as complements of sentences, 303
  continuous forms of, 381
  functions of, 287–288
  noun clauses and, 232
  nouns and, 291
  as objects of verbs, 288
  parallel structures and, 304
  passive forms of, 379, 381
  perfect forms of, 381
  of purpose, 287–288
  as subjects of sentences, 303
  testing on, 308–309, 394–395
  verbs and, 289, 296–297, 369–370, 383
  were +, 325
It, 125, 227, 248, 303

K

Keep, 358

L

Lay / lie, 361–362
Leave, 358
Let, 370
Likewise, 197
Little, 59
Look, 5

M

Make, 370
Many, 59
Mean, 297
Means/manner, phrases of, 360
Measurement, units of, 58

Modal auxiliaries
of abilities, 38
categories of, 33
conditional sentences and, 341, 342
forms of, 33–34
introduction to, 33–34
of logical probability, 34–35
of need/lack of need, 38
with *otherwise,* 321
passive voice and, 262–263
perfect, 328–329
of predictions, 34
of preference, 38
pronunciation of reduced forms of, 34
reported speech and changes in, 213
of social interaction, 36–37
testing on, 43–44
with *wish,* 314
More/less/–er . . . than, 197
Most, 64–65

N

Neither of, 134
Neither . . . nor, 68, 92–93
Never, 9
Nevertheless, 96
Noncount nouns. *See also* Count nouns
as abstract nouns, 49
adjectives and, 59
defined, 49
expressions of quantity and, 59
as mass nouns, 49
nouns that are both count and, 50
pronouns and, 59
quantifiers and, 65
with *so much . . . that,* 202
units of measurement with, 58
None (of), 65, 134
Nor, 89, 91
Not only . . . , 68
Not only . . . but (also), 92–93
Noun(s). *See also* Count nouns; Noncount nouns
abstract, 47
clauses, 101, 102, 211, 214, 218, 223, 227
collective, 77–78
concrete, 47
conjunctions and, 91, 93
defined, 4
infinitives and, 291

Noun(s)—*Cont.*
irregular plurals of, 410
modifiers, 77, 80
of parts of speech, 3
possessive, 284
proper, 71
testing on, 83–84
verbs and, 289
Number of, the vs. *number of, a,* 67

O

Object(s)
direct, 5, 286
gerunds and, 282, 283, 286
indirect, 5
infinitives and, 288
Once, 149, 154
One of, 134
Or, 89, 91
Ordinals, 291
Otherwise, 321, 333
Owing to, 159

P

Parallel structures, 80, 304
Participial phrases, 351, 375–376
Participles, 247, 291, 358, 359, 369–370
Parts of speech, 3
Passive voice. *See also* Active voice
By + agent in, 245
common expressions in, 247
gerunds and, 387–388
get and, 289n
infinitives and, 379, 381
introduction to, 243
it and, 248
modal auxiliaries and, 262–263
perfect tenses and, 251
reduction of clauses to phrases in, 352, 353
in simple tenses, 244–245
testing on, 268–269
verbs and, 247n, 289
Past continuous tense, 15, 17, 166, 258
Past perfect continuous tense, 24, 26, 165
Past perfect tense, 26, 165, 251
Percentages, 65
Perception, verbs of, 359
Permission, asking for, 37

Personal pronouns, 52
Phrase(s)
  adverb, 149–150, 191
  of cause, 159
  of comparison, 196–197
  conjunctions and, 91, 93
  dangling, 367
  defined, 4
  elliptical, 365
  infinitive, 232, 234–235
  of means or manner, 360
  parallel forms and, 80
  participial, 351, 356, 360, 375–376
  quantifiers and, 64, 65
  reduction of clauses to, 351–352, 353–354, 356, 364–365
  of result, 159
  time, 165, 166
Possessive adjectives, 52
Prepositions, 3, 132, 247, 282
Present continuous tense, 15, 16, 149, 154, 258
Present perfect continuous tense, 24, 25
Present perfect tense, 23, 25, 149, 154, 251
Pronoun(s)
  collective nouns and, 78
  defined, 4
  expressions of quantity and, 59
  infinitives and, 297
  object, 196
  of parts of speech, 3
  personal, 52
  quantifiers and, 64, 65
  relative, 101, 107, 127, 129, 130, 132
  reported speech and changes in, 214
  subject, 196
  testing on, 53–54
  verbs and, 289
Pronunciation guidelines, 411
Proper nouns, 71
Propose, 297
Purpose, showing, 191

Q

Quantifiers, 64–65
Quantity, expressions of, 59, 134
Question(s)
  embedded, 217, 235
  as sentence type, 4
  words, 217
  yes/no, 218, 235
Quit, 297
Quotations vs. reported speech, 212

R

Raise vs. *rise*, 362
Regret, 296
Relative pronouns, 101, 107, 127, 129, 130, 132
Remember, 296
Reported speech, 212–213, 214, 234
Requests, 37, 223, 234–235
Rest of, the, 134
Result, showing, 159, 202
Rise vs. *Raise,* 362
Run–On sentences, 107

S

Same . . . as, the, 197
Say, 211n
Seem, 5
Seldom, 9
Send, 358
Sentence(s). *See also* Command sentences; Complex sentences; Compound sentences; Conditional sentences
  defined, 4
  fragments, 108
  run–on, 107
  testing on, 111–112
  types of, 4
Sequence, transitions of, 147
Should, 325
Similar to, 197
Similarly, 197
Simple future tense, 8–9, 10, 245
Simple past tense, 8–9, 165, 166, 245. *See also* Habitual past tense
Simple present tense, 8–9, 149, 154, 245, 341
Since, 154, 159, 365
Smell, 5
So, 89, 91, 202n
So many/much, 202n
So many . . . that, 202
So much . . . that, 202
So that, 191
Some, 59, 64, 65
So . . . that, 202
Sound, 5
Spelling rules, 409–410
Statements, as sentence type, 4

Stop, 297
Subject(s)
defined, 4
forms of, 4
gerunds and, 284, 303
infinitives and, 303
negative adverbs and, 79
two–part, 68
verb agreement, 65, 67, 68, 135
Subjunctive mood, 222, 223, 232, 314, 339–340
Such, 202n
Such . . . that, 202
Superlatives, 63, 195–196, 291

T

Taste, 5
Tell, 211n
Tense(s)
habitual past, 12
preview of, 6
testing on, 173–174
Tense(s), continuous, 15, 258, 353, 381
future, 15, 20
future perfect, 24, 28, 149
past, 15, 17, 166, 258
past perfect, 24, 26, 165
perfect, 24, 251n
present, 15, 16, 149, 154, 258
present perfect, 24, 25
Tense(s), perfect, 23, 251, 354, 381, 388
future, 28, 149
past, 26, 165, 251
present, 23, 25, 149, 154, 251
Tense(s), simple, 8–9, 352
future, 10
past, 11, 165, 166
present, 149, 154
Testing
on adjective clauses, 138–139
on adjectives, 53–54
on adverb clauses, 207–208
on articles, 83–84
on connecting words, 173–174
on gerunds, 308–309, 394–395
on infinitives, 308–309, 394–395
on modal auxiliaries, 43–44
on noun clauses, 239–240
on nouns, 83–84
on passive voice, 268–269
on pronouns, 53–54
Testing—*Cont.*
review of problem areas, 143–144, 276–277, 403–404
on sentences, 111–112, 339–340, 346–347
on subjunctive mood, 339–340
on tenses, 173–174
on verbs, 43–44
That
clauses and, 115, 121, 127–128, 129, 227, 232
urgency and, 222, 223
with *wish,* 314
The, 62–65, 65n, 71
Therefore, 159
These, 64
Those, 64
Though, 178
Thus, 159
Time expressions
adverb clauses / phrases and, 149–150
future continuous tense, 20
future perfect continuous tense, 28
future perfect tense, 28
past continuous tense, 17
past perfect continuous tense, 26
past perfect tense, 26
present continuous tense, 16
present perfect continuous tense, 25
present perfect tense, 23
simple future tense, 10
simple past tense, 11
simple present tense, 9
To, 282, 291
Together with, 68
Too, 291
Transitions, 96, 147, 159, 178, 197, 321
Try, 296

U

Unless, 341
Until, 149, 154, 165
Up to, 165
Up to the time (that), 154
Urgency, 222, 227
Used to, 12

V

Verb(s)
causative, 369–370
collective nouns and, 77–78

Verb(s)—*Cont.*
of emotion, 247n
gerunds and, 283, 296–297, 391
infinitives and, 288, 289, 296–297, 383
intransitive, 5, 243
irregular, 406–408
linking, 5
nonaction, 9
of parts of speech, 3
of perception, 359
(pro)nouns and, 289
subject agreement, 65, 67, 68, 135
testing on, 43–44
transitive, 5, 243
with two-part objects, 358

W

What, 217
When
clauses and, 115, 132–133, 149, 154, 165, 166, 217
elliptical phrases and, 365
infinitives and, 291
Whenever, 154
Where, 115, 132–133, 183–184, 291
Whereas, 185
Whether, 218
Which, 115, 121, 127–128, 129, 134
While, 149, 154, 166, 183–184, 365
Who, 115, 121, 217
Whom, 115, 127–128, 129, 134, 217
Whose, 123, 130
Why, 217
Will, 10
Wish vs. *hope,* 313
Within, 165
Would, 12

Y

Yet, 89, 91

Photo Credits: Chapter 1 Opener: © Spencer Grant/PhotoEdit; p. 6: © Todd Gipstein/CORBIS; p. 12: © Bettmann/CORBIS; p. 13: © CORBIS; p. 22: Eric Lessing/Art Resource; p. 25: Susan Kuklin/Photo Researchers, Inc.; p. 32: © Gary Connor/PhotoEdit; **Chapter 2** Opener: © The Bettmann Archive/CORBIS; p. 48: © UPI/Bettmann/CORBIS; p. 57: © William Whitehurst/The Stock Market/CORBIS; p. 62: The Bettmann Archive/CORBIS; p. 64: Tom McHugh/Photo Researchers, Inc.; p. 70: Bruce Burkhardt/CORBIS; p. 73: © The Bettmann Archive/CORBIS; p. 75: Underwood & Underwood/CORBIS; p. 76: © DPA/The Image Works; p. 79: UPI/Bettmann/CORBIS; p. 81: © Liesl Clark/WGBH, NOVA; **Chapter 3** Opener: © David Young-Wolff/PhotoEdit; p. 89: © Barbara Alper/Stock, Boston; p. 96: Biophoto Associates/Science Source/Photo Researchers, Inc.; p. 100: J. Christopher Briscoe/Photo Researchers, Inc.; p. 101: © Wells/The Image Works; p. 103: © Wolfgang Kaehler/CORBIS; p. 109: © The Bettmann Archive/CORBIS; **Chapter 4** Opener: © Harvey Barad, Photo Researchers, Inc.; p. 115: © Gian Berto Vanni/CORBIS; p. 118: © Bettmann/CORBIS; p. 121: Courtesy Patricia Werner; p. 122: © Jan Butchofsky-Houser/CORBIS; p. 123: © Charles & Josette Lenars/CORBIS; p. 124: © Michael & Patricia Fogden/CORBIS; p. 125: © Macduff Everton/CORBIS; p. 127: © Roman Soumar/CORBIS; p. 132: © George Holton/Photo Researchers, Inc.; p. 136: George Holton/Photo Researchers, Inc.; p. 140: Roger Ressmeyer/CORBIS; p. 141: © Wolfgang Kaehler/CORBIS; **Chapter 5** Opener: © Patrick Ward/CORBIS; p. 148: Courtesy Lea Monaghan; p. 151: © Bettmann/CORBIS; p. 158: © UPI/Bettmann Newsphotos; p. 160: Culver Pictures; p. 161: © Reuters/Bettmann/CORBIS; p. 163,164,168 © The Bettmann Archive/CORBIS; p. 170: © Gianni Dagli Orti/CORBIS; **Chapter 6** Opener: © PhotoDisc Website; p. 176: © Simon Fraser/Science Photo Library/Photo Researchers, Inc.; p. 177: © CNRI/Science Photo Library/Photo Researchers, Inc.; p. 190: © Christopher Briscoe/Photo Researchers, Inc.; p. 192,193: © The Bettmann Archive/CORBIS; p. 197 (*left*): © David A. Northcott/CORBIS; p. 197 (*right*): © Tim Davis/Photo Researchers, Inc.; **Chapter 7** Opener: © Rob Crandall/Stock, Boston; p. 221 (*left*): © Ira Kirschenbaum/Stock, Boston; p. 221 (*right*): © J. Albertson/Stock, Boston; p. 226 (*left*): © Animals/Animals; p. 226 (*right*): © Lawrence Migdale/Stock, Boston; **Chapter 8** Opener: © Michael Grecco/Stock, Boston; p. 243: © PhotoDisc Website; p. 246: © Culver Pictures; p. 251: © Bettmann/CORBIS; p. 253 (*top*): © Culver Pictures; p. 253 (*bottom*): © Runk/Schoenberger/Grant Heilman Photography, Inc.; p. 255: © Michael Newman/PhotoEdit; p. 256: © Mark C. Burnett/Stock, Boston; p. 257 (*left*): © Sean Sprague/Stock, Boston; p. 257 (*right*): © Bob Daemmrich/Stock, Boston; p. 259: © Jean-Claude Lejeune/Stock, Boston; p. 266: © Noel R. Kemp/Photo Researchers, Inc.; p. 267: © Russell D. Curtis; p. 272 (*left*): © Bettmann/CORBIS; p. 272 (*right*): © AFP/CORBIS; **Chapter 9** Opener: © Art Resource; p. 281: © Bettmann/CORBIS; p. 283: © Lynn Goldsmith/CORBIS; p. 285 (*left*): © Ted Streshinsky/CORBIS; p. 285 (*right*): © Bettmann/CORBIS; p. 287: © Victor Englebert/Photo Researchers, Inc.; p. 291 (*left*): © Robert Frerck/Woodfin Camp; p. 291 (*middle*): © Loren McIntyre/Woodfin Camp; p. 291 (*right*): © Victor Englebert/Photo Researchers, Inc.; p. 295: © Art Resource/Giraudon; p. 299: © Art Resource/Bildarchiv Foto Marburg; p. 301 (*top left*): © Tate Gallery, London, Art Resource, NY; p. 301 (*top right*): *Burning of the Houses of Lords and Commons*, October 16, 1834, oil on canvas. 1835, 92.7 × 123.2 cm., J.M.W. Turner, British, 1775-1851, © The Cleveland Museum of Art, Bequest John L. Severence, 42.647; p. 301 (*middle left*): *Mont Sainte-Victoire*, Paul Cezanne, gift of the W. Averell Harriman Foundation in memory of Marie N. Harriman, © 1995 Board of Trustees, National Gallery of Art, Washington; p. 301 (*middle right*): © 2001 Succession H. Matisse, Paris/Artists Rights Society (ARS), New York; Baltimore Museum of Art; p. 301 (*bottom left*): © The Museum of Modern Art; p. 301 (*bottom right*): © Scala/Art Resource; p. 302 (*left*): © Stephanie Dinkins/Photo Researchers, Inc.; p. 302 (*right*): © Bedrich Grunzweig/Photo Researchers, Inc.; p. 304: © Jonathan Blair/CORBIS; **Chapter 10** Opener: Associated Press/GREENPEACE; p. 316 (*top*): © Bob Daemmrich/Stock, Boston; p. 316 (*bottom*): © Matthew McKee; Eye Ubiquitous/CORBIS; p. 317: © AFP/CORBIS; p. 326: Courtesy Patricia Werner; p. 333, 335: Associated Press; p. 337: © Natalie Fobes/CORBIS; p. 340: © Richard Cummins/CORBIS; p. 341: © Bob Kramer/Stock, Boston; **Chapter 11** Opener: © Owen Franken/Stock, Boston; p. 353 (*left*): © Francois Gohier/Photo Researchers, Inc.; p. 353 (*right*): © C. Ray/Photo Researchers, Inc.; p. 263: © Jeremy Homer/CORBIS; p. 364: © UPI/Bettmann/CORBIS; p. 368: Courtesy Patricia Werner; **Chapter 12** Opener: © Forrest J. Ackerman Collection/CORBIS; p. 387: © Lowell Georgia/Science Source/Photo Researchers, Inc.; p. 389: © Everett Collection; p. 390: © Brian Brake/Photo Researchers, Inc.